Diet For A Small Planet

If you've never read DIET FOR A SMALL PLANET you'll find it a warm, caring, human philosophy of how the way we eat affects not only ourselves but our world.

This amazing book is also a complete kitchen guide, filled with tips, suggestions, and delicious recipes—a total guide to eating well.

Diet for a Small Planet
Twentieth Anniversary Edition

Frances Moore Lappé

Illustrations by Marika Hahn

BALLANTINE BOOKS • **NEW YORK**

A Ballantine Book
Published by The Random House Publishing Group
Copyright © 1971, 1975, 1982, 1991 by Frances Moore Lappé

Published in the United States by Ballantine Books, an imprint of The Random House Publishing Group, a division of Random House, Inc., New York, and simultaneously in Canada by Random House of Canada Limited, Toronto.

BALLANTINE and colophon are registered trademarks of Random House, Inc.

ISBN 978-0-345-32120-6

Printed in the United States of America

www.ballantinebooks.com

First Edition: June 1982
Twentieth Anniversary Edition: November 1991

41

For Betty Ballantine, whose foresight, thank God, was better than mine!

Contents

List of Figures

Acknowledgments

In the first edition of this book I included a special acknowledgment to my parents. As I appreciate them even more today than I did ten years ago, I would like to repeat those words: "I wish to thank my parents, John and Ina Moore, who, by having always set the finest example of critical openness to new ideas, made this inquiry possible."

I am indebted to Nick Allen, of the Institute's staff, for his support for this project from its inception and for his inspired and very significant editorial contribution.

Mary Sinclair, Cindy Crowner, and Perri Sloane each contributed cooking talent and other skills to improve the recipes in this book and test the many contributions sent in from around the country. For testing and improving recipes I also appreciate the help of Elizabeth Rivers, Julia Rosenbaum, Claire Greensfelder, Myra Levy, Charles Varon, Katie Allen, Vince Bielski, Elinor Blake, Maria Torres McKay, and the Davis, California, Food for All group—especially Laurie Rubin.

Special thanks go to Jennifer Lovejoy and JoNina Abron, who handled many of my Institute responsibilities so that I could be free to work on this book.

Debbie Fox was the loyal and talented typist of most of this manuscript. Her good humor and her willingness to put up with umpteen drafts will never be forgotten.

Research for this book depended on the help of dozens of people. My special thanks go to Sandy Fritz, Jenny Robinson, and John Moore. I also appreciated the help of Mort Hantman, Tracey Helser, Jim Wessel, Erik Schapiro, David Kinley, Vince Bielski, and Fred Brauneck.

This book benefited greatly from the valuable suggestions of friends and colleagues around the country. I am indebted to Michael Jacobson of the Center for Science in the Public Interest, Marty Strange of the Center for Rural Affairs, William Shurtleff of the Soyfoods Center, to Judy Stone, Robert Greenstein, and Steve Daschle of the Project on Food Assistance and Poverty, to Risk Weissbourd,

Cheryl Rogers, and Tom Joe of the Center for the Study of Welfare Policy of the University of Chicago, and to Bard Shollenberger of the Community Nutrition Institute. I also appreciate the time and thought given to this book by Joan Gussow, Nevin Scrimshaw, Isabel Contento, Keith Akers, Robin Hur, Alex Hershaft, Georg Borgstrom, Douglas McDonald, Donald R. Davis, Stan Winter, Jim Spearow, and V. James Rhodes.

I would also like to thank those to whom I am indebted for recipe sections in the first two editions of this book. Many of the recipes they contributed or helped to develop remain in this edition. First, Ellen Ewald who back in 1970 helped acquaint me with the unknown world of whole foods. Second, Susan Kanor whose special kitchen touch and hard work made developing the recipes for the second edition a great adventure.

For other recipes that I have retained in this new book, I am grateful to Barbara Peter, Carol Ackerman Albiani, Sandye Carroll, Diane Coleman, Nancy Posselt, Jackie Potts, Paul Prensky, Joy Gardner, Nancy Meister, Robin McFarlane, and Jamie Seymour.

For their ideas and editorial suggestions I also want to thank Joseph Collins, Charles Varon, Regina Fitzgerald, Jess Randall, and my parents, John and Ina Moore.

And I appreciate all those at the Institute who put up with me during the period of stress to meet this deadline: Gretta Goldenman, JoNina Abron, Joseph Collins, David Kinley, Jim Wessel, Nick Allen, Jess Randall, Annie Newman, and Diana Dillaway.

Finally, I am grateful to my agent, Joan Raines, for her strong support for my work.

Diet for a Small Planet Twenty Years Later—An Extraordinary Time to Be Alive

I BEGIN THIS introduction to the 20th anniversary edition of *Diet for a Small Planet* with a sense of awe, awe at the rapidity of change. In 1971, I—an intense 26-year-old in search of herself—sat long hours in the U.C. Berkeley library uncovering facts about the global food supply that turned my world upside down. At home in my dining room, working at my manual typewriter, I made seemingly endless protein calculations with a slide rule. And here I am twenty years later, tapping away on my Toshiba "lap top" preparing to FAX this chapter to my editor!

Yes, the pace of technological change has been breathtaking, but our change of consciousness has been yet more dramatic. We who were born in this century are the first generations to experience a perceptible quickening of historical time. The change you or I witness in a lifetime now exceeds what in previous centuries transpired over many, many generations. And we who were born after World II are the first to know that our choices count: They count on a global scale. They matter in evolutionary time. In our species' fantastic rush toward "modernization" we obliterate millions of other species, transfigure the earth's surface, and create climate-changing disruption of the upper atmosphere, all powerfully altering the path of evolution.

More personally, I feel the quickening of time in realizing that what was heresy, what was "fringe," when I wrote *Diet for a Small Planet* just twenty years ago is now common knowledge.

Then, the notion that human beings could do well without meat was heretical. Today, the medical establishment acknowledges the numerous benefits of eating low on the food chain.

Then, anyone who questioned the American diet's reliance on beef—since cattle are the most wasteful converters of grain to meat—was perceived as challenging the American way of life (especially, when that someone came from Fort Worth, Texas—"Cowtown, USA"). Today, the expanding herds of cattle worldwide are not only recognized as poor plant-to-meat converters but are documented contributors to global climate change. They're responsible for releasing enormous quantities of methane into the atmosphere, contributing to global warming. Moreover, commercial invasion of the South and Central American rainforests now implicates cattle ranching in the one-and-one-half acre *per second* destruction of the remaining rainforests worldwide.

Then, anyone who questioned industrial agriculture—fossil fuel and chemically dependent—was seen as a naive "back to the lander." To challenge industrial agriculture was to question efficiency itself and to wish us all back into the fields at hard labor. Today, the National Academy of Sciences acknowledges the threat of agricultural chemicals[1] and even the U.S. Department of Agriculture reports that the small family farm is at least as efficient as the superfarms undermining America's rural communities.[2]

Peeling the Proverbial Onion

What an extraordinary time to be alive! More pointedly, in my case, what an extraordinary time to be middle-aged—to perceive, because I have lived most of half a century, the quickening of time.

And with this awareness of humanity's power to remake, to unmake, our living environment, has come a radical awakening across many disciplines. We thus live in an era of conscious searching, of profound rethinking. It is, I'm convinced, a time of opportunity that may come only once in many centuries. And so, while fear may grip me often, I also feel incredibly privileged to be alive *now*: a time of exploring fundamental questions about who we are and what the role of our species is to be on this lovely planet.

In Part I, you will read "my journey," the path that took me from being the struggling 26-year-old in the U.C. library to being the co-founder of the Institute for Food and Development Policy. In 1981, when I wrote that chapter, my mission was clear. I knew what I had to do. But as the 1980s progressed, I became less sure, and that uncertainty pushed me forward.

Not surprisingly perhaps, I've been thinking in food metaphors all my life—the most persistent being that of the humble onion. I feel I've spent twenty years peeling away at it! Let me now explain by taking you with me through its several layers.

In one sense, what motivated me to write *Diet for a Small Planet* was simple outrage. We feed almost half the world's grain to livestock, returning only a fraction in meat—while millions starve. It confounds all logic. Yet the pattern has intensified. Vast resources move at an accelerating rate toward the production of exports from lands on which people go hungry. Since the 1970s, the rates of growth in food production have been lower in the basic grains and tubers eaten by poor, hungry people than in fruits, vegetables, oil seeds, and feedgrains for meat, eaten largely by the planet's already well-fed minority.

My mission was to awaken people to this simple fact: Hunger is human made. I sought to liberate people from the myth that nature's to blame for the massive deprivation hundreds of millions of people now experience. In writing *Food First* and establishing the Institute for Food and Development Policy in the mid-seventies, however, my mission became more ambitious.

I sought, with my colleagues, to explain *how* human-made institutions create needless suffering. In books like *Aid as Obstacle*, *World Hunger: Twelve Myths*, *Betraying the National Interest*, and *Taking Population Seriously* we described the growing concentration of decision making—from the village level, to the national level, to the level of international commerce and finance. Fewer and fewer people make decisions that have life-and-death consequences for the rest of us. The problem is not scarcity of land or food, I became fond of saying: it is a *scarcity of democracy*.

But, for this phrase to make any sense, I had to probe to the heart and soul of democracy. Surely to have any meaning at all, democracy must be more than a set of formal rules and procedures. After all, many countries—the Philippines, India, and many of the Central American countries—have all the trappings of democracy. Yet their people live in misery. Democracy had to be more—is it less a set of rules, I wondered, than a very human process? A process grounded in several principles that can only be realized by people themselves? First is, perhaps, the *accountability of leadership* to those who have to live with the consequences of their decisions. Second, the related principle of *shared power*, perhaps never equally shared but at least shared to the degree that no one is left powerless, unable to protect themselves and those they love.

In so defining democracy, it became clear to me that wherever there is hunger, democracy has not been fulfilled.

But the better I got at describing the problem, the more intense my frustration. What were the solutions? I could describe the need for greater democracy, making possible, for example, the reforms necessary for the rural poor in the third world to achieve food security and reduce the size of their families. I could describe policy shifts that could do away with homelessness here. But without a practical path for getting there, all my descriptions and prescriptions left me profoundly unsatisfied. I had always enjoyed giving public talks but my enjoyment began to wane. I realized my audiences wanted more from me. And I did not feel able to give it.

I had to go deeper. In the early 1980s, I started reading widely again in political theory and social change. I traveled to countries I thought might have something important to teach. I visited Europe to study the movement for worker participation there. I went to Sweden to examine the much-debated proposal to democratize and decentralize ownership of large industry. In Yugoslavia I studied the troubled path toward worker self-management. I ventured to China to look at its dramatic restructuring of agriculture.

By the mid-eighties my sense of possibilities had been greatly expanded, but I had also come more firmly than ever to believe that no program—no matter how "correct"—could address the problems of our communities and our planet unless many, many more people believed themselves capable of participating in the changes it suggested.

So I was forced to peel away another layer, to go still deeper, again asking why? What blocks us from believing in the possibility of such change—change in the direction of more genuine democracy—and engaging ourselves in the process of bringing it about?

What could possibly be powerful enough to allow us to tolerate and condone as a society what as individuals we abhor? Few of us would allow a child to suffer deprivation in our midst. Yet as a society we do just that. In the United States, we allow one quarter of our children to be born into poverty, which results in twice the chance of their being physically stunted compared to middle-class children. And what could be powerful enough to allow us to destroy majestic redwoods, to dredge breathtaking coastlines, to drain rich wetlands—to obliterate that which has inspired feelings of security, thanksgiving, and awe in human beings over eons of time?

Perhaps, I thought, it's that as individuals we have come to believe we have neither the capacity nor responsibility to do otherwise, to do other than acquiesce to forces beyond our control.

We are in large measure who we believe ourselves to be. I had always believed in the power of ideas to shape our reality, but this concept took on new meaning for me as the 1980s progressed. I came to see that what we believe ourselves to be reflects assumptions so taken for granted that they've become like an invisible ether. We live unconscious of their power. I became convinced that as we approach the 21st century, we remain captured in a set of ideas about ourselves which is a legacy of at least three centuries. This may sound strange, especially from someone arguing the quickening of change. But striking also is continuity, continuity in our ideas of ourselves that we now must consciously examine.

The Power of Ideas

To make myself clearer, let me take you the next step in my own quest, peeling away another layer in my "onion" of discovery.

I wanted to bring to the surface the "big ideas"—the

assumptions about who we are and the nature of our ties to one another—that lie behind our acceptance of the social structures in which we live. I had become convinced that there was only one thing strong enough to explain our behavior—behavior that was needlessly destroying millions of lives each year from hunger and disease, and undermining the integrity of our fragile planet as well. It is the power of ideas. *But how do we get at those ideas?*

My answer in part became: "through talk." We must talk in order to surface underlying assumptions, to nudge ourselves and each other to reflect upon the reasons *why* we think and act as we do. We must talk in order to discover whether our ideas have simply become unexamined habits of mind, habits which thwart instead of aid effective living.

So I decided to stop writing tracts about just what I believe. I wanted to engage those who had never and would never pick up one of my existing books—books they might dismiss because they challenge the status quo.

I wanted to write a dialogue in order to provoke dialogue—to get people talking. So I set out to write in two voices. One voice would speak from the inherited assumptions that make up the dominant, modern worldview; the assumptions that limit the very questions we're allowed to ask. The other voice would be my own, struggling to articulate an emerging alternative. These voices in print became *Rediscovering America's Values*, published in 1989.

In the years of research required to write *Rediscovering*, I became ever surer that indeed we all do carry unexamined mental baggage, now centuries in the making. This metaphorical baggage we now need to put through the "security check." We must open up this baggage, examining it in light of its consequences and for its security threat to our future.

In considering my case, please excuse my audacity in capturing a few centuries in a few sentences.

In the 17th century, René Descartes located the human soul in its mechanical vehicle, the human body. And Isaac Newton offered an exciting metaphor for understanding the interaction of those mechanical vehicles. He discovered laws of motion governing the physical universe. Having just given up on the ever-so-comforting notion of an interventionist God—one able to put the human house aright—we were left with a frightening void. "Ah ha!" we thought, "there must be parallel laws governing the social world governing our interaction with one another."

And what became known as the "mechanistic world view" began to take shape, developed by Western thinkers from the 17th century onward. Dazzling, uninterrupted breakthroughs in technological innovation—from the spinning ginny to steel mills, from bull dozers to dishwashers—permeated ever more aspects of our lives: the ubiquitous presence of machines confirming our sense that indeed the world can best be understood in mechanical terms.

Once absorbing this mechanistic world view, it was easy to assume that parallel laws governed economic life. Our challenge was to identify them, let them freely function and, *voilá*, an economic order would fall neatly into place! Human beings are handily off the hook. No moral reasoning required; the job would be done for us.

Critically important, in the mechanistic worldview, everything can best *be* understood by examining its parts. Human beings become distinct "atoms"—insular beings trapped inside our separate egos. Our radical individualism thus does not result from any moral failing; it derives from *our atomistic nature*. We're constitutionally unable to put ourselves in each others' shoes. We can identify only our own distinct interests. But that's not really so bad after all—for private interests serve, conveniently, to drive the giant social machine. No one put it better than Helvetius in the 18th century:

As the physical world is ruled by the laws of movement, so is the moral universe ruled by the laws of interest.[3]

This view of ourselves has defined the meaning of our most basic social values. Freedom, for example. Freedom is "elbow room": our capacity for self-defense, our success in fending off the intrusion of others. And what better defense than material accumulation? After all, the more we have, the freer we are from dependence upon others. To challenge the unlimited accumulation of material wealth is therefore to challenge the individual's free development. And fairness, what is it? Whatever distribution of rewards follows from each "social atom's" pursuit of its private interests, operating within the "neutral laws" of economic life.

This view of ourselves, driven by narrow self-interest, began to take shape in the 17th century and was picked up in the 18th by many of our nation's founders, including John Adams. He wrote:

> . . . whoever would found a state, and make proper laws for the government of it, must presume that all men are bad by nature.[4]

This combination of notions—social atomism, materialism, and the rule of human affairs by discoverable laws—has had profound implications for the social order we have created. For if indeed we are isolated social atoms, any conscious process of group decision making based on identifying *common* needs—usually called politics—is suspect. We must let absolute laws determine our fate, for self-seeking egos may well twist any other method to their private gain. Any genuine deliberative process is therefore impossible.

Instead of trusting our capacities for common problem solving, we sought desperately, and believed we had found, laws governing the social world—governing life and death matters of economics—laws that determine who eats and who doesn't. The more choices we can leave to these laws, the better off we are.

And what are these absolute laws? In much of the West we have established at least two such laws as almost sacrosanct, and adhered to them in varying degrees of faithfulness. They are:

- the market distribution of goods and services;
- not private property *per se* but a particular variant of this institution: the *unlimited* private accumulation of *productive* property.

And here's where the problem arises. It is not the institutions of the market or private property. The problem is converting these handy tools into fixed laws. What happens then? Human responsibility for consequences goes out the window.

If, for example, an inflating market pushes the price of housing out of reach of families on low incomes, leaving them on the street, hey, that's not the community's fault. That's the market at work! *We're* not responsible for that!

Or take income distribution itself. If it is the result of millions of individual free choices in the market, then as a society we're not responsible for the outcome, no matter how wide the resulting chasm between rich and poor. Never mind that during the 1980s perhaps the greatest transfer of wealth occurred in our nation's history—in this case from the nonrich to the rich—largely as a result of deliberate government and corporate policies. But we're absolved of responsibility, as long as we cling to the myth that individual choices in the market "automatically" determine outcomes.[5]

As the market defines more and more of our lives, even the most sacred of human experiences is up for sale: I was saddened but not surprised that the Reagan era brought "surrogate motherhood." In the 1988 debate over Baby "M," parties wrangled over a contract. Few asked what the renting of a woman's womb portended—a world in which any value could be reduced to a market value.

What if, I asked myself, instead of our masters, the market and private productive property could become mere devices in the service of our values, in the service of community-defined ends? The catch-22 is, of course, that those community ends can only be defined through deliberation—public talk—about our values and common needs—a process precluded by the very assumptions of social "atomism" with its self-seeking limits which we've come unquestionably to accept.

In Search of a New Myth of Being

If social atomism and the universe as machine became the dominant "myths" of the modern era, is there an alternative? What might replace these ubiquitous claims on our collective imaginations?

To suggest an answer, let me return to my life-long focus on food. When I began this quest, I was often dumbfounded when people asked me why I chose *food*. What a funny question, I thought. Everyone knows that all living creatures must eat. If they're not eating, what else matters?

Yet in the 1960s, I only barely understood the implications of my choice to focus on our most direct link to the nurturing earth. Yes, I was aware of being influenced by the birth of environmentalism. In the late 1960s, I attended standing-room lectures on ecology at the "free university" at Berkeley. Most of us were just learning the word for the first time. Something was in the air.

I certainly didn't understand until much later, however, that ecology offered us a new way of thinking about what it means to be a human being.

It's difficult to perceive this possibility in part because the message we hear from environmentalists is too often a scold. "Okay," the environmental preachers tell us, "the party's over. You have all overdone it. Your indulgence must stop! Accept the grim fact that on our little planet we live on limited means, on a fixed income."

Feeling guilty as accused, it's hard to see that while these reprimands may well be deserved there is also a richly positive message for us human beings in the discovery of "nature." Let our guilty feelings not block our capacity to listen. For there is a beautiful irony to appreciate. While the environmental catastrophe sounds the alarm, nature also offers us insights that are essential to addressing not only the environmental crisis but other aspects of social decline as well.

As we begin to see the world through the lens of ecology, subtly, we also begin to reshape our view of ourselves.

To explain, let me again pick up my personal journey.

In 1983, when I began research for what became *Rediscovering America's Values*, I was reacting to the 1980s celebration of narrow self-interest and a materialistic understanding of ourselves. I perceived Reaganism as the last gasp of a tired dogma. In my research and writing, I was struggling to articulate an alternative social understanding of self—self-interest not as narrow selfishness, but as deeply imbedded in relationships.

I was struggling to articulate a vision of social change that took us beyond social atomism and beyond "received" Marxism as well. I was influenced by environmental philosophy, Catholic social teaching, feminist philosophy and historiography. But most fun, I'll admit, was discovering that even within the dominant, Western philosophic tradition were rich insights supporting my own intuitions and life experience. Even from Adam Smith. Yes, the *same* Adam Smith who many view as the Godfather of greed—the supposed celebrator of self-seeking as the engine of the economy. (Officials in the White House during the Reagan years even sported Adam Smith neck ties.) But buried has been Smith's profoundly social vision of human nature.

Whereas in the classic Western philosophic tradition, the individual is poised defensively against society, Adam Smith perceived the individual's sense of self and worth embedded entirely within society. Because we not only need the approval of others, but need to feel that approval is deserved, our individual well-being exists more in relationships *with* others than protection *against* others. In his *Theory of Moral Sentiments*, Smith pointedly reconstructed the Christian precept to love our neighbors as ourselves, writing that:

> . . . it is the great precept of nature to love ourselves only as we love our neighbour; or, what comes to the same thing, as our neighbour is capable of loving us.[6]

This intensely social view of our nature is increasingly confirmed by comparative sociology and anthropology. Indeed, the dominant paradigm's notion of the autonomous individual now appears as philosophical flight of fancy! Its claim to Charles Darwin's imprimatur is suspect when we learn that Darwin clearly believed that evolving human beings could only have expanded their societies because of a "moral sense . . . aboriginally derived from the social instincts."[7] Among primeval people, Darwin observed, actions were no doubt judged good or bad "solely as they obviously affect the welfare of the tribe." Recent studies find the roots of empathy in infancy, noting that infants react to the pain of others as though it were happening to themselves.[8] And psychologists document how human expressions of fellow-feeling respond to a social context which encourages them.[9] In fact, my own intuitions and experience suggest that we ignore our profoundly social nature—our need for approval and to express our feelings for each others' well-being—only at great psychic cost.

But the environmental perspective offers a uniquely moving metaphor for such understanding of self. In 1985, I co-authored an article with environmental philosopher J. Baird Callicott.[10] He, more than anyone I know, views—and eloquently expresses—the social nature of human existence through the lens of ecology. His insights shaped this excerpt from our article:

> Nature is not only human culture's life support system, but its enduring paradigm as well. Human society is not simply embedded in nature. It also imitates nature in crucial ways—as the myths and ceremonies of primal peoples frankly acknowledge.
>
> Ecological science focuses attention on *relationships*. It reveals that organisms are not only mutually related; they are also mutually defining. A species *is what it is because of where and how it lives*. From an ecological point of view, a species is the intersection of a multiplicity of strands in the web of life. It is not only located in its context, *it is literally constituted by its context*.
>
> Once seen through the prism of the biotic community, then, a person's individuality is constituted differently—not by defense against each other but in the peculiar mix of relationships we each bear to family, friends, neighbors, colleagues, and co-workers.[11]

If true, the great environmental awakening we are now experiencing is also reshaping our sense of self. For even the most popular images of ecology involve us in perceiving relationships—the link between acid rain and the forests' health, between the destruction of rainforests in South America and thinning bird populations in North America, between pesticides on crops and the ill health of farmworkers and consumers. They're all about the ties among us and the rest of the natural world. That awareness of *relationship*, I believe, is permeating our consciousness, and ever-so-subtlely eroding the notion that we can stake out our own safety and happiness apart from the well-being of the communities in which we live.

Inescapably, awareness of our environment is also awareness of a "commons"—a reality on which we share dependency and therefore mutual responsibility, a commons which defies division into individual goods. I was struck recently by reports of a survey of American youth's knowledge of geography. A shockingly large share could not name the country that borders the U.S. on the south, but almost all had heard of the ozone hole! Its consequences touch us all.

The environmental crisis teaches perhaps more graphically what is true of all our social problems: The health of the whole is literally essential to the individual's well-being. If we are ultimately interdependent, it becomes silly to think in terms of trade-offs between social integrity and the individual's unfettered pursuit of happiness.

I have come to think of this shift in understanding as moving us from a mechanistic to what might be called a *relational worldview*.

Rethinking Farming and Food

These thoughts provide a framework for what you will find in the chapters that follow. *Diet for a Small Planet* identifies the roots of a wasteful, destructive, and hunger-generating food system in underlying economic "rules." In the pages that follow, you will read about how these unquestioned "rules" drive farmers to overproduce, eroding topsoil, polluting groundwater, and decimating farm communities.

But all that I lay out here can also be understood through the inherited "ether" I've just hinted at—the dominant mechanistic worldview. Why have we accepted these "rules" of economic life? They conform to the notion that there are laws governing the social order, just as laws of motion govern the material world. They "fit" neatly with the view of nature as giant machine. And once nature is so perceived, our job is to tinker, even redesigning nature where necessary.

Nonhuman animals become mere cogs in that machine. First Jim Mason and Peter Singer in their book *Animal Factories*[12] and then John Robbins in *Diet for a New America*[13] have told us in horrifying detail how first poultry and now other farm animals were denied expression of their own nature, constrained to the point of pain and ill-health—and, ultimately, reduced to nothing but "food processors" for human convenience and taste. Farm animals, as I discovered early in my research for *Diet*, are to the U.S. Department of Agriculture mere "units of production."

By the 1980s, the view of nature as machine for our tinkering set the stage for genetic manipulation of a new order. Scientists at the U.S. Department of Agriculture spliced a human growth hormone gene into swine. They were delighted with their success: hogs that gain weight faster and are leaner. Never mind that the animals are arthritic and cross-eyed. These problems, as the Land Institute's Wes Jackson puts it, are just aspects of "fine-tuning" the hog.[14]

If, on the one hand, we condemn modern agriculture because it involves the killing of life to sustain life, do we run the risk of furthering the fundamental fallacy: that we human beings are not really *part of* nature; we stand outside and redesign nature by human-made rules? On the other hand, outrage at the cruel treatment of farm animals by "agribusiness" can lead us to question the whole notion of human beings as outside nature. When we reconnect with our place *in* nature, we may well rediscover respectful patterns of interacting with, and even consuming, animals that have long been sources of human sustenance. For many people, the relationship of indigenous North American peoples to the animals they hunted suggests the possibility that human beings can develop humility, awe, and awareness of ourselves within the ever-renewing chain of life and death. Others, discovering as I have that human beings need eat no flesh to be healthy, understandably arrive at a different point. Why inflict any death that is unnecessary to sustaining life?

My own hope is that as we center the critique of modern agriculture in a critique of the machine model of nature, we will move away from the notion of the rights of animals *versus* the rights of humans. We can begin instead to reconceive an organic whole in which a mutuality of interests can be found. Animals re-integrated into mixed farmsteads, with a rich variety of both animal and plant species, can begin to re-attune human beings to our place in nature alongside other animals, rather than over them, outside nature.

This shift allows activists to move away from a morally self-righteous, self-sacrificial tone and to call others toward a positive vision. A "correct diet," one centered in the plant world, one based in less processed and nonchemically treated foods, is not a "should" as much as a freeing step. It helps us find our place in nature. In so doing, we are reminded of the primary fact of our being—that we are defined by relationships.

Toward a Politics of Hope

But, as we all know, it's one thing to have a vision; it's quite another to know how to manifest it. What could be a process for replacing the mechanistic and atomistic worldview with a relational, ecological vision? By the late 1980s, that was the question that pressed itself on me. What did this new worldview mean for our *real-life, everyday existence* in our complex world?

We human beings can come into harmony with the rest of the natural world, and free ourselves from life-stunting hunger and poverty, only as we together make different public choices—not only in agriculture but also across the full range of concerns. For me, however, suggesting what those different choices *should* be was inadequate—almost suspect—if I couldn't also suggest how we might go about arriving at a broad consensus on those choices and actually putting them into practice in our lives.

Surely we need a process for choosing our future that is consistent with our social nature and reflective of the high stakes we now acknowledge. So, to me a most urgent question was no longer "What is the correct policy?" or "What is my vision of the future?" but rather: "What social processes for arriving at public choices best build on our little-tapped but innate capacities for relatedness inherent in the relational worldview?"

To begin to answer that question means to probe, in order to transform, the very *meaning of democracy itself.*

For democracy in this culture is the term we use to describe the process of coming together to make public choices.

In other words, I had to stop describing the problem and start developing a philosophy of change. If we are in the midst of an historic shift in understanding, the death of the old worldview and the birth of the new, I believe we can each become conscious midwives to the birth. But not unless we are actively envisioning practical alternatives to our modern, alienating notion of politics.

The word "politics" itself has become debased. In polls of today's young people, public officials are typically characterized as unprincipled. Words like "dishonest," "corrupt," "liars," and "puppets" are common descriptions. Clearly we need a richer, stronger, more active vision of democracy to replace the dominant one, which is increasingly alienating, even insulting, to many Americans.

By mid-1990 I was ready to take the next big leap. I was determined to take on this challenge more directly. Food First, the organization I had founded in 1975 with Joseph Collins, was in good hands. It has thrived and had a major impact in part because of support from members who were readers of *Diet for a Small Planet*. It continues to have a powerful role to play. But I needed a vehicle that would allow me to devote all of my energies to these "how" questions.

But I knew I couldn't do it alone. Were there others ready to take the leap with me? Then, in mid-1990 I received a letter of support for my new direction that also offered a brilliant critique. It came from Paul Du Bois, a person about my age with a remarkable career in community organizing and academic and nonprofit leadership posts. Within minutes, I had Paul on the phone. And in less than two months of intense brainstorming and planning, we made the decision: we would throw in our lots together. We would devote ourselves to creating a vehicle for the thousands of people we sensed were—like us—ready to move from complaint or mere protest to positive work for what Paul and I came to call "citizen democracy." Our goal is nothing less than helping citizens transform the very meaning of democracy.

The year 1990 was a heady time for us. In the fall, we incorporated as the Institute for the Arts of Democracy and began a journey worthy of the rest of our lives. By the end of the year we had volunteers on board and several thousand people who'd expressed interest in our work.

In this work, we are, of course, hardly starting from scratch! Worldwide, people are searching for democracy—democracy that *works*. And here at home, in communities all across the nation, people are experimenting with new, more sustainable, effective ways of engaging citizens in public life. The role of our new center is naming, catalyzing, and further developing a search already under way. By "naming" we mean that we see our role in part as articulating an emergent philosophy—giving conceptual shape to what many are already experiencing. This process is itself empowering.

Here I'll just try to give you a taste of what we mean. Please use the coupon at the end of this book to get in touch with us to learn more.

First we acknowledge that anyone searching for real democracy must start with an admission: There exists no functioning model. No current concept of the social order legitimates the central role of *citizens*—their responsibility, their capacities for common problem solving. All inherited models share the mechanistic assumptions. In the now discredited state-socialist model, the *producer* is central—and who makes decisions? The Party. In the capitalist system, the *consumer* is all important—and who makes decisions? Owners of capital. In welfare capitalism a new role is added: the *client*—and who makes decisions? The professional, the "expert" service provider.

In other words, there is no vision of public life that puts citizen responsibility at its center. Thus, none of our inherited models takes seriously the task of creating capable citizens. In fact, "activists" are oddballs. (I recall judging a debate last year for my daughter's high school. All one debater had to do to discredit an opponent was to label her source an "activist"!)

Here in the United States, democracy's become a thin, weak notion, buttressing social atomism. Democracy and government are conflated. Democratic government is viewed as a necessary evil to sort out collisions of competing "social atoms." Government is traffic cop—or, at best, protector of individual rights. Democracy's only economic job is to keep the market functioning smoothly.

Government and politics are something done *for* us—or, more frequently, *to* us. We feel disconnected, far removed, from the decision makers. On the "Phil Donahue Show" last year, an irate member of the audience challenged funding of the Savings and Loan bailout. Leaping to his feet, he exclaimed: "I don't understand why taxpayers have to pay for the bailout, why can't the *government* pay for it!"

Government is *them*. Not us.

This notion reflects our view of democracy itself. Sitting on a long flight last week I chatted with my seat-mates. One was a Marine major; the other an engineer with General Electric. Because they were curious about my work, we started talking about the meaning of democracy. The engineer began quite certain about his views on the subject: "Democracy is the laws we have. It's like they're written in stone. They're fixed. So democracy is protected." In other words, democracy is what we inherited. We were lucky enough to be born into a democracy—there is little left for us to do.

With this perspective, citizenship becomes simply the defensive posture a prudent person assumes to protect her or his solitary self-interest. A recent poll conducted for People for the American Way found that young people hold a markedly passive notion of citizenship. It means not causing trouble. Eighty-eight percent of the teenagers polled thought that getting involved in politics has nothing to do with being good citizens.[15]

While these views dominate, I sense a profoundly different understanding emerging. I think more and more Americans are realizing that the problems we face are simply too great—too deeply rooted, too widespread, and too complex—to be met without our active engagement. Solutions require the ingenuity of those most affected, the creativity that emerges from diverse perspectives, and the commitment that comes only when people know they have a real stake in the outcome. It takes an active citizenry to create public decision making that works—decision making that is accountable and creative enough to address the root causes of today's crises.

In the emerging alternative, democracy becomes no longer a set of static institutions, but a *way of life*. Democracy as a way of life means we each share responsibility for making the whole work. Democracy is not as much structures or laws as *relationships*.

Democracy as a way of life is what the term "citizen democracy" suggests to us. We see its potential emerging in several distinct themes:

Citizen democracy re-dignifies the public realm. It challenges today's privatization of meaning. The 1980s celebrated only private reward—money, career, family. Such was the good life. Neglected was the deep human need for purpose larger than one's self.

Public life is the larger stage—all our relationships in the workplace, school, religious group, social concern organization, or formal political process. It is on this stage that we express our values—including our commitments to our family's future—and develop distinct human capacities that can only be cultivated in public life. It is on this stage that we express our need to "make a difference."

Thus, the most successful community-based citizen organizing today sees itself as preparing people for effective, sustainable public life—not just achieving victory on a given issue. Ernesto Cortes, a founding force in creating the successful Communities Organized for Community Service in San Antonio, calls citizen groups "universities where people learn the arts of public discourse and public action."[16]

For we're not born citizens, as Cortes' words frankly acknowledge. We *learn* the arts of citizenship. That's why the Institute for the Arts of Democracy is an appropriate name for an organization promoting citizen democracy. These arts include active listening, storytelling, dialogue, critical thinking, mediation, creative controversy, the disciplined expression of anger, and reflection.

In a recent speech, Ralph Nader asked: While one can go

to an Arthur Murray dance studio to learn how to dance, where do we go to learn the practice of citizenship? Our answer is that every public encounter—in school, at work, in the community or social group, can become an opportunity for learning.

I'll return to this key theme. Now let me suggest other aspects of citizen democracy coming to life throughout American society.

Citizen democracy is about empowerment through action. Most of us have learned to submerge our common sense, even our own values and tastes, and turn to the "experts"—whether in child rearing, making workplace decisions, or even in decorating our homes. (I recall a few years ago sitting in a café and overhearing a conversation that summed up our sad predicament. One woman confessed to her friend that she felt so intimidated by her interior decorator that she had had to hire a psychotherapist to help her cope!)

We learn at every turn to defer to others "better qualified." But that's changing. Bertha Gilkey, a woman living in the housing projects in St. Louis, got fed up. She wanted to get rid of rampant drugs and crime but was told, she recalls, that "we couldn't do nothing because we were poor folks and not experts." She thought that over for a moment and then responded: "Experts got us into trouble in the first place." Her confidence sparked changes within the project that have transformed it into a desirable place to live and raise a family.[17]

Bertha Gilkey's liberating moment is occurring for more and more of us. With the S&L debacle costing taxpayers the equivalent in real dollars of the entire cost of World War II, with the toxic waste crisis causing vast and needless harm, and with "experts" producing radioactive waste that remains dangerous for millennia while they have no plan for safe storage—more and more citizens are shedding a sense of deference to the authorities "up there."

Understanding citizen democracy as empowering individuals to shoulder responsibility involves us in a radical rethinking of power itself. In the dominant political tradition, power is a one-way force. The cue ball sinks the eight ball in the corner pocket—that's power! As a one-way force, it is also a zero-sum notion: The more I have, the less for you. You must yield to my power, or I to yours. In striking contrast, empowerment as the core of public life returns us to the original meaning of power, from "poder"—to be able. Power is that which enables us to express our interests and values. It is no longer a one-way force, nor zero-sum. Indeed, we can acknowledge the oh-so-frequent instances where my willingness to shoulder responsibility—to assume more power—benefits you. Certainly Bertha Gilkey's story is a case in point: her power catalyzed community power, benefitting the entire housing project and larger community as well.

Citizen politics is values based and values driven. Most of us have also come to think of public life as a series of "issues" driven by narrow interests. But in the most successful citizen initiatives, issues "are dessert, not the main course," as one effective organizer put it.

The main course is our values. What motivates people to act, to get involved? To stay involved? What we care about most—our children's future, peace, security, protecting the integrity and beauty of the natural world, fairness for everybody. These are widely shared values. They manifest in issues. But power in public life derives from consciously naming the values that motivate action.

Such an understanding of motivation belies the dominant understanding of self-interest—simply a synonym for selfishness. Realizing the many dimensions of one's own interests makes it possible to see that they cannot be furthered except in relationships—public and private. In fact, self-interest derives form the Latin *interesse*—"to be among." As political philosopher Bernard Crick puts it:

> . . . the more realistically one construes self-interest, the more one is involved in relationships with others.[18]

Thus, citizen democracy is not about learning to give up one's interests for the sake of others. It is about learning to see one's self-interests embedded in others' interests. From concerns about environmental health and neighborhood safety to effective schools and job security—none can be achieved by oneself. Each depends upon the needs of others being met as well.

In this light, we see that selfishness—narrow preoccupation with self—can actually be an enemy of self-interest. In citizen democracy, self-interest is not to be squelched or simply indulged, but consciously developed in relationships with others. It is the basis of constructive political engagement.

Citizen politics is about solving problems. In today's political world, moral grandstanding and vicious mud-slinging are the order of the day. Poised against this dominant politics is the politics of protest—we've all learned how to decry what we *don't* like.

Citizen politics takes the next step. It is task oriented. It is less concerned about proving our own righteousness or the others' failings than about taking responsibility for solutions. Whether it is citizens developing land trusts to keep down the cost of housing or the Kentuckians for the Commonwealth moving from protest over toxic waste to joining a state taskforce to work out solutions.[19]

But *where* do we learn to be problem solvers, rather than merely good complainers?

At home, at school, at work . . . just about anywhere people come together. Among the most effective classrooms in the country are those in which teachers are encouraging students to learn by tackling real problems in their communities. One of my favorite examples is in a grammar school in Amesville, Ohio, where Bill Elasky proves that his sixth graders can plan and carry out long-term problem-solving projects, given encouragement and back-up.

After a chemical spill in a nearby creek, Elasky's students decided they "didn't trust the EPA." Constituting themselves as the Amesville Sixth Grade Water Chemists, they set out to test the water themselves—and succeeded. In the process they had to divide into teams, assign tasks, plan sampling and testing times, and so on. Soon the Sixth Grade Water Chemists became the town's water quality experts, and their neighbors were buying their water testing services. These kids are learning democracy not by memorizing distant structures of government but by "doing democracy."[20]

Citizen democracy assumes that citizen participation is just as necessary in governing economic life as it is in political life. At the time of our nation's founding, the primary unit of economic life was the family. We were family farmers, shopkeepers, and traders. It made a certain amount of sense to think of economic life as private, and therefore not governed by the same democratic principles that we deemed appropriate to political life.

But in the intervening years, what has happened? The determining unit of the economy is no longer the family. Dominating the economic landscape are giant bureaucracies—non-elected, but nevertheless with more power over the quality of our lives than most governments have. We call them corporations. They determine the location and the quality of many jobs, the health of the environment, and—through their political influence—even broader questions.

Today, the world's four largest corporations enjoy a total revenue greater than the combined gross national products of 80 countries comprising half the world's population. Yet we perceive them as *private* entities, beyond democratic accountability!

Citizen democracy—the concept of ordinary people assuming greater responsibility for public decision making—challenges us to ask whether such categories of public and private still make sense.

More and more citizens are taking responsibility for making democratically accountable such "private" economic structures. A consortium of citizen organizations developed the Valdez Principles, guidelines to ensure that oil companies take measures to avoid oil spills, the consequences of which are broadly public in every sense. The Financial Democracy Campaign is providing a vehicle for citizens to take part in devising a fairer burden-sharing of the federal Saving and Loan bailout.[21]

Evidence of the last 20 years seems definitive on one point: Without democratizing *economic* decision making, reversing environmental decline seems beyond our reach. In his 1990 *Making Peace with the Planet*, Barry Commoner updates his earlier classic, *The Closing Circle*. In the earlier work he predicted that only in the few cases where citizen movements were using government to require economic bureaucracies to change their technologies of production could environmental deterioration be substantially turned around. Commoner's predictions proved correct: Real success in protecting the environment has been achieved in just a few instances: in taking lead out of gasoline, removing DDT from pesticides, and eliminating PCB from the electrical industry.

In other words, once U.S. corporations have been permitted—through citizen *non*involvement in the process—to emit into the environment each year what now amounts to almost four pounds of toxic substances for every person on earth, *it's simply too late*. To dispose safely of this enormous quantity would require several times the profits of the chemical industry. Commoner argues that the record of the last two decades demonstrates that without citizens taking greater responsibility to ensure the halt of production of toxic substances in the first place, there is no solution.[22]

But, taking a position on *anything*, even speaking out in the classroom or workplace, is a scary proposition for most of us. How do we gain the confidence and the capacity to participate in earth-shaping decisions?

Citizen democracy is a learned art. Earlier I noted that we're not born citizens. True, anyone can respond to a few TV ads and pull a lever in a polling booth. But real citizenship is an art. Like the art of dance, music, or sport, we persevere only as we learn to do it well. If we feel awkward or foolish for too long, we'll just stop! On the other hand, if we are learning the particular *challenges* and *rewards* of an art, we continue even if our "performance" is far from perfect. So, too, with active citizenship.

How do we as a society, and as individuals, come to take seriously building our capacities for expressing our values and interests in common problem solving?

The process can begin in family life. In 1985, my children—Anthony and Anna—and I wrote a book together. It's called *What to Do After You Turn Off the TV*.[23] Our idea was to entice families away from letting TV dominate home life, so they might discover the joys of each other's company. We told of our own experience of eight years without TV and interviewed hundreds of other families to capture their experiences. We were struck by how many close families had developed some version of a "family meeting"—a special time when everyone comes together to make plans and talk over problems that might have gone unresolved. Children in such families gain an early start in acquiring the capacities—for dialogue, compromise, mediation, and reflection—that can make them effective citizens.

Above I suggested a critical role for schools in learning the democratic arts. But equally important are the voluntary associations in which the majority of Americans are engaged—through religious affiliations, or in groups like the PTA, the League of Women Voters, Kiwanis, or Greenpeace. Can we come to see such involvements not just as means to solve a particular problem, or to address a given issue, but as occasions for learning the democratic arts, as opportunities for learning that can sustain our involvement throughout our lives?

So many people who become involved in addressing social problems experience early "burn out." If we do not attend to the arts of reflection and evaluation of our progress, if we do not work to perceive how our particular effort is tied to long-term society-wide change, we soon feel like retreating into our private worlds. We deny our need to make a difference in the larger world. We deny ourselves.

As we begin to value the process of democratic renewal itself, seeing our efforts not as stop-gap measures but as engaging in long-term cultural change, we can attend to making that process *rewarding*—consciously measuring our success in incremental steps, deliberately creating celebration and cultural expressions to sustain our energies.

Growing up, most of us learn that "politics" is about staking out a position and defending it. The "art," if there is any, is winning—not listening in order to understand the interests and values of others. If we are locked into pre-set positions, interaction at best hones our arguments but cannot awaken us to new possibilities. Creativity is lost. Thus, in the emerging citizen politics, listening may be the first art. Many are taking its cultivation seriously; one example is the Listening Project.

The Listening Project, a national program based in North Carolina, is a community organizing and outreach tool that uses in-depth, one-on-one interviews with people in their homes. Instead of the usual quick, check-off survey, organizers ask open-ended questions about people's values and concerns. In one home, a middle-aged European-American man complained that the biggest problem he saw was the noisy black teenagers who hung out on the streets and caused trouble. On a simple survey, that one comment might have gotten him labeled as a racist. But the organizers listened. They didn't argue. Their questions encouraged the man to look deeper. As he talked, he began to reflect as well. By the end of the interview, he himself had restated (and re-understood) the problem in his neighborhood as the lack of recreational facilities and opportunities for young people.[24]

These are some of the themes of citizen democracy. What they add up to is a profoundly different approach to social change than most of us are accustomed to. It means, for both Right and Left, breaking the habit of what I call the "manifesto approach" to social change: We decide on the program, and then "sell" it to others, or preferably, "convert" others to our truths. But, if in drawing up our alternative designs, we appear merely as more "experts" with our own brand of specialized knowledge, we do nothing to diminish the sense of powerlessness that people feel. If our process mimics the dominant instrumental view of politics—or of it fuels the polarized, highly moralized brand—we do nothing to encourage prople to take on the joys and frustrations of public engagement. In so doing we fail to address the real crisis. For the real crisis is not that justice, freedom, and biological sustainability have not yet been achieved. It is that people feel increasingly disenfranchised from the public processes essential to their realization.

If this is true, then the real challenge is neither to proclaim beautiful values nor to design elegant answers ourselves; it is to create a politics of practical problem solving—one that is engaging and rewarding, that respects people and allows them to develop their own values in interaction with one another. This means learning, modeling, and mentoring the "democratic arts."

Fully understanding democracy as a process rather than a structure of government means accepting that it can never be fully realized. In his 1990 address to the U.S. Congress, Czechoslovakia's President Vaclav Havel reminded Americans:

One may approach [democracy] as one would the horizon, but it can never be fully attained. . . . You [Americans] have thousands of problems, as other countries do, but you have one great advantage. You have been approaching democracy uninterrupted for 200 years.

Can we come to believe in democracy as an ever-unfolding dynamic to which there can be no final resting point? Such a vision suggests a fragile *ecology of democracy*—democracy as ever-evolving relationships through which people solve common problems and meet deep human needs.

Midwives to the New

The view I have attempted here would allow us finally to leave behind the worthless debate about whether we should address environmental problems by convincing people to alter individual life choices. Or, instead, should we work for changes in our economic rules and structures?

I've held—and believe my intuition confirmed by people's experience during the last 20 years—that so-called structural changes can come only as we reshape our very understanding of ourselves, gain confidence in our intuitive sense of connectedness, and therefore gain courage. That confidence and courage, as I argue throughout *Diet for a Small Planet*, come through making new choices in every aspect of our lives. Gaining confidence in our capacities and values, we're able to challenge messages telling us that market exchange is a virtual divine law whose consequences we must live with; and to question economic dogma making giant corporations "private" and therefore outside democratic accountability.

As we begin to let go of the notion that there are economic laws that take us off the hook, the environmental awakening reminds us that there are indeed laws—*ecological* laws—that we cannot escape.

There is no "away." (Radioactive wastes cannot be stored away because that place doesn't exist.)

And if that is true, then so is the corollary—everything is connected. We can't do just one thing.

And, finally, since in a wink of historical time we have spent our "fossil fuel" savings, we have no choice but to live on our solar budget.

Now these are pretty obvious truths. And the environmental scolds will tell us that these truths determine our limited means, to which we must now resign ourselves. But is this bad news, really? What such a negative casting ignores is the deep human need precisely *for* limits—for what are limits but guidelines, a coherent context for human conduct, helping us make choices?

Looked at thusly, a feeling of relief might come over us instead of panic. For it is unboundedness, endless choices that make people crazy. If little kids need rules to know they're loved and to be happy, perhaps all human beings have that need. Limitlessness means meaninglessness. Nature's very real, nonarbitrary, and universal laws can offer a sense of boundedness, imbuing our individual acts with meaning and giving us direction in making choices.

As we gain the courage to let go of the human-made laws of economic dogma, in which we have sought relief from choice, perhaps we can discover instead the real laws of the biotic community. In this discovery we can take joy in becoming contributing members, not masters, of that community.

Yes, it *is* an extraordinary time to be alive. Can the 21st century be the era in which human beings finally come home, meeting our deep need for security and meaning not in ignoring or conquering, but in living within the community of nature? Now that the stakes are indisputably ultimate, we can break through the limits of the inherited mechanistic worldview and discover the real meaning of the era of ecology—that our very being is dependent upon healthy relationships. We can find in the focus on relationships—the key insight of ecology—the beginning of what we need to meet the multiple crises affecting us, from homelessness to the environmental crisis itself. We can create an *ecology of democracy*—democracy not as fixed structure but as a rich practice of citizen problem solving, grounded in the democratic arts and equal to the challenges of our time.

Amidst such obvious social decline and environmental devastation—yet with the possibility of rebirth—more than anything we each need to find sources of hope. Hope that we can be part of such an historical awakening. Such honest hope, as opposed to wishful thinking, demands hard work. Cynicism is easy. Honest hope comes only as we experience ourselves changing, and are thus able to believe that "the world" can change. For 20 years, responses to *Diet for a Small Planet* have been for me a primary and continuing source of hope—always reminding me of the words of Chinese writer Lu Hsun I have framed on my bedroom wall:

Hope cannot be said to exist, nor can it be said not to exist.
It is just like the roads across the earth.
For actually there were no roads to begin with,
but when many people pass one way a road is made.

Book One

Diet
for a
Small Planet

Preface

I GAVE MY first speech as the author of *Diet for a Small Planet* at the University of Michigan in early 1972. I recall how hard I worked on that speech—locking myself in the basement of my mother-in-law's house while upstairs she cared for my baby son. I remember standing at the podium, shaking like crazy but delivering what I thought was a rousing political speech. Then, the question-and-answer period. A young man far back in the auditorium raised his hand. "Ms. Lappé," he asked, "what is the difference between long grain and short grain brown rice?" In the 1975 edition of this book, I described my reaction:

> I wilted. I had wanted to convey the felt-sense of how our diet relates each of us to the broadest questions of food supply for all of humanity. I had wanted to convey the way in which economic factors rather than natural agricultural ones have determined land and food use. Was I doing just the opposite? Was I helping people to close in on themselves, on their own bodies' needs, instead of using the information to help them relate to global needs?

Five years later, in 1980, before I was to give a lecture at the University of Minnesota, a man approached me. "I have an apology to make to you," he said. "I've been waiting for eight years to make it in person. *I* was that student at the University of Michigan who asked you the difference between long grain and short grain brown rice. I just wanted you to know that, although I am still eating well, *Diet for a Small Planet* also launched me into a broader social commitment. I didn't get stuck—as you thought I did."

You can imagine my surprise. We both laughed hard. And then it dawned on me that, yes, the circle was complete. It was time to do the tenth anniversary edition. It was time to chronicle the change that took me from a narrow, personal concern to the courage to face the bigger questions—questions not so easy to define as the differences among rice varieties.

Part I

Recipe
for a
Personal Revolution

1.

An Entry Point

No one has been more astonished than I at the impact of *Diet for a Small Planet*. It was born as a one-page handout in the late 1960s, and became a book in 1971. Since then it has sold close to two million copies in a half dozen languages. What I've discovered is that many more people than I could ever have imagined are looking for the same thing I was—a first step.

Mammoth social problems, especially global ones like world hunger and ecological destruction, paralyze us. Their roots seem so deep, their ramifications endless. So we feel powerless. How can *we* do anything? Don't we just have to leave these problems to the "experts"? We try to block out the bad news and hope against hope that somewhere someone who knows more than we do has some answers.

The tragedy is that this totally understandable feeling—that we must leave the big problems to the "experts"—lies at the very root of our predicament, because the experts are those with the greatest stake in the status quo. Schooled in the institutions of power, they take as given many patterns that must change if we are to find answers. Thus, the solutions can come only from people who are less "locked-in"—ordinary people like you and me. Only when we discover that we have both the capacity and the right to par-

7

ticipate in making society's important decisions will solutions emerge. Of this I am certain.

But how do we make this discovery?

The world's problems appear so closely interwoven that there is no point of entry. Where do we begin when everything seems to touch everything else? Food, I discovered, was just the tool I needed to crack the seemingly impenetrable facade. With food as my grounding point I could begin to see meaning in what before was a jumble of frightening facts—and over the last ten years I've learned that my experience has been shared by thousands of others. Learning about the politics of food "not only changed my view of the world, but spurred me on to act upon my new vision," Sally Bachman wrote me from New York.

To ask the biggest questions, we can start with the most personal—what do we eat? What we eat is within our control, yet the act ties us to the economic, political, and ecological order of our whole planet. Even an apparently small change—consciously choosing a diet that is good both for our bodies and for the earth—can lead to a series of choices that transform our whole lives. "Food had been a major teacher in my life," Tina Kimmel of Alamosa, California, wrote me.

The process of change is more profound, I'm convinced, than just letting one thing lead to the next. In the first edition of this book I wrote,

> Previously when I went to a supermarket, I felt at the mercy of our advertising culture. My tastes were manipulated. And food, instead of being my most direct link with the nurturing earth, had become mere merchandise by which I fulfilled my role as a "good" consumer.

Feeling victimized, I felt powerless. But gradually I learned that every choice I made that aligned my daily life with an understanding of how I wanted things to be made me feel more powerful. As I became more convincing to myself, I was more convincing to other people. I *was* more powerful.

So while many books about food and hunger appeal to guilt and fear, this book does not. Instead, I want to offer you power. Power, you know, is not a dirty word!

Here's how it began for me . . .

In 1969 I discovered that half of our harvested acreage went to feed livestock. At the same time, I learned that for every 7 pounds of grain and soybeans fed to livestock we get on the average only 1 pound back in meat on our plates. Of all the animals we eat, cattle are the poorest converters of grain to meat: *it takes 16 pounds of grain and soybeans to produce just 1 pound of beef in the United States today*.

The final blow was discovering that much of what I had grown up believing about a healthy diet was false. Lots of protein is essential to a good diet, I thought, and the only way to get enough is to eat meat at virtually every meal. But I learned that, on the average, Americans eat twice the protein their bodies can even use. Since our bodies don't store protein, what's not used is wasted. Moreover, I learned that the "quality" of meat protein, better termed its "usability," could be matched simply by combining certain plant foods. Thus, the final myth was exploded for me.

I was shocked. While the world's experts talked only of scarcity, I had just discovered the incredible waste built into the American meat-centered diet. And nutritionally it was all unnecessary! My world view flipped upside down. Along with many others in the late 1960s, I had started out asking: "How close are we to the limit of the earth's capacity to provide food for everyone?" Then it began to dawn on me that I was part of a system actively *reducing* that capacity.

Hidden Resources Plowed into Our Steaks

What I failed to appreciate fully ten years ago was that the production system that generates our grain-fed-meat diet not only wastes our resources but helps destroy them, too. Most people think of our food-producing resources, soil and water, as renewable, so how can they be destroyed? The answer is that because our production system encourages farmers to continually increase their output, the natural cycle of renewal is undermined. The evidence for this is presented in Part II, but here are a few facts to give you some sense of the threats to our long-term food security:

●*Water costs.* Producing just one pound of steak uses 2,500 gallons of water—as much water as my family uses in a month! Livestock production, including water for U.S. crops fed to livestock abroad, accounts for about half of all water consumed in the United States, and increasingly that water is drawn from underground lakes, some of which are not significantly renewed by rainfall. Already irrigation sources in north Texas are running dry, and within decades the underground sources will be drawn down so far that scientists estimate a third of our current irrigation will be economically unfeasible.

●*Soil erosion.* Corn and soybeans, the country's major animal feed crops, are linked to greater topsoil erosion than any other crops. In some areas topsoil losses are greater now than during the Dust Bowl era. At current rates, the loss of topsoil threatens the productivity of vital farmland within our lifetime.

●*Energy costs.* To produce a pound of steak, which provides us with 500 calories of food energy, takes 20,000 calories of fossil fuel, expended mainly in producing the crops fed to livestock.

●*Import dependency.* Corn alone uses about 40 percent of our major fertilizers. U.S. agriculture has become increasingly dependent on imported fertilizer, which now accounts for 20 percent of our ammonia fertilizer and 65 percent of our potash fertilizer. And even though the United States is the world's leading producer of phosphates for fertilizer, at current rates of use we will be importing phosphates, too, in just 20 years.

A Symbol and a Symptom

The more I learned, the more I realized that a grain-fed-meat diet is not the cause of this resource waste, destruction, and dependency. The "Great American Steak Religion" is both a symbol and a symptom of the underlying logic of our production system—a logic that makes it self-destructive.

Our farm economy is fueled by a blind production imperative. Because farmers are squeezed between rising production costs and falling prices for their crops, their profits per acre fall steadily—by 1979 hitting one-half of what they had been in 1945 (figures adjusted for inflation). So *just to maintain the same income* farmers must constantly increase production—planting more acres and reaping higher yields, regardless of the ecological consequences. And they must constantly seek new markets to absorb their increasing production. But since hungry people in both the United States and the third world have no money to buy this grain, what can be done with it?

One answer has been to feed about 200 million tons of grain, soybean products, and other feeds to domestic livestock every year. Another, especially in the last ten years, has been to sell it abroad. While most Americans believe our grain exports "feed a hungry world," *two-thirds* of our agricultural exports actually go to livestock—and the hungry abroad cannot afford meat. The trouble is that, given the system we take for granted, this all appears logical. So perhaps to begin we must stop taking so much for granted and ask, who really benefits from our production system? Who is hurt, now and in the future?

In this book I seek to begin to answer such questions.

Diet for an Abundant Planet

The worst and best thing about my book is its title. It is catchy and easy to remember. (Although one irate customer stomped into my parents' bookstore to complain that she'd thought she was buying a gardening book, *Diet for a Small Plant.**) But the title is also misleading. To some it connotes scarcity: because the planet is so "small," we must cut back our consumption. So when my next book,

---

* Others in search of my book have told me that bookstore clerks pointed them toward the science-fiction department!

Food First,† came out, with the subtitle *Beyond the Myth of Scarcity,* many people thought I had done an about-face. Yes, my thinking evolved, but for me the message of *Diet for a Small Planet* is abundance, not scarcity. The issue is how we use that abundance. Do we expand the kind of production which degrades the soil and water resources on which all our future food security rests? Do we then dispose of this production by feeding more and more to livestock? The answers lie in the political and economic order we create. The "small planet" image should simply remind us that what we eat helps determine whether our planet *is* too small or whether its abundance can be sustained and enjoyed by everyone. My book might better be called *Diet for an Abundant Planet*—now and in the future.

The Body-Wise Diet

Another part of the good news in this book is that what's good for the earth turns out to be good for us, too. Increasingly, health scientists throughout the world recommend a plant-centered diet. They report that six of the ten leading causes of death in America are linked to the high fat/high sugar/low fiber diet embodied in the Great American Steak Religion. (See Part III, Chapter 1.)

For me, living a diet for a small planet has meant increased physical vitality. And the hundreds of letters I have received testify that my experience is not unique.

The Traditional Diet

Over the years many people have been surprised when meeting the author of *Diet for a Small Planet.* I am not the gray-haired matron they expect. Nor am I a back-to-nature purist. (Sometimes I even wear lipstick!) But mouths

---

† Coauthor Joseph Collins, with Cary Fowler (Ballantine Books, 1979).

really drop open when I explain that I am not a vegetarian. Over the last ten years I've hardly ever served or eaten meat, but I try hard to distinguish what I advocate from what people think of as "vegetarianism."

Most people think of vegetarianism as an ethical stance against the killing of animals, unconventional, and certainly untraditional. But what I advocate is the return to the traditional diet on which our bodies evolved. Traditionally the human diet has centered on plant foods, with animal foods playing a supplementary role. Our digestive and metabolic system evolved over millions of years on such a diet. Only very recently have Americans, and people in some other industrial countries, begun to center their diets on meat. So it is the meat-centered diet—and certainly the grain-fed-meat-centered diet—that is the fad.

I hope that my book will be of value to the growing numbers of people who refuse to eat meat in order to discourage the needless suffering of animals. But I believe that its themes can make sense to just about anyone, whether or not they are prepared to take an ethical stance against the killing of animals for human food.

Many counter the vegetarian's position against killing animals for human food by pointing out that in many parts of the world livestock play a critical role in sustaining human life: only livestock can convert grasses and waste products into meat. Where good cropland is scarce, this unique ability of grazing animals may be crucial to human survival. Intellectually, I agree. But I say "intellectually" because, although using livestock to convert inedible substances to protein for human beings makes sense to me, I found that once I stopped cooking meat, it no longer appealed to me. If all our lives we handle flesh and blood, maybe we become inured to it. Once I stopped, I never wanted to start again. But this view is a strictly personal one, and it is not the subject of this book.

An Escape or a Challenge?

For many who have come to appreciate the profound political and economic roots of our problems, a change in diet seems like a pretty absurd way to start to change things. Such personal decisions are seen simply as a handy way to diminish guilt feelings, while leaving untouched the structural roots of our problems. Yes, I agree—such steps *could* be exactly this and nothing more.

But taking ever greater responsibility for our individual life choices could be one way to change us—heightening our power and deepening our insight, which is exactly what we need most if we are ever to get to the roots of our society's problems. Changing the way we eat will not change the world, but it may begin to change us, and then we can be part of changing the world.

Examining any of our consumption habits has value only to the degree that the effort is both liberating and motivating. Learning why our grain-fed-meat diet developed and learning what does constitute a healthy and satisfying diet have been both for me. In one area of my life I began to feel that I could make real choices—choices based on knowledge of their consequences. Second, the more I learned about why the American diet developed to include not only more grain-fed meat but more processed food, the more I began to grasp the basic flaws in the economic ground rules on which our entire production system is based. I learned, for example, that the prices guiding our resource use are make-believe—they in no way tell us the real resource costs of production. Moreover, I came to see how our production system inevitably treats even an essential ingredient of life itself—food—as just another commodity, totally divorcing it from human need. Slowly it became clear that until the production of our basic survival goods is consciously tied to the fulfillment of human need there can be no solution to the tragedy of needless hunger that characterizes our time—even here in the United States.

We Are the Realists

Some call such views unrealistic, visionary, or idealistic. I respond that it is we who are awakening to the crisis of our planet—and to our own power to make critical changes—who are the realists. Those who believe that our system of waste and destruction should continue are the dreamers. Yes, *we* are the realists. We want to face up to the terrible problems confronting the human race and learn what each of us can do right now. At the same time, we are also visionaries, because we have a vision of the direction in which we want our society to move. In Part IV you will meet some of the people I include in the "we" I've just used, people who are aligning more and more of their life choices in that direction. The lessons their lives embody inspire me. I hope that their insights and the resource guide I've included will be tools to help you take the next step in your own life.

My understanding has changed enormously since the 1975 edition of this book. Some say I realized my book's thesis was "naïve." Some claim that since the first edition of *Diet for a Small Planet* I have become more "political." Others say I have shifted my emphasis away from what the individual should do toward a call for group action. All of these judgments contain some truth, but they are not the way *I* see it.

To explain how I do see it, I've written the next chapter—about my personal journey from desperate social worker to co-founder of an international food action center investigating the causes of hunger in a world of plenty. If I believe so much must change, I must be willing to change myself.

2.

My Journey

"How DID YOU get interested in food? How did you come to write *Diet for a Small Planet?*" Countless times I have been asked these questions. Invariably I am frustrated with my answers. I never really get to explain. So, here it is. This is my chance.

I am a classic child of the 1960s. I graduated from a small Quaker college in 1966, a year of extreme anguish for many, and certainly for me: the war in Vietnam, the civil rights movement, the War on Poverty. That year was the turning point.

While I had supported the U.S. position on the Vietnam war for years, finally I became too uncomfortable merely accepting the government's word. I set out to discover the facts for myself. Why were we fighting? I read everything I could find on U.S. government policy in Vietnam. Within a few weeks, my world began to turn upside down. I was in shock. I functioned, but in a daze. I had grown up believing my government represented me—my basic ideals. Now I was learning that "my" government was not mine at all.

From that state of shock grew feelings of extreme desperation. Our country seemed in such a terrible state that something had to be done, *now*, today, or all hope seemed lost. I wanted to work with those who were suffering the

16

most, so I did what people like Tom Hayden suggested. For two years, 1967 and 1968, I worked as a community organizer in Philadelphia with a national nonprofit organization of welfare recipients—the Welfare Rights Organization. Our goal was to ensure that welfare recipients got what they were entitled to by law.

Most evenings I came home in tears. Perhaps I had helped someone get her full welfare payment, or forced a landlord to make a critical repair. But I realized that even if I succeeded each day in my immediate goal, I was in no way addressing the root causes of the suffering that was so evident to me. The woman I worked most closely with died of a heart attack at the age of forty-five. I was convinced she died of the stress of poverty.

During these years I became *more* desperate, not less. But I just kept on doing what I was doing, because I did not know what else to do.

In 1968 I ended up in graduate school, studying community organizing at the School of Social Work at the University of California at Berkeley. As part of my training, I worked on fair housing policies in Oakland. But this work did nothing to resolve my questions. I was becoming more miserable, more confused.

The Most Important Decision

Then, in the spring of 1969, I made the most important decision of my life (next to the decision to have children, that is): I vowed not to do *anything* to try to "change the world" until I understood why I had chosen one path instead of another, until I understood *how* my actions could attack the roots of needless suffering.

My first step was to drop out of graduate school. This decision was so agonizing it made me physically ill. I was petrified that people would ask me, "What do you do?" and I would have no answer. My identity had been "social worker." Now I would have no identity.

Friends now tease me when I tell this story. They say, "People in the late 1960s in Berkeley would never have asked you what you 'did.' At most, people might have asked, 'What are you into?' " But the truth was, I didn't have an answer to that either.

So there I was, twenty-five years old and adrift. What would I do? In sixteen years of "learning" I had never known whether I had real interests of my own. Yes, I had pleased my teachers and professors. Yes, I had shed my southern accent in my first six months of college, to prove that I wasn't an empty-headed southern female. But all that had been to prove something to others. If I wasn't trying to please a teacher anymore, was there anything left? Any motivation? Any direction? I was skeptical—and afraid.

What gave me the courage to discover my own path? Two things. I knew I couldn't go on as I was; I was just too miserable. At the same time, I was married to a person who gave me absolute emotional support. I was sure Marc would love me even if I never saved the world.

I started studying modern dance and reading political economy—books that attempted to explain the causes of poverty and underdevelopment. Very soon, after only a few months, I began to hone in on food.

Why food? In part I was influenced by the emerging ecology movement and the "limits to growth" consciousness. The first Earth Day was in 1970. Paul Ehrlich's book *The Population Bomb* exploded during this same period, and books like *Famine 1975* appeared. Newspaper headlines were telling us (as they still are) that we had reached the limits of the earth's ability to feed us all.

But part of the reason I chose to focus on food was more personal. I became aware of people around me in Berkeley eating differently from the way I did. Some of the foods I had never heard of—bulgur, soy grits, mung beans, tofu, buckwheat groats. What were all these strange things? I was attracted by the incredible variety of colors, aromas, textures. I remember devouring my first "natural foods" cookbook as if it were a novel. Barley, mushrooms, and dill together? Cheddar cheese, walnuts, and rice? How odd. What would that taste like?

Beyond the Food Battle

As I started experimenting, I found my entire attitude toward food changing. Food and I had always been in battle and had reached a stalemate at about ten pounds more than I really wanted to weigh. To hold that line I had to count calories and feel guilty about what I shouldn't eat. But when I started to learn about food, appreciating the incredible variety I hadn't known before and eating more unprocessed foods, I stopped battling. My appetite began to change. I stopped counting calories. I stopped feeling guilty. I had just one rule: if I was hungry, I would eat; if I wasn't hungry, I would say no. I no longer made the decision about whether to eat based on something external to me, only on how I felt inside.

Dancing also helped me make this change. If food and I had been battling, so had my body and I. In the culture I grew up in, the messages were so powerful that my girlfriends and I were wearing girdles to school by the time we were in junior high. When I began to dance, the old battle—me versus my body—was transformed. Instead of being just a problem to reshape and control, my body became a source of satisfaction and pleasure.

My diet was changing. My feelings about myself were changing. At the same time, I was learning about "world food problems." Soon I was reading everything I could find on food and hunger. Something told me that because food is so basic to all of us, if we could just grasp the causes of hunger we would clear a path to understanding the complexities of politics and economics that overwhelm and paralyze so many.

Following My Nose

I read, took notes. I audited courses from soil science to tropical agriculture. And I found an ideal little study niche

in the agricultural library at Berkeley. In the quiet basement corridors no one bothered me. No one asked me what
I was studying for. The librarians were friendly and helpful.

There I learned to "follow my nose"—a research technique that has served me well for the last twelve years. For
me, this meant not having a grand scheme, not knowing
exactly where I was going. Instead, I responded to the information I was learning, letting it lead me to the next question.

Overall, I wanted to find out for myself just how close
we were to the earth's limits. I wanted to find out for myself the causes of hunger. I wanted to find out what were
the important questions to ask.

Then, in late 1969, in my library-basement hideaway, I
came across certain facts about U.S. agriculture that
changed my life. They changed how I was formulating the
important questions.

First, as I recounted in Chapter 1, I learned that in the
United States over half of the harvested acreage goes to
feed livestock and only a tiny fraction of it gets returned to
us in meat on our plate. I learned that most Americans
consume about twice the protein their bodies can use. Finally, I learned that by combining plant foods one can create a protein of equal "quality" to animal protein.

When I put this all together, I felt like the little boy in
the fairy tale who cries out, "The emperor has no clothes!"
I could barely believe what I was learning, because it flew
so totally in the face of the conventional wisdom. Most
important, I saw that the questions being asked by the experts to whom I had turned for guidance were the *wrong
questions.*

Newspaper headlines and textbooks were all telling me
that we had reached the limits of the earth's ability to feed
people. Famine is inevitable, we were (and are still) told.
Yet my own modest research had shown me that in my
own country the food system was well designed to get rid
of a tremendous abundance of grain created by a relentless
push to increase production. Because hungry people
throughout the world could not afford to buy that grain, it

was fed to livestock to provide more meat to the already well-fed.

Suddenly I understood that questions about the roots of needless hunger had to focus not on the simple physical limits of the earth, but on the economic and political forces that determine what is planted and who eats. I began to realize that the experts' single-minded focus on greater production as the solution to world hunger was wrongheaded. You could have more food and still more hunger.

This realization, besides being the motive for what became *Diet for a Small Planet*, was my first step in demystifying the experts—those credential-laden officials and academics who have the answers *for* us. I thought that if I could write up the facts about how land and grain are wasted through a fixation on meat production, and could demonstrate that there are delicious alternatives, I could get people to question the economic ground rules that create such irrational patterns of resource use.

From a One-Page Handout

So I wrote a one-page handout. I planned to give it to friends and post it where sympathetic souls might read it. But I hesitated. "Oh no, you really should know more about this first," I said to myself. So my message became a five-page handout. Then a seventy-page booklet, which I decided to publish myself. I had it all typed up and had bought the paper to print it on when, out of the blue, a friend told me he was on his way to New York to meet with some publishers, including Betty Ballantine of Ballantine Books. He wanted to show her my booklet. What? He couldn't be serious! In my opinion, it might appeal to 500 people in the greater Berkeley community. But he insisted, and finally I agreed.

I was certain that no New York publisher would be interested in my modest effort, but the idea did make me think that some Berkeley-based publisher might be. So I nervously approached one on my own. Theirs was certainly no New York publishing house, they assured me. This firm considered itself part of the "movement," working to revolutionize publishing to "serve the people." I was impressed. Certainly I wanted my book to reach and serve the people.

Suddenly I was being courted by both the "counterculture" publisher and by Ballantine. At first the choice seemed clear. How could I compromise my principles with a New York publisher? Wouldn't they operate like any other big business—looking only at the profit margin, not the value of my book?

But when Mrs. Ballantine telephoned, I couldn't refuse to see her, could I? It wouldn't hurt just to talk with her.

At the same time, the Berkeley outfit was wining and dining me. They took me to a fine French restaurant to "share" with me what they were sure I would want to know about Ballantine. First, did I know it was controlled by the Mafia? "No, really?" Second, did I know what Ballantine did with leftover books? Well, *they* would tell me. It shredded them and polluted San Francisco Bay with them! For a dutiful child of the ecology movement, this was just too much. I broke down in tears.

A few days later, Mrs. Ballantine arrived in Berkeley. I picked her up at the Durant Hotel, expecting to meet a tough businesswoman—maybe not gloves and hat, but certainly someone who could adequately represent a fat-cat New York firm. Out the door came a middle-aged woman in flowered cotton pants and tennis shoes. Her face was warm and natural. No makeup. Her hair was soft and gray. No coloring. But wait! This couldn't be Betty Ballantine!

Betty Ballantine and I spent the day together. I served her a *Diet for a Small Planet* meal—Mediterranean Lemon Soup and Middle Eastern Tacos. She loved it. I told her my concerns about who should publish the book and how I wanted it to be published. Never did she try to convince me to publish with Ballantine. As she left that evening she said, "Whoever publishes the book, I'll buy it."

What was I to do? All my stereotypes had been smashed. If I couldn't make a decision based on my stereotypes, I had to make one based on which choice would ensure that my book got read by the most people. I knew that Ballantine Books reached into grocery stores, bus stations, and airports. The choice became clear. I chose Ballantine and have never regretted it, although the Ballantines later sold the company to Random House, owned by the multinational conglomerate RCA, which in 1980 sold it to the Newhouse Brothers.

Betty Ballantine kept her word. She did everything I had hoped for. She didn't change a word I had written. She took great care in choosing the graphics.

The Julia Child of the Soybean Circuit

Nineteen seventy-one was a year of tremendous change. My first child, Anthony, was born in June. I moved to Hastings-on-Hudson, New York, in August. *Diet for a Small Planet* was published in September.

Looking back, I realize I still felt like the little boy who says, "The emperor has no clothes." I was terrified when the book first appeared. My message seemed so obvious it couldn't be correct, I thought.

As the author of *Diet for a Small Planet*, I began a new period of my life. But it was not quite what I had bargained for. Ovenight I became the Julia Child of the soybean circuit. I was asked to go on TV talk shows—as long as I brought along my own beans and rice! I was asked to stir them on camera, explaining how to combine protein. As my future colleague Joe Collins later said, "They wanted you to tell people how to lose weight and save money in the coming world food crisis." Such was the intellectual and humanitarian depth of most of these shows.

So I found myself in another apparent ethical dilemma. Did I refuse to be put in the woman's slot on the talk shows, as the writer of a "cookbook," or did I seize the opportunity to reach out to people who would never pick up my book if they knew it was about politics and economics? I chose the latter course. From Boston to San Francisco, from Houston to Minneapolis, I appeared on midday and midnight shows, on morning shows, and on the six o'clock news. Standing there stirring my beans and rice, I would try to get in what *I* thought was important.

The low point of this period came in Pittsburgh on a late-night talk show. Talk-show hosts search for some common ground among their guests; unfortunately that evening the only other guest was a UFO expert. I got only one question the whole evening: "Ms. Lappé, what do you think they eat on UFOs?" I launched from that question into the economic and political roots of hunger. (Now you know why I got only one question.)

Although this was a difficult time, I learned one important rule, useful to everyone in public life—never listen to the questioner, just say what you believe needs to be said!

Rubbing Elbows with the "Experts"

Fortunately, this period of my life came to an end in 1974. In November I attended the World Food Conference in Rome, that much-heralded meeting of government and corporate leaders to design a blueprint to overcome the problem of world hunger. Every major newspaper carried a front-page series on this conference, at which Henry Kissinger announced that in ten years no child would go to bed hungry.

I had gone to Rome at the urging of friends and because I wanted to rub elbows with people who I thought knew a lot more about the problems than I. By now I had two very young children, but I had continued to read and write articles as well as speak and appear on TV. Still, I did not think of myself as especially knowledgeable, certainly not in comparison to the experts gathered in Rome.

Rome was a major shock. People were asking *me* for my opinion. Microphones turned my way. I was asked to appear on a panel of experts. That was pretty startling in itself, but listening to the experts was more shocking still: I discovered that the officials to whom I looked for the answers were still locked into the false diagnoses, and therefore false cures, that I had discarded through my independent study, modest as it was.

This was the second stage in the growing realization which has since formed the basis of my work. I slowly realized that those who have been schooled to direct the powerful institutions which control our economic system are forced to accept and to work within the system that creates needless hunger. Beneficiaries of these institutions, they have been made incapable of seeing outside their boundaries. Rather than preparing them to find solutions, their training has inhibited them from asking questions that could lead to solutions. Those supposed authorities who gathered in Rome in 1974 were still promoting the belief that greater production would solve the problem of hunger, but I had come to see that you could have tremendous production—indeed, I lived in the country with the greatest food abundance in history—and yet still have hunger and malnutrition.

I left Rome feeling I had shed critical layers of self-doubt. I saw more clearly than ever that the real problems in our world—the widespread needless deprivation—will never be solved by the government leaders now in power in most nations. So who will solve them? And how can they be solved? I finally realized that the gravest problems facing our planet today can be solved *only* as part of an overall movement toward a more just sharing of economic and political power, not as separate technical problems. Thus, the solutions will come only when ordinary people, like me and like you, decide to take responsibility for changing the economic order.

In other words, the only way that power will come to be more democratically shared is if you and I take more of it ourselves. If this is true, then the challenge to each of us becomes clear: we must make ourselves capable of shouldering that responsibility.

If I really believed this, then what *I* had to do was clear: I had to take my own work much more seriously. I had to refuse to be dismissed simply as a "cookbook" writer. I had to apply myself with greater diligence than ever in my life.

Finally the veil lifted. I remember feeling like "superwoman" when I returned home that November of 1974. Anything seemed possible. I vowed to completely revise the first edition of *Diet for a Small Planet* and make its political message much clearer. I marched in to talk with the president of Ballantine (the new president, since the Ballantines had sold the company) and presented him with a list of demands concerning the book, its publication date, and its promotion. He agreed to everything.

I completed the revisions in three months, while taking care of two children. It was really a new book. I stressed that I did not believe that a change in the American diet would solve the world food problem. I wrote:

> A change in diet is not an *answer*. A change in diet is a way of experiencing more of the *real* world, instead of living in the illusory world created by our current economic system, where our food resources are actively reduced and where food is treated as just another commodity. . . . A change in diet is a way of saying simply: I have a choice. That is the first step. For how can we take responsibility for the future unless we can make choices now that take us, personally, off the destructive path that has been set for us by our forebears?

I had never worked so hard in my life. It was exhilarating. But when the new book was out (in April 1975) and all the publicity tours were over, I collapsed—from exhaustion, I thought. Soon, however, I learned that fatigue was not my real problem. The real problem was that I did not know where to go next. Here I was, in a suburb of New York, with two small children. I also had a wonderful husband, but his life's work—medical ethics—and his friends who revolved around that work were not mine. I had no political allies and few friends. My isolation overwhelmed me. I sank deeper and deeper into depression. I saw no escape. Only months earlier my confidence had been at its peak, my calling clear. Now I felt more lost than ever. I knew I had power and energy, but I had no idea how to apply it.

Food First: The Challenge

But a seed had been planted even before the new book was out. On Food Day, in March 1975, I lectured at a conference at the University of Michigan. Among the other speakers was Joseph Collins of the Institute for Policy Studies in Washington. He heard part of my lecture (later he told me that the blah vegetarian meals served during the three-day conference left him so hungry he dashed out midway through my speech for some Kentucky Fried Chicken!) and we were introduced afterward. I learned that Joe was beginning work on a book about the political and economic causes of hunger. He, too, had been at the World Food Conference in Rome the autumn before. He had represented the Transnational Institute and had helped write a report for release there which indicted the conference for failing to address the roots of hunger in the political and economic system. Joe was preparing to take off from that document to write a full-length, more popular book.

I thought no more about it until I received Joe's outline in the mail after I got home. He asked if he might visit me to get my perspective on his project. He came, and slowly it dawned on me that Joe wanted me to write the book with him. But how could I? He lived in Washington; I lived in New York. My children were still so tiny. My daughter, Anna, was barely walking. I said no. While my husband encouraged me, I pulled back.

However, I must not have let go of the idea altogether. I remember saying to my husband, "That man is going to write a book I wanted to write. What am I going to do?" But I felt I wasn't ready for a commitment so enormous.

In April I was invited to speak at a church-sponsored retreat in the Midwest. Gathered there were church leaders, the church experts on world hunger. Again I was shocked. I tried to shift the emphasis from a charity approach to one that focused on the political and economic links between Americans and the causes of world hunger. One church leader responded that he wasn't sure that we should criticize our government's policies, because the government can exert its power over the churches and the churches should not take chances. The general level of discussion was so uninformed that again I found myself thinking: as unprepared as I feel to take on this new book project, if not me, who? I knew that people's unwillingness to take chances was a major factor in allowing needless hunger to continue. Was I also unwilling? If I didn't feel prepared, perhaps I could become prepared. All these thoughts went through my mind. But no decision.

After the evening program on the last night of the retreat, a film was shown. On the screen before us were people actually dying of starvation in the Ethiopian famine. I had never seen anything like this before: babies sucking futilely at shriveled breasts; desperate mothers. The narrative told how the corrupt government of Haile Selassie had created this horror.

The decision to write *Food First* came as I watched this film. It was an emotional decision. Intellectually I had decided I wasn't ready and that my responsibility to my family wouldn't allow it, but emotionally I felt there was no choice. I *had* to do what I could do, no matter how impossible it seemed. I called Joe in Washington at midnight and said I would write the book with him if he could move to New York.

Within three weeks Joe had moved to New York. Within six weeks we had a contract with Ballantine.

When Joe and I started to work, I was terrified. Here he was, the most worldly man I had ever known—fluent in six languages and a world traveler since the age of thirteen. He had gone through a demanding Jesuit education; in my twelfth-grade social studies class we had made popsicle-stick models of historical events. I was sure that I would be so intimidated that even before we agreed on the book's outline I'd be a humiliated heap of tears. How could my skills measure up to his?

Well, I was amazed.

Joe treated me as a total intellectual equal. It turned out that rather than being unequal, our skills were—and are—miraculously complementary. Joe is a maniac for detail. He will leave no stone unturned in his research. He's also got a lot of chutzpah, so whatever information we need, Joe can figure out some way to get it. Me, I'm a maniac about organization and deadlines.

So it worked. Instinctively we knew we didn't have to compete. Each of our contributions was essential and appreciated by the other. (No one believes this, but I swear it is true: in writing all 412 pages of *Food First,* Joe and I never disagreed over a single word. We edited and reedited each other's material, but we both knew when we hit just the right phrasing.)

In the next year and a half everything in my life—except my relationship with my children—changed. Instead of just writing a book, Joe and I soon decided to use our advance payment for *Food First* to establish an organization to fill a critical gap. We named it the Institute for Food and Development Policy.

We were aware of the growing number of people asking, why hunger? What can I do? By 1975, when we met, every major church body had established a commission or task force on world hunger. Campus action groups were springing up. In courses ranging from nutrition to geography to world politics, students and professors were asking, what are the causes of and solutions to world hunger?

In addition, a new wave of food co-ops had emerged. Learning from their predecessors (which had begun in the 1930s), these initiatives were democratically managed with the goal of providing quality "whole" foods at lower cost than the supermarket. These co-ops were aware of the larger, political implications of the diet they were promoting and the service they were providing.

These initiatives were not centrally coordinated but represented an embryonic movement. Many people, working on many different projects related to food and farming, were becoming aware of and taking encouragement from one another.

What was missing was an independent research and education center to provide ongoing analysis of the roots of needless hunger to these varied projects. This was the gap we set out to fill. At the time, information and analysis came overwhelmingly from agencies funded by corporations, governments, or churches. Each of these sources, we felt, had a vested interest in maintaining the "hunger myths"—the first and most pervasive being that hunger is caused by scarcity.

Exploding the Hunger Myths*

For us, learning began with unlearning these powerful myths. As we studied, traveled, and interviewed, we were able to cut through the media-repeated themes of scarcity, guilt, and fear. As we worked on the book, certain themes emerged that have grounded our work ever since.

•*No country in the world is a hopeless "basket case."* The illusion of scarcity is a product of the growing concentration of control over food-producing resources. From Bangladesh villages to Wall Street commodity brokerages, fewer and fewer people are deciding how food resources are used and for whose benefit, yet the most wasteful and inefficient food systems are those controlled by a few in the interests of a few.

•*The hungry are not our enemies.* Actually, we and they are victims of the same economic forces. The direct cause of hunger in the third world—the increasing concentration of economic power—is also accelerating here in the United States: 3 percent of U.S. farms now control almost half of farm sales. But concentration of production is only one aspect. Economists warn that monopoly power in the food-processing industry results in close to $20 billion in overcharges to Americans every year.[1]

•*Our role is not to go into other countries to "set things right."* Our responsibility is to remove the obstacles facing the oppressed in the third world—obstacles often created with our tax dollars, such as U.S. economic and military aid that goes selectively to some of the world's most repressive regimes, as in Zaire, the Philippines, and El Salvador.

The logical conclusions of what we were learning put us in conflict with positions we had previously supported, but eventually we came to an understanding that provided us

---

* *World Hunger: Ten Myths,* by Frances Moore Lappé and Joseph Collins, one of our Institute's most popular publications, further explodes these myths. See our address on page 481.

with direction and energy instead of paralyzing us with guilt, fear, or despair.

We worked day and night to write *Food First*. For me the hard work and long hours were not new. What was new was working with other people. For the previous six years I had worked primarily at home or alone in the library. Now I was part of a team. With the advance from Ballantine, Joe and I were able to hire allies like Cary Fowler (now completing a book on the threat of seed patenting) and Robert Olorenshaw to help us. In the process of research and writing I communicated with hundreds more across the country and around the world, people who were willing to offer their ideas and expertise because they believed in what we were doing.

From 1975 on, learning to work as part of a team became a challenge equal to the challenge of writing *Food First* or any of the books I have worked on since. The message of this book and of *Food First* can be distilled into one theme—people can take ever greater responsibility to change the economic ground rules that determine how resources are used, once they understand these rules and can see where to begin. That means we believe in the possibility of genuine democracy. As I began to work in a team, I began to experience this democracy—so abstract and enormous in scope—as something I had to learn to live every day of my life. I discovered how little our society teaches us about how to share power.

A year and a half after we signed the contract, *Food First* was virtually completed. In all the turmoil of that intense work period, Marc and I had separated and he had taken a job with the State of California. To keep the children close to both their parents, we moved the new Institute to California.

On My Own

In January 1977, I landed with my two children, Anthony and Anna, in San Francisco. For the first time I was really on my own. Never before had I alone had to take care of finding housing and schooling for my children, buying a car, dealing with insurance and taxes. Now it was all up to me—and I was terrified. I had spent a year writing about empowerment, yet I was not sure I had inside me what it took to establish my own life. Until that point I hadn't realized how much I had incorporated our society's view of the single mother as social leftover.

Precisely because I had absorbed these images myself, I found my new life a surprise. Rather than experiencing my children as a burden, I discovered that I enjoyed them more than ever. While I was married, I always viewed myself as the mundane Mom—reliable but dull. But I discovered that when I was alone with my kids, I changed. I became more spontaneous. My relationship with each of them got better, closer.

Part of the change came from my decision not to have a TV anymore.* To my great surprise, the children never complained. Even though I work until 5:00 every evening, I am home with them every night they are not with Marc. (We share custody.) Between 6:00 and 9:30 every school night is "our time." We listen to the evening news on listener-supported Pacifica radio station KPFA, and often talk about what we hear. They do their homework at the kitchen table while I read the newspaper. We play games, listen to records, make up dances, do acrobatic tricks in the living room. On longer summer evenings we skate or ride bikes. Every night we have at least twenty minutes of "story time." After story time is "lie-down time"—I lie down by each of them for five minutes or so. This is the one point in the day when we each have the other's total attention. Feelings come out that would never come out otherwise. Sometimes we sing, or I might write messages on their backs for them to guess. Sometimes we just lie there in silence.

While others sometimes see a conflict between my work and my children, I don't. I couldn't accomplish what I do without them. They are my grounding force. They keep me from working so hard that I would run the risk of burning

---

* I cannot overstress the importance of this decision. I commend to you Jerry Mander's beautiful book *Four Arguments for the Elimination of Television* (Morrow Quill Paperbacks, 1977).

out. They pull me back from feelings of despair. They are positive. They welcome each day. With people like that around, no wonder I have energy.

But I want them to see my tears and my anger. I want them to understand the injustice in our society and others. When my daughter was three and my son was six, we lived with a Guatemalan family for four weeks while I studied Spanish. In the town of Antigua, where we lived, as in so many Latin towns, the estates of the wealthy are all behind walls, so you can't see who owns how much. One evening we climbed the hillside behind our home. From the top we looked down on the entire valley. For the first time my children saw that just two families owned huge estates (coffee fincas) covering a large portion of the valley. My son was shocked: "But, Mommy, that isn't fair! Those people have so much. But the people we saw this morning on the way to school were just living alongside the road. They had no houses at all." He continued, "I wonder what would happen if we were giants and we could reach down and take all of the rich people and put them in the poor people's houses and all of the poor people and put them in the rich people's houses."

I didn't answer. I only thought how glad I was that we had come. (I still had no regrets even after they both got amoebic dysentery. I do think, however, that their most enduring memory of Guatemala is not the social injustice but that awful green-brown medicine!)

Building the "Food First" Institute

But I've jumped ahead of my story.

A few weeks after I landed in San Francisco, the rest of the Institute arrived—Joe Collins and David Kinley (formerly with the North American Congress on Latin America and the Corporate Data Exchange). We three—plus the cartons of books and papers, a few filing cabinets, and some typewriters—were *it*. That was four years ago. Now the Institute for Food and Development Policy has ten full-time and six part-time staff, plus at least twenty-five work-study students, interns, and volunteers. We have published fifteen books and booklets, dozens of articles, a Food First slide show, and a Food First comic book. We have given dozens of TV and radio interviews and hundreds of speeches.

Most satisfying is the range of people who are using our work—peasant organizers in the Philippines and Bangladesh, teachers here at home (from classes in political science, economics, and ethics to classes in nutrition), members of church study groups of all denominations, food co-op people, and journalists. In one recent week our work was used as the basis for a front-page *Wall Street Journal* article critical of food aid in Bangladesh, we were quoted in *Newsweek,* and one of our new books was favorably reviewed in the *New York Times Book Review.* Yet we feel certain we have just scratched the surface.

Over the four years since *Food First* was originally published, we have seen a dramatic change in the analysis of hunger by groups that we have been trying to reach. The simplistic overpopulation theories of hunger, for instance, are no longer accepted uncritically. The questions and attitudes of the audiences who hear me speak are also very different. We believe that our work is contributing to that change.

While many discard the overpopulation explanation of hunger, often they still fall back on the idea that greater production alone is the solution; they ignore the most critical issue of control—power. So we have tried to make our message ever clearer: unless we address the issue of power—who is making the decisions—we can never get at the roots of needless hunger.

The official diagnosis is that the poor are poor because they lack certain things—irrigation, credit, improved seeds, good roads, etc. But we ask, *why* are they lacking these things? In studying country after country, it becomes clear that what the poor really lack is power—the power to secure what they need. Government aid agencies focus on the lack of materials; we focus on the lack of power.

Jimmy Carter's Presidential Commission on World Hunger, for example, identified "poverty" instead of overpopulation as the cause of hunger. We disagree. Poverty is a symptom, not a cause. Poverty is a symptom of people's powerlessness.

Nor is this mere semantic nitpicking. From these very different analyses flow very different "solutions"—and very different roles for us as outsiders.

If, as the official diagnosis would have it, the problem is poverty, then the solution is more government foreign aid to provide the goods to increase production. Billions of dollars of foreign aid is justified this way. But the bulk of this aid goes to governments which the United States sees as its military and political allies, including some of the world's most repressive regimes. For fiscal year 1981, just ten countries received over one-third of all U.S. aid.[2] Among them were India, Indonesia, Bangladesh, Pakistan, and the Philippines, with governments internationally notorious for their neglect of the needs of the poor and their repression of those wanting change. In countries where economic control is concentrated in the hands of a few, foreign aid strengthens the local and foreign elites whose stranglehold over land and other productive resources generates poverty and hunger in the first place. Instead of helping, our aid frequently hurts the dispossessed majority.

In a Bangladesh village, tube wells designed to benefit the poorest farmers become the property of the village's richest landlord; in Haiti, food-for-work projects intended to help the landless poor end up as a boon to the village elite; and in Indonesia, rural electrification which was supposed to create jobs in rural industries actually eliminates the jobs of thousands of poor rural women.

We've had to conclude that U.S. foreign assistance fails to help the poor because it is based on two fundamental fallacies: first, that aid can reach the powerless even though channeled through the powerful; second, that U.S. government aid can be separated from the narrow military and economic strategies of U.S. policymakers. In the 1975 edition of *Diet for a Small Planet* I scolded the U.S. government for being so stingy, and called for an increase in U.S. foreign aid. In researching *Food First* and *Aid as Ob-*

stacle,* however, I learned that as a tool of U.S. foreign policy, this aid goes overwhelmingly to the world's most repressive governments, helping to shore up the power of those who are blocking the changes necessary to alleviate hunger and poverty.

Banana Hunger

Six months after we moved to California, I decided that I had to begin traveling in the third world. Since his teen-age years Joe had spent a great deal of time in the third world, especially Latin America. I had been only to Mexico and Guatemala, and then only briefly. I wanted to experience firsthand what I had been studying for so many years.

I chose the Philippines because the United States has particular responsibility for the underdevelopment of that country. The Philippines was once a colony of the United States and has been heavily influenced by U.S. political, military, and corporate ties. During the five years after President Ferdinand Marcos declared martial law in 1972, U.S. military and economic aid to the Philippines leaped fivefold. In the fiscal year 1982 budget, this aid was scheduled to top $110 million—not including rent for military bases, a disguised form of aid.[3]

For years I had read and written about U.S. corporate invasion of third world economies. I wanted to see, hear, and touch the impact of that economic force. For years I had read about grassroots resistance to brutal domination by landed elites. I wanted to meet people who were part of that resistance. What did they want? Were they full of hate and anger? Could they accept people like me as allies, or did they see all North Americans as enemies?

I traveled to the Philippines with my buddy Eleanor McCallie, a founder of Earthwork/Center for Rural Studies, also based in San Francisco. Together we learned about

---

* *Aid as Obstacle: Twenty Questions about Our Foreign Aid and the Hungry*, co-authors Joseph Collins and David Kinley, Institute for Food and Development Policy.

underdevelopment in a way that no statistics could ever convey.

Multinational corporations such as Del Monte and Castle and Cook (Dole) tell us that their investments create the wealth and foreign exchange which the Philippines needs to import essential goods; they're the "engines of development," according to the multinational corporations. We visited the products of their interventions—giant banana plantations they have developed in the southern Philippines over the last ten years.

We met workers paid less than $1.50 a day for back-breaking work, sometimes 12 to 14 hours a day. We went inside their living quarters and tried to imagine what it would be like to live with 24 other women in a room not much bigger than my living room back home, with a small curtain over each woman's bunk providing her only privacy. The bunks were simply hard wooden platforms.

A pregnant woman showed us a large, raw wound on her leg. This, she said, was where another worker had accidentally sprayed her with the fungicide used on the bananas. For the first time we became aware of the terrible danger of pesticides everywhere. Besides the pesticides sprayed regularly on each banana tree and the fungicide sprayed on each bunch as it is packed, planes spray the entire plantation from the air twice a month. Water supplies are left uncovered. The workers are not protected, or even given any warning. In fact, we were told pesticide planes have been used to break up the meetings of workers attempting to organize an effective union.

To Del Monte and Dole, this is development. But development for whom? Small farmers had worked the land for over a generation, yet, as is common in the third world, they had no legal title to it. This made it easier for the corporations to move in. They simply made deals with wealthy local owners of the best banana land. Once these big landowners saw they could make money by producing bananas for Del Monte, Dole, or Standard Brands, they pushed the poor, small farmers off the land, using bribes, false promises of great jobs on the plantations, legal maneuvers, and finally brutal force.

Most of the dispossessed could not get any kind of job on

the plantations. Many ended up even worse off—rising at four each morning to line up near the docks in hopes of being picked to help load the banana boats. They had no job security and no place to live except the crowded, dirty "carton" village set up near the docks.

We might have come home demoralized by the degradation and suffering we witnessed, but we didn't, because we also witnessed the strength of the people.

One morning we got up at four to meet with the men waiting for a day's work on the docks. They told us of their attempts to organize a real union to represent them—and how everything had to be carried out in total secrecy. Anyone known to be organizing never got another work assignment. Living with little food and no security in the carton village should have sapped these men's energy, yet they told of their goals and the secret meetings they were planning. They were not resigned.

Maria, a woman who had worked on the banana plantations and was then working through the church community in basic village-level education, was part of the widespread resistance to the Marcos dictatorship. Petite, soft-spoken, Maria did not fit our image of a revolutionary. (But neither did anyone else we met.) Her commitment was not just to the ousting of a dictator but, most important, to the building of a democratic society from the village up. That was why village-level education was a priority. She and her many allies used drama and song to make political and social problems come to life for the peasants.

We asked our new friends how we in the United States could help them. Without hesitation they told us that we should work to end U.S. government support for the antidemocratic dictatorship that rules their country. Without U.S. aid, Maria told us, the Marcos dictatorship would fall. (In 1981 the Philippines was the sixth largest recipient of U.S. development assistance aid and the seventh largest recipient of U.S. military aid.) She urged us to return home to explain to Americans that our security does not rest in supporting dictators abroad.

Maria helped me to understand that our role is not to empower other people. In fact, we *cannot*. Just as only we can confront the unjust concentration of economic and political power within our society, only the poor in the third world can organize to overcome their powerlessness. We must also understand that wherever people are oppressed, there is *already* resistance. That resistance might appear doomed in light of the mighty forces working against the poor—but many observers belittled the chances of success of our own American Revolution, fought by a minority of colonists. The struggle of the African colonies against Portuguese colonialism was dismissed just two years before its success. And even as late as spring of 1979, many doubted that the Nicaraguans would be able to overthrow the Somoza dictatorship, as they did in July of that year.*

Three years after my eye-opening trip to the Philippines, Joe Collins, David Kinley, and I wrote *Aid as Obstacle: Twenty Questions about Our Foreign Aid and the Hungry*, fully documenting this analysis. In the process, I learned that ending military and economic aid to repressive governments is not a separate "human rights" cause, because where people's human rights are denied, so are their food rights.

Lessons from Africa

In the summer of 1978 I set out again, this time on a different quest. In so much of our work we study and concentrate on what is wrong in the current economic order—the injustice, the waste, the destruction. Yet we know that we will not be successful unless we are also working *for* something. Here we face a tough dilemma: how can we develop a vision without falling into the trap of believing that there is a "model" social order that everyone can simply follow?

In struggling with this dilemma, we came up with the theme of "lessons, not models." While no society has

---

* To understand what has happened in Nicaragua since the fall of Somoza, see our Institute's book, *What Difference Could a Revolution Make? Food and Farming in the New Nicaragua*, by Joseph Collins, 1982.

achieved a model social order, there are powerful lessons that we can learn by studying the experiences of people in other countries, people attempting to establish democratic political and social institutions to meet the needs of all. Behind this belief is the assumption that something new *is* possible—that human beings are capable of building social institutions more life-giving than those known anywhere in the world today.

We try to make "lessons, not models" a basic theme of our work. Yet some people attack *Food First* for offering idealized "models" of alternatives. From these reactions we have learned that our readers—especially North Americans—are not accustomed to thinking in terms of lessons from abroad. Thus, when we praise some feature of another society, we are sometimes accused of suggesting wholesale adoption of their entire system. Wherever possible we seek to break out of this bind by speaking from actual experience and pointing out both the positive and negative lessons to be learned from other societies.

All this explains why I went to Africa in the summer of 1978 with my colleague Adele Negro. I wanted to see what it was like to be in countries where the land is not owned by a small elite and where the government is not merely the brutal defender of the power of this elite minority. We visited two neighboring African countries whose governments claim to be progressive—Tanzania and Mozambique. At the time, Tanzania was in its eighteenth year of independence from British colonial rule, Mozambique its fourth from Portuguese colonial rule.

In neither country did I see the degradation of the majority of people that I had witnessed in northwestern Mexico, the Philippines, or Guatemala. While most Mozambicans and Tanzanians are poor, I did not see decadent wealth flaunted in the face of miserable poverty. I did not see widespread starvation in the midst of abundance.

In Mozambique we visited a cooperative farm. Begun by 33 families in 1976, it included 300 families by the time of our visit. We talked all afternoon to one of its founders. In spite of setbacks of every imaginable kind—flooding, late arrival of seeds, transportation breakdowns, and theft—the cooperative was thriving. The cooperative could not have been organized without the support of the government, which provided the initial loans. Although it was one of a handful of successful cooperatives at that time, it was the kind of organization for development that the government hoped would flourish.

As I talked with the cooperative's founder, I could not help but flash back in my own mind to the banana plantation in the Philippines. In the Mozambican cooperative, every member had one vote. Those who worked the land decided what to grow and what to do with the profits. On the banana plantation the workers were not only powerless but lived in fear of the power of the owner, backed up by the government's military.

It was dusk by the time my host let us leave. Even though I was exhausted and eager to begin the long drive back to the city, he wouldn't let us go until he had taken us out into the well-tended, irrigated fields. For years he had fought against Portuguese colonialism, but he seemed prouder of these budding crops than of the victory over colonialism. For him, the struggle to build a new society was an even greater challenge. And I think he is right: societies formed and deformed over hundreds of years of colonial rule will not emerge within a few years as just societies. Patience is a necessity.

My African trip also showed me the inadequacy of the labels used to describe the two dominant theories of economic organization—capitalism and socialism. Americans are taught to associate capitalism with democracy and socialism with totalitarianism. Yet in the world today we see extremely antidemocratic economic structures in both "socialist" and "capitalist" systems. And we can see democratic elements in both systems, too. In the Philippines, a "capitalist" country, I saw few signs of democratic participation; in "socialist" Mozambique I saw the beginnings of democratic participation from the village up. Every member of the production cooperative had a vote; moreover, everyone could participate in choosing representatives for the country's decision-making bodies, the governing party and the representative assemblies.

As our stereotypes crumble, we have to get better and better at perceiving the important distinctions. Instead of talking in "isms," we must learn to determine how power is actually distributed in a society. For example, both of these African countries have a one-party system, so some might place them in the "totalitarian" category. I learned that what matters most is not the number of parties in the government, but whom the government really represents—and whether it is accountable to the majority of people.

Unlearning our rigid categories means learning to think of every society as in a *process of change* rather than static. (A friend of mine once observed: "What's wrong with Americans is that we want progress without change.") Americans do sense the dramatic changes taking place all around us, and many feel overwhelmed and paralyzed. To break out of our fears, we at the Institute believe, we must first make sense out of these changes—we must understand their roots and their consequences. This is the first step toward moving our society in constructive change. So the Institute has launched a major new investigation. It is not taking me to Maputo, Mozambique, or Davao City, the Philippines. Rather, I am asking: What is the meaning of the critical changes taking place in our food and agricultural system here in the United States?

The Underdevelopment of U.S. Agriculture

Studying third world agricultural problems for ten years, I began to see a pattern of "underdevelopment" that included these three elements: the *concentration of economic power* as the gap between the rich and the poor widens; *dependency and instability* of both the society as a whole and of more and more people within it; and finally, *the mining of agricultural resources* for the benefit of a minority.

The agriculture of so many third world countries can be described in these terms. But what about the United States? Doesn't it have the world's most productive agriculture? Don't we have a system of family farms, not plantations run by a landed elite? And don't we have long-established conservation programs to prevent the mining of our soil and water?

Many believe so, but what I am learning is that each of these patterns of underdevelopment—the kind of society I don't want—is taking hold right here in America.

CONCENTRATION OF ECONOMIC POWER

Control over farmland is becoming increasingly concentrated. In just 20 years, it is predicted, a mere 3 percent of all farms will control two-thirds of farm production.[4] The amount of farmland controlled by absentee landlords will increase. (Already almost half of U. S. farmland is owned by nonfarmers.[5]) Donald Paarlberg, among the most highly regarded agricultural economists in the country, warns us: "We are developing a wealthy hereditary landowning class, which is contrary to American tradition."[6]

U. S. farmland, at present anyway, is actually much less tightly controlled than the rest of the food industry, which is now dominated by what economists call "shared monopolies." This means that in almost any given food category, only four corporations control at least half of the sales. In 33 categories, only four companies control *two-thirds* of the sales. For some foods, the monopoly power is much greater: three corporations—Kellogg's, General Mills, and General Foods—capture over 90 percent of breakfast cereal sales.[7]

Such market power spells profits: between 1973 and 1979, food industry profits rose 46 percent faster than consumer food expenditures. And this monopoly power spells higher food costs for all of us. Monopoly power in the food processing industry results in close to $20 billion in overcharges to American consumers each year, or almost $90 per year for every single American.[8] That's how much more we pay compared to prices in a more competitve food economy.

In fact, at every stage of the food industry concentration is tightening. During just the last ten years 20 "Fortune 500" corporations have acquired at least 60 U. S.–based seed companies.[9] In just ten years the top four pesticide manufacturers increased their control from 33 percent of the market to 59 percent.[10] Just two corporations now control about half of tractor sales.[11]

The meat industry is no exception to these trends. Just three decades ago, cattle were fed in thousands of small feedlots (fenced areas where cattle are fattened for market). During the 1960s, 7,500 feedlots folded each year. By 1977, half of the 25 million cattle fed in the United States passed through only 400 feedlots.[12]

At the next stage of production—beef packing—four corporations control one-third of the market. One of these, Iowa Beef Processors, was just grabbed up by Occidental Petroleum. Having made a killing through its control of one scarce commodity—fossil fuel—Oxy is hoping to do the same with another. Its board chairman told *Business Week* shortly before the 1981 merger: "Food shortages will be to the 1990's what energy shortages have been to the 1970's and 1980's."[13]

While nationally four beef packers control about a third of the market for cattle, what's worrying cattle feeders is how few corporations are *in their vicinity* to bid for their herd; for, regionally, control is even more tightly concentrated. Just three packers, for example, now purchase 70 percent of the feedlot cattle in a major Southwest beef producing area.[14] Cattlemen are sure that such concentrated power depresses the prices they can get for their cattle.

Cattle-feeding, meatpacking, and grain-trading operations used to be owned by separate interests. But today 13 of the 25 biggest feedlot operations are owned or controlled by either meatpacking or grain-trading corporations.[15] Their interest is in keeping the price of feedlot cattle down. Conveniently, these "integrated" firms also control a critically large share of the cattle futures market (trading in contracts for delivery of feedlot cattle), which they can use to depress the price of cattle, helping to drive out of business the smaller feedlots not connected to beef packers. Officers of packing, meat-processing, grain-trading, and feedlot companies also use their insider knowledge to reap incredible personal gain. A 1980 Congressional study revealed that over a 16-month period in 1978 and 1979, those who came out on top in cattle futures trading were a handful of officers in these companies who each profited by an average of $2.5 *million*.[16]

Such concentration of economic power is what I had learned to associate with third world economies.

IMAGES OF THE THIRD WORLD

Miles and miles of coffee or banana trees. Endless fields of sugar cane. Dependency on raw-material production—and dependency on only one or two crops for export. The marketing of these exports through corporations with no accountability, no loyalty to the well-being of the people of the country.

Since these are my images of third world agriculture, you can imagine my alarm as I learned about the parallels in U. S. agriculture.

I began to study the U. S. government's big farm-export push, which began in the early 1970s. Some have called the massive increase in agricultural exports the greatest shock to hit American agriculture since the tractor, and they may be right. In just ten years farm export volume doubled, and in the Corn Belt states almost 30 percent more land came under cultivation—much of it marginal land, highly susceptible to erosion.

Directly related to the export push are two other trends—a reduction in the number of crops produced and the increasing dependence of farmers on foreign markets. In fact, that dependence doubled in only ten years, so that by 1980 almost one-third of farmers' sales went overseas.

What is the significance of these trends for farmers? And for all of us?

Dependence on foreign markets immediately resulted in more volatile commodity prices. The variation in prices farmers received after 1972 was five times greater than during the late 1960s. Boom and bust was the result. While farmers' incomes hit record highs in 1973-74, by 1978 an average farm family's real purchasing power was no greater than it was in the early 1960s. These great income swings hit the moderate-sized family farm the hardest, especially those with big mortgages still to pay off. It favored those farm operators with investments outside farming, those with incomes large enough to weather the price dips, and those with large equity in their land.

THE WINNERS: THE GRAIN TRADERS

If we are right, and the farm export boom has helped only a small minority of farmers, who *has* benefited? We have found that a disproportionate share of the benefits flow to the five major grain-trading companies—Cargill, Continental, Louis Dreyfus, Bunge and Borne, and Andre— that account for an incredible 70 to 80 percent of all U. S. grain trade. What is wrong with that? you may ask.

First, grain traders are able to capture wealth which should rightfully accrue to the farmers. In their role as transporters of farm commodities, traders guarantee themselves a profit because they can add on to their selling price the costs they incur at every transport link in the marketing chain. Because they can pass on costs, grain traders end up profiting while the income of farmers stagnates. Compare the fate of the two: the real income of farmers was about the same at the end of the 1970s as it was in the early 1960s. But the income of the largest trader, the Minneapolis-based Cargill Corporation, has gone up a whopping 441 percent since the late '60s.[17] (And that is *after* adjusting for inflation.)

Second, the interests of the grain traders conflict with the interests of the vast majority of the American people. What consumers and farmers want are stable prices; but traders profit from market *instability*. For grain traders, profit lies in the price *spread*; whether the price goes up or down is less important. Thus, knowledge of price differentials, between locations or between markets, is all that the major firms need to make money.

Third, even though the major grain traders are largely dependent on U.S. producers and U.S. resources, they are virtually unaccountable to the interests of our farm producers or the U.S. government. The grain traders operate in great secrecy and have made themselves immune to many U. S. laws.

Again, take Cargill, the largest. Cargill's major trading arm is Tradax, chartered in Panama and based in Geneva. Cargill calls it an "independent subsidiary," but it is actually 70 percent owned by Cargill and 30 percent owned by the Salevia Foundation—a trust whose beneficiaries are all members of the Cargill and MacMillan families, owners of Cargill.[18] The Panamanian charter gives Tradax (Cargill) significant tax advantages. Based in Geneva, Tradax is protected by Swiss secrecy laws. (Cargill refused to provide some significant information in 1976 Senate hearings, on the grounds that it would be illegal under Swiss law.[19]) Transactions run through Tradax need not all be reported, either to the USDA or to the IRS for tax purposes. This secrecy is both a tax advantage and a trading advantage.

Most major grain-trading firms export grain from every major exporting country in the world. Thus, they have no loyalty to the interests of U. S. producers, and even help to pit foreign producers against U. S. producers.

Fourth, the enormous wealth of the major grain-trading firms gives them power to influence U.S. government policy and to gain access to tax support. The incredible influence of the grain trade came home to us when a high government official confided to us that if he were to question the all-out-for-export strategy, the grain companies would have him out of a job immediately.

Influence helps buy government assistance, too, such as the services of the Foreign Agriculture Service of USDA and even more direct help. Cargill Korea, for example, was started with 95 percent of its financing from the U.S. government. Public assistance has also helped Cargill expand domestically. The Indiana Port Commission, for example, raised $18 million through tax-free revenue bonds for a Cargill-controlled elevator.[20]

Fifth, the size of the major grain traders enables them to prevent competitors—such as farm cooperatives—from entering the export sales market. While farm cooperatives handle 40 percent of domestic grain sales, they have so far garnered less than 10 percent of the export market.

Greater export sales by farm cooperatives might allow more of the money from sales to go to producers.

Sixth, the size of the major grain traders, and the wealth they are accruing as export sales mount, allow them to expand into virtually every aspect of the food industry.

Cargill has used its export bonanza to acquire even more *ships* and *elevator space* at major ports (Cargill and Continental already control half the space);[21] to expand its *poultry operations* (Cargill already ranks fourth in the U. S.);[22] to expand its *animal feed operations* (Cargill is already the nation's second largest producer);[23] and to enlarge its *soybean and sunflower processing operations* (Cargill may already be the largest soybean crusher in the world).

Cargill is also the number one *cattle feeder* in the country.[24] Cargill's new export profits allowed it to purchase the giant *meatpacking firm* Missouri Beef Packers (MBPXL) in 1978. (At that time MBPXL itself ranked 213th of the Fortune 500.) With Cargill's huge assets behind it, it took only one year for MBPXL to push past Swift to become the country's second largest meat packer, just behind Iowa Beef Processors—which itself was just bought by one of the country's biggest oil companies, Occidental, as I just noted. These top two producers are now wiping out smaller competitors. Some investigators suspect that concentration in the meat industry is responsible for a significant chunk of the meat-price increases over the last ten years.[25]

Such increasing vertical integration means that profits, picked up at every stage from raw commodity to sales, accrue to fewer and fewer firms. Not only does this process lead to the concentration of wealth, but it also allows for more market manipulation.

Since our nation was founded, Americans have resisted such economic concentration, believing that mammoth, unaccountable economic units operating behind closed doors are antithetical to democracy. Nevertheless, economic concentration has been quickening and, in the 1980s, it is gaining speed in a "merger mania" blessed by the Reagan administration and fueled by the oil companies' burgeoning profits.

The concentration of economic power, the dependence on unstable international markets, the unaccountability of the most powerful economic forces—all these are characteristics I learned to associate with misery in the third world. But there is a fourth important parallel that we must face—less visible but equally threatening. It is the mining of agricultural resources for short-term gain. In Part II of this book I describe this threat to our food security.

My path has taken me from years of desperation in the 1960s (desperation because I did not understand the root causes of needless suffering) to a study of the roots of third world hunger in the 1970s and, finally, a return home in the 1980s to face the crises in our own food and agriculture system—shockingly similar to systems I have seen in the third world. In this twelve-year process I began to see patterns in what before had been an overwhelming jumble. A framework for understanding began to emerge. Using this framework, I have struggled to identify paths of action that are both meaningful and satisfying. Knowing we can't take on the whole system, where do we begin?

First let me make very clear that I am not suggesting everyone become a "food activist." Yes, I do feel that food problems have a special ability to open doors of understanding—everyone eats and everyone likes to talk about food! But I also believe that most of the gravest problems facing our society today have common roots. Whether the issues be education, health, the legal system, or energy policy, the underlying cause is the distribution of power and wealth which determines how decisions are made and for whose benefit.

In 1980 the Institute published *What Can We Do? Food and Hunger: How You Can Make a Difference.* For this book we interviewed many friends actively involved in transforming our food system into a more democratic and sustainable one. We wanted to know how they kept going in the face of such huge and complex problems. Some of their answers are included in Part IV of this book, "Lessons for the Long Haul."

Power and Responsibility: Changing Ourselves

The first struggle for me and for so many of my friends
has been to reconcile our vision of the future with the com-
promises we must make every day just to survive in our
society. If we attempt to be totally "consistent," eschewing
all links between ourselves and the exploitative aspects of
our culture, we drive ourselves—and those close to us—
nuts! I still remember my annoyance as a friend, sitting
with me in a restaurant in the late 1960s, scornfully picked
the tiny bits of ham out of her omelet.

Who wants to be around someone so righteous that they
make you feel guilty all the time? But while self-
righteousness is not very effective in influencing people,
this does not mean we should not try to make our personal
choices consistent with our political vision. Indeed, this is exactly where we have to begin.

If the solution to needless hunger lies in the redistribution of decision-making power, we must become part of
that redistribution. That means exercising to the fullest our
power to make choices in our daily life. It means working
with other people to force the few who have more power to
share it with the majority. It also means preparing ourselves to share responsibility with others in areas that we
now leave to unaccountable "experts" and politicians.

All this implies taking ourselves seriously, which for
years I found difficult. In part, taking ourselves seriously
means taking responsibility for how our individual life
choices either sustain or challenge the antidemocratic nature of our society.

What do we eat? What we eat links us to every aspect of
the economic order. Do we allow ourselves to be victimized
by that structure, or do we choose a diet that the earth can
sustain and that can best sustain our own bodies? Answer-
ing that question is the basis of Book One, explored in
depth in Parts II and III.

Where do we shop? Do we support the handful of supermarket chains that are tightening their grip over food? In

more than a quarter of all U. S. cities, four chains control at least 60 percent of all sales. That tight control means monopoly power and monopoly prices. In 1974 Americans were overcharged $660 million due to concentration of control by supermarket chains alone.[26] Or do we support the growth of a more democratic alternative, the mushrooming network of consumer- and worker-managed retail food cooperatives, which already have more than 3 million patrons? Their consumers have much greater influence over what is sold and where the products come from. Part IV includes a partial list of the addresses of this network and some excellent books for those interested in starting their own food co-ops.

In school, how do we study? Are we studying to please the professor, or to hone our knowledge to heighten our own power? Are we studying toward a narrow career path, or to prepare ourselves for a life of change?

How do we try to learn about the world? Only through the mass media, whose interpretations and choice of stories reinforce the status quo? Or do we seek alternative sources of information that discuss the lessons which we might learn from our counterparts here and abroad? The publications listed in Appendix A suggest some possibilities.

Where do we work? One of the greatest tragedies of our economic system is that few people are able to earn a livelihood and still feel that they are making a meaningful contribution to society. So many jobs produce either weapons of destruction or frivolous nonessentials. Therefore, our struggle is first to find a livelihood that reflects our vision of the world. If that is not possible, then we can do what more and more people are doing—find the least destructive job that pays, then devote our creative energies to unpaid work. (Some of the volunteers at our Institute have chosen this path.) But just as important are these questions:

How do we work? Are we challenging the arbitrary hierarchies that we were taught to accept? Are we struggling to create structures in which responsibilities are shared and accountability is broadened—so that we are accountable not just to one boss but to one another and to ourselves?

Do we work alone (as I tried to do for too many years)?

Or do we join with others to learn how to share decision-making power and to experience the excitement of collaborative work? (All the projects I have undertaken in the last six years have involved teamwork, and I'm convinced that the whole is greater than the sum of our individual contributions.)

How do we choose our friends? Do we surround ourselves with people who reinforce our habits and assumptions, or do we seek out people who challenge us?

Obviously these are only some of the questions that we must ask ourselves as we become part of the redistribution of power. Every choice we make that consciously aligns our daily life with our vision of a better future makes us more powerful people. We feel less victimized. We gain confidence in ourselves. And the more convincing we are to ourselves, the more convincing we are to other people.

The less victimized we are by forces outside us, the freer we become. For freedom is not the capacity to do whatever we please; freedom is the capacity to make intelligent choices. This implies knowledge of the consequences of our actions. And that is what this book is all about—gaining the knowledge we need to make choices based upon awareness of the consequences of those choices.

Overcoming Hopelessness: Taking Risks

According to a 1980 Gallup Poll, Americans are more "hope-less" than the people of any other country polled except Britain and India. Fully 56 percent of Americans queried believed the coming year would be worse than the past year. These findings come as no surprise. Hopelessness is a growing American malady. Increasingly, Americans feel alienated from "their" government—witness the lowest voter turnout since 1948 in the Reagan-Carter contest. Americans increasingly perceive that their government operates in the interests of a privileged minority.

This hopelessness is born of the feelings of powerlessness I have been talking about. Consciously working to make our lives more consistent is the first step in attacking the powerlessness that generates despair—but only the first step.

Taking more responsibility for ourselves—and for the impact of our choices in the world—we start *changing ourselves.* This is the key to overcoming hopelessness. Unless we experience ourselves changing, can we really believe that illiterate peasants in the Philippines, El Savador, or Chile can change? (After all, they face much greater obstacles and much stronger messages telling them of their own incapacity.)

If, then, belief that "the world" can change depends on changing ourselves, how do we start?

I believe there is only one way—we must take risks. There is no change without risk. To change, we must push ourselves to do what we thought we were incapable of doing.

What do we risk?

We risk being controversial. Personally, I hate being controversial! I hate it when people attack my views—or, worse, attack me. I remember burning inside when a well-known university president tried to dismiss my views on U. S. support for the Marcos dictatorship in the Philippines. "What does *she* know?" he said. "She's just a cookbook writer." I was outraged when a speaker sympathetic to agribusiness who shared the platform with me several years ago in Minneapolis tried to dismiss my positions by suggesting that I was getting personally wealthy from *Diet for a Small Planet* royalties and therefore was a hypocrite. (Royalties have allowed me to work full time on food and hunger issues, and have helped pay the bills at the Institute for Food and Development Policy. The money I earn from speeches goes directly to the Institute.) I grew up wanting everyone to like me (preferably, to love me!), but to change myself and to try to change the world, I have to accept that many people will *not* like me.

We risk being lonely. Maybe this is even harder. Changing yourself often means taking independent positions that those closest to you cannot accept. For me, this meant deciding I no longer wanted to be married. At the prospect of being on my own, I experienced the greatest pain and terror I had ever felt. I can't deny that I do feel lonely sometimes, but I came to realize that many of the most important things I wanted to do, I could only do alone. Yes, I do work in a team. I enjoy our meetings, making plans and reacting to each other's work. But when it comes right down to getting the words on the page, it is me and the typewriter. I came to learn also that there is a reward for being alone in order to do what I believe in: I feel connected to others who share my vision, not only to others at the Institute but to a growing network of people throughout the world.

We risk being wrong. Taking controversial positions is hard enough, but how do we deal with our fear of being wrong? Part of the answer for me was discovering that those learned academics and government officials—whom I had believed—are wrong. They may be mostly correct in their statistics, but how useful are statistics if their questions are the wrong questions? Those "experts" intimidate so many of us and use their grasp of trivial detail to avoid asking the important questions. (In Rome in 1974, all the experts were asking, "How can we increase food production?" But I had already learned that many countries were increasing food production faster than their population grew and yet had more hunger than ever.)

In learning not to fear being wrong, I had to accept that to ask the important questions is to ask *big* questions—and this inevitably entails crossing many disciplines. If you have read our book *Food First,* you know what I mean. The material spans dozens of disciplines, from anthropology to climatology to nutrition to economics. When you ask big questions, it is impossible to be an "expert" in everything that you study. But instead of being paralyzed by that realization, I try to keep in mind the advice of a wise friend. "If you ask a big question you may get something wrong," Marty Strange told me. "But if you ask a small question— as most narrow academics do—it doesn't matter if you're wrong. Nobody cares!"

My positions have changed as I have learned. In the process, I have become more convinced that acting out of sheer emotion, even genuine compassion, is not enough. If we are serious about committing our lives to positive social change, we must always be learning, and accepting the logical consequences of what we learn as a basis for what we do.

Yes, we must be able to risk—risk being controversial, risk being lonely, risk being wrong. Only through risk-taking do we gain the strength we need to take responsibility—and to be part of the redistribution of political and economic power essential for a solution to needless hunger.

But How Do We Learn to Take Risks?

Few people change alone. As I have already suggested, we must choose friends and colleagues who will push us to what we thought we could not do. But we must select friends who will "catch" us, too, when we push ourselves too far and need to be supported. Wherever we are, we must not be content to work alone. Only if we experience the possibility and the rewards of shared decision-making in our own lives—in our families, our schools, our community groups, our workplaces—will we believe in the possibility of more just sharing of decision-making in our government and economic structures.

Second, we must learn to associate risk with joy as well as pain. Despite my parents' struggle against racism and McCarthyism through the Unitarian church they founded, the cultural messages were so strong that I grew up believing that the "good life" we all are seeking would be a life without risk-taking. This was my "sailboat" image of the good life. First you work to acquire your sailboat (husband, kids, etc.), then you set your sails, and off into the sunset. Of course, I assumed that you might have to adjust the sails now and then. But, short of hurricanes, I thought of life as a continuous and relatively riskless journey.

Well, at the age of thirty-seven my view of the good life is different. I discovered that a life without risk is missing *the* ingredient—joy. If we never risk being afraid, failing, being lonely, we will never experience that joy that comes only from learning that *we can change ourselves*.

Third, we can gain inspiration from our counterparts around the world whose lives entail risks much greater than ours. But this requires our seeking out alternative news sources, because the mass media rarely show us the courageous struggles of ordinary people. Learning about our counterparts around the world, we'll come to realize that we do not have to start the train moving. It is already moving. In every country where people are suffering, there is resistance. Those who believe in the possibility of genuine democracy are building new forms of human organization. The question for each of us is, how can we board that train, and how can we remove the mighty obstacles in its way?

But none of what I have presented here makes much sense unless we develop a perspective longer than our life-times. Glenn, a volunteer at the Institute, joked with us before he moved to the East Coast. "For a while I consid-ered getting into your line of work—you know, trying to change the world—but I decided against it," he told us. "The problem is that you can go for *weeks* and not see any change!"

We laughed. Glenn was right. It took hundreds and hundreds of years to create the web of assumptions and the unchallenged institutions of exploitation and privilege that people take for granted today. It will take a very long time to create new structures based on different values. But rather than belittling our task, this realization—seeing our-selves as part of a historical process longer than our life-times—can be a source of courage. Years ago I read an interview with I. F. Stone, the journalist who warned Americans about U. S. involvement in Vietnam long be-fore antiwar sentiment became popular. He was asked, "How can you keep working so hard when no one is listen-ing to you?" His answer: "I think that if you expect to see the final results of your work, you simply have not asked a big enough question." I've used Stone's answer in several books and probably too many speeches! For me it sums up an attitude we all must cultivate. I call it the "long-haul perspective."

A book on how our eating relates us to a system that destroys our food resources and deprives many of their right to food would seem, on the surface, to carry a mes-sage of guilt and self-denial. But not this book!

I don't think the solution to the tragedy of needless hunger lies in either guilt or self-denial. It lies rather in our own liberation. If we do not understand the world, we are bound to be its victims. But we do not have to be. We can come to see the tragedy of needless hunger as a tool for understanding.

We can discover that our personal and social liberation lies not in freedom from responsibility but in our growing capacity to take on greater responsibility. The organizations and publications listed in Part IV can help—as tools through which we can transform ourselves from victims of change to makers of change. We can choose to seize these tools—not just on behalf of the hundreds of millions who are hungry, but for our own liberation as well.

Part II

Diet
for a
Small
Planet

1.

One Less Hamburger?

I REMEMBER RIDICULING Hubert Humphrey's comment that if we all just ate one less hamburger a week, the hunger crisis would be conquered. Yet even while I scoffed at that notion in 1974, my own writing was often taken to be saying the same thing. In the 1975 edition I asked my readers to pretend they were seated in a restaurant, eating an eight-ounce steak—and to appreciate that the grain used to produce the steak could have filled the empty bowls of 40 people in the room.

The first two editions implied that our grain-fed-meat diet denied grain to the hungry abroad who lacked the resources to feed themselves. But as I did research for *Food First,* my view began to shift. I came to learn that virtually every country has the capacity to grow enough food for its people. No country is a hopeless basket case. Moreover, only a minuscule fraction of our food exports ever reach the hungry.

Much of our research for *Food First* focused on the food-producing potential of some of the world's most densely populated countries, such as Bangladesh, and some of the most agriculturally resource-poor countries, such as the nations south of the Sahara Desert, known as the Sahel.

In Bangladesh, we learned, enough food is already produced to prevent malnutrition; if it had been fairly distributed, grain alone would have provided over 2,200 calories per person per day in 1979.[1] And the stunning agriculture potential of Bangladesh, where rice yields are only half as large as in China, has hardly been tapped. I was struck by the conclusion of a 1976 report to Congress: "The country is rich enough in fertile land, water, manpower and natural gas for fertilizer, not only to be self-sufficient in food but a food exporter, even with its rapidly increasing population size."[2]

We focused on the Sahel because severe famine threatened the region in the years just before we began *Food First*. We saw so many TV images of hungry people dying on desolate, parched earth that we were certain that if ever there were a case of nature-caused famine, this had to be it.

But to our dismay, we learned that with the possible exception of Mauritania (a country rich in minerals), every country in the Sahel actually produced enough grain to feed its total population even during the worst years of the drought of the early 1970s.[3] Moreover, in a number of the Sahelian countries production of *export* crops such as cotton, peanuts, and vegetables actually increased.[4]

In researching what became *Diet for a Small Planet*, I was struck by the tremendous abundance in the U.S. food system, and I assumed that many other countries would be forever dependent on our grain exports because they did not have the soil and climate suitable for basic food production. But I learned that while the United States is blessed with exceptional agricultural resources, third world countries are not doomed to be perpetually dependent on U.S. exports.

I learned that what so many Americans are made to see as inevitable third world dependence on grain imports is the result of five forces:

1. A small minority controls more and more of the farmland. In most third world countries, roughly 80 percent of the agricultural land is, on average, controlled by a tiny 3 percent of those who own land.[5] This minority underuses and misuses the land.

2. Agricultural development of basic foods is neglected,

while production for export climbs. Elites now in control in most third world countries prefer urban industrialization to basic rural development that could benefit the majority. Of 71 underdeveloped countries studied in the mid-1970s, three-quarters allocated less than 10 percent of their central government expenditures to agriculture.[6] Moreover, as the majority of people are increasingly impoverished, the domestic market for basic food shrinks. So food production is oriented toward the more lucrative foreign markets and the tastes of the small urban class. The meager investment in agriculture which does take place is primarily private investment in export crops. In Asia, for example, "the new export-oriented luxury food agribusiness is undoubtedly the fastest growing agriculture sector," the prestigious *Far Eastern Economic Review* notes. "Fruit, vegetables, seafood and poultry [from southeastern Asian countries] are filling European, American and, above all, Japanese supermarket shelves."[7]

3. More and more basic grains go to livestock. As the gap between rich and poor widens, basic grains are fed increasingly to livestock in the third world, even in the face of deepening hunger for the majority there. Not only is more and more grain fed to animals, but much land that could be growing basic food is used to graze livestock, often for export. Two-thirds of the agriculturally productive land in Central America is devoted to livestock production, yet the poor majority cannot afford the meat, which is eaten by the well-to-do or exported.[8]

4. Poverty pushes up population growth rates. The poverty and powerlessness of the poor produces large families. The poor must have many children to compensate for their high infant death rate, to provide laborers to supplement meager family income, and to provide the only old age security the poor have. High birthrates also reflect the social powerlessness of women, exacerbated by poverty.[9]

5. Conscious "market development" strategies of the U. S. government help to make other economies dependent on our grain. (See "The Meat Mystique," Part II, Chapter 3, to learn how market development works.)

These forces that generate needless hunger are hidden from most Americans, so when they hear that the poorest underdeveloped countries are importing twice as much grain as they did ten years ago, Americans inevitably conclude that scarcity of resources is their basic problem. Americans then urge more food exports, including food aid.

In writing *Food First*, however, we learned that two-thirds of U.S. agricultural exports go to the industrial countries, not the third world, and that most of what does go to the third world is fed to livestock, not to the hungry people. In writing *Aid as Obstacle: Twenty Questions about Our Foreign Aid and the Hungry*, we learned that chronic food aid to elite-based, repressive governments not only fails to reach the hungry in most cases, it actually hurts them. Food aid, we found, is largely a disguised form of economic assistance, concentrated on a handful of governments that U.S. policymakers view as allies. Because food aid is often sold to the people by recipient governments, it serves as general budgetary support, reinforcing the power of these elite-based governments. In 1980, ten countries received three-quarters of all our food aid.[10] Among them were Egypt, India, Bangladesh, Indonesia, Pakistan, and South Korea. Notorious for their neglect of the poor, such governments block genuine agrarian reform that could unchain their country's productive potential. Indonesia, for example, squanders its spectacular oil wealth—$10 billion in 1980—on luxury imports, militarism, and showy capital-intensive industrial projects which don't even provide many jobs.

What I have just said does not diminish our responsibility to send food to relieve famine, as was needed in Kampuchea in 1980 and Africa in 1981. (Note that disaster and famine relief are only 11 percent of our government's food aid program.) But even in the face of famine, as in Kampuchea or Somalia, we learned, the U.S. government often operates more out of political than humanitarian considerations—to the detriment of the hungry. Famine relief funds channeled through private voluntary agencies often have a better chance of helping.

In writing *Food First* and the books that followed, I had to learn some painful lessons. In the back of my mind I was always asking, what does all of this mean for the message of *Diet for a Small Planet*?

If our food is not getting to the hungry, if our food exports actually prop up some of the world's most repressive governments, then why exhort Americans to feed less grain to livestock? Why not pour even more of our grain into livestock, so that at least it does not block needed change abroad?

At the same time I was asking myself these questions, I was studying the agricultural system in the United States. In the process, *Diet for a Small Planet* took on new and deeper meaning. The first edition of this book explained how our production system takes abundant grain, which hungry people can't afford, and shrinks it into meat, which better-off people will pay for. But I didn't fully appreciate that our production system not only reduces abundance but actually mines the very resources on which our future food security rests.

2.

Like Driving a Cadillac

A FEW MONTHS ago a Brazilian friend, Mauro, passed through town. As he sat down to eat at a friend's house, his friend lifted a sizzling piece of prime beef off the stove. "You're eating that today," Mauro remarked, "but you won't be in ten years. Would you drive a Cadillac? Ten years from now you'll realize that eating that chunk of meat is as crazy as driving a Cadillac."

Mauro is right: a grain-fed-meat-centered diet *is* like driving a Cadillac. Yet many Americans who have reluctantly given up their gas-guzzling cars would never think of questioning the resource costs of their grain-fed-meat diet. So let me try to give you some sense of the enormity of the resources flowing into livestock production in the United States. The consequences of a grain-fed-meat diet may be as severe as those of a nation of Cadillac drivers.

A detailed 1978 study sponsored by the Departments of Interior and Commerce produced startling figures showing that *the value of raw materials consumed to produce food from livestock is greater than the value of all oil, gas, and coal consumed in this country.*[1] Expressed another way, one-third of the value of *all* raw materials consumed for all purposes in the United States is consumed in livestock foods.[2]

How can this be?

66

The Protein Factory in Reverse

Excluding exports, about one-half of our harvested acreage goes to feed livestock. Over the last forty years the amount of grain, soybeans, and special feeds going to American livestock has doubled. Now approaching 200 million tons, it is equal in volume to all the grain that is now imported throughout the world.[3] Today our livestock consume ten times the grain that we Americans eat directly[4] and they outweigh the human population of our country four to one.[5]

These staggering estimates reflect the revolution that has taken place in meat and poultry production and consumption since about 1950.

First, beef. Because cattle are ruminants, they don't need to consume protein sources like grain or soybeans to produce protein for us. Ruminants have the simplest nutritional requirements of any animal because of a unique fermentation "vat" in front of their true stomach. This vat, the rumen, is a protein factory. With the help of billions of bacteria and protozoa, the rumen produces microbial protein, which then passes on to the true stomach, where it is treated just like any other protein. Not only does the rumen enable the ruminant to thrive without dietary protein, B vitamins, or essential fatty acids, it also enables the animal to digest large quantities of fibrous foodstuffs inedible by humans.[6]

The ruminant can recycle a wide variety of waste products into high-protein foods. Successful animal feeds have come from orange juice squeeze remainders in Florida, cocoa residue in Ghana, coffee processing residue in Britain, and bananas (too ripe to export) in the Caribbean. Ruminants will thrive on single-celled protein, such as bacteria or yeast produced in special factories, and they can utilize some of the cellulose in waste products such as wood pulp, newsprint, and bark. In Marin County, near my home in San Francisco, ranchers are feeding apple pulp and cottonseed to their cattle. Such is the "hidden talent" of livestock.

Because of this "hidden talent," cattle have been prized for millennia as a means of transforming grazing land unsuited for cropping into a source of highly usable protein, meat. But in the last 40 years we in the United States have turned that equation on its head. Instead of just protein factories, we have turned cattle into protein disposal systems, too.

Yes, our cattle still graze. In fact, from one-third to one-half of the continental land mass is used for grazing. But since the 1940s we have developed a system of feeding grain to cattle that is unique in human history. Instead of going from pasture to slaughter, most cattle in the United States now first pass through feedlots where they are each fed over 2,500 pounds of grain and soybean products (about 22 pounds a day) plus hormones and antibiotics.[7]

Before 1950 relatively few cattle were fed grain before slaughter,[8] but by the early 1970s about three-quarters were grain-fed.[9] During this time, the number of cattle more than doubled. And we now feed one-third more grain to produce each pound of beef than we did in the early 1960s.[10] With grain cheap, more animals have been fed to heavier weights, at which it takes increasingly more grain to put on each additional pound.

In addition to cattle, poultry have also become a big consumer of our harvested crops. Poultry can't eat grass. Unlike cows, they need a source of protein. But it doesn't have to be grain. Although prepared feed played an important role in the past, chickens also scratched the barnyard for seeds, worms, and bits of organic matter. They also got scraps from the kitchen. But after 1950, when poultry moved from the barnyard into huge factorylike compounds, production leaped more than threefold, and the volume of grain fed to poultry climbed almost as much.

Hogs, too, are big grain consumers in the United States, taking almost a third of the total fed to livestock. Many countries, however, raise hogs exclusively on waste products and on plants which humans don't eat. When Nobel Prize winner Norman Borlaug heard that China had 250 million pigs, about four times the number here, he could hardly believe it. What could they possibly eat? He went to China and saw "pretty scrawny pigs." Their growth was slow, but by the time they reached maturity they were decent-looking hogs, he admitted in awe. And all on cotton leaves, corn stalks, rice husks, water hyacinths, and peanut shells.[11] In the United States hogs are now fed about as much grain as is fed to cattle.

All told, each grain-consuming animal "unit" (as the Department of Agriculture calls our livestock) eats almost two and a half tons of grain, soy, and other feeds each year.[12]

WHAT DO WE GET BACK?

For every 16 pounds of grain and soy fed to beef cattle in the United States we only get 1 pound back in meat on our plates.[13] The other 15 pounds are inaccessible to us, either used by the animal to produce energy or to make some part of its own body that we do not eat (like hair or bones) or excreted.

To give you some basis for comparison, 16 pounds of grain has twenty-one times more calories and eight times more protein—but only three times more fat—than a pound of hamburger.

Livestock other than cattle are markedly more efficient in converting grain to meat, as you can see in Figure 1; hogs consume 6, turkeys 4, and chickens 3 pounds of grain and soy to produce 1 pound of meat.[14] Milk production is even more efficient, with less than 1 pound of grain fed for every pint of milk produced. (This is partly because we don't have to grow a new cow every time we milk one.)

Now let us put these two factors together: the large quantities of humanly edible plants fed to animals and their inefficient conversion into meat for us to eat. Some very startling statistics result. If we exclude dairy cows, the average ratio of all U.S. livestock is 7 pounds of grain and soy fed to produce 1 pound of edible food.[15] Thus, of the 145 million tons of grain and soy fed to our beef cattle, poultry, and hogs in 1979, only 21 million tons were returned to us in meat, poultry, and eggs. *The rest, about 124 million tons of grain and soybeans, became inaccessible to human consumption.* (We also feed considerable quantities

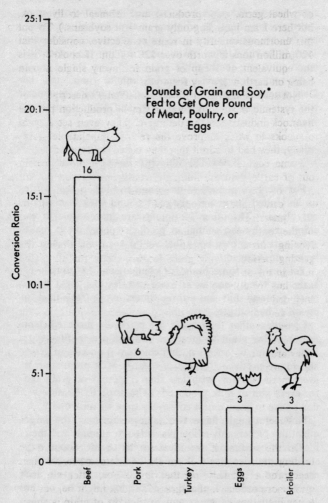

Pounds of Grain and Soy*
Fed to Get One Pound
of Meat, Poultry, or
Eggs

Conversion Ratio

Beef — 16
Pork — 6
Turkey — 4
Eggs — 3
Broiler — 3

Figure 1. A Protein Factory in Reverse

Source: USDA, Economic Research Service, Beltsville, Maryland.
*Soy constitutes only 12% of steer feed and 20–25% of poultry.

of wheat germ, milk products, and fishmeal to livestock, but here I am including only grain and soybeans.) To put this enormous quantity in some perspective, consider that 120 million tons is worth over $20 billion. If cooked, it is the equivalent of 1 cup of grain for every single human being on earth every day for a year.[16]

Not surprisingly, *Diet for a Small Planet*'s description of the systemic waste in our nation's meat production put the livestock industry on the defensive. They even set a team of cooks to work to prove the recipes unpalatable! (Actually, they had to admit that they tasted pretty good.)

Some countered by arguing that you get *more* protein out of cattle than the humanly edible protein you put in! Most of these calculations use one simple technique to make cattle appear incredibly efficient: on the "in" side of the equation they included only the grain and soy fed, but on the "out" side they include the meat put on by the grain feeding *plus* all the meat the animal put on during the grazing period. Giving grain feeding credit for all of the meat in the animal is misleading, to say the least, since it accounts for only about 40 percent. In my equation I have included only the meat put on the animal as a result of the grain and soy feeding. Obviously all the other meat, put on by forage, would have been there for us anyway—just as it was before the feedlot system was developed. (My calculations are in note 13 for this chapter, so you can see exactly how I arrived at my estimate.)

The Feedlot Logic: More Grain, Lower Cost

On the surface it would seem that beef produced by feeding grain to livestock would be more expensive than beef produced solely on the range. For, after all, isn't grain more expensive than grass? To us it might be, but not to the cattle producer. As long as the cost of grain is cheap in relation to the price of meat, the lowest production costs per pound are achieved by putting the animal in the feedlot as soon as possible after weaning and feeding it as long as it continues to gain significant weight.[17] This is true in large part because an animal gains weight three times faster in the feedlot on a grain and high-protein feed diet than on the range.

As a byproduct, our beef has gotten fattier, since the more grain fed, the more fat on the animal. American consumers have been told that our beef became fattier because *we* demanded it. Says the U.S. Department of Agriculture: "most cattle are fed today because U.S. feed consumers have a preference for [grain]fed beef."[18] But the evidence is that our beef became fattier *in spite of* consumer preference, not because of it. A 1957 report in the *Journal of Animal Science* noted that the public prefers "good" grade (less fatty) beef and would buy more of it if it were available.[19] And studies at Iowa State University indicate that the fat content of meat is not the key element in its taste anyway.[20] Nevertheless, more and more marbled "choice" meat was produced, and "good" lean meat became increasingly scarce as cattle were fed more grain. In 1957 less than half of marketed beef was graded "choice"; ten years later "choice" accounted for two-thirds of it.[21]

Many have misunderstood the economic logic of cattle feeding. Knowing that grain puts on fat and that our grading system rewards fatty meat with tantalizing names like "choice" and "prime," people target the grading system as the reason so much grain goes to livestock. They assume that if we could just overhaul the grading system, grain going to livestock would drop significantly and our beef would be less fatty. (The grading system was altered in 1976, but it still rewards fattier meat with higher prices and more appealing-sounding labels.)

But what would happen if the grading system stopped rewarding fatty meat entirely? Would less fatty meat be produced? Would less grain be fed? Probably only marginally less. As long as grain is cheap in relation to the price of meat, it would still make economic sense for the producer to put the animal in the feedlot and feed it lots of grain. The irony is that, given our economic imperatives that produce cheap grain, most of the fat is an inevitable consequence of producing the cheapest possible meat. We got fatty meat not because we demanded fatty meat but because fatty meat was the cheapest to produce. If we had demanded the same amount of leaner meat, meat prices would have been higher over the last 30 years.[22]

The Livestock Explosion and the Illusion of Cheap Grain

If we are feeding millions of tons of grain to livestock, it must be because it makes economic sense. Indeed, it does "make sense" under the rules of our economy. But that fact might better be seen as the problem, rather than the explanation that should put our concerns to rest. We got hooked on grain-fed meat just as we got hooked on gas-guzzling automobiles. Big cars "made sense" only when oil was cheap; grain-fed meat "makes sense" only because the true costs of producing it are not counted.

But why is grain in America so cheap? If grain is cheap simply because there is so much of it and it will go to waste unless we feed it to livestock, doesn't grain-fed meat represent a sound use of our resources? Here we need to back up to another, more basic question: why is there so much grain in the first place?

In our production system each farmer must compete against every other farmer; the only way a farmer can compete is to produce more. Therefore, every farmer is motivated to use any new technology—higher yielding seeds, fertilizers, or machines—which will grow more and require less labor. In the last 30 years crop production has virtually doubled as farmers have adopted hybrid seeds and applied ever more fertilizer and pesticides. Since the 1940s fertilizer use has increased fivefold, and corn yields have tripled.

But this production imperative is ultimately self-defeating. As soon as one farmer adopts the more productive technology, all other farmers must do the same or go out of business. This is because those using the more productive technology can afford to sell their grain at a lower price, making up in volume what they lose in profit per bushel. That means constant downward pressure on the price of grain.

Since World War II real grain prices have sometimes

fluctuated wildly, but the indisputable trend has been downward. The price of corn peaked at $6.43 per bushel in 1947 and fell to about $2.00 in 1967. In the early 1970s prices swung wildly up, but then fell to a low of $1.12 in 1977, or about *one-sixth the price 30 years earlier*. (All prices are in 1967 dollars.)[23]

This production imperative doesn't fully explain why production of feed doubled after 1950. In the 1950s the problem of agricultural surplus was seen as too much of certain crops, such as wheat, cotton, and tobacco; so government programs subsidized cutbacks of certain crops, but allowed farmers to expand their acreage in others, such as the feed crops barley, soybeans, and grain sorghum. In Texas, for example, sorghum production leaped sevenfold after cotton acreage was limited by law in the 1950s.[24]

But neglected in this explanation of the low price of grain are the hidden production costs which we and future generations are subsidizing: the fossil fuels and water consumed, the groundwater mined, the topsoil lost, the fertilizer resources depleted, and the water polluted.

Fossil Fuel Costs

Agricultural production uses the equivalent of about 10 percent of all of the fossil fuel imported into the United States.[25]

Besides the cost of the grain used to produce meat, we can also measure the cost of the fossil fuel energy used compared with the food value we receive. Each calorie of protein we get from feedlot-produced beef costs us 78 calories of fossil fuel, as we learn from Figure 2, prepared from the work of Drs. Marcia and David Pimentel at Cornell. Grains and beans are from 22 to almost 40 times less fossil-fuel costly.

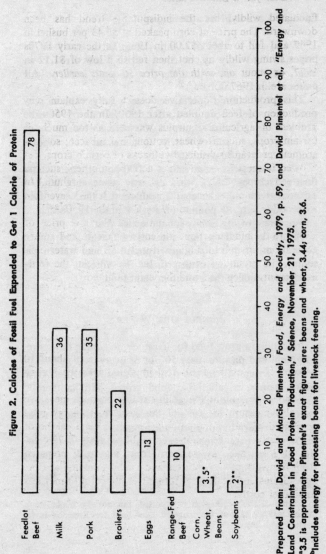

Figure 2. Calories of Fossil Fuel Expended to Get 1 Calorie of Protein

Feedlot Beef	78
Milk	36
Pork	35
Broilers	22
Eggs	13
Range-Fed Beef	10
Corn, Wheat, Beans	3.5*
Soybeans	2**

Prepared from: David and Marcia Pimentel, Food, Energy and Society, 1979, p. 59, and David Pimentel et al., "Energy and Land Constraints in Food Protein Production," Science, November 21, 1975.

a3.5 is approximate. Pimentel's exact figures are: beans and wheat, 3.44; corn, 3.6.
bIncludes energy for processing beans for livestock feeding.

Enough Water to Float a Destroyer

"We are in a crisis over our water that is every bit as important and deep as our energy crisis," says Fred Powledge, who has just written the first in-depth book on our national water crisis.*

According to food geographer Georg Borgstrom, to produce a 1-pound steak requires 2,500 gallons of water![26] The average U.S. diet requires 4,200 gallons of water a day for each person, and of this he estimates animal products account for over 80 percent.[27]

"The water that goes into a 1,000-pound steer would float a destroyer," *Newsweek* recently reported.[28] When I sat down with my calculator, I realized that the water used to produce just 10 pounds of steak equals the household consumption of my family for the entire year.

Figure 3, based on the estimates of David Pimentel at Cornell, shows that to produce 1 pound of beef protein can require as much as fifteen times the amount of water needed to produce the protein in plant food.

MINING OUR WATER

Irrigation to grow food for livestock, including hay, corn, sorghum, and pasture, uses 50 out of every 100 gallons of water "consumed" in the United States.*[29] Other farm uses—mainly irrigation for food crops—add another 35 gallons, so agriculture's total use of water equals 85 out of every 100 gallons consumed. (Water is "consumed" when it doesn't return to our rivers and streams.)

Over the past fifteen years grain-fed-beef production has been shifting from the rain-fed Corn Belt to newly

---

* *Water: The Nature, Uses and Future of Our Most Precious and Abused Resource* (New York: Farrar, Straus & Giroux, 1981).

---

* Some of this production is exported, but not the major share, since close to half of the irrigated land used for livestock is for pasture and hay.

Figure 3. Amount of Water to Produce 1 Pound of Protein from Various Food Sources

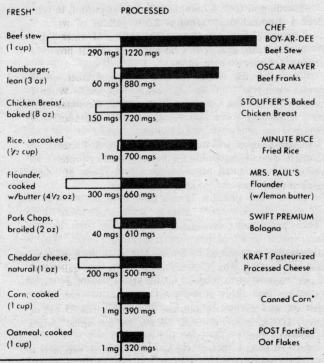

FRESH*		PROCESSED
Beef stew (1 cup)	290 mgs	1220 mgs — CHEF BOY-AR-DEE Beef Stew
Hamburger, lean (3 oz)	60 mgs	880 mgs — OSCAR MAYER Beef Franks
Chicken Breast, baked (8 oz)	150 mgs	720 mgs — STOUFFER'S Baked Chicken Breast
Rice, uncooked (½ cup)	1 mg	700 mgs — MINUTE RICE Fried Rice
Flounder, cooked w/butter (4½ oz)	300 mgs	660 mgs — MRS. PAUL'S Flounder (w/lemon butter)
Pork Chops, broiled (2 oz)	40 mgs	610 mgs — SWIFT PREMIUM Bologna
Cheddar cheese, natural (1 oz)	200 mgs	500 mgs — KRAFT Pasteurized Processed Cheese
Corn, cooked (1 cup)	1 mg	390 mgs — Canned Corn*
Oatmeal, cooked (1 cup)	1 mg	320 mgs — POST Fortified Oat Flakes

*roughly 2000 mgs sodium = 1 tsp salt (total daily recommended maximum)

Source: Dr. David Pimentel, Cornell University, 1981.
ªIncludes irrigation water.

irrigated acres in the Great Plains. Just four Great Plains states, Nebraska, Kansas, Oklahoma, and Texas, have accounted for over three-fourths of the new irrigation since 1964, and most of that irrigation has been used to grow more feed. Today half of the grain-fed beef in the United States is produced in states that depend for irrigation on an enormous underground lake called the Ogallala Aquifer.[30]

But much of this irrigation just can't last.

Rainwater seeps into this underground lake so slowly in some areas that scientists consider parts of the aquifer a virtually nonrenewable resource, much like oil deposits. With all the new irrigation, farmers now withdraw more water each year from the Ogallala Aquifer than the entire annual flow of the Colorado River. Pumping water at this rate is causing water tables to drop six inches a year in some areas, six feet a year in others. And lower water tables mean higher and higher costs to pump the water. The Department of Agriculture predicts that in 40 years the number of irrigated acres in the Great Plains will have shrunk by 30 percent.[31]

In only two decades Texans have used up one-quarter of their groundwater.[32] Already some wells in northern Texas are running dry, and with rising fuel costs, farmers are unable to afford pumping from deeper wells. Why is this water being mined in Texas? Mostly to grow sorghum for the feedlots which have sprung up in the last decade.

When most of us think of California's irrigated acres, we visualize lush fields growing tomatoes, artichokes, strawberries, and grapes. But in California, the biggest user of underground water, more irrigation water is used for feed crops and pasture than for all these specialty crops combined. In fact, 42 percent of California's irrigation goes to produce livestock.[33] Not only are water tables dropping, but in some parts of California the earth itself is sinking as groundwater is drawn out. According to a 1980 government survey, 5,000 square miles of the rich San Joaquin Valley have already sunk, in some areas as much as 29 feet.[34]

The fact that water is free encourages this mammoth waste. Whoever has the $450 an acre needed to level the land and install pumping equipment can take groundwater for nothing. The replacement cost—the cost of an equal amount of water when present wells have run dry—is not taken into consideration. This no-price, no-plan policy leads to the rapid depletion of our resources, bringing the day closer when alternatives must be found—but at the same time postponing any search for alternatives.

Ironically, our tax laws actually entice farmers to mine groundwater. In Texas, Kansas, and New Mexico, land-owners get a depletion allowance on the groundwater to compensate for the fact that their pumping costs rise as their groundwater mining lowers the water table. Moreover, the costs of buying the equipment and sinking the well are tax-deductible. Irrigation increases the value of the land enormously, but when the land is sold the profits from the sale are taxed according to the capital gains provisions; that is, only 40 percent of the difference between the original cost of the farm and its sale price is taxed as ordinary in-come. The rest is not taxed at all.

Few of us—and certainly not those whose wealth de-pends on the mining of nonrenewable resources—can face the fact that soon we will suffer for this waste of water. Don-ald Worster, author of *Dust Bowl: The Southern Plains in the 1930's* (New York: Oxford University Press, 1979), interviewed a landowner in Haskell County, Kansas, where $27.4 million in corn for feed is produced on about 100,000 acres of land irrigated with groundwater. He asked one of the groundwater-made millionaires, "What happens when the irrigation water runs out?"

"I don't think that in our time it can," the woman re-plied. "And if it does, we'll get more from someplace else. The Lord never intended us to do without water."[35]

The Soil in Our Steaks

Most of us think of soil as a renewable resource. After all, in parts of Europe and Asia, haven't crops been grown on the same land for thousands of years? It's true, soil should be a renewable resource; but in the United States, we have not allowed it to be.

We are losing two bushels of topsoil for every bushel of

corn harvested on Iowa's sloping soils, warned Iowa state conservation official William Brune in 1976.[36] Few listened. "It can take 100 to 500 years to create an inch of topsoil," but under current farming practices in Iowa, an inch of topsoil "can wash away in a single heavy rainstorm," Brune said after the spring rains in 1980. On many slopes in Iowa we have only six inches of topsoil left.[37]

Few would argue with Brune. Few would dispute that our topsoil loss is a national catastrophe, or that in the last two decades we have backpedaled on protecting our topsoil, or that in some places erosion is as bad as or worse than during the Dust Bowl era. Few dispute that excessive erosion is reducing the soil's productive capacity, making chemical fertilizers ever more necessary while their cost soars. The only dispute is how many billions of dollars topsoil erosion is costing Americans and how soon the impact will be felt in higher food prices and the end of farming on land that could have been abundant for years to come.

Since we began tilling the fields in our prime farming states we have lost one-third of our topsoil.[38] Each year we lose nearly 4 billion tons of topsoil from cropland, range, pasture, and forest land just because of rain-related water erosion.[39] That 4 billion tons could put two inches of topsoil on all of the cropland in Pennsylvania, New York, and New Jersey.[40] Adding wind erosion, estimated at 3 billion tons, we hit a total erosion figure of nearly 7 billion tons a year.[41]

Robin Hur is a mathematician and Harvard Business School graduate who has spent the last year documenting the resource cost of livestock production for his forthcoming book. "How much of our topsoil erosion is associated with crops destined for livestock and overgrazing of rangeland?" I asked him. "Most of it—about 5.9 billion tons," he calculates, including erosion associated with exported feed grains. This is true not only because feed crops cover half of our harvested acres, but because these crops, especially corn and soybeans, are among the worst offenders when it comes to soil erosion. According to the Department of Agriculture, one-quarter of all soil erosion in the United States can be attributed to corn alone.[42]

MINING THE SOIL

The loss of billions of tons of topsoil threatens our food security only if we are losing topsoil faster than nature is building it. The difficulty is knowing how fast nature works. The most widely accepted rule of thumb is that we can lose up to five tons of topsoil per acre per year without outpacing nature's rebuilding rate—yet one-third of the nation's cropland already exceeds this limit, the Department of Agriculture estimates, and one out of eight acres exceeds the limit almost three times over.[43] This is bad enough, but many soil scientists challenge the standard itself, suggesting it applies only to the top layer of the soil. Soil formation from the underlying bedrock may proceed *ten times* more slowly.[44] If these scientists are correct, we are mining the soil on most of our cropland.

LOST SOIL, LOWER YIELDS

In some areas we are already experiencing lower yields due to erosion and the reduction in fertility it causes. The Department of Agriculture estimates the annual dollar value of the loss just from water erosion at $540 million to $810 million.[45] Adding wind erosion may increase that estimate by 30 percent.

"In our area of Nebraska you see hilltops eroded—completely naked," says Marty Strange of the Center for Rural Affairs. "Yet farmers are still getting 90 to 95 bushels of corn an acre. Farmers don't believe they are losing productivity." They use chemicals to make up for the soil's lost natural fertility, but the cost of fertilizer has risen 200 percent since 1967 and is likely to keep rising. Higher production costs must ultimately mean higher food prices.

We also pay in our taxes, for billions of dollars have gone toward conservation measures (although this spending is shrinking, while the need increases). Moreover, the soil washed from farmlands ends up in rivers, streams, and reservoirs. Dredging sediment from rivers and harbors, the reduction in the useful life of reservoirs, and water purification—these costs amount to $500 million to $1 billion a year.[46]

Thus, the direct and indirect costs of soil erosion already approach *$2 billion a year*.

BUT WHY?

Why is soil erosion accelerating, despite 34 Department of Agriculture programs related to soil and water conservation? There are several reasons:

• the increased tillage of soil so fragile it probably should have remained uncultivated. The government estimates that 43 percent of the land used for row crops in the Corn Belt is composed of highly erodible soils.[47]

• the increased planting of row crops, especially the feed crops corn and soybeans, which make the land particularly susceptible to erosion.

• the growing neglect of conservation practices, including the removal of shelterbelts planted during the Dust Bowl era to protect the soil. By 1975 the total real value of soil conservation improvements had deteriorated over 20 percent from its peak in 1955.[48]

These are the reasons, but what are the causes? Unfortunately, they lie in the economic givens that most Americans take as normal and proper. Squeezed between ever higher costs of production and falling prices, farmers must increase their production. They plant more acres, including marginal land susceptible to erosion, and they plant what brings the highest return, even if this means continuous planting of the most erosion-inducing crops, corn and soybeans. "The most erosive production system—continuous corn—produces the highest net income," according to researchers at the University of Minnesota.[49]

Fertilizers: Becoming Import-Dependent

To determine a price for grain which reflects all its costs would also mean looking at the fertilizers required to mask our lost fertility and continually increase production. Higher yields and continuous cropping deplete soil nutrients, so that ever greater quantities of fertilizer must be used. This vicious circle caused our nation's use of chemical fertilizer to increase fivefold between the 1940s and the 1970s. Just in the last ten years, the use of ammonia (for nitrogen fertilizer) has increased by almost 200 percent and that of potash by almost 300 percent.[50] Corn, the major national feed grain, which occupies about 23 percent of all our cropland, uses more fertilizer than any other crop—about 40 percent of the total.[51]

Because fertilizer has been relatively cheap, farmers have been encouraged to apply ever greater quantities in their desperate struggle to produce. As with topsoil and groundwater, we squander fertilizer resources today without considering the consequences tomorrow. One of the consequences of our heavy consumption of fertilizer is increasing dependence on imports. Americans might be alarmed at how our dependence on imported strategic metals can be used to justify U.S. political or even military intervention abroad. Americans would probably be even more alarmed about becoming dependent on imported food. But is being dependent on the fertilizer needed to produce food really much different?

Let's look at the three major types of fertilizer:

Nitrogen fertilizer. We won't run out of nitrogen, since it makes up about 78 percent of our air, but the price of natural gas, used to make ammonia, the most common nitrogen fertilizer, has risen so rapidly that we have begun to import ammonia from countries with cheap supplies of natural gas. We now import about 20 percent of our supplies.[52]

Potash. Today we import about 85 percent of our potash (from Canada), and by the year 2000 we are expected to import 90 percent.[53]

Phosphate fertilizer. The U.S. is the world's leading producer, but our high-grade reserves will probably be exhausted over the next 30 to 40 years at the current rate of use, according to a 1979 government report. "We will probably move from assured self-sufficiency and a dominant exporter position to one of increasing dependency on possibly unreliable foreign sources of supply," says the ominous report. "Since phosphates are a fundamental necessity to agriculture . . . *the situation . . . is somewhat analogous to that now being experienced with oil*"[54] (my emphasis).

Livestock Pollution

Some people believe that although we feed enormous quantities of high-grade plant food to livestock with relatively little return to us as food, there is really no loss. After all, we live in a closed system, don't we? Animal waste returns to the soil, providing nutrients for the crops that the animals themselves will eventually eat, thus completing a natural ecological cycle.

Unfortunately, it doesn't work that way anymore. Most manure is not returned to the land. Animal waste in the United States amounts to 2 billion tons annually, equivalent to the waste of almost half of the world's human population.[55] Much of the nitrogen-containing waste from livestock is converted into ammonia and into nitrates, which leach into the groundwater beneath the soil or run directly into surface water, thus contributing to high nitrate levels in the rural wells which tap the groundwater. In streams and lakes, high levels of waste runoff contribute to oxygen depletion and algae overgrowth.[56] American livestock contribute five times more harmful organic waste to water pollution than do people, and twice that of industry, estimates food geographer Georg Borgstrom.[57]

Cheap Water for Cheap Grain

In a true accounting, the two bushels of topsoil washed away with every bushel of corn grown on Iowa's sloping land would be seen as a subsidy to our cheap grain. In other words, if we were to use all of the conservation measures we know of to prevent this erosion, the cost of producing our grain would go up, as it would if we were to add in all of the costs of dredging the soil from our waterways or charge for feedlot pollution. Failing to account for these costs amounts to hidden subsidies. But in addition, you and I as taxpayers are paying *direct* subsidies right now.

Our tax dollars have paid for more than one-half of the net value of all irrigation facilities in the United States as of 1975.[58] Since the turn of the century the federal government has sponsored 32 irrigation projects in 17 western states where 20 percent of the acreage is now irrigated with the help of government subsidies. A recent General Accounting Office study concluded that even though farmers are legally required to repay irrigation construction costs, in the cases studied the repayments amounted to less than 8 percent of the cost to the federal government.[59]

In some of the projects, the irrigators pay even less. Take the Fryingpan-Arkansas Project near Pueblo, Colorado. This half-billion-dollar project helps farmers grow corn, sorghum, and alfalfa for feed. The GAO calculated the full cost of water delivered to be $54 per acre-foot, but the farmers are being charged only 7¢ per acre-foot.[60] (And the GAO's "full cost" is based on an interest rate of 7½ percent.) According to *Fortune* magazine, the huge California Central Valley irrigation project is being subsidized at a rate of $79,000 a day.[61]

Cheap water encourages farmers to grow livestock feed. "Because water is so cheap, its use is based on its price and not its supposed scarcity," observes *Fortune*. "Many farmers . . . use inferior land to grow low value crops that require large amounts of water, like alfalfa and sorghum" for feed.[62]

Government subsidies are so large that "the market value of the crops to be grown with federal water is less than the cost of the water and the other farming supplies used to grow those crops," the government study concluded.[63] But Robin Hur has an even dimmer view of the economics of federal irrigation. After studying federal irrigation in the Pacific Northwest, he calculated that in six major projects the value of the crops produced doesn't cover even the cost of the water alone!

Federally subsidized irrigation water helps keep grain

cheap. It also helps make people rich. To a farmer with 2,200 irrigated acres in California's Westlands district, the federal water subsidy is worth $3.4 million—that's how much more the land is worth simply because of what the government contributes to irrigation.[64]

A key 1902 federal law stipulated that beneficiaries of the subsidized irrigation were to be small farmers *only,* those owning no more than 160 acres. But the law has never been enforced, despite suits filed by National Land for People and others seeking the irrigated land they are legally entitled to. Today one-quarter of the federally subsidized irrigated land is owned by a mere 2 percent of the landholders, who own far more land than the legal limit. In California, for example, over a million and a half acres of federally subsidized water are controlled illegally—that is, by farms over the legal acreage limit.[65] Southern Pacific alone controls land almost 700 times the legal limit for an individual. (All told, Southern Pacific owns almost 4 million acres in three states.[66])

Tax Benefits at the Feedlot, Too

Besides directly and indirectly subsidizing the feedlot system by keeping the price of grain low, we taxpayers also subsidize the feedlot operations themselves. Tax laws favoring feedlot owners and investors in feedlot cattle shift the tax burden onto the rest of us. While these tax advantages were cut back in 1976, there are still "income tax management strategies" that can benefit cattle owners who contract with feedlots to fatten their cattle, putting on the last 200 to 600 pounds of each head.[67] According to a Department of Agriculture report, the law that allows farmers to use cash accounting for tax purposes can also profit investors in feedlot cattle, especially those with high nonfarm incomes seeking to reduce their taxable income. More than a quarter of "custom feeding" clients in the Southern Plains are such outside investors, including doctors, lawyers, and bankers.[68]

Agricultural economists V. James Rhodes and the late

Joseph C. Meisner of the University of Missouri offer this observation of tax favors to feedlot operations:

> Subsidies to large-size feedlot firms, indirect though they be, would tend to lead to survival and growth of those firms on a basis of other than economic efficiency. . . . If the nation seeks to subsidize beef production, direct grants to feedlot firms is an alternative. Then, true economic costs of the subsidies would be more apparent. However, in a world of growing concern for energy supplies, the beef industry would seem to be a most unlikely recipient of national subsidy.[69]

A Fatal Blindness

After reading this account of the resource costs of our current production system, you probably are amazed that more people are not aware and alarmed. I am continually amazed. Again and again I have to learn this lesson: often those with the most information concerning our society's basic problems are those so schooled in defending the status quo that they are blind to the implications of what they know.

As I was preparing this chapter I came across a book that read as if designed to be the definitive rebuttal to *Diet for a Small Planet*. Three noted livestock economists conclude that "total resource use in this [livestock] production has decreased dramatically."[70] To arrive here, they had, of course, to ignore such hidden costs as I've just outlined—the fossil fuel used, the water consumed (including groundwater that is irreplaceable), the topsoil eroded, and the domestic fertilizer depleted as we attempt to make up for our soil's declining fertility. They also ignore feedlot pollution and hidden tax subsidies. All this I would have expected. What really shocked me was their attempt to prove that we are producing more meat using *less* resources. Their evidence? A decline in labor used and a dramatic drop in acres devoted to feed grains between 1944 and about 1960, while meat production rose. What they fail to tell us is that about one-third of our total cropland was released from feed-grain production between 1930 and 1955 by the rapid replacement of grain-consuming draft animals by fuel-consuming tractors. *Thus, much of the decline in feed-grain acres had nothing to do with increased efficiency of meat production.* Just as appalling, these economists ignore the fact that livestock eat more than feed grains. Since 1960 there has been a spectacular rise in soybean use as animal feed. Tripling since 1960, acres in soybeans now exceed two-thirds of total acres in feed grains.[71] (Almost half of those acres are used to feed domestic livestock,* the rest for export.) Soybeans are not even mentioned by these economists as a resource in livestock production.

While it is useful to keep these gross oversights in mind for the next time we feel cowed by an "authority" questioning *our* facts, they sidetrack us a bit from the basic argument used by such defenders of the status quo. Most economists defend our current meat production system by arguing that feeding grain to livestock is the cheapest way to produce meat. The fatal blindness in this argument is attention only to price. As we have seen, the price of our grain is an illusion. It results from the powerlessness of farmers to pass on their costs of production and the fact that so many of the costs of production—topsoil and groundwater, for example—carry no price at all.

In writing this chapter I came to realize more clearly than ever that our production system is ultimately self-destructive because it is self-deceptive; it can't incorporate the many costs I've outlined here. It can't look to the future. And it blinds those closest to it from even seeing what is happening. Thus, the task of opening our eyes lies more heavily with the rest of us—those less committed to protecting the status quo. As awakening stewards of this small planet, we have a lot to learn—and fast.

But now, let's turn abroad. If the food-producing resources of our country—one blessed with exceptional agricultural wealth—are threatened, what does this production system mean for countries much less well endowed?

---

* The protein concentrate made from soybeans is an excellent livestock ration, and the oil extracted is used to make margarine, salad oil, etc.

3.

The Meat Mystique

ALL THAT I have said so far might give the impression that the shift toward a meat-centered diet is an American craze. It is not. Throughout the world, more and more grain is being fed to livestock and people are eating more meat—at least, those people who can afford it. When I first wrote *Diet for a Small Planet* ten years ago, about one-third of the world's grain went to feed livestock. Today livestock consume close to one-half the world's grain output; and, by 1985, livestock are expected to eat even more grain than people do.[1] The portion of the world's wheat being fed to livestock has doubled since the late 1960s.[2] And increasingly, even basic staple foods of the poor, such as the tuber cassava, are used as livestock feed.

Grain feeding to livestock outside the United States increased more than twice as fast as population in the 1970s. In Brazil, for example, 44 percent of the staple food crops, mainly grains, are now fed to livestock; in Mexico, 32 percent.[3] In the Soviet Union, not only does a third of the domestically produced grain go to livestock, but the government has made huge foreign purchases of grain to satisfy the Russian people's demand for meat. The 18 million tons of grain which the Russians bought from us in the infamous 1972 Russian grain deal went largely to feed live-stock.

Meat consumption is rising in countries where diets traditionally centered on rice, fish, and soy foods. Thirty years ago, for example, the Japanese people ate almost no meat, but by 1980 meat contributed 20 percent of the calories in the Japanese diet and meat consumption was continuing to rise.[4]

Two questions seem worth exploring. First, why do people want more meat? (Just about everybody seems to want more than they have.) Second, how is it possible that more and more grain is used to produce meat when at least a quarter of the world's people go without even the basic grain they need?

The most obvious answer to the first question is: meat tastes good. And once any food is considered a favorite, other foods, such as vegetables, are neglected. Mushy string beans accompany the chopped steak plate at Denny's to give it the variety of a classic "home-ec" meal, but don't expect a taste thrill if you eat them!

Meat, especially beef, is also a status symbol. I remember an ad in a progressive newsmagazine for $7-a-pound mail-order steaks. Buy these "when you want to impress your brother-in-law," the ad proclaimed. Like drinking Coca-Cola and wearing Levi's, eating beef is a symbol of the American way of life, imitated from Tegucigalpa to Tokyo. Rising urban middle classes eagerly adopt a meat diet to show how far they have come from the villages where they ate rice, fish, and vegetables.

The Korean diet has historically been based on vegetable protein. But, as Shirley Dorow, a Lutheran missionary who has lived for many years in South Korea, wrote me, "average consumption of beef has risen about 15 pounds a year per person. This means, of course, that some people never eat beef and a few are eating it regularly, for it is a status food."

And to some, I'm convinced, there is an association between meat eating and masculinity. How many women have I heard sigh with pretended exasperation (but real pride) that their husbands are unyielding "steak and potatoes" men. As I was writing this book one of the more amusing letters I received was from a woman in Maine who told me that her efforts to get a good friend to eat more plant foods and less meat got nowhere. He told her that if he didn't eat a lot of meat he would not be able to make love to his wife.

Thus, to challenge a meat-centered diet is to challenge a whole set of feelings and associations. For many, realizing that a meat-centered diet does not bring greater well-being but in fact risks to their health has been one step in rethinking their definition of "progress" or "development." But let's turn to my second question: how can it be that even in the third world countries more and more grain is used to produce meat while in many of those countries the majority go without the basic food they need?

The answer to this question is much easier than the answer to the first. The sad truth is that those who want and need the grain cannot afford to buy it, so livestock get it. And this is truer every day as the poor are pushed off their lands by the more powerful landowners and as new technology denies the landless poor the jobs they need if they are to buy food.

In researching *Food First* I began to understand that when the "experts" praise underdeveloped countries for "upgrading their diets," the diet of the majority is often being downgraded. This "upgrading" of diets, reflected in statistics showing greater per capita consumption, often means that the well-off minority is eating up hundreds of pounds of grain in the form of meat while the majority is denied even a minimal grain diet.

Brazil is an extreme and tragic example. There, as I've said, almost half of the basic grains go to feed livestock while the majority of the rural poor suffer from malnutrition. Black beans, long the source of cheap protein for the poor, are now expensive and out of the reach of many. The reason? Landowners have shifted from growing black beans to what is more profitable—growing soybeans for livestock feed for domestic and export markets.

The growing power and wealth of the elite in many third world countries means that scarce foreign exchange, often earned by agricultural exports, is used to import feed instead of basic development goods for the benefit of the

poor majority. During the 1970s half of the increased livestock feeding abroad relied on imported feed, primarily
from the United States.[5]

Exporting the Steak Religion

Most Americans assume that our farm exports go to feed
the hungry world. Few appreciate that most of these exports go to other industrial countries, and, overall, *two-
thirds of all of our agricultural exports go to feed livestock.*[6] As noted earlier, U.S. farm exports have doubled in
just one decade. Much of that spectacular increase is due
to feed grain exports, which have leaped fourfold.

The United States has done its part to create a world of
hamburger and wheat bread lovers, even in cultures that
have thrived for centuries on rice, soy, and fish. From its
beginnings in the 1950s, U.S. food aid was officially
viewed as a tool for developing commercial markets.[7] American officials understood that food aid could be a foot in
the door for converting a nation's taste and food system to
dependence on the United States, first on "aid" food, then
on commercial exports. The strategy has worked: among
the largest importers of U.S. grain are countries, like South
Korea and Taiwan, that not long ago were major recipients
of food aid.

But at least most food aid went directly to feed people
(mainly the better off); more and more of the current
commercial shipments to such countries go into livestock
production. This shift to livestock feeding in the third world
was encouraged by a provision in our food aid program
during the 1960s. We allowed a percentage of the local
currency used to repay food aid loans to be lent at very low
interest rates to U.S. corporations. Over 400 U.S. corporations benefited. Some were food firms, such as Ralston
Purina, Peavey, and Cargill, which used the cheap loans to
establish grain-fed-poultry operations abroad. The development of feed grain markets in the third world was also
encouraged by a law that allowed the federal Commodity
Credit Corporation to lend American companies money—

over $120 million by 1976—to purchase agricultural commodities. The companies then sell them in the foreign markets, using the proceeds to establish operations there.

At the same time that food aid was introducing Asian tastebuds to U.S. wheat, and to poultry fed on U.S. grain, the Foreign Agricultural Service (FAS) of the U.S. Department of Agriculture was pushing "aggressive foreign market development" to beat out the "stiff competition" in the race for increased agricultural exports. The Foreign Agricultural Service's cooperation with food export industries includes "market intelligence," "trade servicing," and "product promotion."[8]

If an American corporation wants to know whether it would be profitable to enter a certain market, it turns to one of 100 or so U.S. agricultural attachés in foreign countries. These government employees first make sure the company's product can legally be imported, then call in "professional taste panels" to see if it is acceptable to local tastes. If the company's product makes it past these steps, the FAS helps sponsor a market test.

In addition, the FAS sponsors exhibits around the world for the benefit of U.S. producers. One favorite exhibit is a full-scale reproduction of an American supermarket. Since the United States exports 44 percent of all the wheat in the world trade, the FAS also helps sponsor schools to teach people how to cook with wheat where it is not a traditional food. In Japan the FAS has sponsored a beef campaign, noting that it is "aimed at better-class hotels and restaurants catering to the tourist trade."[9] Its efforts there have also helped to account for the success of fast-food outlets like McDonald's, 90 percent of whose ingredients are imported. Although American-style fast-food outlets began operating in Japan only in 1970, by the end of the decade these chains had taken over a substantial portion of all such sales, displacing many traditional rice, fish, and noodle bars.

Our export strategy thus rests not on shipping our food to a world of hungry people, but on molding the tastes and habits of a relatively small class of people able to afford imported food, making them dependent on products and styles that they never wanted before. American policymakers are encouraging other countries to become more and more food-dependent on the United States, and the United States itself is becoming more and more economically dependent on food exports. Reading the FAS material, one would think that the survival of our nation rested on its success in creating one more hamburger lover in the world.

Meat Imports

We hear almost exclusively about the export side of our agricultural trade. Few Americans are aware that we are also among the world's top agricultural importers. For every dollar our agricultural exports earn we pay out close to 50 cents importing food and other farm products. About one-quarter of those imports are meat and other livestock products, worth almost $4 billion in 1979.[10]

Less than six percent of the meat we ate over the last decade was imported. While small in relation to total U.S. consumption, it represents an enormous food resource in relation to the needs of people in some of the countries where it is produced.

As I was finishing this book I received a letter from Sue Pohl of Hillsdale, Michigan. In the early 1970s she lived with her two children in Honduras. "While I was there I experienced the damage our meat-eating habits can do," she wrote. "In 1973 President Nixon increased the quota of imported meat to keep U.S. meat prices down. Instantly many kinds of meat disappeared from our local market, including liver, which I relied on for my iron in our limited diet. (Eggs were in chronically short supply and had to be saved for the children.) So great was the greed of the Honduran meat producers that the government had to issue a decree that a certain percentage of meat must be reserved for the country's own people."

In exporting the Great American Steak Religion we are exporting a desire for the impossible. The earth could never provide the majority of its people with the grain-fed-meat-centered diet that Americans take for granted. If everyone in the world were to eat the typical American diet, the acreage under cultivation worldwide today would have to double.

4.

Democracy at Stake

I HAVE TALKED of the resources and outright subsidies hidden in our cheap-grain-fed meat and how we are promoting this pattern of eating around the world. But I have left out perhaps the most critical lesson of all: how the production system that mines our resources also undermines social values we cherish. We have been taught that our production system rewards hard work and efficiency while providing abundant food for all, but it actually rewards waste, wealth, and size—and the hungry go without food no matter how much is produced. This is the most painful lesson I have had to learn in the last ten years.

The Blind Production Imperative

In our production system, farmers' profits are in a continually tightening squeeze—between rising costs of production and falling prices for their crops. Their profits are squeezed because farmers are largely price *takers* who must confront price *makers* both when they buy what they need to make the land produce and when they sell their crops.

The first price makers are the manufacturers of farm inputs. Tractor manufacturers, for example, can pass on their rising costs to farmers in the form of higher prices, because farmers must have tractors and there are only a handful of manufacturers. The same holds true for fuel, pesticides, fertilizers, seeds, and other farming inputs. Farmers, however, cannot pass on their higher costs, because in selling their crops farmers meet the second price maker: the marketplace. Farm commodity sales may be the last truly competitive market, with thousands of units competing against one another. Farmers have to take whatever price they can get from relatively few major buyers. Going prices are determined largely by supply and demand, not by the farmers' costs of production.

Because they are at the mercy of price makers both in buying farm inputs and in selling their crops, farmers' profits per acre fall steadily. By 1979 profits per acre in real terms had sunk to one-half the level of 1945.[1] Because of their greater volume of sales, many large farms can survive these lower profits per acres, but smaller farms, *even if more efficient,* may not survive while receiving the very same price per bushel. Thus, ever lower profit margins favor size and force the smaller farms to try to become even larger. Moreover, simply to maintain the *same* income all farmers must try to increase production and lower production costs, regardless of the ecological or human consequences.

So Earl Butz's infamous "Get big or get out" was not a snide crack—it was sound economic advice. But who has the opportunity to "get big"? Only those farmers whose operations are already quite large, particularly those who have considerable equity in their land. They have the advantage when it comes to taxes, government payments, and marketing their crops.

But control of the land is key. Because of this incessant pressure to expand, the most limiting factor in production—land—steadily inflates in value. "Thus, simply owning land comes to be rewarded more highly than producing food on it," Marty Strange, co-director of Nebraska's Center for Rural Affairs, told me. "In other words, unearned wealth is a bigger factor today in farm expansion than earned income from farming." (For example, a typical farmer with 80 percent of his land paid for had an annual net income of $18,500 in 1978, but the value of the land itself increased by $34,600 that year, according to a 1979 government study.[2]) As the wealth of those with considerable equity soars, they have the collateral to buy out their neighbors down the road. By the mid-1970s almost two-thirds of all farmland sales involved the expansion of existing farms, a reversal of the 1950s, when two-thirds of farmland sales resulted in new farms.[3]

In this process, over four million farms have gone out of business in the last 40 years. Of those remaining, the top 3 percent now control almost half of all farm sales. By the year 2000, if trends continue, this 3 percent will control two-thirds of all farm output.[4]

In place of owner-run farms and widely dispersed control of our land, we see the possibility of what former Secretary of Agriculture Bob Bergland called a "landed aristocracy"; that is, more and more of the actual farming in this country will be done by tenants, sharecroppers, and day laborers.[5] Already in the "family farm" heartland of Iowa, more than half of the farms in some counties are operated by tenants or sharecroppers.[6] And those farms which are still owner-run will operate increasingly under contract to large export and processing firms. Newcomers, except the most wealthy, will be barred from entering farming.

The practice of better established, bigger farms gobbling up smaller ones is commonly defended on the grounds of more efficient production, yet already over half the value of all crops in the United States is produced on farms *larger* than can be justified on the ground of efficiency.[7] Moreover, costs of production on small to moderate-sized farms are often *lower* than on the biggest farms, according to the Congressional Research Service.[8]

Greater production and growing markets have always been held out to farmers as keys to their prosperity, but the most straightforward facts of our agricultural history deny this promise:

Our agricultural output has almost doubled in the last 30 years,[9] and agricultural exports have doubled just since 1970, yet the real purchasing power of an average farm family in 1978 was about the same as in the early 1960s.[10] And even this average masks the economic devastation of many (those unable to expand) and the meteoric rise of a minority. Eighty thousand dollars is the *average* net income of the 3 percent at the top, those who now control almost half of U.S. farm sales. The tiny group of 6,000 farms that captures 20 percent of farm sales now enjoys an average annual net income of roughly half a million dollars.[11] At the same time, if two-thirds of American farms tried to live off the sales of their crops alone, their income would fall below the poverty line. Their average income hovers close to the national median only because of increased nonfarm income.[12] And *that* average hides the continuing reality of rural poverty.

Thus, production itself, and efforts to dispose of it through livestock and exports (or, most recently, gasohol), can no longer be accepted as a solution to the plight of the farmer. For we can see where this blind production imperative has taken us—away from values that Americans have always associated with democracy, and toward a "landed aristocracy"; away from dispersed control over the land, and toward a highly concentrated pattern of control; away from a system rewarding hard work and good management, and toward one rewarding size and wealth alone. As I suggested earlier, ours is becoming the kind of farm economy that I have seen at the root of so much injustice and misery in the third world.

Production Divorced from Human Need

We view our production system as rational, but what makes it go? It is motivated by this year's profits to the individual producer. We proudly cite abundant production as proof of the system's success. But "Does it produce?" cannot be the only question we ask. In judging our system, we must also ask, is it sustainable? Is it fair to its producers? I have already answered "No" to these questions. But the ultimate question which we must answer is, *does it fulfill human needs?* Production divorced from human need is not rational.

Our production is staggering: over four acres of cropland and pasture are producing food for each person in America. (That's the equivalent of about four football fields just for you!) We produce so much food that although roughly one-fifth is wasted altogether—simply plowed under or thrown out—we are still able to export the output of every third acre harvested. In fact, our production has been so great that one of the biggest government headaches over the last four decades has been the mountains of costly "surpluses."

Yet despite our abundance and the fact that our food prices do not reflect the true costs of production, middle-income families—$15,000 to $25,000 a year—must spend almost 29 percent of their income to eat a "liberal" food plan (as defined by the Department of Agriculture). Poor families must spend from one-half to two-thirds of their income just to buy a "low-cost" food plan.[13]

What's more, there is hunger in America.

"Hunger here?" The Dutch reporter interviewing me looked puzzled. "There can't be. I've never seen anything like your supermarkets. So much food. So many different kinds."

But I have learned that hunger can exist anywhere, within any society that has not accepted the fundamental responsibility of providing for the basic needs of its most vulnerable members—those unable to meet their own needs. And ours, sadly, is such a society. I found myself feeling ashamed when I learned that other societies with which we might compare ourselves—France, Sweden, West Germany—demonstrate by their welfare programs that they do accept this social responsibility. In a recent study of social benefits to needy families with children in eight major industrial countries, the United States ranked among the lowest. In France, a single, unemployed mother caring for two children would receive in benefits 78 percent of the average wage of that country. In Sweden, 94 percent. But in the United States she would receive only 54 percent—and in many parts of our country, much less.[14] (While benefits in other countries are uniform, in our system a person living in the South is likely to get as little as half the benefits of someone living in the Northeast, for example.)

Despite our staggering abundance, millions live in utter deprivation. Who are those denied access to America's abundance?

They are the elderly. Fifteen percent have incomes below the poverty line, and that percentage has begun to climb.[15] Forty percent of all unmarried elderly women in the United States live in poverty.[16]

They are children, and the mothers who must stay home to take care of them. Twelve million American children live below the poverty line, and poverty among inner-city children is climbing at a horrifying rate: between 1969 and 1975 poverty among related children under five rose, for example, 68 percent in Ohio and 49 percent in New Jersey.[17]

They are the disabled and those unable to find work. By the late 1970s, Americans were being asked to accept as normal an unemployment rate double that of a decade earlier.

In addition to the people who cannot work or cannot find a job, there are many Americans trying to support a family on the money they earn working for the minimum wage. You can work full-time for the minimum wage and still fall below the poverty line.

All told, 29 million Americans—about one in eight of us—live below the poverty line, which the government sets at about $8,400 for a family of four.[18] Poverty-line income amounts to $583 a month, but family incomes of $300 to $400 are more typical. To grasp how there can be hunger and other needless deprivation in our country, all I have to do is try to imagine meeting the needs of myself and my two children on $400 a month.

Many would like to deny that hunger and poverty exist in America. Just after Ronald Reagan's election as President, his chief adviser on domestic affairs declared that poverty had been "virtually wiped out in the United States." Since our system of government aid had been a "brilliant success," he added, it "should now be dismantled."[19] What irresponsible ignorance.

First, our welfare programs do not lift people out of poverty. *Even including food stamp benefits, in few states does welfare bring families even up to the poverty line.*[20] In half the states these programs do not bring families even to 75 percent of the poverty standard.[21] The second fallacy in this statement is that there could ever be a time when government welfare programs are no longer needed. This attitude reflects an unwillingness to accept responsibility for those who—in any society—cannot care for themselves, no matter how bright the economy looks.

But what about hunger? Even though poverty cannot be denied, haven't food stamps eliminated hunger? There is no doubt that food stamps have helped enormously, but they have not eliminated hunger. First, food stamps alone, at about 45 cents per meal, are not enough to supply an adequate diet.[22] The Department of Agriculture concluded that the diets of 91 percent of those families whose food spending is at the level of the food plan on which food stamp allotments are based are nutritionally deprived.[23] If they possibly can, most people supplement their food stamps with cash. But if you are trying to support a family on $400 a month, that means you'll probably have to squeeze some food money out of the rent or heating bill.

Other evidence exists to prove the reality of hunger in America. Poor children have actually been shown to be physically stunted compared to their middle-class counterparts. A Center for Disease Control study in the mid-1970s documented that up to 15 percent of the poor children examined showed symptoms of anemia and 12 percent were stunted in height.[24] Dr. Robert Livingston of the University of California at San Diego told us that "poor children have measurably smaller head circumferences than those in families with adequate income."[25]

Our infant death rate is another powerful indictment of our society. Because the infant mortality rate (deaths of babies less than one year old per 1,000 live births) in part reflects the nutrition of the mother, it is often used to judge the overall nutritional well-being of a people. Even though per person spending on health care has leapt tenfold in less than 20 years,[26] our infant mortality rate ranks 16th in the world, almost double that of Sweden or Finland.[27] In the United States, 14 babies die for every thousand born alive. This national average is "not enviable," the journal *Pediatrics* sadly notes.[28] But averages do not uncover the real tragedy. Among *nonwhite* babies the infant death rate is 22 per thousand, about the same as that of an extremely poor country like Jamaica.[29] Even assuming much better reporting of infant deaths here, this comparison should alarm us.

Even averages among nonwhites mask the extreme deprivation in some communities. In the Fruitvale area of Oakland, California, just across the San Francisco Bay from my home, the infant death rate is 36 per thousand. And in the capital of our nation the rate is 25 per thousand, approximately that of Taiwan.[30]

Perhaps the most convincing evidence of hunger amid abundant production comes from the few people who have the courage to go into our communities to meet and talk with those who are suffering from lack of food. One such person is a woman I met five years ago when we both participated in a Philadelphia "hunger radiothon," 24 hours of commercial-free radio in which all the breaks were used to tell people about hunger and its causes. Investigative reporter Loretta Schwartz-Nobel spoke about people starving in Philadelphia. As I was writing this book, I heard from Loretta again. This time she sent the manuscript that documented the hunger—even starvation—that she had witnessed. Her evidence includes many passages like this one, quoting an elderly former civil service worker in Boston:

> I've had no income and I've paid no rent for many months. My landlord let me stay. He felt sorry for me because I had no money. The Friday before Christmas he gave me ten dollars. For days I had had nothing but water. I knew I needed food; I tried to go out but I was too weak to walk to the store. I felt as if I was dying. I saw the mailman and told him I thought I was starving. He brought me food and then he made some phone calls and that's when they began delivering these lunches. But I had already lost so much weight that five meals a week are not enough to keep me going.
>
> I just pray to God I can survive. I keep praying I can have the will to save some of my food so I can divide it

up and make it last. It's hard to save because I am so hungry that I want to eat it right away. On Friday, I held over two peas from lunch. I ate one pea on Saturday morning. Then I got into bed with the taste of food in my mouth and I waited as long as I could. Later on in the day I ate the other pea.

Today I saved the container that the mashed potatoes were in and tonight, before bed, I'll lick the sides of the container.

When there are bones I keep them. I know this is going to be hard for you to believe and I am almost ashamed to tell you, but these days I boil the bones till they're soft and then I eat them. Today there were no bones.[31]

If your reaction is that Loretta has simply ferreted out a handful of senile old people who refuse government help, read her book *Starving in the Shadow of Plenty* (Putnam, 1981). She is convinced that the people she met are only the tip of the iceberg. "It's happening all over the city," said a social worker in the community where this starving woman lived. "They can't get welfare; they're too old for the job market and too young for Social Security. What can we tell them to do? Tell them to go to the hospital and get treated for malnutrition?" In a Mississippi community, Dr. Caroline Broussard told Loretta, "Whole families come here malnourished. But what's worse is that we know for every hungry child or adult we see here in this clinic there are 20 to 30 others in the area we are not getting to." And in New York City, according to the Community Service Society and a number of public officials, 36,000 people are living on the streets. Again, we think of homeless street people as a third world tragedy. Yet their numbers are increasing right here in America.

Illusion of Progress

Most Americans believe that since the late 1960s we've made steady progress in eliminating hunger and poverty, due to the introduction of food stamps, school lunch programs, and supplemental feeding programs for pregnant and nursing women. And it's true that these programs have had an impact. In 1967 the Field Foundation sent a team of physicians to investigate hunger in America. Their tour of depressed communities riveted national attention on hunger. Ten years later another Field Foundation team of physicians returned to the same localities. Their 1979 report noted "fewer visible signs of malnutrition and its related illnesses," although "hunger and malnutrition have not vanished." They attributed the improvement *not* to overall economic progress for the poor: ". . . the facts of life for Americans living in poverty remain as dark or darker than they were 10 years ago. But in the area of food there is a difference. The Food Stamp Program, the nutritional component of Head Start, school lunch and breakfast programs, and to a lesser extent the Women-Infant-Children (WIC) feeding programs have made the difference."[32]

Clearly there was progress for those who received the benefits. But these benefits are totally inadequate. (A Texas family of four, for example, is expected to make do on $140 a month in welfare benefits.)[33] Moreover, poverty programs have never reached all those in desperate need of them. The food stamp program reached only half of those eligible for most of its life, reaching two-thirds of those eligible only after rule changes in 1977.[34] Programs for pregnant women and young children have served only one-quarter of those eligible.[35]

Moreover, the value of all our welfare programs has been declining over the 1970s because, except for food stamps, benefits are not tied to inflating prices. And now even food stamp benefits are falling behind. The poor are the worst hit by inflation because they spend a much larger share of their income on necessities, and the prices of necessities (housing, food, fuel, medical care) rose twice as fast as nonnecessities in the 1970s. Inflation has cost welfare recipients 20 percent of their purchasing power over the decade.[36]

In sum, if the lives of the poor have improved at all over the last two decades it has been, for the most part, not because of increases in job-related incomes but because of government programs, such as the grossly inadequate health and food assistance I've just discussed. And even these gains are being reduced by inflation and cut by President Reagan and the Congress elected in 1980.

As to the alleviation of poverty itself? New figures from the Census Bureau show that gains made since the mid-1960s had been virtually wiped out by 1980, even *before* the Reagan administration began to ax social-welfare programs. And in 1981 the nation experienced one of the biggest increases in poverty since the early 1960s, when the Bureau first started collecting poverty statistics. In early 1982, a county administrator in South Carolina told *The New York Times* how he experiences poverty's tightening grip: "The population of the jail has tripled, even though there has been no increase in serious crime," he said. "People get themselves arrested on some minor violation so they can get a meal or two, and I can prove that."[37]

"We're at risk of turning back the clock to a time when hunger and malnutrition were common in this country," Nancy Amidei told me. Nancy is director of the Food Research and Action Center in Washington, D.C. Over the last year she has talked throughout the country with low-income people who are already being affected by the Reagan budget cutbacks. What they told her can be summed up by 82-year-old Luisa Whipple who told a congressional committee, "I plead with you not to cut back the food stamp program, because as you cut back food stamps you cut back on our health and you cut back on our lives."

Every society must be judged as to how well it meets the basic needs of those unable to meet their own, and on whether it provides a living wage to all those able to work. Our society fails on both counts. How can we act on this judgment? First, we must keep alive in our minds the reality of hunger amid the massive squandering of food resources, for only a sense of moral outrage can keep us probing *how* our society evolved so as to divorce production from human need—and only a sense of moral outrage can force us to question our everyday life choices, asking just how each choice either shores up or challenges the economic assumptions and institutions that generate needless suffering. The "what can we do?" is then answered, not in one act but in the entire unfolding of our lives.

What we eat is only one of those everyday life choices. Making conscious choices about what we eat, based on what the earth can sustain and what our bodies need, can remind us daily that our whole society must do the same— begin to link sustainable production with human need. And choosing this diet can help us to keep in mind the questions that we ourselves must be asking in order to be part of that new society—questions such as, how can we work to ensure the right to food for all those unable to meet their own needs, and a decent livelihood for all those who can work? How do we counter false messages from the government and media blaming the poor and hungry for their own predicament?

Ironically, the notion of relating food production to human needs might strike most Americans as a "radical" idea. We know we're in trouble when common sense seems extreme! But maybe it hasn't gone that far yet. "We've been going at it from the wrong end in the past," Agriculture Secretary in the Carter Administration Bob Bergland admitted. "This country must develop a policy around human nutrition, around which we build a food policy, and in that framework we have to fashion a more rational farm policy."[38]

5.

Asking the Right Questions

ONCE WE UNDERSTAND how the ground rules of our economy force greater production yet bypass the hungry, we
realize that grain-fed meat is not the cause of our problems. It is a symptom and, for me, a powerful symbol of
what is wrong.

If grain-fed-livestock production and consumption were
the cause of our problems, then producing and eating less
would be the answer. Today Americans *are* eating less
beef—16 pounds per person less than in 1976.* What has
been the impact?

Some ranchers, desperate to maintain their livelihood,
are planting crops on pastureland. In early 1981, when Eu-
gen Schroeder of Palisade, Nebraska, realized that he stood
to lose $200 on each head of cattle, he plowed one-fifth of
the 5,000 acres he had previously used for pasture.[2] Along
with thousands of other farmers, Schroeder found that it
was more profitable in 1981 to grow corn for export than
to produce cattle. Thus, given the production imperative
basic to our system, a decline in beef eating which helped

---

* This drop in beef consumption was made up for by 10 pounds
per person more of both pork and poultry.[1]

undercut ranchers' profits led to a potentially *more* damaging use of our soil and water, at least in the short term.

Similarly, although the low price of grain is one reason why so much goes to feed livestock, more expensive grain would not be the answer. Would it reduce the mining of our resources? Alone, no. If grain were more expensive, the push to produce it would be even greater, to take advantage of the higher price.

The disturbing discovery is that there is no single change that could alter the self-destructive path we are on. Many things will have to change. But this does not mean that we can wait until they can all happen at once! Eating less grain-fed meat is not the answer in itself, but if this step means that more and more of us will be asking *why* the current American diet developed and *what can we do* to alter the forces behind it, then we are on our way.

The first step is uncovering the right questions.

As long as we focus single-mindedly on increasing production and then on finding ways to dispose of it—through livestock, exports, or gasohol—we can neatly avoid asking the most critical social questions. As our nation was being built, we did not learn how to ask these questions. The continent's vast natural resources, the delusion of "Manifest Destiny" which led Americans to seize most of the United States from its native inhabitants and Mexico, the cheap labor offered by slavery—all these allowed Americans to evade critical questions of justice, resource efficiency, and sustainability in our agriculture. After 200 years we face the consequences: the production system which has provided such abundance for most Americans is now beginning to threaten our food security.

It turned out to be easier to develop new seeds, new machines, and new ways to use grain than to deal with issues of power: how decisions are made and for whose benefit, taking into account not only the immediate return but the long-term impact of these decisions. Our national blindness to the issues of power—how to share it fairly and effectively—has been aided by myths deeply rooted in our national consciousness. So we must begin by looking inside ourselves.

First, a belief that paralyzes many people is the notion

that human beings are motivated solely by selfish interests. As a result, democratic economic planning, based on cooperative decision-making instead of a battle of vested interests, is viewed as impossible. And people are bound to doubt any movement or organization claiming to be based on cooperative principles, because if human nature is inherently selfish, people will not cooperate willingly. Claims of cooperation must be masks for coercion.

But look at your own life and the historical record; human beings are much more complex than this. Sure, we all have self-interests. The species would not have survived without them! But most people also want their lives to have meaning beyond themselves. And this is one right denied so many Americans—the "right to feel useful."

So the question is not how to extinguish individual self-interest in the interests of society, but how to begin to build economic and social structures in which the individual can serve her or his own interests and the community's interests at the same time. There need not be an irreconcilable conflict.

The tragedy is that under our current economic ground rules, many feel they must choose: either ravage our resources today to stay in business or conserve these resources and run the risk of bankruptcy.

Second, we must examine the myth that the essence of democracy is the unbridled freedom of the individual. But wait . . . every responsible society limits people's freedom. In our society freedom is limited by wealth. Those who have wealth have many options; those without wealth have many fewer. Today the "freedom" to own farmland is denied to virtually all those without it, except the few with great wealth. So the question is not *whether* freedom is limited, but *how*. Is our way fair? Is there a more just and democratic way?

Once we accept the myth of unbridled freedom, then placing a ceiling on an individual's "success" is seen as undemocratic. So Americans defend anyone's right to accumulate unlimited wealth. But isn't this a frontier concept? On the frontier it appeared as if there were enough resources for everyone. But the frontier has disappeared; there's only so much farmland in the United States and now it's shrinking, not growing. Yet we give some the right to own 100,000 acres when we know this denies dozens of farm families the right to own any land at all. Is this democratic?

Third, we must probe our deep fear that social planning is always alien and handed down from the top. Hearing the word "planning," we immediately see a grim-faced Politburo officer handing down production quotas. Our stereotypes make us blind to the similarly antidemocratic planning that takes place in our own economy. Industry and government executives here speak English instead of Russian, but their power over our lives may be just as profound as that of economic decision-makers in the Soviet system.

So the question is not *whether* we should have planning. Every society has planning. The issue is *what kind and by whom*. (In Sweden, for example, a committee of local residents decides who can bid on farmland that is for sale, if it is to be sold outside the family. Typically, these committees try to ensure that it does not go to the larger farmers.) But so narrow is our view of planning that it is hard even to imagine developing democratic, accountable planning mechanisms controlled locally and coordinated nationally. In our blind fear we hand over our power—to the unaccountable. What is grown depends only on what will sell to those with money, not on what is needed by those without money. So production is not accountable to need. Neither is production accountable to our children and grandchildren, who will need the resources squandered today. Processing and marketing decisions, moreover, are accountable only to the boards of directors of a handful of corporate giants, as we'll see in Part III.

We have the information to break out of these old fears and misunderstandings. After 200 years we can see where they have taken us. And we can learn from what we see. The destruction of resources, the emergence of a landed aristocracy, and hunger in America are *not necessary*. Shocked into this realization, we can begin to imagine the shape of an economic system truly consistent with democracy. What we need now is courage.

I can't offer you a set of how-to's to get us moving in the direction of greater democracy, although Part IV shows you what some other people are doing. But here I would like to offer certain principles that have evolved as the basis of all my work over the last ten years. While there is no blueprint for how we can transform our society, the first step is to develop a sense of the direction in which we want to move—an orientation that more and more people will come to share, so that our distinct tasks become ever more complementary and therefore ever more effective. Here is what I would like to offer to the building of such an orientation.

My Grounding Principles

1. Because scarcity is not the cause of hunger, increasing production alone is not the solution. The solution can be found only by addressing the issue of power. Thus, "development" must be redefined, here and in the third world, not merely in terms of more production or consumption, but first and foremost in the changing relationships among people. Development must be the process of moving toward genuine democracy, understood as the ever more just sharing of political and economic power.

2. Just as "development" must be redefined to encompass the concept of power, so must "freedom." For what is freedom without power? Freedom to complain about what's wrong in our society without the power to do anything about the problems is virtually meaningless. Thus, *freedom from* interference is only part of what democracy means. We must also have *freedom to* achieve what makes life worth living—the freedom to have safe and satisfying work; the freedom to enjoy security in the form of food, housing, and health care; the freedom to share in decisions affecting our workplace, community, and nation; and the freedom to share in the responsibility of protecting our resources for coming generations.

3. The concepts of economic and political democracy are

inseparable. As the eminent jurist Louis Brandeis said, "We can have democracy in this country or we can have great wealth in a few hands, but we can't have both." Thus, democracy must go beyond the ballot box. It must include the wide dispersion of wealth and control over resources. It must entail the development of accountable, flexible planning structures for resource use from the community to the national level. And the concept of democracy must not stop when we go to work each morning; it must involve the opportunity for self-management in the workplace.

Political and economic democracy are inseparable concepts because where wealth is in the hands of relatively few, laws regulating control over society's basic resources are made in their interest. What's more, this minority's economic might allows it to defy laws not in its interest. (In the United States such monopolies as American Telephone and Telegraph defy antitrust laws; likewise, in California a handful of corporate farming giants have for decades flouted federal law prohibiting their profiting from tax-funded irrigation.)

4. Democracy is not a static model to be achieved once and for all. "Democracy," said William Hastie, "can easily be lost, but is never finally won. Its essence is eternal struggle." Thus, every society is in a process of change and must be judged by the *direction* in which it is moving—toward a more just distribution of power or toward more and more tightly held power. Sadly, I believe my own society is moving away from democracy, toward greater and greater concentration of economic and political power.

5. Within every society, "capitalist" or "socialist," those who have power tend to increase their power. The *only* way to move in the opposite direction is for those who have less power—that means *us*—not only to resist this tendency but to actively take part in the redistribution of power. That means taking on greater and greater responsibility ourselves. In other words, movement toward genuine democracy can happen only when ordinary people realize that they have both the right and capacity to help make the important political and economic decisions in their society.

With these five grounding principles, the critical question becomes, how can we take part in the redistribution of power? I hope that Part IV will help you answer this question yourself.

Part III

Diet for a Small Planet Revisited

1.

America's Experimental Diet

To EAT THE typical American diet is to participate in the biggest experiment in human nutrition ever conducted. And the guinea pigs aren't faring so well! With a higher percent of our GNP spent on medical care than in any other industrial country and after remarkable advances in the understanding and cure of disease, the life expectancy of a forty-year-old American male in 1980 was only about six years longer than that of his counterpart of 1900.

Why haven't our wealth and scientific advances done more for our health? Medical authorities now believe that a big part of the answer lies in the new American diet—an untested diet of high fat, high sugar, low fiber, which is now linked to six of the ten leading causes of death. (See Figure 4.)

The first two editions of this book are full of nonmeat recipes, just as this one is. But in my discussion of nutrition I stuck to the protein debate because I wanted to demonstrate that we didn't need a lot of meat (or any, for that matter) to get the protein our bodies need. Now I think I missed the boat, for the *Diet for a Small Planet* message can't be limited to meat. At root its theme is, how can we choose a diet that the earth's resources can sustain *and* that

117

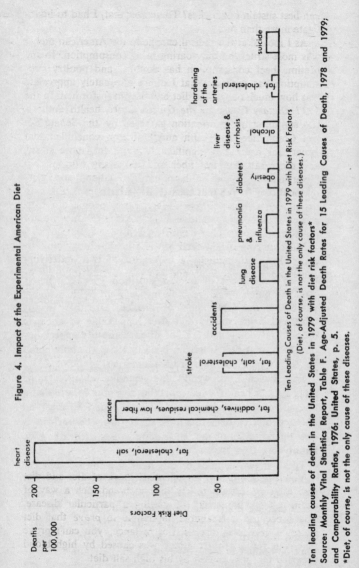

Figure 4. Impact of the Experimental American Diet

Ten leading causes of death in the United States in 1979 with diet risk factors*
Source: Monthly Vital Statistics Report, Table F. Age-Adjusted Death Rates for 15 Leading Causes of Death, 1978 and 1979; and Comparability Ratios, 1976: United States, p. 5.
*Diet, of course, is not the only cause of these diseases.

can best sustain our bodies? To answer that, I had to investigate more than meat.

As I looked at the radical change in the American diet, I was most struck by our soaring meat consumption. In my lifetime beef consumption has doubled and poultry consumption has tripled. What I didn't adequately appreciate was how much our *entire* diet had been transformed. In the 1977 *Dietary Goals for the United States,* health authorities summing up information gathered by the Senate Select Committee on Health and Nutrition concluded that Americans are eating significantly more fat, more sugar, and more salt, but less fiber and too many calories. No fewer than 16 expert health committees, national and international, now agree that each of these changes is linked to heightened risk of disease.[1] Many other people are concerned that the food additives and pesticide residues we are ingesting may also pose health hazards.

Most striking is that each of these health-threatening dietary changes is actually a byproduct of two underlying ones: *more animal food,* and *more processed food.* "Processed" simply means that between the ground and our mouths someone takes out certain things and puts in other things—and not always things that are good for us. The problem is not that Americans are adding more sugar and salt to their recipes or cooking with more fat; the problem is that these are being added *for* us. All we have to do is take the fatty, grain-fed steak from the meat counter, the potato chips from the shelf, or the Big Mac from its styrofoam package.

Eat at Your Own Risk

You'll notice that when scientists speak of diet and disease they are careful to say that such-and-such a way of eating affects the "risk" of getting a particular disease. That's because it is almost impossible to *prove* that diet causes a particular disease. For instance, you can't prove that your father's heart attack was caused by high blood pressure that was caused by his high salt diet.

Scientists must largely rely on "guilt by association." By comparing populations, they can observe which diets are associated with which types of disease. But comparing different societies with different diets is less than convincing, since there is always the possibility that genetic differences among populations and other environmental factors play a decisive role. So the most telling observations are those of a single population group which changes its diet. Here is a sampling of such evidence:

• The traditional Japanese diet contains little animal fat and almost no dairy products. Japanese who migrate to the United States and shift to a typical American diet have a dramatically increased incidence of breast and colon cancer.[2]

• The citizens of Denmark were forced to reduce their intake of animal foods by 30 percent during World War I, when their country was blockaded. Their death rate simultaneously fell 30 percent, to its lowest level in 20 years.[3] Denmark's experience was not unique: in a number of European countries, where World War II forced people to eat less fat and cholesterol and fewer calories, rates of heart disease fell.

• In some third world countries a small class of urbanites have adopted the new American diet over the last 20 years. Coronary heart disease now occurs more and more frequently in some of those countries, such as Sri Lanka, South Korea, Malaysia, and the Philippines, the World Health Organization reports.[4]

Other important evidence comes from different diet and disease patterns in populations that are similar in most other ways. For example, a study of 24,000 Seventh Day Adventists living in California showed that the nonvegetarian Adventists had a three times greater risk of heart disease than those eating a plant food diet.[5]

In her fascinating, thoroughly researched book *Jack Sprat's Legacy* (Richard Marek, 1981), Patricia Hausman convinced me that health authorities around the world virtually all agree: the typical American diet is a high-risk diet. The "debate" over the risks associated with the new American diet is perpetuated by the media and vested interests in the meat, dairy, and egg industries, who have spent millions of dollars trying to publicly deny these risks, despite overwhelming evidence to the contrary.

Eight Radical Changes in the U.S. Diet

The food industry was quick to attack the Senate Select Committee on Nutrition and Human Needs for daring in 1977 to suggest a change in the American diet. How ironic. Never has a people's diet changed so much so fast as ours has over the last 80 years. And that change, as we shall see, has been in large part caused by the food industry itself.

I have looked at each of these changes and asked, what are the risks associated with this change? And *why* the change? (By the way, the best detailed source on the "Changing American Diet" is an excellent book by that name (1978) written by Letitia Brewster and Michael Jacobson of the Center for Science in the Public Interest in Washington, D.C.)

I will discuss each change separately, but as nutritionist Dr. Joan Gussow wisely observes, our bodies don't experience these changes separately. "One of the handicaps of most 'scientific' investigations of the impact of dietary change is that each is studied separately, whereas the greater threat may be their cumulative impact," says Dr. Gussow. So we have to look at the whole cluster.

Dangerous Change No. 1: Protein from Animals Instead of Plants

Contrary to what I thought, the dramatic change is *not* in our protein consumption. It has actually varied little over the last 65 years, fluctuating between 88 grams and 104 grams per person per day (roughly twice what our bodies can use). The change is in how our protein is packaged. Sixty-five years ago we got almost 40 percent of our protein from grain, bread, and other cereal products. Now we only get 17 percent of our protein from these sources. In their place, animal products, which then supplied about half of our protein, now contribute two-thirds.[6]

U.S. consumption of animal products began to climb after World War II, with beef consumption almost doubling and poultry consumption almost tripling by the late 1970s.[7]

THE RISKS

There is no medical consensus about the risks of diets high in protein generally or about diets high in animal protein specifically. (There is general agreement about the risks of what results from this new "packaging" of our protein—more fat and less fiber. But I'll deal with those risks later.) While no consensus exists, there are some intriguing warning signals.

The Senate Select Committee notes: "One series of investigations found that diets that derive their protein from animal sources elevate plasma cholesterol levels to a much greater extent than do diets that derive their protein from vegetable sources. Another line of basic research demonstrated that, in almost all cases, high protein diets are more atherosclerotic than are low protein diets."[8] (Atherosclerosis is a hardening of the arteries caused by fatty deposits accumulating along the artery walls.)

High-protein diets have also been linked to osteoporosis, the thinning of the skeleton, in some studies. Osteoporosis, which now affects four out of five elderly American women, occurs when calcium is drawn from the bones, weakening them. Pain, fractures, and even the collapse of part of the vertebrae can result. Because more calcium is excreted in the urine in a high-protein diet, this kind of diet may promote osteoporosis. (Apparently, eating more calcium doesn't help.) One recent investigation found that animal protein did contribute to increased calcium excretion. But there is still much that's not understood.[9]

Dangerous Change No. 2: More Fat

Americans eat 27 percent more fat than did our grandparents in the early 1900s. And more than one-third of that increase has come just in the last ten years. As a result, fat's contribution to our total calorie intake climbed from 32 to 42 percent, though there are signs that the average may be lowering.

THE RISKS

The risks appear to lie in too much total fat, too much saturated fat, and too much cholesterol. Saturated fats, found in animal foods and in some vegetable foods (especially palm and coconut oil), and cholesterol, found only in animal foods (especially eggs, some seafood, and organ meats), generally increase the blood cholesterol level. Eating saturated fat raises blood cholesterol levels more than does eating cholesterol itself.[10] As Patricia Hausman explains in *Jack Sprat's Legacy*, the higher the blood cholesterol, the greater the rate of fatty deposits that harden the arteries. The more severe the fatty deposits in the arteries, the greater the risk of heart disease, stroke, and other complications of atherosclerosis.

Reducing the cholesterol in the diet does not automatically reduce the cholesterol in the blood for everyone. There may be genetic factors which determine why some people respond to lowered dietary cholesterol and others do not. But to be on the safe side, it would seem prudent to assume that lowering our cholesterol consumption will make a difference.

In a survey of 200 scientists in 23 countries, 92 percent recommended that we eat less fat to reduce our risk of heart disease.[11] In addition to increased risk of heart disease, says Hausman, "studies, spanning up to 40 countries worldwide, confirmed that the total amount of fat in the diet does correlate with some forms of cancer. Studies link six forms of cancer with dietary fat, including cancers of the breast and colon, two of the top cancer killers in the United States."[12]

Dietary Goals for the United States suggests we return to a diet in which 30 percent of our calories come from fat, instead of the 42 percent we're averaging now. (The Japanese, notable for their low incidence of heart disease, traditionally have gotten only 10 percent of their calories from fat. Unfortunately, this is rapidly changing as hamburger joints displace the traditional rice, fish, and noodle bars.)

The good news is that eating polyunsaturated fats— safflower, sunflower, corn, and soybean oils—actually *lowers* the blood cholesterol levels, and may help control hypertension as well.[13] So the recommendation is that at the same time as we reduce our total fat, we shift from animal fats and palm and coconut oils to more of these polyunsaturates.

Where Is the Fat in Our Diet?

We are eating more fat, not because we are pouring more oil on our salads or frying more foods at home. Again, we are letting someone else ut the fat in for us. In our "choice" and "prime" steaks, grain has been turned into fat. In those french fries at Burger King, a very low-fat food—the potato—has been transformed into one in which most of the calories are from fat, mostly saturated fat.

Where is the fat in our diet?

In animal foods. Over half the fat in the American diet comes from animal foods, with red meat alone contributing almost one-third. Although our consumption of butter and lard has fallen drastically (Americans eat about one-quarter the butter we ate in 1910),[14] we're eating much more fat in meat, poultry, cheese, and margarine. We're eating two or three times as much of these foods as we did in the mid-1940s.

In fattier meat. Not only do we eat more meat and poultry, but those products contain more fat today than in our grandparents' time. As we've seen, one important effect of grain feeding is to put on more fat. During their last 120 to

150 days before slaughter, cattle are fattened up (or "finished," as cattlemen say) so they will receive USDA's "choice" or "prime" grade rating and command a premium price. A choice-grade carcass has about 63 percent more fat than one fed less grain and graded only "standard." (In the last several years the meat industry has begun to respond to the public's concern about fat by offering more lean meat and even a few reduced-fat processed meats, such as hot dogs.)

In snack foods. Just as important in explaining our increase in fat consumption are snack foods—french fries, potato chips, corn chips, crackers, and other snack foods. Eating potato chips, we get 63 percent of calories from fat—fully double the recommended proportion for our total diet. Even in Ritz crackers, we get 46 percent of the calories from fat.[15]

In other processed fat surprises. Ironically, some of the processed foods we purchase in an attempt to avoid fat or cholesterol have more fat than the product we are trying to avoid. Nondairy coffee whitener, for example, has three times the fat of natural half-and-half.[16]

Prepared foods such as TV dinners and fast foods also contribute to the fat surge in the American diet. In a Big Mac or Kentucky Fried Chicken or a TV dinner, Americans are getting about half their calories from fat.[17] At home we *could* eat a meal with just as much fat, but once we pass under the Golden Arches we have no choice.

The vegetable oils most commonly used in processed foods—coconut and palm kernel oils—contain largely saturated fats, the type medical authorities warn us against. Virtually all of the fat in powdered coffee whitener is saturated fat.[18] So is the fat used in processed foods such as "breakfast bars" and some imitation ice creams. Thus, even though we might never use coconut or palm oil in our own kitchens, if we eat a processed diet we get plenty of these saturated vegetable fats. They now account for 16 percent of total vegetable oil consumption.

Dangerous Change No. 3: Too Much Sugar

Since the turn of the century Americans have doubled their daily sugar dose; just since 1960 it's gone up 25 percent. One-third of a pound of sugar is now consumed each day for every man, woman, and child in America.[19]

THE RISKS

The problem with sugar is both what it does to us and what it displaces. The link between sugar and tooth decay is well established. In virtually all societies studied, the incidence of tooth decay rises as people eat more sugar. Half of all Americans have no teeth at all by the time they reach the age of fifty-five.

Sugar also fills us up with calories while giving us no nutrients or fiber. Filled on sugar calories, we inevitably eat less of other nutrient-rich foods such as breads and cereals, fruits and vegetables. Unfortunately, sugar makes us need the nutrients in these foods even more. Sugar increases the body's need for thiamin and perhaps the trace mineral chromium as well, according to Dr. Jean Mayer.[20]

WHERE IS THE SUGAR IN OUR DIET?

As with fat, Americans are not buying more sugar and confections directly. In fact, Americans are eating significantly less candy today than they did in the early 1940s. Candy has its ups and downs, but per capita intake has been falling steadily since 1970.[21] The household use of sugar has dropped to half of what it was in the early 1900s.[22]

We are eating more sugar because it is being added *for us* by the food-processing corporations and we are eating more of their processed foods.

Since the early 1900s the per capita consumption of sugar in processed fruits and vegetables has tripled. So much sugar is added to processed fruits and vegetables that Americans eat almost as much sugar in these foods as they do in cake and candy. Since the early 1900s, the per capita use of sugar in beverages, mainly soft drinks, has increased almost sevenfold.[23] By 1976 the equivalent of 382 twelve-ounce cans of soft drinks—each with six to nine teaspoons of sugar—was consumed for every person in the country—up about two and one-half times just since 1960.[24] (The next time you reach for a Coke, remember that you're about to drink the sugar equivalent of a piece of chocolate cake, including the icing.) Fully one-quarter of our intake of cane and beet sugar now comes from soft drinks.[25] Among processed foods, cereals and baked goods give us the most sugar; the country's second most popular breakfast cereal, Sugar Frosted Flakes, is *half* sugar.[26]

Dangerous Change No. 4: Too Much Salt

Americans now eat 6 to 18 grams of salt (sodium chloride) a day—10 to 30 times the average human requirement, and as much as three times the recommended level.[27] *Dietary Goals for the United States* recommends that we eat no more than one teaspoon of salt (5 grams) a day (about 2,000 mg of sodium). Since the average human *requirement* for salt is probably one-twentieth the recommended maximum of one teaspoon, there is virtually no danger of insufficient salt even if we never add salt to any food ourselves.[28]

THE RISKS

Health scientists are widely agreed that high salt intake markedly increases the risk of hypertension, or high blood pressure, and they estimate that as many as 40 percent of the older people in the United States are susceptible to hypertension. High blood pressure increases the risk of heart attack and stroke. High-salt diets also cause edema, or water retention, in some people.

WHERE IS THE SALT IN OUR DIET?

Again, as with fat and sugar, the problem is not so much that Americans are reaching for the saltshaker more often. The greater problem is that many Americans eat two to three times the recommended daily intake without ever seeing a grain of salt. In a Kentucky Fried Chicken dinner, for example, you consume a teaspoon of salt—enough for a whole day.[29]

Not only does fast food come salt-laden, so do many processed foods. (See Figure 5.) A mere ounce of processed Swiss cheese—less than you might put in a sandwich—has almost one-quarter teaspoon salt. Natural Swiss cheese has one-sixth that much.[30] A frozen beef dinner contains almost a full teaspoon of salt, 20 times as much as an unsalted hamburger.[31] Two hot dogs give you one-half teaspoon, as does a cup of Campbell's soup.

Almost all canned vegetables are salt-heavy. Fresh or frozen corn, for example, has almost no salt; but a cup of canned corn has 20 percent of the salt recommended for a whole day. Even processed foods that we think of as sweet are really salty, too. One piece of cake made from a devil's food cake mix contains as much salt as a 1½-ounce bag of potato chips.[32]

Other salt-laden foods are cured meats, such as smoked ham, chipped beef, and corned beef, and the pickles Americans love on hamburgers.

In addition to the invisible salt in processed foods, Americans are eating more and more salted snacks. In 1980 Americans spent almost $4 billion on potato chips, nuts, corn chips, pretzels, and prepopped popcorn.

Dangerous Change No. 5: Too Little Fiber

Until very recently, most of us did not know that lack of fiber in the diet was a risk; most of us didn't even know

Figure 5. Sodium* in Fresh versus Processed Foods

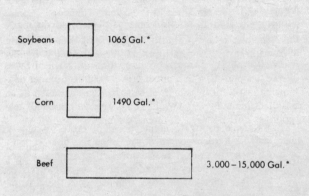

Soybeans — 1065 Gal.*

Corn — 1490 Gal.*

Beef — 3,000 – 15,000 Gal.*

Adapted with permission from Center for Science in the Public Interest, Washington, D.C.
*Roughly 2,000 mg sodium = 1 tsp. salt (total daily recommended maximum).

what fiber was. Scientists define dietary fiber as the skeletal remains of plant cells that are not digested by our bodies' enzymes.

As significant as any other change in the human diet over the last 20,000 years is the "fiber revolution." The diets of our early ancestors probably contained ten times the dietary fiber of contemporary diets.[33] Our long digestive tract undoubtedly evolved to handle this higher-fiber diet. The antifiber revolution has taken its most extreme form in the United States, where today 70 percent of our calories come from food containing little or no fiber.[34]

The fiber in fruits, grains, beans, seeds, and vegetables differs, and serves different beneficial functions. Some, for example, shorten the time it takes food to pass through the intestines; others promote the growth of bacteria useful in altering potentially harmful substances. So it is important to eat a variety of fiber.

THE RISKS

Of all the diet-disease connections, the role of dietary fiber may be hardest to pin down, since the fiber content of our diet has no direct biochemical effects but promotes physical and secondary physiological changes. Nevertheless, low-fiber diets have been implicated in heightened risk of bowel cancer and other intestinal diseases. "Dietary fiber appears to aid in reducing the onset and incidences of diabetes, cardiovascular disease, diverticulosis, colon and rectal cancer, and hemorrhoids," states Dr. Sharon Fleming of the Department of Nutritional Sciences at the University of California, Berkeley.[35] More than one scientist believes that fiber in the diet appears to be even more strongly linked to reduction of blood cholesterol levels than does a lowering of fat consumption.[36] Another problem associated with lack of fiber is plain old constipation.

WHY SO LITTLE FIBER IN OUR DIETS?

Whole cereals, fruits, vegetables, and legumes (peas, beans, lentils) are good fiber sources. But we are eating less of many of these fiber foods and more of foods without fiber. For example, we eat less than half the flour and cereals our grandparents ate in 1910,[87] and the refined cereal products we do eat have been stripped of their fiber. A slice of white bread has only one-eighth the fiber of a slice of whole wheat bread. (See Figure 6.) Since 1930 we have cut our fresh fruit consumption by one-third.[88] The amount of dried beans in our diets has dropped by a third since its peak in the 1930s. One of the few fiber foods whose consumption is not declining is fresh vegetables.

As with fat, the real reasons for lack of fiber in the American diet are the increase in animal foods (which have no fiber to begin with) and the increase in processed foods (which have theirs removed).

Figure 6. Fiber in 4 Slices of Bread and Other Foods

White bread	.2 gm
Whole wheat bread	1.6 gm
Rye bread	1.1 gm
1 small apple	1.0 gm
½ cup cooked dry beans	1.5 gm
1 cup grated carrots	1.0 gm
¾ cup raw cabbage	.8 gm

Dangerous Change No. 6: Too Much Alcohol

Ever since Prohibition, Americans have been drinking more alcohol. They drank the equivalent of 2.69 gallons of *pure* alcohol per person in 1975, 24 percent more than during the 1961–65 period. Of course, this figure is misleading, because while many people drink little or no alcohol, others drink far more than their share.[39] The biggest increases have come in wine, with 490 million gallons sold in 1979, and beer, up from 82 million barrels in 1950 to 175 million barrels in 1979.[40] (Some 25 percent of the cereal grains directly consumed in the United States are used to make alcoholic beverages.[41])

Alcoholic beverages offer us few nutrients but lots of calories—210 calories per day in the average adult diet in 1975. (Again, this is misleading: since many Americans drink no alcohol, others must get 500 or even 1,000 calories a day from alcoholic drinks.[42])

THE RISKS

Alcohol leads to cirrhosis of the liver, the sixth leading cause of death in the United States. It can also cause birth defects and mouth cancer. Even more deadly is alcohol's effect in traffic accidents: half of all traffic deaths involve a drinking driver. Moreover, alcoholism destroys—only more slowly—the lives of millions of Americans every year.

Despite these undisputed dangers, sales of alcoholic beverages amount to more than $45 billion a year. Anheuser Busch, which controls 26 percent of the beer market, spends $120 million a year on advertising, and the alcohol industries have enormous political power.[43]

Dangerous Change No. 7: More Additives, Antibiotic Residues, and Pesticides

FOOD ADDITIVES

"It is impossible to know exactly how many pounds of artificial colors, flavors and preservatives we ingest annually" is the sober assessment of Letitia Brewster and Michael Jacobson. In *The Changing American Diet*, these authors note that the only accurate records made public are the amounts of coal-tar-based colors certified each year by the Food and Drug Administration. But Brewster and Jacobson suggest that the increase in the use of food coloring is probably a pretty good indicator of the increase in other additives. The use of certified food coloring has increased about *elevenfold* since 1940.[44]

THE RISKS

The debate over the risks of food additives continues. The Center for Science in the Public Interest, co-founded by Jacobson, has spent ten years looking into these risks. Jacobson's first book, *Eater's Digest* (Doubleday, 1972), is a valuable encyclopedia of food additives and their risks.

"But there are hundreds of common additives," I said to Michael Jacobson in a recent phone conversation. "What do *you* tell people to do?" He answered with a list of five additives about which he believes there is enough evidence to warrant concern.

Read labels and avoid these additives, Michael suggests. "But it's not so difficult," he says. "Basically, if you avoid junk food, you'll avoid most of them."

ANTIBIOTICS

Livestock consume nearly half of the 25 million pounds of antibiotics produced in this country every year, an output that has shot up 400 percent in the last 20 years. Livestock eat most of these antibiotics in their feed, which contains low-level doses to enhance growth and prevent disease. Penicillin and tetracycline are the most common.[45]

Cancer-causing sulfa residues from antibiotics are still occasionally found in pork above the levels now considered safe, according to my former husband, pathologist Marc Lappé, author of *Germs That Will Not Die: The New Threat of Antibiotic-Resistant Bacteria* (Doubleday/ Anchor Press, 1981). In addition, the carcinogenic growth hormone DES has been discovered in some cattle, even after its banning several years ago.

Marc and other scientists fear that such widespread use of antibiotics in animals could lead to the evolution of bacteria resistant to common antibiotics. "The drugs are used

	Where You Find It	Suspected to Increase Risks of
Caffeine	3 Cokes have as much as 1 cup of coffee	Birth defects and other reproductive problems when consumed by pregnant women, fibrocystic breast disease (breast lumps), irritability, insomnia
Saccharin	"Diet foods" (diet soda accounts for half of all saccharin used)	Bladder cancer
Nitrite	Hot dogs, bologna, bacon, sausage, etc.	Cancer*
BHT†	Many processed foods, such as potato chips, oils, and yeast	Cancer
Colorings	Many processed foods, especially candy, soft drinks, and gelatin desserts	Cancer

*The debate about whether nitrites are cancer-causing continues. But what is often overlooked, according to the Center for Science in the Public Interest, is the fact that even if nitrites themselves are not shown to cause cancer, nitrosamines may be formed from the nitrites either in cooking or in the digestive process, and nitrosamines have been linked to cancer.

†Butylated hydroxytoluene (BHT) prevents oils from oxidizing and becoming rancid. But it increases the shelf life of a product only slightly and is not necessary if one consumes the product within a normal time range.

in livestock production in total disregard of the possibility that they could create resisistant bacteria which might directly or indirectly cause disease in humans, or even human epidemics," Marc warns.

The Food and Drug Administration is now considering banning the use of penicillin and certain types of tetracycline in animal feed.

The antibiotic explosion is just one more aspect of the destructive production imperative. Since poultry producers can get as much as 12 percent more weight gain from the same amount of feed when antibiotics are used, they feel they have no economic choice. Antibiotics also reduce disease and death, problems greatly exacerbated by the large-scale, high-density livestock production our economy encourages.

PESTICIDES

Pesticide use doubled from 1966 to 1976, reaching about 600 million pounds of active ingredients. When livestock eat tremendous volumes of treated grass and grain, pesticide residues concentrate in their tissues. Not surprisingly, a Food and Drug Administration study of our diet found the most (22 percent) pesticide detections in meat, fish, and poultry. (Virtually all the detections of DDT were in this group.) Oils and fats were next, with 18 percent of all detections.[46]

Studies of human breast milk offer strong evidence linking animal fat in the diet with heightened concentrations of pesticides. Stephanie Harris, formerly with the Environmental Defense Fund, told me that her study, using matched controls, found a significant correlation between pesticide levels in breast milk and the diet of the mother. "The more animal fats in the diet, the more pesticides we found in the mother's milk," Stephanie told me. "To reduce our intake of pesticides," she suggests, "means not only cutting back on our meat intake but also on full-fat dairy foods—butter, whole milk and fatty cheeses."[47]

Our national intake of DDT is going down. But you might be surprised that there is any DDT in our food at all, since it was banned for use here in 1972. Unfortunately, the life span of organochlorine pesticides already introduced into the environment ranges from 7 years to over 40 years. And while the amount of DDT in our food may be going down, our intake of other pesticides, like malathion, toxaphene, and captan, is going up.[48]

THE RISKS

No one knows. Our intake of pesticides does not exceed what the government calls safe "tolerance" levels. But these toxicity standards are established on the basis of short-term toxicity tests on small animals. They tell us little about the long-term risks to humans.

Moreover, when officials of the Environmental Protection Agency checked up on Industrial Biotest Laboratories, the mammoth lab which conducted most of the studies establishing the "safe" levels for pesticides consumed by Americans, it found that more than 75 percent of the tests audited were invalid. They involved faulty test procedures or downright falsification of data.[49]

We may not know for 10 to 20 years (or we may never know) the true health risks of pesticides in our food. In the meantime, one way to reduce our exposure is to limit our intake of meat, poultry, fish, and fats. Fruits and vegetables come next in line as carriers of pesticides. Chemists recommend that we wash commercially produced fruits and vegetables with detergent to reduce the amount of pesticides we eat.

In 1981 our Institute published *Circle of Poison: Pesticides and People in a Hungry World*, a book by David Weir and Mark Schapiro. It reveals that American chemical corporations are legally exporting to the third world pesticides that have been banned or heavily restricted in the U.S. Residues of these banned pesticides have been found in some of the food we import. Therefore, avoiding imported meat, fruits, and vegetables makes sense as another way to lower your pesticide intake.

Dangerous Change No. 8: Too Many Calories

I probably don't have to present evidence to convince you of one of the key consequences of the new American diet. A government study confirms what our scales are telling us: as of the early 1970s the average American man was six pounds heavier and the average woman seven pounds heavier than their counterparts of 15 years earlier.[50] Twenty percent of all Americans are either clinically overweight or obese.[51]

THE RISKS

Extra pounds can aggravate hypertension and heart disease.[52] (Even a 10 percent reduction in weight can lower blood pressure significantly, according to a recent study.[53]) It is less widely known that obesity is also believed to promote diabetes.

But why are Americans getting fatter?

We are not eating more calories, but we are burning up less because our lives are more sedentary. Moreover, with the typical American high-fat, low-fiber, high-sugar diet you can eat a lot of calories without eating very much bulk, so you just don't feel full. A gram of fat has more than twice as many calories as a gram of carbohydrate. This means that for the calorie "cost" of just one pat of butter or two bites of hamburger, you could eat a whole cup of plain popcorn, a slice of bread, most of a small potato, a cup of strawberries, or an entire head of lettuce.

Eating more plant food and less animal food allowed me not only to shed my extra ten pounds (never achieved as a chronic dieter) but to maintain the same weight for the last ten years. And my experience is apparently not exceptional. Says the *Journal of the American Dietetic Association:* "Persons who were previously omnivores and became vegetarians in adulthood report weight loss rather than gain."[54] It suggests that increased physical activity might also play a part, as was true for me. Most important, I was liberated from the stifling preoccupation with weight that plagues so many Americans.

The Good News

The flip side of the message in this chapter—that so many of our most dreaded diseases are related to the food we now eat—is the good news: we can reduce our chances of getting these diseases since *we* control what we eat. And it's easy. We don't have to memorize a book of tables and walk through the grocery store with an electronic calculator, adding up grams of fat, salt, and sugar. Since the eight threats to our health derive mainly from animal foods and processed foods, achieving a healthy diet involves only a few steps: reducing our consumption of animal foods (limiting eggs to three a week and cutting back on full-fat dairy products), enjoying a variety of *whole* foods, and using safflower, sunflower, corn, or soybean oil at home. Remember, what the medical authorities are recommending today is not some newfangled way of eating that requires a Ph.D. to put together. It is a pattern of eating that sustained human life for thousands of years.

The lesson is clear: the more we let the food industry create what we eat, the more we expose ourselves to risk. The more control we take over our diet, the better able we are to reduce those risks. (I am not suggesting a corporate plot to make us sick; it is simply that the logic of corporate expansion is frequently in direct conflict with our body's logic, as we'll see in the next chapter.)

And the word is getting out. Americans *are* starting to modify their diets, at least in part for reasons of nutrition and health. Many people nationwide have cut back on fatty meat, eggs, and oil, while eating more fruits and vegetables.

The single most important first step in rediscovering the traditional, healthy diet is *changing where you shop.* As long as you are wading through 15,000 choices in a supermarket, coming up with something healthy will seem like an incredible challenge. But if you are shopping in a community cooperative store filled with whole foods and foods from local producers, all your senses will be tantalized— but in the right direction for your health. Part IV lists some cooperative networks and some excellent guides to getting such a cooperative food store going in your community.

2.

Who Asked for Fruit Loops?

AT A PARTY not long ago I was talking with a man I hardly knew about the ideas in this edition—how I was struggling to grasp the forces *behind* these eight radical and risky changes in the American diet. "Well, don't blame the corporations," he told me. "If people are stupid enough to eat junk food, they deserve to get sick. Naturally corporations are going to make what sells best."

I think he summed up pretty well how most Americans view these changes in our diet. They are seen as the more or less inevitable consequences of combining the corporate profit motive with human weakness. And since you can't change either, why stew about it?

I'm convinced that this view is popular because while it *appears* to assign responsibility (to the gullible individual), it is really a way to evade responsibility for our economic ground rules. Once accepted, these ground rules justify such practices as feeding 145 million tons of grain to livestock. And they make the expensive, energy-consuming, life-threatening changes in our national diet inevitable.

To understand corporate logic, pretend for a few minutes that you are the chief executive of Conglomerated Foods, Inc.

From the Point of View of Conglomerated Foods, Inc.

Get off the elevator on the top floor. Enter the executive suite. Say hello to your secretary, settle down in your big leather chair, and gaze for a moment out the picture window. Think. How would *you* make Conglomerated Foods prosper? Even if you don't have a degree from Harvard Business School, I think you'll find that certain obvious strategies come to mind.

Ah, yes . . . first *expand sales*. But how?

The "Takeover" Strategy

Your most obvious step in expanding sales is to squeeze out, or buy out, smaller, often regional, producers. (As Proctor & Gamble did when they bought a small southwest coffee company called J. A. Folger about ten years ago.[1]) Then you launch an advertising blitz and a deluge of coupons and even reduce the price of your product below your cost. (You can follow International Telephone & Telegraph's example—it sold its Wonder, Fresh Horizons, and Home Pride breads at a loss to drive smaller bakeries out of the market.[2]) Since you're a conglomerate selling many different products, you can make up for any losses simply by raising prices in your other product lines. And why not expand your sales overseas through takeovers? (As Borden did when it bought Brazil's biggest pasta manufacturer.[3])

THE IMPACT OF YOUR STRATEGY

Walking into the supermarket, customers still see Aunt Nellie's Pickles and Grandma's Molasses. This illusion of diversity hides the reality that your strategy has succeeded making the food industry one of the most tightly controlled in America. In the scramble to capture national markets, *half* of American food companies have been bought out or closed down during my lifetime. Most of them were not inefficient producers; they simply could not withstand the financial muscle of the cash-laden conglomerates.

Take Beatrice Foods, for example, a company whose name is unknown to most Americans. This one company has bought out more than 400 others.[4] Names like Tropicana, Milk Duds, Rosarita, La Choy, Swiss Miss, Mother's, and Aunt Nellie's, and even Samsonite and Airstream—all these should really be called "Beatrice."

As a result of the surge of takeovers, 50 of the remaining 20,000 companies have emerged at the pinnacle. These 50 corporations now own two-thirds of the industry's assets. Based on present trends, these 50 firms—one-quarter of 1 percent of them all—will control virtually *all* the food industry's assets in another 20 years.[5]

By the 1970s the supergiants had begun to gobble up the giants. In what *Business Week* called the "great takeover binge," Pillsbury plunked down $152 million for Green Giant (frozen vegetables). For $621 million, R. J. Reynolds seized Del Monte's vast fruit and vegetable empire. Nabisco merged with Standard Brands (Chase & Sanborn coffee, Blue Bonnet margarine, Planter's peanuts, etc.).

Now, in most food lines—such as breakfast cereals, soups, and frozen foods—four or fewer firms control at least half of the sales. (See Figure 7.) Economists call that a "shared monopoly"—and with it come monopoly prices, an estimated $20 billion in overcharges to consumers each year.[6] Anticompetitive practices cost consumers a 15-cent "monopoly overcharge" on every dollar's worth of cereal, according to a four-year study by the Federal Trade Commission.[7]

And who's to resist? The combined budget of the antitrust divisions of the Justice Department and the Federal Trade Commission is $20 million a year, the sum that a corporate food giant can put into promoting just one "new" processed food. Spending only $20 million to counter the monopoly abuses in a trillion-dollar economy is what Ralph Nader calls a "charade."[8]

The "Grab a Bigger Market Share" Strategy

But now where are you? In most major food categories, a few giants now make over half the sales. Proctor & Gam-

Figure 7. Control of Our Food by Shared Monopolies*

Industry	PERCENT OF SALES CONTROLLED BY TOP FOUR COMPANIES
Coffee, ground	51
Oil, salad and cooking	51
Peanut butter	51
Baked goods, dry cookies	52
Fish and seafood, canned	58
Cigars	59
Beans, canned and dry	65
Corn, wet milling	65
Grain mill products, mixes, and prepared flours	70
Milk, canned	70
Spice	70
Baked goods, dry crackers	71
Chocolate and cocoa	71
Milk, dried	73
Cereal, to be prepared	80
Cigarettes	80
Coffee, instant	81
Tomato products, catsup	81
Baking powder and yeast	86
Dessert mixes	86
Grain mill products, refrigerated doughs	87
Soft drinks, bottling	89
Soft drinks, syrup	89
Cereal, ready to eat	90
Gum	90
Soup	92
Baby food	95

Source: Food Price Investigation, Senate Hearings, 1973.
*When as few as four firms control in excess of 50 percent of the sales of a given food line, economists usually find "oligopolistic" practices, such as overcharging, in comparison to prices under more competitive conditions.

ble (Folger's) and General Foods (Maxwell House, Sanka) together control nearly 60 percent of the ground-coffee market.[9] Kellogg's, General Foods, and General Mills divvy up 90 percent of the dry-cereal market.[10] Campbell's alone controls nearly 90 percent of the soup market.[11] And on it goes. Industry studies show us that at least half of the shoppers in a supermarket buy mainly the top two brands, even though they usually cost more. So you've got to become number one, or at least number two. You'll have to lure some customers away from the other Big Food companies. But you can't compete in ways that hurt your long-term profits—like offering better quality or lowering prices. Hmmm. Why not up the advertising budget? And you can come up with some eye-catching "new" products in some eye-catching new packages. If you can't compete in price or quality, you must compete in visibility —and the more snazzy the packaging, the more visible. With more products, you can squeeze your competitors off the supermarket shelf.

To create consumer loyalty, you have to have brand names. And that's a lot easier with processed foods. (You did stick labels on bananas, but lettuce and mushrooms were a lot more trouble.) And since you want to sell the products from your giant assembly lines all over the country, you'll need to add such delicacies as BHT and polysorbate for indefinite "freshness."

THE IMPACT OF YOUR STRATEGY

Food advertising costs shot up from about $2 billion a year in 1950 to a record $13 billion in 1978.[12] "On the average, six cents of every dollar we spend on processed foods will go directly to buy ad time on television and other promotion," says food researcher and writer Daniel Zwerdling. "But when we buy one of industry's hot-selling brands, we pay far, far more. In a recent year, breakfast eaters who bought Kellogg's Country Morning, a so-called 'natural cereal' that better resembled crumbled cookies, paid 35 cents of every dollar merely to finance Kellogg's ads. . . ."[13] But the costs of the ads themselves are only a fraction of what the consumer ends up paying for advertising. Because advertising is power, people are willing to pay more for a highly advertised brand-name item than they would for exactly the same product sold under a less well-known or store brand name. (See Figure 8.)

Since launching just one new item nationwide can cost as much as $20 million, only the corporate giants can afford to play this game.[14]

Because of the huge expense of advertising, Zwerdling concludes, the advertising strategy and the takeover strategy are closely tied: "Food corporations merge in part to amass the financial power they need to launch massive advertising campaigns."[15] Other studies confirm that the more any industry relies on advertising, the faster the concentration of market power.[16]

More eye-catching packaging was also part of your strategy. What has this done for us? Well, by 1980 the cost of the package exceeded the cost of the food ingredients for a fourth of the food and beverage product industry. (Soft drink containers cost two times as much as their contents; beer containers five times as much!) Over the last decade packaging costs have gone up 50 percent faster than the labor costs in our food. Today one out of every 11 dollars we spend on food and drink goes to pay for packaging.[17]

And the impact of your new product strategy? "In the beginning, there was just Campbell's chicken rice soup," quips journalist A. Kent MacDougall. "Today, besides chicken with rice soup, Campbell Soup makes chicken gumbo, chicken noodle, chicken noodle-Os, curly noodles with chicken, cream of chicken, creamy mushroom"[18] plus five others. That's what economists call "product proliferation." ("To grow dramatically you have to introduce new products," says General Foods' Peter Rosow, general manager of the company's dessert division.) It's the battle of the giants for supermarket shelf space. And it works. Today, just five companies use 108 brands of cereal to control over 90 percent of cereal sales.

Such product proliferation requires more and more shelf space. Just since the early 1970s, shelf space devoted to candy and chewing gum has gone up 75 percent; that for dog and cat food, 80 percent.[19] All this means bigger stores, more clerks—costs which must mean rising prices.

Figure 8. The Price of a Brand Name

	Price of House Brand	Price of Name Brand		Percent Higher
Flour, all-purpose, 10 lb.	$1.35	$2.75	Gold Medal, Pillsbury	104
Salt, iodized, 26 oz.	.22	.33	Morton	50
Sugar, granu-lated, 5 lb.	1.89	2.49	Domino	32
Corn oil, 1 qt.	1.99	2.25	Mazola	13
Spaghetti, 1 lb.	.59	.85	Mueller's	44
Rice, enriched, parboiled, 32 oz.	1.05	1.69	Uncle Ben's	61
Nonfat dry milk, ten 1-qt. envelopes	3.79	4.49	Carnation	18
Cut green beans, 16-oz. can	.30	.50	Libby's	67
Raisin bran, 20 oz.	1.19	1.63	Kellogg's	37
Orange juice, frozen concen-trate, 16 oz.	1.04	1.49	Minute Maid	43
Graham crackers, 16 oz.	.79	1.09	Nabisco	38
Peanut butter, smooth, 12 oz.	.83	1.15	Jif, Peter Pan	39
Coffee, instant, 6 oz.	3.19	3.99	Nescafé, Folger's	25

Source: Center for Science in the Public Interest, 1980.

And product proliferation, almost by definition, means more processed foods. You can't easily proliferate new fruits. If you want endless varieties of colors, flavors, and shapes, the answer is more and more processing and ever greater use of food colorings and flavorings. Firms like International Flavors and Fragrances are delighted by your product proliferation strategy. They introduce more than 5,000 scents and 2,000 flavors each year, and estimate that three-quarters of what we buy at the supermarket contains either artificial flavors or scents.[20]

The energy cost of all this processing is staggering. We use twice as much energy to process our food as to produce all of our nation's crops, according to the Department of Agriculture.[21] And the energy our food system uses off the farm is rising much faster than that used on the farm. The energy consumed in food processing and transportation doubled between 1960 and 1973.[22]

Food processing generates yet another cost that few of us ever think about—water pollution. Food processing corporations in the United States contribute more waste to water pollution than does our entire human population.[23]

Not only do we pay for this processing, for burgeoning advertising, for bigger stores and the labor to stock them, but we also pay for the "research and development" of these "new" foods. In 1981 just one company—General Foods—budgeted almost $100 million for developing "new" foods. Food corporations tell us that they are responding to our needs, yet rarely do we get a glimpse of how new products really come to be. This description from Foremost-McKesson is a candid exception.

According to a company spokesperson, the first step is a brainstorming session that produces all kinds of crazy ideas. Typically, only 50 out of 200 ideas are chosen for a preliminary technical analysis. These 50 are presented to "focus groups" of sophisticated consumers (formerly called housewives), and their reactions whittle the number down to 10 ideas, leading to perhaps 5 prototype products. Then test marketing brings the selection down to one.

We, the consumers, ultimately foot the bill—even if the product never makes it. Foremost-McKesson, with $3.3 billion in annual sales, spent a whole year and $200,000 developing "Quick 'n Saucy" sloppy joe lunches, then ditched them before they ever hit the supermarket.[24]

While product proliferation has gone wild, with 60,000 brand-name processed food items introduced in ten years, only 100 basic foods still account for three-quarters of the food we eat.[25] Doesn't this suggest that the billions of dollars spent on processing, advertising, and packaging are peripheral to our real diet? Most of us have plenty of variety with a minuscule fraction of what is offered.

The "Don't Just Make It, Serve It" Strategy

More than a third of America's food dollars are spent on food eaten away from home. To profit on this trend, you'll need to buy into the fast food business and spread your stores throughout the nation.

The Impact of Your Strategy

Into every city and town enter the fast food outlets, their invasion often fueled by the big money their new conglomerate owners can put behind them. (See Figure 9.) The same food giant that brings us Pillsbury flour brings us Burger King hamburgers. The same conglomerate that feeds our dogs Gainesburgers feeds us Burger Chef hamburgers. The same multinational company that brings us Pepsi serves us Pizza Hut pizzas. These giant corporations have driven out of business the roadside diners and Mom and Pop cafés which once served us local specialties and real cooking—soda biscuits, corn bread, and homemade soup. After a tour of over 26 fast food restaurants in a five-mile stretch outside Tucson, MIT nutritionist Judith Wurtman reported: "Despite the number and variety of these places, their menus were relatively similar . . . pancakes, doughnuts, fried or 'char'-broiled meats, hotdogs, fried potatoes, soft drinks and soft ice cream. . . . None served carrots, chopped liver, whole wheat bread, vegetable soup, baked potatoes, yogurt, skim milk, bananas or broccoli."[26] Forced to select foods only from these places, she concluded, "one might begin to feel deprived." Deprived not only in variety but nutritionally, too, because the fast food joints hit us with every nutritional hazard from high fat to high salt to low fiber.

Figure 9. Who Owns the Fast Food Giants?

Chain	Owner
Burger King	Pillsbury Co.
Burger Chef	General Foods
Jack-in-the-Box	Ralston Purina
Kentucky Fried Chicken	Heublein Co.
Pizza Hut	PepsiCo., Inc.
Arby's Roast Beef	Royal Crown Cola
A & W Root Beer	United Brands

All but Royal Crown Cola are among the 200 largest industrial corporations in the country.

The "Cut the Calorie" Strategy

Now that you've captured the national market, how can you expand U.S. sales? Our population is growing very slowly. And while some Americans might aspire to owning 20 pairs of shoes, most can eat only three meals a day. Since you can't produce bigger people, you could launch a "fat is beautiful" campaign. No, that might not go over . . . Why not just take the calories out of food? That will appeal to the weight-watchers, and since the food will have no calories, people can eat almost unlimited amounts!

This ingenious sales expansion strategy also increases your profit on each item. For while you can charge the consumer the same price, or even a premium price, manufacturing low-calorie "foods" costs you less. Saccharin is cheaper than sugar. "Light" beer costs less to produce.

THE IMPACT OF YOUR STRATEGY

Diet sodas and low-cal foods are born. By the late 1970s, three diet sodas were among the top ten best-selling soft drinks in America.[27] By using less expensive ingredients but charging the same for diet sodas, soft drink makers are overcharging American consumers $300 million each year, estimates the Center for Science in the Public Interest. No one's added up the overcharges for "light" beer, but buying

Michelob Light means paying a higher price for regular Michelob plus water.[28]

The "Salt Plus Soft Drink" Strategy

Now there must be another angle on this. Since people can eat only so much at any given meal, what about *between* meals? Can't you make some progress there? Snack food—that's it! With plenty of salt and sugar. Bet you can't eat just one! (And if more people are eating salty snacks, certainly that must help push up your soft drink and beer sales.)

THE IMPACT OF YOUR STRATEGY

Americans bought almost $4 billion in salty snack foods in 1979. Since 1949, soft drink consumption has increased almost four times.[29]

The Popcorn Institute even arranged for joint popcorn-Coke ads on television in the 1950s.[30] Enormously successful, the campaign led to more and more Americans munching and sipping in front of their TVs. The connection was completed in 1965, when PepsiCo bought Frito-Lay Corp., makers of Fritos corn chips and Lay's potato chips, and the first company to sell $1 billion worth of snack foods in one year.[31]

So far you've explored five possible strategies to expand sales. The second path to corporate prosperity is to ring up more profit on every item you sell.

The "Up the Price for the Same Ingredients" Strategy

Raw produce and even unprocessed frozen foods aren't so profitable. But if you turn these ingredients into some "new" specialty, you can charge more for them. "The biggest growth and profit potential lies in prepared foods—frozen entrees, vegetables in special sauces and 'ethnic' combinations—products that command higher margins for the producers," *Forbes* advises.[32]

THE IMPACT OF YOUR STRATEGY

Your strategy means higher prices and more and more processing. In fact, that seems to be a recurring theme here! How else can you take macaroni (55 cents a pound), add a bit of "dried cheese" and some chemicals, and convince consumers that Betty Crocker will stretch their food budget with Hamburger Helper? Hamburger Helper costs $2.38 a pound; a few aisles away hamburger itself sells for just $1.50. (By the way, Hamburger Helper is 23 percent sugar, according to *Consumer Reports*.)

The "Reduce Your Costs" Strategy

If you can cut your costs while charging the customer the same price, your profits will rise. To do this, you can use fewer expensive ingredients, more of cheaper ones, invent cheap flavorings that taste like quality ingredients, and use synthetic flavor enhancers or MSG while reducing the amount of real, expensive ingredients. You can also try to use fewer ingredients which are imported or in unreliable supply. After all, if the prices of basic ingredients are constantly changing, your financial planning becomes a nightmare.

THE IMPACT OF YOUR STRATEGY

Your strategy has led to more salt, more sugar, more artificial flavors. To clam chowder with an almost invisible portion of clam, but the clam flavor enhanced by one whole teaspoon of salt in every cup. To "chocolate" candy bars with little chocolate. (Cocoa prices are unpredictable.) To soft drinks sweetened with saccharin. (Saccharin costs about one-tenth as much as sugar.) And to raspberry and blueberry pies actually made from apples and flavorings. (Berries are too expensive.)

But What's Good for Conglomerated . . .

Your logic as a Conglomerated Foods executive was impeccable. There was only one problem: virtually *every one* of your sales strategies added one more health risk for everybody who buys your products. More salt, more sugar, more fat, less fiber, more additives (not to mention higher prices and more energy wasted).

Ironically, at least four of our giant food corporations—Borden's, Nestlé, General Foods, and Kellogg's—were started by men whose prime motive was to make people healthier. Dr. Kellogg was a strict vegetarian working in a world-famous sanatorium when the first wheat flakes were developed in 1894.[33] Yet the logic of corporate profit-seeking is so powerful that today Kellogg's boasts two of the most sugared cereals. General Foods, the same company that was launched with Postum by a man who wanted to free us from the evils of caffeine, now sells seven brands of coffee plus Pop Rocks and Dream Whip.[34]

The man I met at the party would respond: "But people *buy* the stuff. And more than ever. So it must be what they want."

While he's right that Americans are buying more and more high-risk foods, this justification for defending the status quo doesn't hold up.

First of all, the same corporations that sell us food also control virtually all of the information bombarding us every day about food. The top 50 food firms control 90 percent of all food advertising on TV. A typical television-watching child is exposed to between 8,500 and 13,000 food and drink commercials each year.[35] Hundreds of times a week Americans hear that nutritionally empty foods will actually make our lives better: Coke "adds life"; Betty Crocker cake mixes help us show our love better; Jell-O helps us "have fun." In other words, health-risky food is continuously promoted as an antidepressant in a society where depression is epidemic. (Valium was the most widely prescribed drug in America in the last decade.)

TV's power of persuasion is well demonstrated by the history of presweetened cereals, disclosed in a Senate hearing on TV advertising aimed at children. When the cereal industry first introduced presweetened cereals, before World War II, consumers vetoed them. Yet now they are among the best-selling cereals. Sidney Margolius testified, "I attribute this [change] largely to the development of television as a very powerful selling medium for children, and I think if we had television before World War II, the housewives would not have been able to reject it [presweetened cereal]."[36]

Almost half of all TV commercials are for cereals, candy, and gum. The sweetest cereals of all—some half sugar—have the highest advertising budgets.[37] TV advertising promotes such low-nutrition foods specifically to children. General Foods' Tang was advertised 24 times on Saturday mornings, but only once each on Sunday and Monday evenings, according to one study. Similarly, Nabisco aired its Cream of Wheat commercial only once—on a Monday evening—but 16 Nabisco commercials for its Chips Ahoy, 12 for its Fig Newtons, and 16 for its Oreo cookies were shown on Saturday mornings during a two-week period.[38] The food corporations know what they are doing. Almost half the time children are successful in influencing what their parents buy, according to surveys by psychologist Joanne Paley Galst. Other studies have shown that the more time children spend watching TV, the stronger their desire for advertised foods—and the more they eat of them.[39]

Needless to say, very few unprocessed foods are advertised.

Does it make sense to say that the risky new American diet is what people *want,* when their choices are so heavily influenced by the corporations which have the most to gain by these choices?

PepsiCo and Nabisco and General Foods also benefit from the fact that although the sugar and salt in high-risk foods are not biologically addictive, as far as we know, they often seem to be psychologically addictive. From my own experience, from the experience of friends, and from dozens and dozens of letters I have received over the years, I'm convinced that "the more you eat, the more you want." (On the other hand, the less you eat, the less you want.)

Whose Convenience?

The explosion of processed foods is frequently explained as a response to the needs of working women. "Working wives haven't the time to cook, and they've got the money to pay a bit more for frozen foods," is how *Forbes* puts it.[40] There is some truth to this, but the presumption is always that cooking with whole foods is more time-consuming than using "convenience" foods. Yet in my own experience this is simply not true, although it takes some extra time and thought to change habits in the beginning. If you know what to have on hand for easy meals, shop in a small whole-foods store (which takes much less time than a supermarket), and lay out your kitchen so that everything, including a few time-saving utensils, is within easy reach, whole-food cooking can be fast and convenient. (I discuss these points in more detail in Book Two.)

Thousands of processed foods and mammoth supermarkets purport to save us time. But do they really? Although the average time spent in preparing food in an urban household fell by half an hour between the 1920s and the late 1960s, we never really gained more free time, according to a *Journal of Home Economics* report.[41] With longer distances to stores, bigger stores, and other complexities of life, an extra 36 minutes each day were used in food marketing and record keeping. We actually lost 6 minutes!

Another reason processed foods have taken over is that they require less imagination. (There are no instructions on a raw potato, says Michael Jacobson, but there are on a box of instant potatoes.) While I believe people are inherently creative, so much in our culture stifles creativity. Uniform images of what is beautiful, acceptable, and of high status bombard us. And the easiest way to be sure that we don't deviate from those images is to buy what is *pre*packaged and *pre*pared. In cooking and eating whole foods, however, we break loose from these standardized images. By taking charge of our food choices, we gain confidence in our judgment and creativity. Feeling less like simpleminded followers of instructions in one area of our lives can help us feel capable of assuming responsibility in unrelated areas.

A Right or a Privilege?

The man I met at the party who claims that Americans are getting what they ask for also was concerned about any attempt to interfere with corporations' "right" to advertise what they want, to whomever they want. "We can't violate their First Amendment rights," he said.

He got me thinking. When they advertise, *are* General Foods and Coca-Cola exercising their First Amendment rights? A lot of Americans would agree that they are. But, I wondered, should we include in the definition of "free speech" the capacity to dominate national advertising? Isn't there something amiss in this definition of rights?

Perhaps the concept of "rights" should be limited to those powers or possibilities which are open to *anyone*. For example, our right to say what we think, to associate with whom we please, and to practice whatever religion we choose. These are rights. But actions such as advertising on TV, open only to those with vast wealth, should be called something else—perhaps "privileges." For how many of us could spend $340 million a year for advertising, as General Foods does? The $20 million spent just to promote one new sugared cereal amounts to more than 40 times the entire budget of the Center for Science in the Public Interest, which has provided vital information for this book.

Ideally, I suppose, there would be no such privileges in a society. If it were impossible for everyone wanting to participate in an action to do so, some would be selected on the basis of merit or some other fair system open equally to everyone. But that is pretty dreamy. So what can we do in the present, when there *are* privileges because some are incomparably more wealthy than others?

We can work to limit the privileges of wealth and to make those with wealth and power accountable to us all.

In campaigns for public office, for example, we have already limited the privileges of wealth by limiting the size of any one contribution. Why not regard access to TV advertising the same way? If we placed a low ceiling on the amount of money that any one company could spend on TV advertising, this would diminish the privileges now held by a handful of giant corporations. As we have seen, it's because the biggest corporations can spend such enormous sums on advertising that they can squeeze out the smaller producers—and then charge us more.

Once we realize that advertising is a privilege, not a

right, isn't it reasonable to grant that privilege only on certain conditions? An obvious condition would be that the advertising—with its proven power to influence—not be used to promote products that threaten our well-being. Society has already banned cigarette advertising on TV. There is virtually unanimous opinion in the health community that high-sugar, low-nutrition foods—those which monopolize TV advertising—threaten our health. So why not ban advertising of candy, sugared cereals, soft drinks, and other sweets?

As long as our society rewards wealth by allowing it such disproportionate ability to influence public opinion, we cannot build a genuine democracy in America. But our vision must extend beyond the need to make advertising responsible to society's well-being. The theme of this book is that we must work toward more democratic decision-making structures governing all aspects of our resource use. Those who process and distribute our food must be accountable, not just to their shareholders but to a broad, representative, elected, and recallable group of Americans whose concerns are wider than expanding sales and increasing profits. Only through such structures can we put into action our choices affecting the health and well-being of our earth and our bodies.

Where Do We Begin?

If this vision of a genuine democracy seems a long way off, we might be tempted to give up. Or we might look around us for signs of change and ask, how can we support them? We might look at ourselves, at our own lives right now. To build a democracy in America, we must redistribute power. We can be part of that redistribution *right now* by taking greater and greater responsibility for our own lives and the problems right in our own communities. I have met and heard from thousands of people across the country who are realizing that the redistribution of power in America begins with them.

Michelle Kamhi is one. She lives in New York City's Upper West Side. In 1978 she decided that if the diet in her son's school lunchroom—Twinkies, white bread, and bologna—was to change, it was up to her. "But how to change things?" she wrote. "Answer: form a committee, however small. Our Nutrition Committee at first consisted of one other concerned parent and myself." From these two parents grew an innovative program on teacher and parent education. Kindergartners tried making their own whole wheat flour and bread. Third-graders, who were studying "desert people," experimented with Middle Eastern delicacies, using beans and whole wheat pita bread. So nutrition entered the classroom not as a negative "don't" but as a positive and tasty "do."

And nutrition entered the lunchroom, too, according to Michelle.

> Raw carrot and celery sticks are displacing mushy canned vegetables. Fruits canned in syrup have been banished in favor of fresh fruits on most days; occasionally, unsweetened canned pineapple or applesauce is substituted. No more white bread; only whole wheat is served. And meats containing nitrates/nitrites have been banned, thanks to a school-wide poll of parents.

Nutrition also entered the regular curriculum:

> The day my son came home with a vocabulary list of "glucose, maltose, dextrose, fructose, honey, corn syrup, etc.," I could see that my efforts had begun to reap benefits close to home. His second-grade class's assignment was to see how many packaged foods containing hidden sugar he could find at home. This was a perfect example of how teachers were using the information disseminated at the workshops. . . .[42]

Learning about food was obviously a powerful first step for Michelle, and her decision to seize the power she had is changing hundreds, maybe thousands of lives.

I have heard from many other people like Michelle. In Part IV, "Lessons for the Long Haul," I've tried to capture what their experiences have to teach us. But first let's tackle the protein debate, because that was where *Diet for a Small Planet*—and the vision it embodies—began over ten years ago.

3.

Protein Myths: A New Look

HAVING READ OF the vast resources we squander to produce meat, you might easily conclude that meat must be indispensable to human well-being. But this just isn't the case. When I first wrote *Diet for a Small Planet* I was fighting two nutritional myths at once. First was the myth that we need scads of protein, the more the better. The second was that meat contains the *best* protein. Combined, these two myths have led millions of people to believe that only by eating lots of meat could they get enough protein.

Protein Mythology

Myth No. 1: Meat contains more protein than any other food.
Fact: Containing 20 to 25 percent protein by weight, meat ranks about in the middle of the protein quantity scale, along with some nuts, cheese, beans, and fish. (Check the "quantity" side of Figure 14, "The Food/Protein Continuum.")

Myth No. 2: Eating lots of meat is the only way to get enough protein.
Fact: Americans often eat 50 to 100 percent more protein than their bodies can use. Thus, most Americans could *completely eliminate* meat, fish, and poultry from their diets and still get the recommended daily allowance of protein from all the other protein-rich foods in the typical American diet.

Myth No. 3: Meat is the sole source for certain essential vitamins and minerals.
Fact: Even in the current meat-centered American diet, nonmeat sources provide more than half of our intake of each of the 11 most critical vitamins and minerals, except vitamin B12. And meat is not the sole source of B12; it is also found in dairy products and eggs, and even more abundantly in tempeh, a fermented soy food. Some nutrients, such as iron, tend to be less absorbable by the body when eaten in plant instead of animal foods. Nevertheless, varied plant-centered diets using whole foods, especially if they include dairy products, do not risk deficiencies.

Myth No. 4: Meat has the highest-quality protein of any food.
Fact: The word "quality" is an unscientific term. What is really meant is usability: how much of the protein eaten the body can actually use. The usability of egg and milk protein is greater than that of meat, and the usability of soy protein is about equal to that of meat. (Check the "Usability" side of Figure 14.)

Myth No. 5: Because plant protein is missing certain essential amino acids, it can never equal the quality of meat protein.
Facts: All plant foods commonly eaten as sources of protein contain *all* eight essential amino acids. Plant proteins do have deficiencies in their amino acid patterns that make them generally less usable by the body than animal protein. (See the "Usability" side of Figure 14.) However, the deficiencies in some foods can be matched with amino acid strengths in other foods to produce protein usability equiva-

lent or superior to meat protein. This effect is called "protein complementarity."

Myth No. 6: Plant-centered diets are dull.

Fact: Just compare! There are basically five different kinds of meat and poultry, but 40 to 50 kinds of commonly eaten vegetables, 24 kinds of peas, beans, and lentils, 20 fruits, 12 nuts, and 9 grains. Variety of flavor, of texture, and of color obviously lies in the plant world . . . though your average American restaurant would give you no clue to this fact.

Myth No. 7: Plant foods contain a lot of carbohydrates and therefore are more fattening than meat.

Fact: Plant foods do contain carbohydrates but they generally don't have the fat that meat does. So ounce for ounce, most plant food has either the same calories (bread is an example) or considerably fewer calories than most meats. Many fruits have one-third the calories; cooked beans have one-half; and green vegetables have one-eighth the calories that meat contains. Complex carbohydrates in whole plant foods, grain, vegetables, and fruits can actually aid weight control. Their fiber helps us feel full with fewer calories than do refined or fatty foods.

Myth No. 8: Our meat-centered cuisine provides us with a more nutritious diet overall than that eaten in underdeveloped countries.

Fact: For the most part the problem of malnutrition in the third world is not the poor quality of the diet but the inadequate quantity. Traditional diets in most third world countries are probably more nutritious and less hazardous than the meat-centered, highly processed diet most Americans eat. The hungry are simply too poor to buy enough of their traditional diet. The dramatic contrast between our diet and that of the "average" Indian, for example, is not in our higher protein consumption but in the amount of sugar, fat, and refined flour we eat. While we consume only 50 percent more protein, we consume eight times the fat and four times the sugar. Our diet would actually be improved if we ate more plant food.

In earlier editions of *Diet for a Small Planet* I concentrated on the "meat protein mystique," explaining why the body needs protein, how protein is ranked according to its usability by the body, and how you can combine plant proteins to create a protein mix that is just as usable by the body as is meat protein.

But it was the possibility of combining two or more less-usable proteins to create one of a better "quality" that most intrigued me. This neat trick is called "protein complementarity" and is explained fully in the next chapter. It doubly intrigued me when I realized that such food combinations evolved as the mainstay of traditional diets throughout the world.

Virtually all traditional societies based their diets on protein complementarity; they used grain and legume combinations as their main source of protein and energy. In Latin America it was corn tortillas with beans, or rice with beans. In the Middle East it was bulgur wheat with chickpeas or pita bread felafel with hummus sauce (whole wheat, chickpeas, and sesame seeds). In India it was rice or chapaties with dal (lentils, often served with yogurt). In Asia it was soy foods with rice (in southern China, northern Japan, and Indonesia), or soy foods with wheat or millet (in northern China), or soy foods with barley (in parts of Korea and southern China). In each case, the balance was typically 70 to 80 percent whole grains and 20 to 30 percent legumes, the very balance that nutritionists have found maximizes protein usability.

"Anglo students in Tucson had always put down the Chicanos for their 'starchy' diet," *Arizona Daily Star* reporter Jane Kay told me. "But after your book came out, the Chicanos felt vindicated because it showed that the food the Mexican people in Tucson eat—lettuce, cheese, tortillas, and beans—is better than the all-American hamburger and fries."

When I first wrote *Diet for a Small Planet* in 1971, the idea that people could live well without meat seemed much more controversial than it does today. I felt I had to prove to nutritionists and doctors that because we could combine proteins to create foods equal in protein usability to meat, people could thrive on a nonmeat or low-meat diet. Today, few dispute that people can thrive on this kind of diet. In fact, more and more health professionals are actually advocating less meat precisely for health reasons, reasons I discussed in "America's Experimental Diet."

In 1971 I stressed protein complementarity because I assumed that the only way to get enough protein (without consuming too many calories) was to create a protein as usable by the body as animal protein. In combatting the myth that meat is the only way to get high-quality protein, I reinforced another myth. I gave the impression that in order to get enough protein without meat, considerable care was needed in choosing foods. Actually, it is much easier than I thought.

With three important exceptions, there is little danger of protein deficiency in a plant food diet. The exceptions are diets very heavily dependent on fruit or on some tubers, such as sweet potatoes or cassava, or on junk food (refined flours, sugars, and fat). Fortunately, relatively few people in the world try to survive on diets in which these foods are virtually the sole source of calories. *In all other diets, if people are getting enough calories, they are virtually certain of getting enough protein.* (Babies, young children, and pregnant women need some special consideration, which I'll discuss later.) This is true because the vast majority of unprocessed foods can supply us with enough protein to meet our daily protein allowance without filling us with too many calories. In Appendix D I present a simple rule of thumb for judging any food as a protein source. There you'll see that most plant foods excel—meaning that you could eat just one food and get enough protein.

The simplest way to prove the overall point is to propose a diet which most people would consider protein-deprived and ask, does its protein content add up to the allowance recommended by the National Academy of Sciences? In Figure 10 I have put together such a day's menu—with no meat, no dairy foods, and no protein supplements. Even without accounting for improved protein usability due to combining complementary proteins, this diet has adequate protein without exceeding calorie limits.

Figure 10. Hypothetical All-Plant-Food Diet (Just to Prove a Point)

Breakfast	Calories	Total Protein (Grams)
1 c. orange juice	111	1.7
1 c. cooked oatmeal	148	5.4
½ oz. sunflower seeds	80	3.5
1 tbsp. brown sugar	52	0
3 tbsp. raisins, dried seedless	87	0.9
Lunch		
2 tbsp. peanut butter	172	7.8
2 slices whole wheat bread	112	4.8
1 tbsp. honey	64	0.1
1 apple, medium, raw	87	0.3
2 carrots, small, raw	42	1.1
Dinner		
1 c. cooked beans	236	15.6
1 c. cooked brown rice	178	3.8
3 stalks broccoli (approx. 1 1/3 c.)	52	6.2
4 mushrooms, large, raw	28	2.7
2 tbsp. oil	248	0
1 c. apple juice, fresh canned	109	0.3
½ banana, medium, raw	64	0.8
Snack		
1½ c. popcorn, cooked with oil	123	2.7
Total	**1,993**	**57.7**
National Academy of Sciences (NAS) recommended allowance for 128-lb. woman eating typical American diet	2,000	44
NAS recommended allowance adjusted for less usable protein in plant food diet, assuming no improvement in protein usability due to combining protein. (See page 172.)	2,000	55

Clearly this diet contains much more protein, 57.7 grams, than the National Academy of Science's recommendation of 44 grams of protein for an average American woman eating a typical American diet. But this allowance assumes that two-thirds of that protein is highly usable animal protein. Since my hypothetical daily menu contains no animal protein, and since I am trying to show that protein complementarity is not essential, let's adjust the National Academy's recommendation upward to what it would be for a plant food diet, assuming no protein complementarity. The allowance rises to about 55 grams. Yet my hypothetical diet *still* exceeds the allowance.

In the example, I used the weight and protein allowance of a typical American woman. But the same pattern would hold true for *any weight* person, since the protein allowance and calorie needs rise proportionately as body weight increases. For men, getting enough protein without exceeding calories limits is even a slight bit easier. (Men are allowed 2 more calories for every gram of protein than are women.)

Note that my hypothetical diet, while not intentionally protein-packed, is a healthy one. It contains few protein-empty foods, only sugar, honey, oil, an apple, and apple juice. They comprise only about 25 percent of the calories. The more of these protein-empty foods one eats, the more the rest of the diet should be filled with foods with considerable protein.

But a number of the world's authorities on protein believe that the current recommended daily protein allowance may be too low. At the Massachusetts Institute of Technology, three-month-long experiments, with subjects consuming the recommended amount of protein in the form of egg, for most subjects resulted in the loss of lean body mass and a decrease in the proteins and oxygen-carrying cells of the blood.

If the recommended allowance were pushed up by one-third, as some scientists believe it should be, would it then be difficult to eat enough protein without meat?

The average American woman's recommended allowance would then be 59 grams of protein. At this higher level, combining protein foods to improve the usability of the protein would become more important. But in this hypothetical day's diet there are already complementary protein combinations (peanut butter plus bread, beans plus rice) which would bring the usability of the protein up closer to that assumed in the recommended allowance. To be totally safe, however, one might want to replace one of the protein-empty foods with an additional protein food if maintaining an all plant food diet. (For example, replacing the sugar and honey with grain or vegetable.)

Very few Americans, however, eat only plant foods. Even most vegetarians eat some dairy products. So in Figure 11 let's look at basically the same day's diet but this time put in two modest portions of dairy foods, one cup of skim milk and a one-inch cube of cheese. These changes bring the total protein up to 71 grams—well above even the highest standard recommended by some nutritionists.

Protein Individuality

But scientists studying the differences in individual needs for nutrients warn us that even the most prudently arrived at recommendations, claiming to cover 97.5 percent of the population, should not be followed blindly.

R. J. Williams at the University of Texas is one of the best-known of these scientists. He points out that if beef were the only source of protein, one person's minimum protein needs could be met by two ounces of meat; yet another individual might require eight ounces.[1] These two extremes represent a *fourfold difference.* The recommended allowance of the National Academy of Sciences nonetheless assumes that a twofold variation between the highest and the lowest needs will cover 95 percent of the population.) Donald R. Davis, also at the University of Texas, recently reviewed the literature on individual needs for amino acids, protein's building blocks. Within small groups of subjects, differences ranged up to ninefold, states Davis.[2]

In addition, the recommended allowances of protein are calculated for healthy people. Ill health and age, as well as genetic differences, could result in greatly differing needs.

Figure 11. Hypothetical Mixed Plant and Dairy Diet (Just to Prove a Point)

Breakfast	Calories	Protein (Grams)
1 c. orange juice	111	1.7
1 c. cooked oatmeal	148	5.4
½ oz. sunflower seeds	80	3.5
1 tbsp. brown sugar	52	0
1 c. low-fat milk	88	8.8
Lunch		
2 tbsp. peanut butter	172	7.8
2 slices whole wheat bread	112	4.8
1 tbsp. honey	64	0.1
½ apple, medium, raw	43	0.2
1 carrot, small, raw	21	0.6
Dinner		
1 oz. cheddar cheese (1 inch square)	112	7.0
1 c. cooked beans	236	15.6
1 c. cooked brown rice	178	3.8
3 stalks broccoli (approx. 1 1/3 c.)	52	6.2
4 mushrooms, large, raw	28	2.7
2 tbsp. oil	248	0
1 c. apple juice, fresh canned	109	0.3
½ banana, medium, raw	63	0.8
Snack		
1 c. popcorn, cooked with oil	82	1.8
Total	**1,999**	**71.1**
Protein allowance one-third above 1980 recommendation of the National Academy of Sciences (44 grams)	**2,000**	**59**

Genetic differences may play a role not only in our needs but also in our taste for foods (which may or may not be related to needs). In a recent study, adult identical twins were found more similar in their choices of foods, including the protein density of the diet, than were fraternal twins.[3]

Effects of Stress

Even more surprising, any individual's need for protein can vary a lot. Physical stress—pain, for example—or psychological stress—even from exam pressure—can push your protein need up by as much as one-third. But remember, most of us eat almost twice the protein our bodies can use, so we can easily get the "extra" protein needed under stress from the protein already in most of our diets.

A World Health Organization report[4] discussed these stress conditions: (1) *heat:* unacclimatized individuals lose nitrogen (a primary component of protein) in heavy sweating; (2) *heavy work:* athletes and others may need additional protein when they are increasing their muscle mass, although the amount needed is not likely to be large (some studies, though not widely substantiated, suggest an additional 25 percent intake over the totals recommended here if you are building muscle mass); (3) *inadequate energy intake:* when overall calorie intake is not adequate, some dietary protein is used for energy and thus is not available to meet protein needs; (4) *infection:* infections, especially acute ones, cause some depletion of body nitrogen due to increased urinary excretion and poor intestinal absorption (as with diarrhea); these losses need to be replaced with additional protein during recovery.

The obvious conclusion is this: we should suspect any diet "expert" who claims that we *all* would do better on a high-protein or a low-protein diet. Instead of following a recommended allowance blindly, we should become better observers of our own body's well-being, developing what protein researcher Williams calls "body wisdom." Part of body wisdom is being aware of how you feel—your energy level, general health, and temperament. (Certain nutritional deficiencies negatively affect appetite and choice of foods, so just feeling "satisfied" is not enough.) Body wisdom also involves being a wise observer of your body's condition: many types of nutritional deficiencies show up as deterioration in the hair, skin, and nails and in the slow healing of wounds.

Why Do We Need Protein Anyway?

Given protein's importance to the body, perhaps it is not so surprising that a certain mystique grew up around it. We simply cannot live on fats and carbohydrates alone. Protein makes up about one-half of the nonwater components of our bodies. Just as cellulose provides the structural framework of a tree, protein provides the framework for animals. Skin, hair, nails, cartilage, tendons, muscles, and even the organic framework of bones are made up largely of fibrous proteins. Obviously, protein is needed for growth in children. Adults also need it to replace tissues that are continually breaking down and to build tissues, such as hair and nails, which are continually growing.

But talking about the body's need for "protein" is unscientific. What the body needs from food are the building blocks of protein—amino acids, specifically the eight that the body cannot manufacture itself, which are called "essential amino acids." Even more precisely, what the body actually requires are the carbon skeletons of these essential amino acids that the body cannot synthesize, although it can complete them by adding nitrogen, if the nitrogen is available. The body needs many more amino acids than just these eight essential ones. The body can, however, build the others *if* it has sufficient "loose" or extra nitrogen to build with. Thus, what is popularly referred to as the "protein" the body needs to eat are the eight essential amino acids and some extra nitrogen.

The body depends on protein for the myriad of reactions that we call "metabolism." Proteins such as insulin, which regulate metabolic processors, we call "hormones"; other proteins, catalysts of important metabolic reactions, we call "enzymes." In addition, hemoglobin, the critical oxygen-carrying molecule of the blood, is built from protein.

Not only is protein necessary to the basic chemical reactions of life, it is also necessary to maintain the body environment so that these reactions can take place. Protein in the blood helps to prevent excess alkalinity or acidity, maintaining the "body neutrality" essential to normal cellular metabolism. Protein in blood serum participates in regulating the body's water balance, the distribution of fluid on either side of the cell membrane.

Last, and of great importance, new protein synthesis is needed to form antibodies to fight bacterial and viral infections.

How Much Is Enough?

The protein allowances I use in this book are those recommended by the Committee on Dietary Allowances of the National Academy of Sciences, Food and Nutrition Board. It's interesting to learn how the committee arrives at these recommended allowances. Keep in mind that the procedure is full of *assumptions* (some of which are disputed within the scientific community), *estimates,* and *averages.* Realizing this, R. J. Williams's advice takes on even greater importance: observe your own body carefully to find out what is best for you.

To come up with the recommended allowance for an entire population, the committee followed four steps:

Step 1. Estimating average need. Since nitrogen is a characteristic and relatively constant component of protein, scientists can measure protein by measuring nitrogen. To determine how much protein humans need, experimenters put subjects on a protein-free diet. They then measure how much nitrogen is lost in urine and feces. They add to this an amount to cover the small losses through the skin, sweat, and internal body structure. For children, additional nitrogen for growth is added. *The total of these nitrogen losses is the amount you have to replace by eating protein,* and is therefore the basis of the average protein requirement for body maintenance—24 grams of protein for a 154-pound man (also expressed as .34 gram of protein per kilogram of body weight).

Step 2. Adjusting for individual differences. To allow for individual differences and to cover 97.5 percent of the population, the committee sets this protein requirement 30 percent above the average, arriving at 30 grams per day of protein for a 154-pound man, or .45 gram per kilogram of body weight per day. This assumption that 30 percent above the average requirement will cover 97.5 percent of the population is one of the issues in dispute by nutritionists.

Step 3. Adjusting for normal eating compared to experimental conditions. Scientists have discovered that protein is used less efficiently when people are eating a normal diet containing some extra protein than when they are eating at or near their protein requirement, as they do under experimental conditions. Apparently, when people are deprived of protein their bodies compensate by more fully using what's there and excreting less. So to account for the less efficient use of protein in ordinary eating patterns, the committee adds another 30 percent. This brings the allowance up to 42 grams for a 154-pound "average" American man, .57 gram per kilogram of body weight per day.

Step 4. Adjusting for protein usability. The protein in our food is not fully used by the body. The above estimates are all based on an ideal "reference protein" (I'll explain this fully in the following section). Scientists estimate the average usability of protein in the U. S. diet at 75 percent Therefore, the allowance of 42 grams of protein for a 154-pound male is pushed up to 56 grams because it is assumed that only 75 percent of what is eaten is actually used. For a 128-pound woman, the average American female, the corresponding allowance is 44 grams.

So now you know how the National Academy of Sciences arrived at the recommended protein allowances that are used throughout this book. Since it is set 30 percent above the average, it is *more than most people need*. Some protein authorities, however, believe that the allowance still may not be high enough to include 97.5 percent of the population.

Special Needs

While I've said that protein complementarity is not necessary for most of us, it does come in handy for those who must increase their protein intake without increasing calories. This is true for those whose bodies are under special stress, especially pregnant and breast-feeding women. A pregnant woman is advised to up her protein intake by an additional 30 grams a day (a 68 percent increase) but her calorie intake by only 300 calories (a 15 percent increase). A breast-feeding woman is advised to add 20 grams of protein to her diet but only 500 more calories; that would be 45 percent more protein but only 25 percent more calories. With these high protein needs, it becomes important to make the most of all the protein you eat, and combining complementary protein can help do that.

Many are concerned about the protein needs of children. Actually, they do not need more protein in relation to their calorie intake than adults. But because infant and young children cannot digest certain plant foods as easily as adults, some special care is needed in meeting their needs on a largely plant food diet. Michael and Nina Shandler have provided guidance for parents in *The Complete Guide and Cookbook for Raising Your Child as a Vegetarian* (Schocken Books, 1981). It also contains sound nutritional advice for pregnant women.

4.

Protein Complementarity: The Debate

IN THE PREVIOUS chapter I tried to dispel the myth that you need lots of meat to get the protein you need, while confessing that *Diet for a Small Planet* had helped create a new myth—that to get the protein you need without meat you have to conscientiously combine nonmeat sources to create a protein that is as usable by the body as meat protein. Protein complementarity is not the myth; it works. The myth is that complementing proteins is *necessary* for most people on a low- or nonmeat diet. With a healthy varied diet, concern about protein complementarity is not necessary for most of us.

Nonetheless, for several reasons, I would like to explain briefly protein complementarity. The first reason is that it is useful for people with a considerably higher than average protein need, including pregnant and breast-feeding women. Second, understanding protein complementarity does disprove any notion that animal protein is uniquely qualified to meet nutritional needs. But perhaps my real reason is simply that it fascinates me, particularly since I realized that complementary protein combinations evolved spontaneously as the basis of virtually all of the world's great cuisines.

If all proteins were the same, there would never have been a controversy about preferable sources for humans;

only quantity would matter. Proteins, however, are not identical. The proteins which our bodies use are made up of 22 amino acids in varying combinations. As already noted, 8 of these amino acids cannot be synthesized by our bodies; they must be obtained from outside sources. These 8 essential amino acids (which I will refer to as "EAAs") are tryptophan, leucine, isoleucine, lysine, valine, threonine, the sulfur-containing amino acids (methionine and cystine), and the aromatic amino acids. (Histidine is also necessary for children.)

Our bodies need all of the EAAs simultaneously in order to carry out protein synthesis. If one EAA is missing, even temporarily, protein synthesis will fall to a very low level or stop altogether. We also need the EAAs in differing amounts. In most food proteins all of the EAAs are present, but one or more of the EAAs is usually present in a disproportionately small amount, thus deviating from the most utilizable pattern. These EAAs are called the "limiting amino acids" in a food protein.

Let us put together these three critical factors about protein:

Of the 22 necessary amino acids, there are 8 that our bodies cannot make but must get from outside sources.

All of these 8 must be present simultaneously.

All of these 8 must be present in the right proportions.

What does this mean to the body? A great deal. If you eat protein containing enough tryptophan to satisfy 100 percent of the utilizable pattern's requirement, 100 percent of the leucine level, and so forth, but only 50 percent of the necessary lysine, then as far as your body is concerned, you might as well have eaten only 50 percent of *all* the EAAs. Only 50 percent of the protein you ate was used *as protein*. The protein "assembling center" in the body cells uses the EAAs at the level of the "limiting amino acid"; that is, at the level of whichever EAA happens to be least present. The surplus amino acids are released to be used by the body as fuel as if they were carbohydrates. Figure 12 gives you a graphic illustration of what this means.

One reflection of how closely the amino acid pattern of a given food matches that which the body can use is what nutritionists term the "biological value" of a food protein.

Roughly, the biological value is the proportion of the protein absorbed by the digestive tract that is retained by the body. In other words, the biological value is the percentage of absorbed protein that your body actually uses. There is, however, another question: how much gets absorbed *to begin with* by the digestive tract? That is what we call "digestibility." So the protein available to our bodies depends on its biological value *and* its digestibility. The term covering both of these factors is "net protein utilization," or NPU. Quite simply, NPU estimates how much of the protein we eat is actually available to our bodies. (See Figure 13.)

The NPU of a food is largely determined by how closely the essential amino acids in its protein match the body's one utilizable pattern. Because the protein of egg most nearly matches this ideal pattern, egg protein is used as a model for measuring amino acid patterns in other food. The amino acid pattern of cheese nearly matches egg's pattern, while that of peanuts fails utterly. You can guess then that the NPU of cheese is significantly higher than that of peanuts. The difference is great—70 as compared to about 40.

In Appendix D I provide basic protein information on over a hundred commonly eaten foods. I give the amount of usable protein (total protein adjusted by NPU scores), their amino acid strengths and weaknesses, and the contribution of one serving to meeting an average person's daily protein allowance.

In the last few years, nutritionists have learned that the NPU ratings (see Appendix C) tend to overestimate the usability of protein by the body; that is, the NPU values we use are too high. Most of these ratings were determined in experiments in which people's protein intake was grossly inadequate. At this low level, it turns out, the body uses protein more efficiently than when the diet contains adequate protein. This is especially true for the less usable plant proteins.[1] What this means is that in a protein-adequate diet, we may have to eat slightly more of any given food to get the amount of usable protein indicated. Scientists are now proceeding with experiments based on this new understanding, but in the meantime, all we have are the current NPU scores.

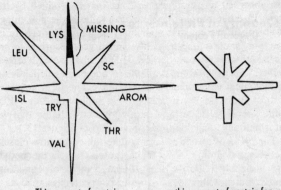

This amount of protein in the food becomes...

...this amount of protein for your body to use.

Figure 12. The Problem of a "Limiting Amino Acid"

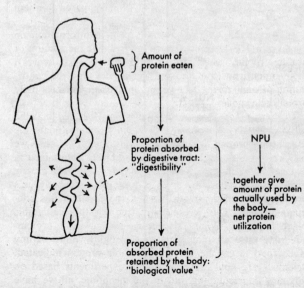

Amount of protein eaten

Proportion of protein absorbed by digestive tract: "digestibility"

NPU

together give amount of protein actually used by the body— net protein utilization

Proportion of absorbed protein retained by the body: "biological value"

Figure 13. What Is "NPU"?

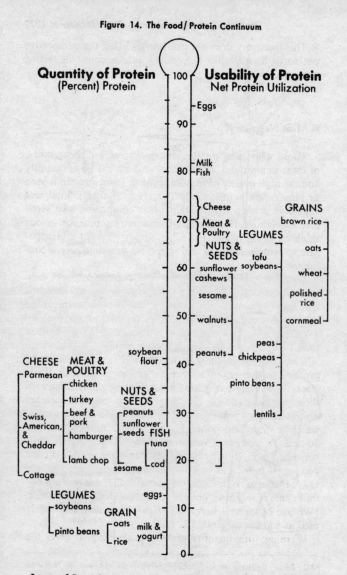

Figure 14. The Food/Protein Continuum

Source of Data: Department of Agriculture Handbook No. 8, 1968; and
The Amino Acid Composition and Biological Value of Some Proteins,

This discovery does not call into question the perspective put forth here. It has been taken into account in setting protein allowances.

Is Meat Necessary?

Those who insist on the superiority, or indispensability, of meat as a protein source focus on both the large quantity and the high quality of protein in meat. Plant protein is seen as inferior on both counts. The result is that animal and vegetable protein are thought of as comprising two separate categories. In fact, this is a common mistake in our thinking about protein. It is much more useful and accurate to visualize animal and vegetable protein along a continuum.

Figure 14, "The Food/Protein Continuum," will help you see the range of protein variability on two scales: protein quantity, based on the percent of protein in the food by weight; and usability, based on the NPU of the protein. (Weights for grains and legumes are calculated for *cooked* food.)

Quantity. When judging foods with the percentage of protein as the criterion, generalization is difficult. It is clear, however, that plants rank highest, particularly in their processed forms. Soybean flour is over 40 percent protein. Next come certain cheeses, such as Parmesan, which is 36 percent protein. Meat follows, ranging between 20 and 35 percent. Cooked beans, peas, and lentils have between 5 and 10 percent protein; though it might surprise you, eggs, milk, and yogurt are in the same range. There are, of course, other plants—some fruits, for example— that contain too little protein to even appear on the scale. (We are concerned here only with plants that are widely used as sources of protein.)

Warning: this quantity scale is misleading. It gives the

FAO, Rome. Courtesy of Dr. Isabel Contento, Department of Nutrition Education, Teachers College, Columbia University; adapted from chart in 1971 edition of *Diet for a Small Planet.*

percent by weight, yet the real issue in evaluating a protein source is not weight but calories. Can we get enough protein from a food without getting too many calories? Looked at from this angle, most plant foods qualify and some excel. Eating vegetables such as broccoli, cauliflower, mushrooms, and spinach, *you get the same amount of protein for each calorie that you get with meat.* But it would be difficult to get a full day's protein allowance from cauliflower (unless you were prepared to eat 20 cups!). Nonetheless, such vegetables can contribute substantially to meeting our protein needs.

Usability. The protein usability scale generally ranges from NPU values of about 40 to 94. Clearly, animal protein occupies the highest rungs of this scale. Meat, however, is not at the top. It places slightly above the middle, with an average NPU of 67. At the top are eggs (NPU of 94) and milk (NPU of 82). The NPUs of plant proteins generally range lower on the continuum, between 40 and 70. But protein in some plants, such as soybeans and whole rice, approaches or overlaps the NPU values for meat.

Complementing Your Proteins

Because different food groups have different amino acid strengths and weaknesses, eating a mixture of protein sources can increase the protein value of a meal; here's a case where the whole is greater than the sum of its parts. The EAA deficiency in one food can be countered by the EAA contained in other food. For example, the expected biological value of three parts bread and one part cheddar cheese would be 64 percent if eaten separately. Yet, if eaten together, their biological value is 76 percent because of the complementary relationship. The "whole" is greater largely because cheese makes up for bread's lysine and isoleucine deficiencies. Such protein mixes *do not result in a perfect protein* that is fully utilizable by the body (only egg is near perfect). But combinations can increase the protein quality as much as 50 percent above the average of the items eaten separately.

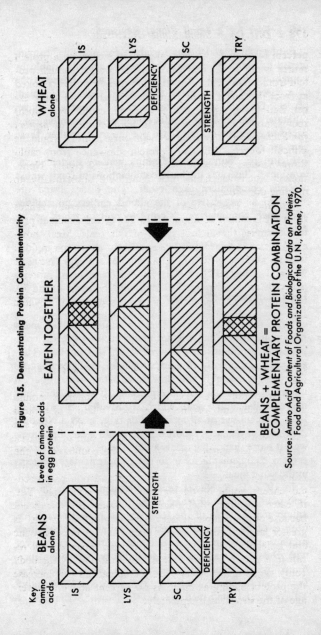

Figure 15. Demonstrating Protein Complementarity

Source: Amino Acid Content of Foods and Biological Data on Proteins, Food and Agricultural Organization of the U.N., Rome, 1970.

BEANS + WHEAT =
COMPLEMENTARY PROTEIN COMBINATION

Eating wheat and beans together, for example, can increase by about 33 percent the protein actually usable by your body. Figure 15 will help you see why. It shows the four essential amino acids most often deficient in plant protein. On each side, where beans and wheat are shown separately, we see large gaps in amino acid content as compared to egg protein. But if we put the two together, these gaps are closed.

Figure 16, "Summary of Complementary Protein Relationships," illustrates the basic combinations of foods whose proteins complement each other. The dishes listed are meant to be suggestive of the almost endless possibilities using each combination. (Complete protein tables are in Appendix E.)

The Complementarity Debate

Since the first edition of *Diet for a Small Planet*, many have pointed out that it is not really necessary to eat complementary proteins *in the same meal,* as I implied. They are right, technically. But experimental evidence suggests that protein assembly will slow down after several hours if all of the amino acids are not present. "If a diet lacks only one essential amino acid, which is provided several hours later, efficient use of all amino acids falls," says a National Academy of Sciences report.[2] So it would seem that unless we eat more than three meals a day, the only way to *ensure* protein complementarity is to eat complementary proteins in the same meal.

In 1972, E. S. Nasset reported evidence of an "amino acid pool" that could make up for any deficiencies in the amino acid patterns of the food we eat. Nasset's work has been cited by many to suggest that eating complementary proteins may be irrelevant. But most nutritionists disagree with Nasset. His amino acid pool theory "has been questioned by a number of workers and the results presented so far do not support Nasset's theory," reports a 1978 study.[3] This view is confirmed by MIT's Nevin Scrimshaw, a

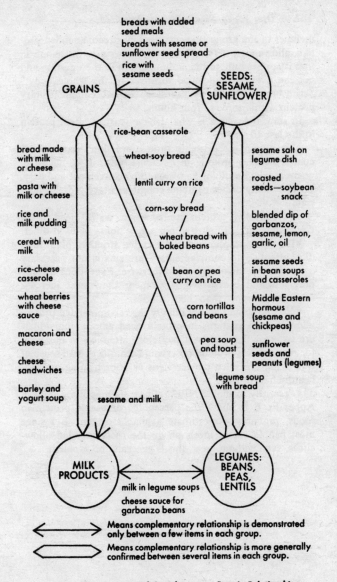

Figure 16. Summary of Complementary Protein Relationships

member of the group that sets the UN's recommended protein allowances: "The Nasset Hypothesis is fallacious in that it applies only to the amino pattern in the intestine and not the overall amino acid turnover of the whole body." Scrimshaw adds, "It *is* necessary to eat complementary protein within three to four hours."[4]

In sum, then, here is what I have learned about protein in the last 10 years:

•To obtain more usable protein we don't have to eat complementary proteins *in the same meal,* if we have frequent meals. But doing so seems to be convenient and easy, since so many dishes combine complementary proteins anyway.

•For effective protein use, however, we do need to eat complementary proteins within a few hours of each other.

•For most people, even those eating strictly a plant food diet, attention to complementary proteins is not necessary as long as the diet is healthy otherwise. Exceptions include pregnant and breast-feeding women; they must increase their protein more than their calories.

•*No one* should accept blindly the recommended protein allowances. Variations in protein need among individuals are so great that we must pay close attention to our need for more or less protein, observing both our overall sense of well-being and such danger signs as poor healing and unhealthy hair or nails.

•Presently available NPU ratings, such as those used in Appendix E to show the percentage of usable protein in foods, probably overestimate available protein. But since most people eat at levels above the recommended allowances, even without meat, this is generally no problem.

Part IV

Lessons
for the
Long Haul

1.

What Can We Do?

To BE PART of building a more democratic society, one in which our economic structures are accountable to people's needs, what can we do? Since we can't take on the whole system at once, where can we start? How can we find others to work with, people who will not only help us accomplish our goals but also help us change ourselves?

I've found that food issues have a special ability to open doors. Everyone has an opinion about food, because everybody has to eat! But, as I have said, I'm not suggesting that everyone should become a food activist. Our society's gravest problems have common roots, so we can work in many areas—toward better schooling or health care systems or toward safe energy policies—and we will affect all the others.

In a dozen years focused on food problems, traveling back and forth across the United States, I've met hundreds of other people working on everything from food co-ops in Michigan to investigating center-pivot irrigation in Nebraska to water rights in California. I consider all these people allies, and some have become close friends, even if we get to see each other only a few times a year.

But I always fear that people who have never been involved in work for social change believe that people already intensely engaged are somehow different from themselves. They assume: "Well, she must have *always* been self-motivated and had direction. *I* could never be that way." In my experience, this perception is just not accurate, certainly not when I look at the progression in my life. One goal of this book and of the book *What Can We Do? Food and Hunger: How You Can Make A Difference,** which Bill Valentine and I wrote in 1980, is to demystify the people already involved—to show that we all must undergo the same struggles. None of us is spared the uncertainties. It may look easier for the other person, but it probably isn't. For *What Can We Do?* we interviewed two dozen food and hunger activists in the United States and Canada and tried to find out what makes them tick. How did they get involved? How do they see their work changing the food system? And what keeps them going? In this chapter I would like to share some of their responses as well as those from people around the country who wrote to me as I was preparing this edition.

Use What We Have

As I was working on the final draft of this chapter, the popular balladeer Harry Chapin died in an automobile accident. He was thirty-eight. I was deeply affected, because Harry's life reflected many of the themes in this book—especially this chapter. Joe and I first met Harry in 1976, when *Food First* and our Institute were just being born. The year before, Harry and radio talk-show host Bill Ayres had founded World Hunger Year as a vehicle for their work against hunger.

What first struck us was Harry's drive to learn. I guess we'd assumed that entertainers who got involved in "causes" were not too concerned about the facts; they were out to prove they had a heart, not just an ego. But Harry was different. We sent him the drafts of the *Food First* manuscript and we held informal seminars to discuss our

* Published by the Institute for Food and Development Policy, 1980.

findings. I felt that what appealed to Harry most was that ours is a message of hope.

While Harry's fame came from his hits "Taxi" and "Cat's in the Cradle," his most fervent fans were those who had seen him in concert. In his concerts Harry broke all the "pop star" rules. He needed no gimmicks. It was just Harry—in simple street clothes, with no props. Harry sang ballads about the pathos of everyday life—and between songs told people of the tragedy of needless hunger—yet he left his audiences uplifted. How did he do it? By the force of his character, grounded in certain core beliefs. One he called the "nudge factor." To him this meant the power of even a small minority to bring about enormous change—if that minority just cared enough. In Harry's presence, you *had* to believe, for it seemed as though even a minority of one could do the impossible.

When someone like Harry Chapin is gone, we feel an enormous void. But we can use the lessons his life taught to take up the challenge of filling that void. Perhaps the most important lesson is to use what we have. He started with what he had—musical talent and incredible energy—and used them to open doors for millions of people. He was directly responsible for the birth of three antihunger organizations and, through these, several more. One spinoff was the New York City Food and Hunger Hotline, through which hungry people can get emergency help and support in coping with the government food programs. Harry also made major contributions to our Institute during the early years when we needed help most. In addition, Harry did benefit concerts for dozens of other causes. He gave away several million dollars.

Harry used his fame as a singer in other imaginative ways. For example, he was able to convince radio station managers in ten major cities all over the country to hold "world hunger radiothons"—24 hours of commercial-free air time, during which all the breaks were filled with information and insight about the causes of hunger. And the shows were not just "Harry's shows." His staff, led by Jeri Barr and Wray McKay, did the tiresome work of drawing in local spokespeople to tell about the problems and the struggles right in the local community. The goal: to ignite local activism.

Harry started with what he had and used it. That's the challenge of his life to us.

The First Step Is the Hardest

From Harry Chapin, from the many, many people I have met in the last ten years, I learned that we must each begin from where we are. Each person's interests, passions, abilities, age, and geographical location affect the actions one can—and wants to—take. In seeking a focus for action, many choose to look close to home, doing what they can right now, and then taking the next step as it comes.

Cathy Adrian of Santa Barbara, California, was working in a doughnut shop when she became interested in food problems ten years ago. "I began to see things in a different light," she explains. "A spark had been set off inside me that has continued to get stronger.

"I started talking to my customers who were friends about nutrition and found myself talking people out of buying coffee and doughnuts," she remembers. "It goes without saying that I felt out of place at the doughnut shop." Today she works as a teacher's aide for special-education preschoolers. At the food co-op where she shops, she has set up two bulletin boards because "I needed a way to effectively share information. I want to help people become more aware and, most importantly, become *active*."

Twelve years ago Joan Gussow was forty, at home with two children, and working two days a week on a book project she was less than enthusiastic about. When that work was completed, Joan said, "I kept asking myself, '*Now* what are you going to do when you grow up?' " When she first thought of going back to school to study nutrition, the idea frightened her. "I realized that I had my last chemistry course in 1949!" Joan said. "But, being more honest with myself, I realized that my main reservation was nutrition's dull *image*. (Let's face it, nutrition is not one of the high-prestige fields.) But that's a pretty crummy reason for not doing something you believe in . . . just because other people don't think it's important. I told myself, if *you* think it is important, make it important."

Joan is now head of the Department of Nutrition and Education at Teachers College, Columbia University, a sought-after speaker, and author of *The Feeding Web: Issues in Nutritional Ecology* (Bull Publishing, 1978).

In retrospect Joan believes that the decision to go back to school to study nutrition was probably the first real decision in her whole life. "Yes, I responded to offers, and in other instances there seemed to be no choice, so I went through whatever door opened," she says. "But in this case *I* made the decision because of what I thought was important. And I've never regretted it."

Bob Pickford, who works for the Federation of Ohio River Co-ops in Columbus, says he "became involved in co-op work as a consumer at a food cooperative, looking for higher-quality food than was available in the supermarket, or a little less expensive food.

"I spent more time at the co-op, began to understand a little bit about what a food cooperative was, and started to work as a volunteer. Since then I've worked as a paid worker in several stores, and now as a paid employee in the warehouse." The Federation operates a central warehouse and about 100 buying associations in Ohio, West Virginia, Kentucky, and Indiana. It places a few cents' tax on every product from the third world and uses that fund for educational projects and donations to groups addressing the roots of hunger.

"If you asked me 12 years ago, I wouldn't have believed that I could be doing work on enforcing a law that would provide access to inexpensive, highly productive agricultural land for thousands of small family farmers," explains Maia Sortor of National Land for People in Fresno, California. "I used to earn my living doing commercial art for products I could no longer stomach. And now I do graphics for the purpose of educating people about how they can get more control over their lives and stomachs."

Marilyn Fedelchak, who farms 320 acres in Churdan, Iowa, works with the U. S. Farmers' Organization, seeking a fair income for farmers. "When I married a farmer," she says, "I looked forward to living in rural America. I thought I would be close to nature and be part of a community . . . I guess I got involved because I think there is still hope for the kind of rural America that I wanted to live in."

Leah Margulies, a leader of the Nestlé infant-formula boycott at the Interfaith Center on Corporate Responsibility in New York, recalls, "Ten years ago I was a housewife. I was pretty despairing about changing my life. I first got involved through the women's movement, in a collective studying how multinational corporations are expanding their markets overseas. What I started to think about initially was the way women's realities are formed by economics. I started to question whether or not the kind of people that are being created by the necessity of ever-expanding sales of consumer goods are really the kinds of people we in the women's movement wanted to be!"

The Interfaith Center where Leah works coordinates efforts by church denominations and agencies to use their power as shareholders to raise questions of social justice within corporations. Every shareholder in a corporation has the right to introduce resolutions suggesting changes in corporate policy, and the Interfaith Center has used these resolutions to force discussion of bank loans to repressive governments, the portrayal of women and minorities on television, and unfair labor practices.

The Center works closely with INFACT, a national coalition of 450 local organizations trying to prevent the advertising of infant formula to third world mothers. (Once mothers get hooked on using formula, their breast milk dries up, but often third world mothers are too poor to buy as much formula as their babies need. They are forced to stretch it with water that is frequently unsanitary or with other nonnutritious substitutes. So millions of babies die who might have lived if their mothers had breast-fed them instead of believing the suggestion of Nestlé and other multinationals that bottle feeding is "modern" and better for babies.)

Ten years ago Michael Jacobson was getting his doctorate in biochemistry at MIT. He had no particular interest in food. "In 1970, I'm not even sure I'd ever heard of a 'whole grain,' " says Michael. "I was spending all my life in the library and with test tubes. But I was dying to do something—anything—that would touch our immediate social problems. So I took a chance. I signed on as an intern with Ralph Nader. Since I had the science degree, my assignment was to look at the hazards of food additives. And out of that summer eventually came my first book, *Eaters' Digest* (Doubleday, 1972).

Within a year, Michael and two other scientists had launched the Center for Science in the Public Interest, a Washington-based public interest group which now boasts 25,000 members. Its nutrition education materials are used by thousands of teachers around the country. And its public advocacy has helped alert the country to dangers of the new American diet I describe in Part III. The Center has taken on the food industry in fighting for accurate food labeling and against hazardous additives. It has exposed the shocking collusion among industry officials, government regulators, and "objective" academics.

Trapped by the pressure of exams and term papers, students often feel they just can't get involved in the kind of social change work they most want to do. But students at the University of Oregon decided that what they *could* change was the nature of the courses on world hunger being taught right in their own university. Brad Oppermann and two classmates organized their own for-credit course, "World Hunger and You," through the sociology department. "It's been going for two years and now attracts 30 to 40 students," writes Brad.

For Kathleen Cusick, the decision to stop eating meat was the first step which led her to work with Rural Resources, a Loveland, Ohio, group which has helped set up tailgate farmers' markets in Cincinnati and a Citizen's Alliance to fight a proposed sewer project in a nearby rural community.

"It began with the negative emotional responses I got from people even to that one personal decision not to eat meat," she recalls. "The more I followed through on that decision, and discovered why I made it, the more I discovered that my decision to become involved in food work was something that very few people were doing.

"It was frightening because for a long time there was really no support," she remembers. "This kind of decision—to be an organzier or activist—really has to be made with some community support. Otherwise it can turn you into a loner, and make you very ineffective and unhappy."

Working with Others

"What keeps me going," Kathleen explains, "is that I feel I'm on a frontier. I feel that the whole group is on a cutting edge, able to share a sense of vision, and able to support each other personally in our work."

For Leah, as for Kathleen, working with other people has made all the difference. "Working in groups is the most important thing because you can get support from other people and test your ideas," Leah says. "I discovered that a lot of things I thought were true were not. When I kept my thoughts to myself, I didn't have an audience to check them. Once I started interacting in groups I got challenged on my ideas, on the way I lived, on my capacity as a person."

"You have to find some kind of core group, maybe only two or three people that you can relate to value-wise," adds Jody Grundy, who works with Kathleen Cusick at Rural Resources. "They can be a renewing source of energy for work that is often isolating and lonely. We three women in Rural Resources have a sense we can do anything!"

To do more than we think we can do, most of us need a push. For some this means taking a position in which a lot more is expected of us than we feel prepared for. Keith Jardine, one of the key people in the Canadian People's Food Commission (a two-year-long nongovernmental initiative to involve people at the grassroots in analyzing problems of the Canadian food system), told us, "I began with the Commission as a volunteer, and when a staff position opened, I was hired. I suddenly found myself helping to organize this enormous project. I had no particular training or experience, other than a minimal amount of educational work in my food co-op. Most of my experience was shuffling boxes around." From the experience with the Commission, Keith concluded, "If I changed, then other people can!"

Direct Experience of Oppression

Many people first got involved by "playing the hand they were dealt," but for others personal travel in the third world (even a vacation trip to Mexico or Jamaica) or a stint in the Peace Corps or VISTA made the difference. Their life directions were profoundly altered when they put themselves as close as possible to the deprivation and oppression which previously they had only read about.

Larry Simon was a college professor before he joined Oxfam-America, a development organization based in Boston. "I suppose what changed me the most was not reading or intellectually grasping the structures of oppression but having the opportunity to actually go to Latin America, to talk to peasants, to talk to cane-cutters working for Gulf + Western Corporation, to feel the incredible repression in the air, to taste and smell the awful, needless poverty."

Sue Penner found that her work as a Peace Corps nurse in Honduras sensitized her permanently to the injustice of needless suffering. "When you've seen the poor kids, the babies that are shrivelled up like little old men, the ashen faces of women *dying* of anemia, the men with stunted bodies and stooped shoulders, it somehow makes you start thinking," she writes. "It's awfully hard to forget. It's awfully frustrating just sitting down there pushing penicillin into the bodies of sick babies who couldn't have died if they'd just had *food* to eat!"

As a participant in a Jesuit Volunteer Corps program, Annie Newman worked one day a week at a soup kitchen frequented by the poor and down-and-out in the Latino area of San Francisco. "I grew up in a middle-class family in Phoenix, so working at the soup kitchen shocked me at first," says Annie, who also works at our Institute. "Seeing how badly our society takes care of these abandoned people really strengthened my commitment to working for change."

From Larry's, Sue's, and Annie's experiences, we can derive a powerful lesson: to cut through our own self-doubts and indecision about what we should be doing with our lives, it is often necessary to experience the real oppression which so many people face every day. Of course, such firsthand experience will always be vicarious; we will always "have a plane ticket in our pocket," as Larry Simon puts it. Nonetheless, seeing firsthand the suffering with which so much of the world lives can sometimes jolt us into taking our own life choices more seriously.

Remaining Critical—Especially Self-critical

"Playing the hand one is dealt" does not mean simply taking the most obvious step uncritically. Working with pressing issues close to home must go hand in hand with an evolving analysis, an analysis constantly used to evaluate your own work. Larry Simon's experience in the third world took him from an academic setting to more active participation at Oxfam-America. But having made that step, he did not suspend his critical analysis. Within only a few years Larry was examining not only the projects Oxfam supports in the third world but also the context in which those projects operate. Finally he concluded that Oxfam should not work in certain countries where government repression is so strong that it precludes the existence of any organization working for redistribution of power, the only kind of organization which Oxfam wants to support.

Hard Work and Balance

"Corporate executives work hard. Peasant organizers work hard," Leah Margulies points out. "So must we." Leah actually made a conscious decision to move to fast-paced New York City so she could "learn how to work hard." Hard work and self-discipline were frequently mentioned by the people we interviewed.

This might appear to contradict the fact that these people are full of energy and excited about their work. Their lives tell us that passionate involvement must link risk, self-discipline, and hard work, with release and comfort to achieve a balance. Perhaps those committing their lives to social change today have learned something from the 1960s, when many people "burned out." Leah Margulies, for instance, plays flute and bass and has performed regularly in a women's band and a theater group.

Balancing one's life to avoid burning out is an essential part of an attitude that working for justice is not just something to do for a few years before settling down into a more conventional life. Rather, the activists we talked to see themselves as part of a historical process longer than their own lifetimes.

"We're in this for the long haul," says John Vlcek of the Nashville-based Agricultural Marketing Project. "We've got to realize that even if we work our entire lifetime we'll only have a certain impact, and a lot of that impact is going to be seen only after we're gone."

The most common link we found in talking to people working in the food and hunger movement was the tremendous change they felt in their individual lives. They began to experience themselves as initiators of change in others. For them, the possibility of change is no longer just theoretical. Leah moved from seeing herself as a dependent housewife to becoming a major policymaker in an international movement which has affected millions. John Vlcek and Bob Pickford have seen how the ideas of a few food activists could grow, within a few years, into programs of direct marketing and co-op stores that affect tens of thousands of people. As Keith Jardine said, "If I changed, then other people can!"

I hope that the testimonies in this chapter show that getting involved—taking on the challenge of "what can we do?"—can bring extraordinary satisfaction.

But, after reading a draft of this chapter, Cathy Lerza, a founder and director of the Washington-based National Family Farm Coalition, protested: "Frankie, you make it sound too heavy and serious. Actually, I've had a great time the last ten years! I *want* to come to work each morning. I love the people I work with. How many Americans can feel that way?

"You make it sound like working for social change is harder than the lot of most people. But no, it's the people who feel that they have no reason to get up in the morning who are in worse shape. If I weren't doing what I am, my life would be so much less interesting. I think I'm pretty damn lucky!"

What everybody wants is what Cathy's found—something she feels passionate about. That's the common thread uniting the people I've quoted here. My central hope for this book is that it's given you some clues as to how others have made that discovery—so that you might make it for yourself.

But, so many say, what difference can *one* of us make? The problems are so enormous. And they are right. Nothing any one of us can do will make a big difference. Yet, the irony is that the world is changing every day in response to individual choices; and that is the *only* way it can change—by individuals making up their minds to act.

When we realize that no one individual act will make much difference, when we appreciate how many things have to change at once, self-doubt and despair come in the door. I believe this is inevitable. But the door is also open to another realization: if it is true that many things must change at once, we can put behind us the futile struggle to figure out *the* way to change the world and get on with the work right at hand—the injustices, the needless suffering, the destruction of resources right in our own communities.

And once we grasp how profound the problems are, we also can let go of our futile efforts to overcome our despair once and for all. The people quoted in this chapter may seem basically satisifed with their lives, but their satisfaction does not come from protecting themselves from uncertainty. They accept periodic uncertainty, loneliness, and self-doubt as facts of life. Their satisfaction comes in knowing they can face those feelings and go on. So, more than a guaranteed recipe for action, more than perfectly formed analysis, we need courage—courage to face despair and go on.

And remember: we don't have to start the train moving. It is moving! Our struggle is to figure out how to board that train, bringing on board all the creative energy we can muster.

2.

How to Plug In

TAKING THE FIRST step is easier today than it was two decades ago when I first wrote *Diet for a Small Planet*. Literally thousands of citizen organizations have emerged, addressing both immediate problems in their communities and global problems of historical impact.

But *how* can you find out about them? And *how* can you choose those through which you can learn and act for positive change? Instead of including a list of organizations here as I have in earlier editions—one that of necessity must be partial and impermanent—I suggest the following:

First, I've noticed that most of us get involved through someone we know. So look around. Turn to friends and acquaintances who are already involved in something they care about deeply. This may mean seeking out new friends. Whom we choose as friends can be among the most important decisions of our lives. We can choose those who challenge us to take risks—to try on new ideas and new actions.

Another step in finding others to work with for constructive change is to broaden one's reading. Bring new books and periodicals into your home in which you can find out about citizen initiatives that would probably not appear on the nightly news. In Appendix A, I've included a short list of books and periodicals for you to consider.

I also suggest that you write to the two organizations which I know best, both for ways to get involved and for further "leads."

For more depth on issues related to food, land, and third world development, I suggest you write to Food First (the Institute for Food and Development Policy), 145 Ninth Street, San Francisco, CA 94103. Food First will send you further reading and action ideas, membership information, as well as a guide to other related organizations working for constructive change.

I also suggest you write to the organization I co-founded with Paul Du Bois in 1990, the Institute for the Arts of Democracy, 700 Larkspur Landing Circle, Suite #199, Larkspur, CA 94939. We are developing programs to bring forth a more active democracy in which citizens are re-claiming authority in public life—in the schools, the media, the workplace, and at every level of government. We call this work "Building Citizen Democracy." We'd love to have your participation. Please write to us to find out about joining with us and to receive a list of publications. We and Food First are especially looking for volunteers and interns to work with us.

Book
Two

Eating
Well
on a
Small Planet:
Complementary
Protein Recipes,
Menus,
Tips

Preface

In 1980, when I decided to write a Tenth Anniversary Edition, I sent out a call for help. I mailed hundreds of fliers and put notices in newsletters and magazines asking people to contribute their favorite complementary protein recipes. The response was incredible. Hundreds of people not only sent recipes but also their very thoughful suggestions for how to make the book better.

At first I found it hard to write this edition—to go back to what I had written so many years ago. But these letters kept me going. Many people described their own personal journey over the last ten years. Their words made more bearable the isolation I feel when I write. I felt I had friends all over the country who were urging me on. No longer did I feel like I was going backward; instead I could use this new book to move forward, by taking the time to reflect on what I had learned.

You'll recognize these new recipes by the names of contributors at the top. Bill and Akiko Shurtleff, authors of the *Book of Tofu, Miso,* and *Tempeh,* deserve a special thanks, since I used several of their excellent recipes.

All of these new recipes and those that have been substantially revised are indicated by an asterisk(*) on each Contents page.

When I was growing up my brother and I used to say that although our mother was no gourmet cook, she was perhaps the best short-order cook in the world. Judging from the reaction to the first edition of this book, I'd say that a lot of other Americans have the same approach to cooking as my mother. They like recipes that they can whip up from memory, vary according to what they have on hand, get on the table in a hurry, but that have a flair of originality to them.

This is certainly the way I try to cook most of the time, except for those special meals for friends when the extra preparation time and care add to the pleasure of the occasion. So in this edition I have divided the recipes into sections that reflect my own cooking habits.

The first and largest section is "Meatless Meals in a Dish." (Suggestions for salad or vegetable accompaniments are given, too.) If the beans or grains for these dishes can be taken from the refrigerator or freezer already cooked, virtually all of these dishes would appeal to even my "short-order" mom. Others are quick even starting from scratch.

The next section, "Meatless Menus for Special Occasions," gives complete dinner menus to help you plan when you have the time for more elaborate dinners.

Following these main sections, you'll find recipes for "All the Extras"—snacks, appetizers, breakfast foods, baked goods, and desserts. Most of these dishes, from the main dish recipes to snacks and desserts, use complementary protein combinations.

Part I

Tips for Making Meals Without Meat

1.

What Is a Meal Without Meat?

WHEN AS CHILDREN we asked our mothers, "What's for supper, Mom?" the shorthand answer always came back "Pork chops" . . . "Chicken" . . . "Meat loaf." The meat course defined the meal.

These menus, which many of us take for granted, are inherited from our physically active forebears. But in our mechanized society we often need many less calories each day than did our great-grandparents, who worked the fields, carried water, and washed by hand. This fact has become well known, if not well heeded. The trouble is that it is virtually impossible to avoid consuming too many calories per meal as long as you define a meal as meat-vegetable-starch-salad-bread-and-dessert. It just can't add up any other way than *too much*.

But once meat is no longer the center of the menu, then the whole pattern of habit falls apart. Anything goes. We are free to respond to our own appetites in planning menus. In my family what seems most natural is a one-dish meal into which we put our care and imagination, accompanied by one simple side dish such as salad, good hearty bread, or a steamed vegetable. Therefore, the majority of the recipes in the book, and all those in the first section of the recipes, are not merely main-dish ideas but really "meal-dish" ideas—meals in themselves with (if you choose) the addition of a simple salad, etc.

In focusing on how to get protein without meat in the first two editions of this book, I fear I reinforced a preoccupation with protein. In this edition I've tried to correct for that, emphasizing how much easier it is than most of us thought to get the protein we need. (My "Hypothetical Diets" in Figures 10 and 11 make this point.) Once we lower our estimation of the amount of protein our bodies need, and realize how many foods provide protein—even those, such as green vegetables, that we've never thought of as protein sources—we gain much more flexibility in meal planning. We no longer have to pack scads of protein into a dish filled with cheese and eggs. We can use more vegetables, grains, and fruit. We achieve greater variety and lighter meals.

Letting go of the meat-starch-vegetable formula and experimenting with new foods was, for me, satisfying in yet another way. Because there is no Betty Crocker of plant foods telling me what a dish *should* be like, I became more experimental. I recall the first nonmeat dinner party I ever gave, for which I made a walnut-cheddar loaf. Never too confident about my cooking, I was comforted by the thought that at least no one would be comparing my dish with Julia Child's version (who else ever tasted walnut-cheddar loaf?). After you become comfortable with the ingredients, you will become a creator, taking foods that are in season and on hand and creating your own favorites.

But let me offer one important caveat that I also included in the first edition of this book: don't expect yourself to change overnight. Start with one new menu a week, or one new ingredient, until you gradually build up a repertoire of dishes you enjoy. Suddenly changing lifelong habits of any kind on the basis of new understanding does not strike me as very realistic or even desirable, however great the revelation. At least, this is not the way it has worked for me.

Why Meatless?

In Book One I explained the difference between the diet I advocate and "vegetarianism." I said that what I advocate is a return to the traditional diet on which our bodies evolved—a plant-centered diet in which animal foods play a supplemental role. But the recipes in my book have always been meatless. Isn't this a contradiction? If I'm not advocating a totally meatless diet, then why don't the recipes contain meat? Well, here's where the personal and the intellectual parts of me come together. Intellectually, I believe that meat has a role to play in human nutrition, since livestock can convert nonedible substances into high-grade protein for people—and in some parts of the world, where cropland is scarce but grazing land plentiful, they seem to play an essential role. Personally, I don't like to cook with meat and I feel much better when I don't eat it. However, my personal preference for a basically meatless diet should not deter others from using this book. If you do not want to eliminate meat completely, you can still use almost any of the recipes, simply adding small quantites of meat. Eating meat occasionally and adding small quantities to plant-centered meals does not violate the themes of this book.

The Calorie and Dollar Costs of Protein

Other questions people often have about plant-centered versus meat-centered diets concern the dollar cost differences and the calorie "cost" differences, so here are two charts that, at a glance, give you a sense of how a variety of foods rank. Figure 17 tells which foods give you the most protein for the fewest calories. Figure 18 tells you which are the cheapest protein sources.

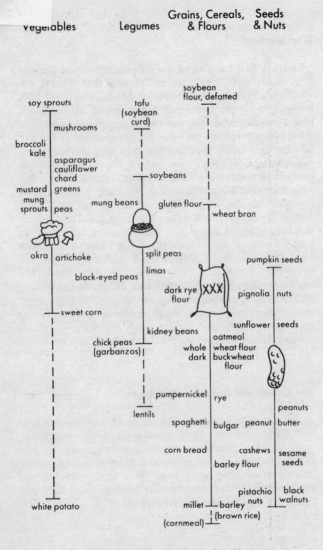

Vegetables	Legumes	Grains, Cereals, & Flours	Seeds & Nuts

soybean
flour, defatted

soy sprouts

tofu
(soybean
curd)

mushrooms

broccoli
kale

asparagus
cauliflower
chard
greens

soybeans

mustard
mung
sprouts   peas

mung beans

gluten flour

wheat bran

okra   artichoke

split peas

limas

pumpkin seeds

black-eyed peas

dark rye
flour   XXX   pignolia   nuts

sweet corn

sunflower   seeds

kidney beans

chick peas
(garbanzos)

oatmeal
whole   wheat flour
dark   buckwheat
flour

pumpernickel   rye

peanuts

lentils

spaghetti   bulgar   peanut   butter

corn bread

cashews   sesame
seeds

barley flour

pistachio   black
nuts   walnuts

millet —— barley
(cornmeal)   (brown rice)

white potato

Figure 17. Calorie "Cost" Per Gram of Usable Protein

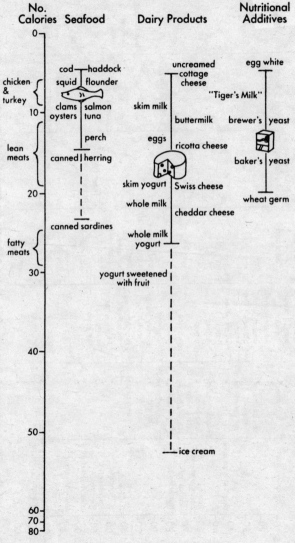

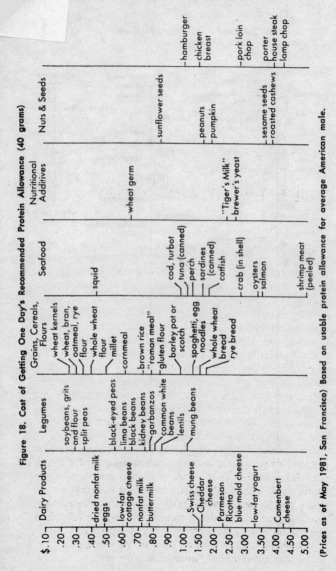

Figure 18. Cost of Getting One Day's Recommended Protein Allowance (40 grams)

(Prices as of May 1981, San Francisco) Based on usable protein allowance for average American male.

2.

"But It Takes Too Much Time . . ."

. . . IS ONE OF the most common reactions to the suggestion of cooking with whole foods. I used to resist making even so-called quick breads from scratch. How could they be as quick as a ready-made mix? But when I began to want dishes that demanded I start from scratch, I decided to test myself. How much more time did it actually take to make my corn bread recipe than to use a commercial corn bread mix? Hardly any more time at all! Both required that I get out bowls and utensils, mix the batter, oil the baking pan, pour in the batter, put it in the oven, clean the mixing utensils and then the baking pan. The only difference was that with my recipe I had to combine a few more ingredients—a really minor part of the whole operation.

But people continue to tell me that they can't wait for the long cooking time necessary when using whole foods, can't take time to chop fresh vegetables and hand-make exotic ethnic dishes. Still, while the actual time my stove is in use may be longer than it takes to fry a hamburger, I am sure that I do not spend any more of my time on food than they do. So what is the secret? Part of the secret is:

1. knowing what to have on hand for easy meals;
2. taking advantage of "intentional leftovers";

ips for Making Meals Without Meat

nging where you shop;
andy kitchen layout and time-saving utensils.

What to Have on Hand

There are probably certain foods that you always have, that you shop for automatically because you know that with these basic ingredients you can always produce a good meal. As you begin to change your eating habits, your buying and stocking habits will change too. To help you, I made a list of the items that I am virtually never without. Many of these foods are probably in your kitchen right now, but perhaps it never occurred to you that you could build a meal with many of them. Of course, in each of these categories there are many, many more possibilities, but with these items you could make *any* of the recipes in this book. (You might have to substitute a little, but that is part of the fun!)

Again, I am not suggesting that you go out and buy a whole lot of new ingredients all at once. If you have a friend who uses whole grains, legumes, and seeds, ask if you might just have some samples to get you started. (That's how I got started, with the help of a dear friend, Ellen Ewald.) One of the many advantages to shopping at a food co-op is that you can buy many grains, flours, pastas, etc., loose from bins, so you can buy very small quantities.

Another way to begin is to find a friend who would also like to experiment. Together you might buy one-pound quantities of a few new things, split them, then compare experiences and reactions to your new menus. This way you will not be making such a big initial investment that you will feel it *has* to "work" all at once. Or, if you are on your own, just find one recipe that looks good to you. Buy any ingredient you don't already have, then try discovering all the other possibilities for it. You'll be amazed at the variety that is possible when cooking with plant foods.

Here are my basic pantry items for easy meals, with

some tips on how I use them. (For basic cooking instructions, see Appendix C.)

DAIRY PRODUCTS

Nonfat dry milk. In hot cereal, baked goods, soups, blender drinks, white sauces.

Low-fat cottage cheese or ricotta cheese. The basis of sauces, salad dressings, casseroles, pancake filling, pie filling, or simply a delicious spread on bread.

Low-fat yogurt or buttermilk. A dressing for fruit salad, in blender fruit drinks, cold summer blender soups, and sauces (especially with curries). You can use buttermilk in place of yogurt wherever you don't need yogurt's thickness. It's much cheaper, too.

SOY FOODS

Tofu (soybean curd) has a mild flavor and the consistency of firm custard. It readily absorbs the flavors with which it is cooked. Uncooked, tofu can be blended for salad dressings and sauces. Lightly sautéed with vegetables and seasonings, it becomes a main dish. Actually, tofu can be used in almost any kind of dish, as you'll see in the recipes that follow. Tofu and soy milk also can be used in place of milk in virtually any recipe.

Tempeh (a fermented soy curd) and *miso* (a fermented soy paste) are also favorites of growing numbers of Westerners. They lend themselves to many different types of dishes. The best source of information about soy foods, including hundreds of delicious recipes, are the books of Bill and Akiko Shurtleff, *The Book of Tofu, The Book of Miso,* and *The Book of Tempeh* (Ballantine Books).

QUICK-COOKING GRAIN PRODUCTS

Bulgur (partially cooked, i.e., parboiled wheat, usually cracked). For breakfast cereal, dinner grain, soup thicken-

...alad with vegetables. (Couscous is similar but
...ed, and usually more expensive.) Bulgur's nutty
...nhanced by sautéing before steaming.

Flours—whole wheat, soy, corn. Endless possibilities!

NUTS AND SEEDS

Sunflower and ground sesame seeds (nutritionists have
advised that sesame seeds should be ground for digestibility; this can be easily done in the blender or with a mortar
and pestle). Used in baked goods, salads, as a toasted topping, in casseroles, stuffing, granola, with peanuts for
snacking. Toasting lightly brings out the flavor.

Peanuts and peanut butter. In bean croquettes, casseroles, salads, cookies, candy, vegetable sauce for pasta,
curries.

QUICK-COOKING DRY LEGUMES

Split peas (green or yellow). Soups, curries, sauces, with
rice, in rice patties, loaves.

Lentils. Same uses.

Soy grits (partially cooked, cracked soybeans; also called
soy granules). In hot cereals, baked goods, in small
amounts with other grains, in spaghetti sauce or bean chili,
soups—or in just about anything for extra protein. Soy grits
have a very mild taste and absorb the flavor of whatever they
are cooked with.

OIL AND MARGARINE

You'll notice that in this edition I have replaced butter
in the recipes with margarine or oil. For my reasoning, I
refer you back to the "America's Experimental Diet" chapter in which I discuss the importance of reducing our intake
of cholesterol. I recommend that you use natural magarine,
which does not contain chemical additives. The best vege-

table oils for your health are polyunsaturated. They in
safflower, sunflower, corn, and soybean oils.

FRESH FOODS

These are fresh foods that keep well. With these three
vegetables you can, as a friend put it, always create a meal
out of nothing.
Carrots. In carrot and onion soup, bread, grain dishes,
salad, curries.
Onions. French onion soup, in casseroles, curries.
Potatoes. In soups, salads, casseroles, pancakes.

CANNED FOODS

Kidney and garbanzo beans. In stews, chili, tacos,
puréed for sandwich fillings, curries. (I use canned beans
only when I am really rushed and have used up my freezer
store of leftover cooked beans.)
Tomatoes. In soups, casseroles.
Spaghetti sauce. In pasta dishes, as topping for bean croquettes, eggplant platters.
Tuna fish. In casseroles, sandwiches, salads, rice fritters.
Minced clams. In chowder, spaghetti sauce, dips,
spreads, fritters.
Beets. Add beautiful color and interest to vegetable,
tuna, lettuce, or spinach salads.
Corn. In casseroles, fritters, soups, stews, pancakes.

FREEZER FOODS

Leftover beans. Always cook at least twice what the recipe calls for and store the rest for instant meals.
Middle Eastern flatbread (pita) and tortillas. Use for authentic foreign dishes and for instant sandwiches with all
types of fillings. (Cheese melted on tortillas makes a quick
and delicious snack—and kids love it.)

Add color, taste, and nutrition to soups,

SEASONINGS ("SEASONED STOCK")

Powdered vegetable seasoning. Use in just about any-thing. Look around and you can find vegetable seasonings that are made from natural ingredients, without preserva-tives or salt. Use with water whenever the recipe calls for Seasoned Stock, or sprinkle on whenever you think extra flavor might be needed.

You can make your own seasoning to sprinkle on a little extra flavor. Here's a suggestion from Alice Green of San Francisco: take 3 sheets of nori (pressed seaweed, avail-able in Asian or natural foods stores) and toast one side of each sheet over a gas burner (to enhance the flavor). Then roast ¼ cup of sesame seeds in a dry skillet until golden. Crumble the nori and combine with seeds in a small jar with a tight lid. Shake well. (I would add that you might want to put the seeds in a blender or grind them to release flavor and aid their digestibility.) This is good on all grain and vegetable dishes, Alice says.

Herbs. You can substitute fresh herbs for dried herbs, or vice versa, by using the following rule of thumb in the reci-pes that follow: for every teaspoon of dried herbs, use roughly one tablespoon of fresh. But be careful to taste as you go: herbs vary greatly in strength. *Unless otherwise in-dicated, the recipes call for dried herbs.*

Intentional Leftovers

Prepared foods are popular because it *is* nice, when you are exhausted after a long day, to just take a delicious dish out of the refrigerator, heat, and serve.

But why not make your own TV dinners? Again, it is a question of habit. If we get into the habit of preparing more than we will eat in one meal and freezing the rest (in containers that can go right into the oven, if appropriate), then we can have our favorite foods there ready for us when we are too tired to cook.

Cook extra beans for the freezer—to be added later to soups, casseroles, or salads. Also, cooked grain keeps well for about four days in the refrigerator. My children like to add milk or buttermilk and a touch of brown sugar (and sometimes some nuts) to leftover brown rice or bulgur for instant cereal. Cooked potatoes also keep well in the refrigerator for at least that long. They can become a quick salad (delicious with other vegetables and a vinaigrette dressing), hash browns, or dozens of other delicious potato dishes.

Shopping

One of the most effective ways to change how you eat is to change how you shop. In a giant supermarket that offers (or should I say bombards us with) 15,000 items, finding healthy foods seems like a struggle. If we shop in a smaller, whole foods cooperative store, we are surrounded by foods that not only tempt our palates but are good for us. A second argument for shifting to a whole foods store is time. Even though I measure out the quantities myself, it takes me less time to shop at the Noe Valley Community Store than at the supermarket. Maybe this is because I know exactly where everything is and I don't have to walk down long aisles of items I would never buy. In addition, shopping in my community whole foods store probably seems even quicker than it is, because I enjoy it. A supermarket trip seems like an ordeal to endure. A trip to the community store is a totally different experience. Everyone there seems to want to be there, including the people who work there.

Cooking with grains, legumes, nuts, and seeds also means that in one shopping trip you can buy enough to last a few months.

Kitchen Shortcuts

KEEPING IT ALL WITHIN REACH

Preparation time is not just how long something takes to cook; it's getting the ingredients to the cooking stage, too. That's why the organization of your kitchen is all-important.

All that wasted space at the back of your kitchen counters could be a beautiful and handy storage area for your whole foods. All you need are large glass jars with tight-fitting lids. Giant peanut butter or pickle jars are good. Flours, seeds, beans, lentils, even pasta and milk powder can be kept within easy reach. The variety of color and texture will add an attractive touch to your kitchen, too. Also, being able to see all the ingredients can be a spur to the imagination. I inevitably end up tossing in a little of something that I had not planned to, just because I see it there on the counter.

Measuring utensils can also be in easy reach of your basic ingredients. Get measuring cups with long handles with holes in them for hanging. Hang them on hooks from a cupboard over your storage jars, if possible. Measuring spoons can also be hung on a hook. Just think how much time you might save if you never again had to fumble through the utensil drawer for measuring cups or spoons! As soon as I wash mine I hang them on their hooks. That way I never have to dry them and always know where they are.

SIMPLE KITCHEN TIME-SAVERS

No-hassle cooking with plant foods requires a few basic tools. The small investment of money will pay off in hours and hours of time saved. Here are some no-kitchen-should-be-without suggestions.

Pressure cooker. Even though I recommended using a

pressure cooker in the first edition of this book, many friends tell me that they don't use one. So let me underline again the usefulness of this old-fashioned tool. Beans that would require hours of soaking and cooking take only 35 to 45 minutes, with no soaking. Grains cook in less than half an hour; potatoes and carrots for soups and stews cook in a few minutes. I think using a pressure cooker is a matter of getting into the habit. Becoming comfortable with it may take some time, but it's worth it. I have found the technique very simple, and have never had any trouble.

I also devised a foolproof method for pressure-cooking grains. I bought a stainless-steel mixing bowl that fits inside my pressure cooker and is about one inch shorter than the inside height of the cooker. I fill the pressure cooker with about three inches of water and put the grain or beans I am cooking in the bowl, with enough water to cover the food plus about one inch. I put the bowl inside the cooker and cook it per conventional pressure cooker instructions. This method is quick—I never have to measure the water, because I just add water to a level one inch above the food—and it is impossible to scorch the food because of the water between the bowl and the pressure cooker.

You can also use this method to cook two items separately in the same pressure cooker. Simply put one food in the pressure cooker, with the same amount of water as you would ordinarily use in a pressure cooker, and the other food in the stainless-steel bowl, with water to cover plus about one inch.

If you don't want to try it my style, simply follow the basic cooking instructions that come with your pressure cooker, or see Appendix C. New pressure cookers are too expensive for some budgets, but a friend of mine found an almost-new one for $5 at a secondhand store.

Vegetable chopper. Never again pass over a recipe because you don't want to take the time to chop vegetables with a knife. You don't have to. If you are not as adept with a knife as Julia Child, you'll want a vegetable chopper. I have a plunger-type blade in a round plastic case.

Salad spinner. Originating in France, this round plastic device (about the size of a big salad bowl) cuts my salad-making time at least in half. You simply put all the greens in it, cover with water, and wash. Pour out the water and then spin the greens dry in seconds.

Vegetable steamer. A perforated metal sheet on short legs, with leaves that open to cover the bottom of the pot. You put an inch of water under the steamer, and the steam from the water cooks the vegetables, which retain their vitamins and form.

Garlic press. Never again will you have the frustration of trying to mince a tiny clove of garlic with a knife. Just put the clove in and squeeze. Widely available, and cheap. You can either mince or press the garlic in the recipes that follow.

Blender. This useful gadget will help you make instant soups and spreads as well as your favorite shakes and sauces. Again, you can pick up a good used one at a secondhand store or flea market.

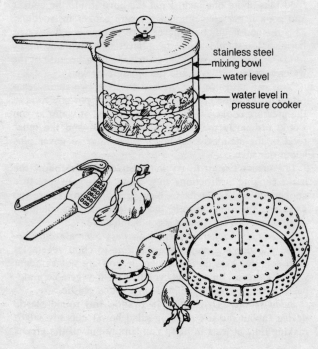

stainless steel mixing bowl

water level

water level in pressure cooker

3.

Understanding Protein Complementarity

MOST OF THE recipes that follow combine foods whose proteins are complementary. In Book One, Part III, I explained protein complementarity—how by combining certain protein foods we can create one more usable by the body than the two eaten separately. I went on to say that what I had learned since my earlier books is that concern about "complementing" our proteins is probably not necessary for most people. *Even without meat*, the average person who eats a varied diet of whole foods and only modest amounts of sugar and fat is getting his or her recommended protein allowance. Remember that stress—from disease, physical exertion, or psychological pressure—can increase your body's need for protein. But since the recommended protein allowance is higher than most people need anyway, most of us would still be covered without concern about eating complementary proteins, even under stress. Then why bother with complementary proteins?

People are different. We don't all fit the averages. Some scientists believe, for example, that current protein allowances do *not* cover 97.5 percent of the population, as they claim to. If you are an individual with an unusually high protein need, then combining foods to maximize the usable protein *is* important, especially when you are under stress.

But how do you know if you are one of those people? There is no simple answer. All you can do is observe your health and how rapidly you heal. You can try diets with different protein levels and see what feels right for you. If you feel that you have an exceptionally high need for protein, consult the tables in Appendix E to learn the best foods for upping your protein intake.

But there is another minority whose need for protein is exceptionally high—pregnant and breast-feeding women. A pregnant woman needs 30 additional grams of protein; a breast-feeding woman, 20 grams. The complementary protein recipes will be of special value to them.

So, one reason that I have stuck to complementary proteins in the recipes that follow is that they are of benefit to this minority. But the rest of us benefit, too, for complementary protein combinations make for delicious recipes—they are combinations that formed the basis of the world's traditional cuisines. We use them naturally in our cooking without even being aware of it. The three most common complementary protein combinations are:

1. Grains (rice, corn, wheat, barley, etc.) + legumes (peas, beans, lentils).
2. Grains + milk products.
3. Seeds (sesame or sunflower) + legumes.

How much more usable protein do you get by eating complementary proteins together compared to eating them separately?

No one knows precisely. For the first two editions of this book I used as my basic source *Amino Acid Content of Foods and Biological Data on Protein*, published by the Food and Agriculture Organization of the United States (Rome, 1970). I took the proportions of foods that produced the highest scores in tests with experimental animals. They indicated that when foods are combined in certain proportions as much as 50 percent more of the protein is usable by the body, compared to these same foods eaten separately. But there has been much scientific debate on the best ways to determine the usability of protein. Animal studies are now viewed as imprecise indicators of how usable a protein would be by humans. Rats, often used in these experiments, have a considerably different balance of amino acid needs. A recent book, *Nutritional Evaluation of Protein Foods* (The United Nations University World Hunger Programme, Food and Nutrition Bulletin, Supplement 4), edited by Peter L. Pellett and Vernon R. Young, describes the state of the uncertainty about the best way to determine the usability of proteins by humans. So, while we cannot pin down *exactly* how much more usable protein we get by eating certain foods in combination, as I tried to do in previous editions, it is safe to say that the increase is significant. That fact is not disputed in the scientific community. But for this edition I have deleted the charts that indicate exact proportions of complementary proteins. They give an impression of more precision than currently exists in our understanding.

Another change you'll find in this edition is that I don't refer to my recipes as "High-Protein Meatless Meals." I don't think we need to worry about "high" protein. If we get "some" protein in most of the foods we eat, we'll easily meet our protein needs.

In sum, what I've learned over ten years is that it is easier than I thought!

Part II

Meatless
Meals
in a Dish

1.

Sauces That Make a Meal

Sauces That Keep
* Korean Barbecue Sauce
* Indonesian Peanut Sauce (Gado-Gado)
* Tofu Spaghetti Sauce
* Cashew Gravy

Quick Sauces
  Fettuccine al Marco
  Mushroom Stroganoff
  Pesto Genovese-American
* Emptying the Fridge

---

*New recipe.

HERE ARE EASY-to-make sauces that can turn any combination of vegetables, pasta, your favorite grain, or sautéed tofu into a delicious dinner. Most of them keep well in the refrigerator—some for as long as two or three weeks. Others can be frozen and taken out any morning for a quick evening meal.

Korean Barbecue Sauce

About 1 cup

A favorite of Joan Donaldson-Van Voorhees of Pennville, Michigan, this is the recipe that converted my ten-year-old diehard anti-tofu son. Joan writes that "the maple flavor is what makes it special and from Michigan," but it is awfully good even with honey. Served with (or over) brown rice, it makes a meal.

1 to 4 tablespoons toasted ground sesame seeds	2 tablespoons sesame oil
3 green onions, chopped	2 tablespoons maple syrup or honey
4 cloves garlic, minced	2 to 4 tablespoons sherry
¼ cup soy sauce	⅛ teaspoon pepper

Stir or blend until thoroughly mixed. Marinate slices of tofu in the sauce for several hours, grill, and serve with sauce.

This sauce keeps for weeks in the refrigerator. Try marinating whole mushrooms in it, for a special appetizer.

Complementary protein: soy (tofu) + sesame + rice

Indonesian Peanut Sauce (Gado-Gado)

Serves 6

Public-interest lawyer Kathy Severens of Rosalie, Nebraska, served this beautiful dish to a group of friends as we sat around a picnic table in the yard of her home, a converted country schoolhouse. It's easy and quick to make, but can be very festive for special occasions. I once created a striking platter by making a bed of fresh spinach leaves and covering it with a layer of red cabbage leaves. The steamed mixed vegetables went on top, with a bowl of sauce in the center.

Traditionally Gado-Gado is served over steamed vegetables and/or grain. Choose a variety of colorful vegetables; Kathy suggests starting with leafy vegetables such as spinach or Chinese cabbage, then adding string beans, zucchini, and cauliflower. Cooked cubed potatoes are almost always included.

2 tablespoons oil
6 cloves garlic, minced
1 medium onion, finely chopped
1 tablespoon fresh grated ginger (or more, to taste)
1 teaspoon red chili powder (or more, to taste)

2 tablespoons soy sauce
¼ cup tomato sauce
Juice of ½ lime or lemon
2 cups coconut milk,* low-fat milk, or soy milk
2 cups peanut butter

Heat oil and sauté garlic and onion until onion is translucent. Add ginger and cook 2 minutes. Add remaining ingredients and cook gently 5 to 10 minutes, being careful not to let mixture burn. Serve it on vegetables, grains, or sautéed tofu.

For the best flavor, make the sauce a day ahead of serving time. It keeps well for a couple of weeks in the refrigerator.

Complementary protein: peanuts + rice or other grain

*You can use 1 cup grated or slivered unsweetened coconut soaked in 1 cup warm water for an hour.

Tofu Spaghetti Sauce

8 servings

A favorite of Bill and Akiko Shurtleff of the Soyfoods Center in Lafayette, California.

2 tablespoons oil or margarine
1 to 2 large cloves garlic, minced
2 onions, minced
21 ounces firm tofu, cut into ½-inch cubes or crumbled
10 medium mushrooms, sliced (about 1½ cups), or 1 medium zucchini, chopped (about 2½ cups)
1¼ cups chopped celery (2 to 3 stalks)
1 cup chopped carrots (2 medium)
2½ cups chopped green peppers (about 2 peppers)

10 cups peeled and chopped tomatoes, or two 8-ounce cans tomato sauce and one 6-ounce can tomato paste
1 teaspoon salt (if using fresh tomatoes)
3 tablespoons soy sauce
2 tablespoons honey
1½ bay leaves
1 teaspoon basil
½ teaspoon oregano
Dash thyme
Dash marjoram

In a large skillet or heavy pot, heat oil and sauté garlic and onions for 1 minute. Add tofu and sauté 4 to 5 minutes. Add mushrooms and sauté 1 minute. Add remaining ingredients, bring to a boil, and simmer over low heat for 1 hour, stirring frequently.* For best flavor, refrigerate overnight to let flavors marry. Remove bay leaf, reheat, and serve over hot pasta. If desired, sprinkle with Parmesan cheese.

Complementary protein: soy (tofu) + wheat

*If you are using canned tomato sauce, simmering can be for as little as 10 minutes.

Cashew Gravy

1½ cups gravy

Inspired by a recipe from Barbara Cuomo of Freedom, Maine. Heat and serve over your favorite vegetables with grain or pasta.

½ cup cashews	1 teaspoon lemon juice
½ cup water	2 tablespoons whole wheat flour
2 tablespoons nonfat milk powder	2 tablespoons grated coconut (optional)

Process in a blender until smooth. Adjust consistency by adding water.

Complementary protein: nuts + grain

Fettuccine al Marco

4 servings

This dish may not be as rich-tasting as Fettuccine Alfredo, but it has a lot fewer calories and a lot more protein—and it is delicious!

½ pound fettuccine or other noodles*	½ cup parsley
1½ cups ricotta or cottage cheese	2 cups spinach leaves (optional*)
¼ cup Parmesan cheese	Salt and pepper to taste
½ cup yogurt	Garnish: your choice of herbs (such as fresh basil), and sliced black olives or fresh parsley

Start cooking the pasta. In a blender, process cheeses, yogurt, parsley, spinach, and salt and pepper until very smooth. When pasta is al dente, drain and toss with sauce. Garnish with herbs and olives and serve immediately.

Complementary protein: wheat + milk products

---

*Spinach noodles provide an attractive contrast if you make the sauce without spinach leaves; otherwise, use white pasta for contrast.

Mushroom Stroganoff

4 servings

With a favorite green salad and Italian dressing, this may be the most elegant "instant" dish you've ever made.

½ pound flat egg noodles	2 tablespoons fresh or 1 tablespoon dried parsley
1 tablespoon margarine	3 dashes Worcestershire sauce
1 small onion, finely chopped	1 cup cottage cheese
½ pound mushrooms, halved (if small, leave some whole)	½ cup yogurt
1 to 2 cloves garlic, crushed	Salt and pepper to taste
	Garnish: fresh parsley

Start cooking the noodles. Heat the margarine and sauté the onion, mushrooms, and garlic until onion is translucent;

add parsley when onion is almost done. Stir in Worcestershire sauce. In a blender, process cottage cheese, yogurt, and salt and pepper until smooth. Remove vegetables from heat and stir in blender mixture. Serve immediately over hot noodles and garnish with more parsley.

Complementary protein: wheat + milk products

Pesto Genovese-American

6 servings

This dish has a subtle and absolutely unique flavor—especially when served with hot or sweet marinated Italian peppers and garlic bread.

½ cup olive oil
2 cloves garlic
3 tablespoons pignolia nuts or
sunflower seeds
¼ teaspoon pepper

2 cups chopped fresh basil
1 cup freshly grated Parmesan cheese or ½ cup commercial grated Parmesan
1 pound linguine

In a covered blender, process oil and garlic on high speed until smooth. Let stand for 15 minutes. Remove inner cap or cover of blender and gradually add nuts and pepper, blending until smooth. A little at a time, add basil. Stir mixture down with a thin scraper (turn blender off first) and add Parmesan cheese. Cook linguine and drain, reserving ½ cup cooking water. Toss linguine with reserved water, transfer to a large heated platter, pour on sauce, and toss with two forks until evenly blended. Serve with additional grated Parmesan, if you wish.

Complementary protein: nuts + wheat + milk products

Emptying the Fridge

3 servings

This recipe is a variation on San Franciscan Terry Gilbreath-Hart's suggestion for a quick and tasty way to use just about any leftover vegetables you have on hand. The essence is a delicious white sauce that lends itself to endless adaptation. The cabbage and carrots called for here were what happened to be in *my* refrigerator.

Oil for sautéing
1 onion, chopped
½ head cabbage, coarsely chopped
2 carrots, coarsely chopped
¾ teaspoon grated fresh ginger
1 tablespoon soy sauce
1 clove garlic, minced
Pepper to taste

2 tablespoons flour
2 tablespoons margarine
½ cup low-fat condensed milk
½ cup low-fat milk
1/3 to ½ cup yogurt
¼ cup Parmesan cheese
Salt and pepper to taste
Garnish: ¼ cup toasted sesame seeds or chopped walnuts

Heat oil in a large skillet and sauté vegetables until barely tender. Add ginger, soy sauce, garlic, and pepper. In a saucepan, brown flour in margarine and add milk, a little at a time, stirring until sauce rethickens between each addition. Take sauce off the heat and add yogurt, Parmesan cheese, and salt and pepper, if necessary. Stir sauce into vegetables. Garnish and serve over noodles, rice, or boiled spinach.

Complementary protein: milk + grain

2.

Something from the Oven

Baked Italian
* * Spinach Lasagne Special
* * East-Meets-West Lasagne
* Ricotta Lasagne Swirls
* Spaghetti for Peanuts

With a Mexican Flavor
* * Enchiladas Gomez Style
* Enchilada Bake
* Easy Mexican Pan Bread
* * South of the Border Bake

Vegetable Bake
* * Baked Stuffed Anything
* Sue's Famous Vegetable Squares
* Spinach-Rice Pot
* Sesame Eggplant Parmesan

Bean Bake
* * Bolinas Soyburgers
* Broiled Falafel Patties
* Savory Stuffed Peppers
* Garbanzo Bake

Cheese Bake (mostly low-fat)
* * Pasticcio
* * Greek Cheese and Spinach Wedges
* Noodle-Cheese "Soufflé"
* Golden Parsley Potatoes

---

*New recipe.

WHILE THE COOKING time for these dishes may be longer than for stove-top meals, your actual work time is no greater. Most can be easily adapted to the food you have on hand. Remember, never feel you have to follow the recipe to the letter; just try to keep the major protein ingredients the same or in the same proportion. After trying just a few, you will see that none of them deserve that drab old label, "casserole."

Spinach Lasagne Special

6 to 8 servings

What's special about this lasagne is that it calls for no tomato sauce and uses low-fat cheese, so that its taste isn't heavy. Peggy Ritter of Bellingham, Washington, won "Best Entree" in a nutritional-awareness contest with it. Her recipe calls for 3 eggs combined with the cheese mixture. I eliminated the eggs to cut down on cholesterol; you can achieve their congealing effect by adding 2 or 3 egg whites.

2–3 tablespoons oil
½ pound lasagne noodles (about 12 noodles)
2 cloves garlic, minced
1 medium onion, chopped
2 tomatoes, chopped
10 medium mushrooms, sliced
½ teaspoon each oregano, basil, and rosemary

2 tablespoons chopped fresh parsley
1 pound spinach, washed, drained, and chopped
1 cup low-fat cottage cheese
½ cup grated Parmesan cheese
8 to 10 ounces grated mozzarella cheese

Cook noodles until al dente, drain, and set aside. Preheat oven to 350°F.

Heat oil in a big skillet and sauté garlic, onion, tomatoes, and mushrooms. When onion is translucent, add herbs and spinach, stirring until spinach is wilted. Simmer.

Reserving ½ cup mozzarella cheese, in a large bowl combine cheeses. Pour vegetables into cheese mixture and mix thoroughly. Layer noodles alternately with vegetable-cheese mixture in an 8x13-inch baking pan. Top with reserved mozzarella and more Parmesan cheese, if desired. Bake for ½ hour. Let sit 5 to 10 minutes before serving.

Complementary protein: milk products + grain

East-Meets-West Lasagne

6 to 8 servings

A nondairy favorite of Bill and Akiko Shurtleff of the Soyfoods Center in Lafayette, California, who point out that "tofu takes the place of ricotta cheese and provides protein complementarity for the lasagne." Delicious hot or cold.

8 ounces whole wheat lasagne noodles
2 tablespoons oil for sautéing
1 clove garlic, minced
1 onion, chopped
8 ounces mushrooms, sliced (about 10 medium)
2 cups chopped celery
1 green pepper, chopped
2½ cups tomato sauce (two and a half 8-ounce cans)
1¼ cups tomato paste (two 6-ounce cans)
2 tablespoons soy sauce
2 tablespoons honey
1 teaspoon each cumin, basil, and oregano
28 ounces firm tofu, mashed

Cook noodles, drain, and set aside. Preheat oven to 350°F.

Heat oil in a skillet and sauté garlic for 30 seconds. Add onion and mushrooms and sauté 3 to 4 minutes. Add celery and green pepper and sauté 3 minutes. Add remaining ingredients except tofu, bring to a boil, and simmer 3 minutes. Spread a third of this sauce in the bottom of a 9x13-inch baking dish. On top of it put half the noodles, then half the tofu. (Sprinkle on 1 tablespoon nutritional yeast, if desired.) Repeat the layers of sauce, noodles, and tofu (and optional yeast). Top with the remaining tomato sauce. Bake 25 to 30 minutes.

Complementary protein: soy (tofu) + wheat

Ricotta Lasagne Swirls

4 servings

This is an especially attractive dish, and it is much lighter than most Italian-style pasta dishes. Serve with a green salad and garlic bread.

8 lasagne noodles	Oil for sautéing
2 pounds spinach	2 cloves garlic, minced
2 tablespoons Parmesan cheese	½ cup chopped onion
1 cup ricotta cheese (½ pound)	2 cups tomato sauce
¼ teaspoon nutmeg	½ teaspoon basil
Salt and pepper to taste	½ teaspoon oregano

Cook noodles until al dente, drain, and set aside. Preheat oven to 350°F.

Wash spinach, put in a pan with a tight-fitting lid, and steam over low heat until it is limp but not mushy, about 7 minutes. Chop and mix with the cheeses, nutmeg, and salt and pepper. Coat each noodle with 2 to 3 tablespoons of the mixture along its entire length, roll up, stand on end, and put in a shallow baking pan. Heat oil, sauté garlic and onion until onion is translucent, mix with tomato sauce, herbs, and salt and pepper to taste, and pour this sauce over the rolled-up noodles. Bake for 20 minutes.

You can substitute your favorite prepared spaghetti sauce for the sauce suggested here.

Complementary protein: wheat + milk products

Spaghetti for Peanuts

4 servings

This dish makes a great supper with a tossed green salad and/or any fresh green vegetable, steamed or sautéed.

2 cups broken spaghetti (preferably whole wheat)	2 cups buttermilk or low-fat milk
2 to 4 tablespoons margarine	½ onion, finely chopped
3 tablespoons whole wheat flour	3 drops hot pepper sauce
½ teaspoon salt (optional)	½ cup sliced black olives
1 teaspoon dry mustard	1 cup grated cheddar cheese
¼ teaspoon pepper	1 cup chopped peanuts
	Topping: 1/3 cup bread crumbs

Cook spaghetti until tender, drain, and set aside. Preheat oven to 350°F.

Heat margarine in a medium saucepan and add flour, salt, mustard, and pepper; stir until flour is browned. Add buttermilk, onion, and pepper sauce and stir until thickened. Put half the spaghetti in a casserole and top with half the olives, cheese, and peanuts. Repeat layers. Pour sauce on top and sprinkle with bread crumbs. Bake for 25 minutes.

Complementary protein: legume (peanuts) + milk and
milk product + wheat

Enchiladas Gomez Style

6 servings (2 enchiladas each)

Inspired by a favorite recipe of Bob Gomez of Berkeley.

12 corn tortillas
1 pound firm tofu
3 zucchinis
Two 6-ounce cans tomato paste
2 cups water
One 10-ounce can tomatillos or
    whole tomatoes, undrained

One 4-ounce can whole green
    chilis
1 large onion, chopped
2 to 3 cloves garlic, minced
1½ tablespoons curry powder
1 tablespoon oregano or basil
8 ounces Monterey jack cheese,
    grated
2 large carrots, grated

Steam tortillas individually. Preheat oven to 350°F.

Slice tofu into 12 strips, each about 1½ ounces. Slice zucchinis lengthwise into 12 strips and steam until tender.* In a blender at medium speed, briefly process (in batches, if necessary) tomato paste, water, tomatillos, chilis, onion, garlic, curry powder, and oregano. Dip each tortilla in this sauce and lay flat in a large casserole. On each put 1 strip tofu, 1 slice zucchini, ½ ounce cheese, and about 2 tablespoons carrot. Roll up. Pack the filled tortillas in the casserole and pour the remaining sauce over them. Sprinkle on the remaining cheese and bake for ½ hour.

Complementary protein: soy (tofu) + corn + milk product

---

*Steaming is not necessary, but otherwise the baking time must be increased.

Enchilada Bake

4 servings

This dish goes well with a fruit salad. Try the Fine Fruit Salad for a pleasant taste contrast.

Oil for sautéing
1 onion, chopped
1 clove garlic, minced
5 to 6 mushrooms, sliced
1 green pepper, chopped
1 small can corn (optional)
1½ cups cooked kidney or pinto beans (½ cup uncooked) or 1 pound tofu (squeeze out water with a towel), crumbled
1½ cups stewed tomatoes
1 tablespoon chili powder
1 teaspoon ground cumin
½ cup red wine
Salt to taste
6 to 8 corn tortillas
½ to 1 cup grated Monterey jack or other cheese
½ to 1 cup combined ricotta cheese and yogurt, or blended cottage cheese and yogurt
Garnish: black olives

Preheat oven to 350°F. Heat oil in a large skillet and sauté onion, garlic, mushrooms, green pepper, and corn. Add beans, tomatoes, spices, wine, and salt and simmer 30 minutes. Put a layer of tortillas in an oiled casserole. Top with a layer of sauce, 3 tablespoons grated cheese, and 3 tablespoons cheese-yogurt mixture. Repeat layers, ending with a layer of sauce. Add a little of the cheese-yogurt mixture and garnish with olives. Bake for 15 to 20 minutes.

Complementary protein: beans + corn + milk products

Easy Mexican Pan Bread

6 servings

I've gotten letters from people telling me how much they liked this recipe. With a fresh salad (try putting in some avocado), it can be a light meal in itself. If you are serving a crowd, make this along with other dishes with a Mexican touch. Using dark beans—kidney or black beans—makes it colorful.

½ cup dry beans	1 tablespoon chili powder (or more to taste)
2 tablespoons oil for sautéing plus 2 tablespoons more	½ teaspoon ground cumin
1 large onion, chopped	1 green pepper, diced (optional)
2 cloves garlic, minced	½ teaspoon salt
1 egg, beaten	1/3 cup grated Monterey jack or other cheese
1 cup cornmeal	¼ cup sliced black olives
2 teaspoons baking powder	Garnish: chopped fresh onion and/ or tomato (optional)

Cook beans with extra water; drain, reserving ¾ cup of the cooking liquid. Preheat oven to 350°F.

Heat oil in an ovenproof skillet and sauté onion and garlic until onion is translucent. Remove half the onion and garlic to a bowl and add the cooked beans and reserved liquid, egg, 2 tablespoons oil, cornmeal, baking powder, chili powder, cumin, green pepper, and salt. Mix well and return to the skillet, but do not stir—the onion should stay on the bottom. Bake for about 15 minutes. Just before it is done, sprinkle with grated cheese and olives, and continue baking until the cheese melts. Garnish before serving.

Complementary protein: beans + corn + milk product

South of the Border Bake

4 servings

A favorite of Chynna Goldstein of Mill Valley, California, who writes: "I usually double the recipe so that I have enough for two meals . . . that is, if we don't make pigs of ourselves and eat it all the first time around. Delicious with green salad and whole wheat sourdough French bread." Elinor Blake, who adapted this recipe for the book, says, "It looks beautiful when cooked—soufflé-like—and tastes wonderful."

Oil for sautéing
1 small onion, chopped
2 eggs or 3 egg whites
2 cups low-fat milk
1 cup shredded sharp cheddar cheese
1 cup raw whole-kernel corn
¾ cup garbanzo beans (chickpeas)
¼ cup chopped seeded green chilis
5 corn tortillas (6-inch diameter), cut in quarters
½ cup grated sharp cheddar cheese
1 cup chopped tomatoes
¼ cup chopped fresh parsley (optional)

Preheat oven to 350°F. Heat oil and sauté the onion until translucent. Beat the eggs in a bowl and add the milk, shredded cheddar, corn, beans, chilis, and sautéed onion. Line the bottom and sides of a 10-inch glass pie pan with tortilla pieces and fill with mixture in bowl. Sprinkle with grated cheddar, tomatoes, and parsley. Bake until firm in the center and brown on top, about 40 to 45 minutes.

Complementary protein: beans + corn + milk and milk product

Baked Stuffed Anything

2 to 3 servings

A creation of Mary Sinclair of Albany, California, and Julie Rosenbaum of Ann Arbor, Michigan, both of whom helped test many of the recipes in this book. Serve with a green salad and crusty French bread.

1 medium eggplant or 2 large zucchinis or 1 medium squash
2 tablespoons oil for sautéing
1 onion, chopped
1 green pepper, diced
4 mushrooms, sliced
1 clove garlic, minced
½ teaspoon coriander

¼ teaspoon cumin
Black pepper
Few dashes Tabasco sauce or ¼ teaspoon cayenne pepper
½ cup cooked rice
½ cup low-fat cottage cheese
¼ cup chopped fresh parsley
3 tablespoons pignolia nuts or sunflower seeds

Cut the eggplant in half and scoop out the flesh. Set the shells aside. Preheat oven to 350°F.

Heat oil in a skillet and sauté the eggplant flesh, onion, green pepper, mushrooms, garlic, spices, and Tabasco for about 15 minutes. Turn off the heat, let cool 2 to 3 minutes, and add the rice, cottage cheese, parsley, and nuts. Mix well. Put the eggplant shells in a shallow baking dish and fill with sautéed mixture. Cover with foil and bake for 45 minutes. Remove the foil and bake another 10 minutes.

Complementary protein: rice + milk product + nuts

Sue's Famous Vegetable Squares

5 to 6 servings

Sue Kanor of Hastings-on-Hudson, New York, was the "artist in the kitchen" who helped develop many of the recipes for the 1975 edition of this book. Lots of fresh parsley and celery give these squares a light taste that is irresistible.

1¼ cups combined soybeans and raw peanuts, cooked together (about 1/3 cup uncooked beans and ¼ cup peanuts)
4 tablespoons margarine
4 stalks celery, minced
2 carrots, grated
¼ pound mushrooms, chopped

1 onion, minced
½ cup chopped fresh parsley
½ to 1 cup coarsely chopped walnuts
½ cup wheat germ
1 egg
¼ cup water or Seasoned Stock
Salt and pepper or soy sauce to taste

Preheat oven to 350°F. In a blender, grind the cooked soybeans and peanuts. In a large saucepan, melt margarine and sauté celery and carrots for 5 minutes. Add mushrooms and onion and cook until onion is translucent. Turn off heat and add soybean-peanut mixture, parsley, nuts, wheat germ, egg, water, and salt and pepper. Add more water if necessary; the mixture should have the consistency of loose stuffing. Pack the mixture into a shallow pan in a layer no more than ¾ inch high. Bake until the loaf is dry, about 30 minutes. Cool for a few minutes and cut into 2- to 3-inch squares. To complete the protein complementary, serve with rice and/or bulgur.

Complementary protein: soy + peanuts + wheat + rice

Variation: Add this simple mushroom cream sauce for a truly elegant dish.

Mushroom Cream Sauce

2 cups mushrooms, sliced thin
2 tablespoons margarine
1 tablespoon flour

1½ cups low-fat milk
Salt and pepper to taste
Dash of Worcestershire sauce

Sauté mushrooms in margarine until soft. Add flour to coat the mushrooms and stir; cook to toast the flour. Add milk, salt and pepper, and Worcestershire sauce. Stir over heat until sauce thickens.

Complementary protein: wheat + milk

Spinach-Rice Pot

4 servings

I once made this casserole on a TV talk show, and the stage crew loved it. Serve it with a contrasting vegetable, such as sautéed carrots or yellow squash.

2 cups cooked brown rice (¾ cup uncooked)
¾ cup grated cheddar cheese
2 eggs, beaten
2 tablespoons chopped fresh parsley

½ teaspoon salt
¼ teaspoon pepper
1 pound fresh spinach, chopped
2 tablespoons wheat germ
1 tablespoon melted margarine

Preheat oven to 350°F. Combine rice and cheese. In a separate bowl combine eggs, parsley, salt, and pepper. Add the two mixtures to the spinach and pour into an oiled casserole. Mix wheat germ and magarine and spread on top. Bake for 35 minutes.

Complementary protein: rice + wheat + milk product

Sesame Eggplant Parmesan

4 servings

Even eggplant haters like this dish. It is easy, but elegant enough for guests. A meal by itself with a fresh green salad, it can become a heartier dinner if you add your favorite pasta or rice as a side dish, or as a bottom layer under the eggplant.

Oil for sautéing
1 medium eggplant, sliced ½ inch thick
2 cups marinara or spaghetti sauce
¼ teaspoon each oregano, thyme, and rosemary (optional)

½ onion, grated
½ green pepper, grated
1 carrot, grated
¼ cup grated Parmesan cheese
½ cup toasted ground sesame seeds
½ pound mozzarella cheese, sliced

Preheat oven to 350°F. Heat oil in a skillet and sauté eggplant slices until browned and becoming soft. Remove eggplant and add to skillet the sauce, herbs, onion, green pepper, carrot, Parmesan cheese, and sesame seeds. Simmer 15 minutes. Arrange the eggplant slices on a large ovenproof platter or in a shallow 2-quart casserole. Cover with sauce and top with mozzarella slices. Bake for about 15 minutes.

Complementary protein: sesame seeds + milk products

Bolinas Soyburgers

4 servings

Elizabeth Rivers of Bolinas, California, adapted these burgers from the Soybean Croquette recipe in the 1975 edition of this book. She developed them to please her kids, and says, "Kids love these—even when they hate 'health food.' "

1 cup cooked soybeans (½ cup uncooked) or 1 cup soybean sprouts
½ cup peanuts
½ cup walnuts (optional)
3 tablespoons tomato paste
1 onion, cut in chunks
½ cup bread crumbs
3 tablespoons oil (optional)
1 tablespoon soy sauce
3 cloves garlic
½ teaspoon chopped chili pepper
Juice of 1 lemon or 1 tablespoon vinegar
¼ to ½ cup chopped fresh parsley
1 egg, beaten
Up to ¼ cup water
2 tablespoons sesame seeds
Coating: bread crumbs or wheat germ

Mash soybeans. Preheat oven to 350°F.

Leaving some chunks for texture, in a blender process the peanuts, walnuts, tomato paste, onion, bread crumbs, oil, soy sauce, garlic, chili pepper, lemon juice, parsley, egg, and water. Remove from the blender and stir in sesame seeds and mashed soybeans. Mold into burgers, roll in bread crumbs, and put on a baking sheet. Bake for 40 minutes. Serve in pita bread with lettuce and tomato, or shredded cabbage with guacamole or hot tomato sauce (salsa). Before they're all gone, stick some of the burgers in the freezer for a quick meal later.

Complementary protein: soybeans + peanuts + sesame + wheat

Broiled Falafel Patties

About ten 3-inch patties

Falafel is a traditional Middle Eastern food. We added the complementary protein (milk) without losing the special original flavor.

2 cups cooked garbanzos (¾ cup uncooked)
½ cup parsley clusters
¼ cup sesame butter
2 cloves garlic, minced
¼ cup dry milk
1 egg, beaten with 1 tablespoon water

½ teaspoon dry mustard
1 teaspoon cumin
½ teaspoon chili powder
Celery salt to taste
Salt and pepper to taste
1 teaspoon Worcestershire sauce
Oil as needed

Preheat oven to 350°F. Purée the beans and parsley in a blender, then put mixture in a mixing bowl and add remaining ingredients except oil. Mix well and spoon by tablespoonsful onto an oiled baking sheet. Flatten each patty and brush with oil. Bake until crusty and golden, about 15 minutes, or broil for a few minutes on each side, basting with more oil if necessary. Serve with lettuce and tomato and tahini (seasame butter), or put in warm pita bread (or any sandwich bun) that has been slit open, with lettuce on top and a little mayonnaise-ketchup or Thousand Island dressing. (Make bite-size patties for great hors d'oeuvres.)

Complementary protein: beans + sesame + milk

Savory Stuffed Peppers

6 servings

Pinto beans are good in this.

2¼ cups cooked beans (1 cup
uncooked)

2 tablespoons oil for sautéing

½ onion, chopped

1 cup chopped celery

¾ cup bean sprouts (optional)

2 cups canned tomatoes (drain
and reserve liquid) or 3 fresh
tomatoes, chopped

One 12-ounce can corn

½ teaspoon basil

1 tablespoon chopped fresh
parsley

1 teaspoon each dillweed and
cayenne pepper (or less, to
taste)

¼ teaspoon cumin

Salt to taste

6 green peppers, seeds and
membranes removed

2/3 cup grated Monterey jack or
other cheese

Preheat oven to 400°F. Mash beans. Heat oil in a skillet and sauté onion, celery, and bean sprouts. Stir in tomatoes, tomato liquid, corn, mashed beans, herbs, cayenne pepper, cumin, and salt; add additional liquid if the mixture is very dry. Fill the peppers with the stuffing, top with cheese, and put in a pan, adding an inch of water (to keep peppers from burning). Bake for 25 to 30 minutes, replenishing water in pan if necessary.

Complementary protein: beans + milk product

Garbanzo Bake

4 servings

This hearty, rich-tasting loaf is easy to prepare. A favorite from the 1975 edition, it goes well with any steamed or sautéed vegetable and is good hot or cold, or as a sandwich spread. For a really hearty meal, serve it with your favorite cooked grain.

2 cups cooked garbanzos (2/3 cup uncooked)
2 cups bread crumbs (preferably whole wheat; stale bread is fine)
1½ cups hot Seasoned Stock
2 tablespoons oil for sautéing
2 onions, chopped
1 small can water chestnuts (optional)

½ cup sesame seed meal
2 tablespoons sesame butter
¼ teaspoon each thyme, coriander, and nutmeg
1 bay leaf
¼ cup chopped fresh parsley
½ teaspoon salt
3 tablespoons soy sauce
2/3 cup grated Monterey jack or other cheese

Preheat oven to 325°F. Mash beans and set aside. Soak bread crumbs in hot stock. Heat oil in a skillet and sauté onions and water chestnuts until onions are translucent. Add sesame seed meal and sesame butter and sauté until lightly browned. In a bowl, combine bread crumbs with sauté mixture and add herbs, salt, soy sauce, and mashed beans. Put in a loaf pan and bake for 20 minutes, sprinkle cheese on top, and bake another 10 minutes.

Complementary protein: beans + sesame seeds + wheat + milk product

Pasticcio

3 to 4 servings

A favorite recipe of Sue Pohl, Hillsdale, Michigan. Serve with a Greek salad or your favorite tossed salad.

½ pound macaroni
1 cup lentils
1 small onion, chopped
2 medium carrots, finely chopped or grated
2–3 cloves garlic, minced
1 tablespoon soy sauce
½ teaspoon rosemary
2¼ cups water

2 cups low-fat cottage cheese
¼ cup whole wheat flour
½ cup grated Parmesan cheese
1 egg
1 cup low-fat milk
1 teaspoon salt (optional)
½ teaspoon nutmeg
1 teaspoon cinnamon
Topping: wheat or bran flakes or bread crumbs

Cook macaroni until al dente, drain, and set aside. Preheat oven to 350°F.

In a saucepan, cook lentils with ½ cup onion, carrots, garlic, soy sauce, rosemary, and water until water is absorbed (about 20 minutes). In a bowl, combine cottage cheese and flour and add the rest of the onion and the Parmesan cheese, egg, milk, salt, nutmeg, and cinnamon.

Pour half the macaroni into a 9x9-inch baking pan or casserole. Pour over it a third of the cheese sauce, then make a lentil layer, topped with another third of the sauce. Add remaining macaroni and top with remaining sauce. Sprinkle on topping for a crusty texture. Bake for 35 minutes or until browned.

Complementary protein: wheat + milk and milk products + legume

Greek Cheese and Spinach Wedges

6 to 8 servings

Simpler than a quiche, this dish has a distinctive and rich taste. It was improved from the 1975 edition by Myra Levy and Charles Varon of San Francisco.

2 or 3 egg whites	¼ pound feta cheese, crumbled
2 cups part-skim-milk ricotta cheese	1 pound spinach, washed and chopped or torn
1/3 cup whole wheat flour	Garnish: black olives, halved

Preheat oven to 350°F. Beat egg whites, ricotta cheese, and flour until smooth. Add feta cheese and spinach and mix thoroughly. Pack into a large pie plate or baking dish and garnish. Bake for approximately 45 minutes.

Complementary protein: wheat + milk products

Noodle-Cheese "Souffle"

6 to 8 servings

This is a delicious and elegant dish. Serve it with green peas and a fresh fruit salad (chopped apples, bananas, oranges, etc.) with a yogurt and honey dressing.

½ pound whole wheat or wheat-soy noodles	1 pound cottage cheese (about 2 cups)
3 eggs, separated	1 cup yogurt
¼ cup butter, melted (optional)	½ to 1 cup raisins (optional)
2 tablespoons honey	Topping: whole wheat bread crumbs or wheat germ
	Butter

Cook noodles, drain, and set aside. Preheat oven to 375°F.

Beat egg yolks and mix with butter, honey, cottage

cheese, and yogurt. Beat egg whites until stiff and fold into yolk-cheese-yogurt mixture, along with raisins and noodles. Sprinkle on topping and dot with butter. Bake for 45 minutes.

Complementary protein: wheat + milk products

Golden Parsley Potatoes

4 servings

For a light dinner, I serve this with a spinach salad containing red onion, sliced beets, and other leftover cold vegetables. This simple dish is easy to prepare and beautiful to see.

1 pound potatoes, unpeeled	1 cup cottage cheese
1 cup grated cheddar cheese	1 tablespoon dried parsley
2 onions, sliced	Salt and pepper to taste
1 or 2 eggs	Topping: chopped fresh parsley

Preheat oven to 350°F. Cook potatoes until tender and slice. In a small casserole, layer potatoes, cheddar cheese, and onions. In a blender or by hand, thoroughly mix the egg, cottage cheese, dried parsley, and salt and pepper. Pour sauce over potatoes and cheese. Bake until golden, about 20 to 30 minutes. Top with chopped fresh parsley.

Complementary protein: potatoes + milk products

3.

International Meals from the Top of the Stove

Indian curry flavors
* Sabji (Lentil Curry)
* Summer Curry
  Song of India Rice
* Fried Spiced Tofu

Chinese style
* Sweet and Sour Tofu
  Super Sweet and Sour Tempeh
* Chinese Cabbage, Northern China Style

Latin style
* Joan's Brazilian Rice
  Spanish Bulgur

Other cultures
* Mjeddrah
  Greek-Style Skillet with Mint
  Roman Rice and Beans
  Potato Latkes
  Sweet and Sour Stuffed Cabbage

All-American
* Homemade Tofu Burgers
  Creamed Celery Sauté

---

*New recipe.

THESE MEALS ARE simple to prepare. Many take very little time at all (especially if you have leftover rice and/or beans in the refrigerator or freezer). They underline my advice given earlier: the real trick in saving time (besides using a pressure cooker) is always to cook at least twice the amount of beans that you are going to use for the recipe and freeze what you don't use. Grains will keep for several days in the refrigerator. If, however, you have a pressure cooker, you can cook the rice in the 20 minutes or so that it will take you to sauté the vegetables, set the table, etc. I'm sure that if you use a pressure cooker or use already cooked grains and legumes, none of these recipes will take more than 30 minutes.

To guide you in your own creations, here are the easiest ways to get more usable protein into your top-of-the-stove dishes: with grains, use soy grits (just cook them along with the grain), any milk product (milk, nonfat dry milk, yogurt, cheese, etc.), or sunflower or ground sesame seeds. With grain, beans, peas and lentils, use any milk product or seeds. With peanuts, use seeds.

Sabji (Lentil Curry)

4 servings

A favorite recipe of Deborah Wheeler of Mar Vista, California. She writes: "Have a curry party—you supply the rice and curry and have each guest bring several condiments. Once we had 23 different condiments!"

Deborah Bridge of Orono, Maine, sent a similar recipe (she added the cauliflower)—and the Indian name, Sabji. She learned the recipe from Indian friends, and writes that it evokes memories of "long evenings discussing Indian culture, disarmament, reform, revolutionary movements, chatting and watching TV . . . That was the real beginning of my political education and commitment to hungry people here and in developing nations. This recipe is a favorite from that year."

1 cup lentils or waxed dahl (yellow split peas)	1 to 2 cloves garlic, minced
¼ teaspoon salt	2 tablespoons Indian curry powder
¾ cup brown rice	1 cup fresh or frozen peas
¼ cup soy grits	Cayenne pepper to taste
3 tablespoons oil for sautéing	1 cup yogurt
2 cups chopped onions	½ cucumber, chopped
½ head cauliflower, broken into pieces and coarsely chopped (optional)	Condiments: chutney, raisins, chopped nuts, coconut

Cook lentils and salt in 2 cups water until they lose their distinct shape, about 25 minutes. In another pot, cook rice and soy grits in 2 cups water, about 30 to 45 minutes. Heat oil in a large skillet and sauté onions, cauliflower, and garlic until onions are translucent. Stir in curry powder, sauté briefly, and add lentils, peas, cayenne pepper, and water as needed, about ¼ cup. Simmer about 15 minutes. In a small bowl, combine yogurt and cucumber.

To serve, put condiments in bowls on the table. Serve lentils over rice, with a generous dollop of yogurt-cucumber sauce for coolness. Everyone chooses their own condiments.

Instead of prepared curry powder, Deborah Bridge adds to the sauté mixture 2 teaspoons each coriander, mustard, and cumin seeds and 1 teaspoon whole red chili peppers, and stirs in 1 teaspoon turmeric before the last 15 minutes of cooking.

Complementary protein: lentils + rice

Summer Curry

6 servings

A favorite of Ping Ho and Doris Harkson of Palo Alto, California.

5 cups cooked brown rice (2 cups uncooked)
1 cup toasted sunflower seeds
1 cup raisins
1½ cups orange juice
¾ teaspoon nutmeg
1½ teaspoons Indian curry powder (or more to taste)

3 zucchinis, sliced
3 carrots, sliced
3 Pippin or tart apples, cored and chopped
3 bananas, sliced
1 cup yogurt
Grated rind of 2 oranges

Mix rice, sunflower seeds, raisins, orange juice, nutmeg, and curry powder and heat just to warm through. Steam zucchinis, carrots, and apples until barely tender and add bananas. Serve vegetable-fruit mixture over rice. Top each serving with yogurt and orange rind.

Complementary protein: rice + sunflower seeds + milk product

Song of India Rice

3 to 4 servings

Green peas make a good accompaniment to this dish; or, to be traditional, serve cooked yellow lentils (dahl).

1 tablespoon margarine
1 tablespoon curry powder
½ cup cashews and raisins
1 onion, sliced
1 apple, cored and sliced

3 cups cooked brown rice and soy grits (granules) (about 1¼ cups uncooked rice and 2 tablespoons soy grits)
Salt and pepper to taste
Yogurt

Heat margarine and sauté curry powder, cashews and raisins, onion, and apple. Add rice and grits and salt and pepper and mix well. Serve with yogurt.

Variations: Cook rice and soy grits with the raisins and part of the curry powder; the raisins plump up and the rice absorbs the flavor of the curry.

Add 1 teaspoon coriander seeds.

Instead of cashews, raisins, and apple, try 1 cup chopped mixed dried fruit and 1 cup mixed nuts, including some ground sesame seeds. Reduce curry powder by ¼ to ½ teaspoon and substitute the same amount of cloves.

Complementary protein: rice + nuts + soy + milk product

Fried Spiced Tofu

3 to 4 servings

A favorite of Eric Dunder of Greenbush, Maine. We served this at an Institute potluck while testing recipes for the Tenth Anniversary Edition. It was gone in minutes.

1 pound tofu	2 cloves garlic, minced
1 tablespoon oil	2 tablespoons soy sauce
½ teaspoon turmeric	⅛ cup nutritional yeast
½ teaspoon each sweet basil, thyme, ground cumin, and curry powder	

Drain tofu, pat dry, and cut into ½-inch cubes. Heat oil (in a wok, if you have one) and sauté tofu over high heat for 5 minutes. Pour out excess water, reduce heat, and add turmeric; stir until tofu is uniformly yellow and add basil, thyme, cumin, and curry powder. Add garlic (and perhaps a little more oil to prevent sticking) and increase heat; then add soy sauce and yeast. Sauté until golden brown. Taste and add more soy sauce, if desired.

Good hot or cold in sandwiches or tacos, or as a side dish.

Complementary protein: soy (tofu) + grain

Sweet and Sour Tofu

4 servings

Diane Brenner of Greenbush, Maine, submitted this recipe in a special recipe contest at the University of Maine, held to help find great meals for this edition.

1 cup pineapple juice
¼ cup soy sauce
¼ cup vinegar
¼ cup crushed tomatoes
1 tablespoon cornstarch or arrowroot powder
1 teaspoon ginger

2 pounds tofu
3 tablespoons sesame or other oil
2 green peppers, sliced in 2-inch strips
1 carrot, thinly sliced
One 20-ounce can pineapple chunks

Drain pineapple, reserving 1 cup of the juice, and set aside. In a bowl, mix pineapple juice, soy sauce, vinegar, tomatoes, cornstarch, and ginger. Drain tofu, pat dry, and slice into 1-inch cubes. Heat oil and sauté tofu for 10 minutes. Add peppers and carrots and sauté for 3 minutes. Add sauce to the sauté mixture and cook, stirring, until sauce thickens but carrots are still somewhat crisp, about 5 minutes. Add pineapple chunks and heat through. Serve over brown rice.

Complementary protein: soy (tofu) + grain

Super Sweet and Sour Tempeh

4 servings

Less well known to Americans than tofu, tempeh is a fermented soy food with a firmer texture and, many think, a more interesting taste. Not only is this sweet and sour sauce different from the preceding one, but the cooking method is different. Coating the tempeh before frying locks out some of the frying oil and locks in the seasoning. This recipe, from Akiko and Bill Shurtleff of the Soyfoods Center in Lafayette, California, converted the staff of the Institute to tempeh fans.

½ cup water
2 teaspoons salt (reduced to 1, if desired*)
½ teaspoon ground coriander

1 clove garlic, minced
10 ounces tempeh
¼ cup cornstarch or arrowroot powder
Oil for deep frying

Mix water, salt, coriander, and garlic in a bowl. Cut tempeh into chunks, 1x1x½ inch thick, and dip quickly in mix. Drain in a colander or on paper towel. Coat tempeh pieces with cornstarch. Heat oil in a wok, skillet, or deep fryer and deep-fry tempeh until golden brown, 3 to 4 minutes. Drain briefly on paper towel.

---

*Much of the salt is not absorbed by the tempeh.

Sweet and Sour Sauce

1 tablespoon oil (plus 1 teaspoon dark sesame oil, if desired)
1 onion, chopped
1¼ cups water
2½ tablespoons honey
4 teaspoons soy sauce

1 tablespoon vinegar
1 tablespoon tahini (sesame butter)
½ teaspoon freshly grated ginger
1 green onion, finely chopped
2 to 3 teaspoons cornstarch or arrowroot powder

Heat oil in a medium skillet and sauté onion for 4 to 5 minutes. Add water, honey, soy sauce, vinegar, tahini, ginger, and green onion and bring to a boil. Dissolve cornstarch in 2 tablespoons water and stir into sauce; cook until sauce thickens.

Put tempeh chunks in a serving dish and pour sauce over it. Serve as is, or over cooked rice or noodles. Nice hot or cold.

Complementary protein: soy (tempeh) + sesame + rice (or wheat)

Chinese Cabbage, Northern China Style

4 servings

A favorite of Julya Ripsam of Alamosa, Colorado. Use a Chinese wok or simply your favorite big skillet.

2 tablespoons dark sesame oil
1 tablespoon fresh grated ginger
1 head Chinese cabbage, cut in 1x2-inch pieces
1 cup sliced mushrooms
3 tablespoons soy sauce (or more or less, to taste)
½ teaspoon cayenne pepper or crushed peppers
10 to 16 ounces tofu, cut in 1-inch squares

Heat oil and sauté ginger briefly. Add Chinese cabbage and mushrooms and sauté a few minutes. Add soy sauce and cayenne pepper and cook for a few minutes. Add the tofu and cook 5 to 10 minutes.

That's it. Serve over brown rice for a quick and unusual dinner.

Complementary protein: soy (tofu) + grain

Joan's Brazilian Rice

6 servings

A favorite of Joan Francis of Boscobel, Wisconsin, this turns out to be more than just rice with peppers and onions. Toasting makes the rice nuttier. Sprinkling feta cheese on top would be great, too. For a delicious variations, you may wish to substitute this rice dish for the Rice with Green Chili Sauce recipe in Brazilian Evening.

2 tablespoons olive oil
½ cup sesame seeds
2 cups uncooked brown rice
2 tablespoons margarine

2 to 3 hot chiles (or to taste), chopped (1 small can)
1 onion, chopped
3 cups water
2 cups coarsely chopped tomatoes
½ cup lemon juice

With the olive oil, in a deep skillet or Dutch oven, briskly stir sesame seeds and rice for a few minutes, until slightly translucent and toasty-smelling. In another skillet, heat oil and margarine and sauté peppers and onion until the onion is translucent. Add vegetables to the seeds and rice and add water; bring to a boil, turn flame down, and simmer, covered, until water is absorbed, about 40 minutes. Add tomatoes and lemon juice, cover, and let sit for 5 minutes.

Complementary protein: sesame seeds + rice

Spanish Bulgur

2 servings

This dish is lighter than Spanish rice and just as tasty. The beans make it into a whole meal. A good accompaniment is sliced cucumber and tomato salad with Vinaigrette Dressing.

2 tablespoons oil
1 clove garlic, minced
½ cup chopped green onions
½ green pepper, diced
1¼ cups bulgur
1 cup cooked kidney or pinto
  beans (about ¼ to ½ cup
  uncooked)

1 teaspoon paprika
Salt to taste
⅛ teaspoon black pepper
Dash cayenne pepper
1 No. 2 can tomatoes

Heat oil and sauté garlic, green onions, green pepper, and bulgur until bulgur is coated with oil and onions are translucent. Add beans, paprika, salt, black pepper, cayenne pepper, and tomatoes. Cover and bring to a boil, then reduce heat and simmer until liquid is absorbed and bulgur is tender, about 15 minutes, adding more liquid if necessary.

Complementary protein: wheat + beans

Mjeddrah

3 to 4 servings

This is the favorite recipe of Jennifer Raymond of *The Best of Jenny's Kitchen*. She writes, "Don't let the name [pronounced *mi-jed-rah*] put you off. This is a wonderful, basic food—one of the most popular dishes in the Middle East. No wonder! According to Biblical scholars, Mjeddrah is the 'mess of pottage' for which Esau sold his birthright to Jacob. When you taste its simple, hearty flavor, you'll see why."

1½ cups lentils, rinsed
4 cups water
3 to 3½ tablespoons olive oil

2 large onions, coarsely chopped
½ teaspoon salt
¾ cup brown rice

Bring lentils and water to a boil, then reduce heat, cover, and simmer for 25 minutes. Heat 2 tablespoons oil in a skillet and sauté onions and salt until onions are translucent. Heat remaining oil in another skillet and sauté rice for 3 minutes. Combine lentils, onions, and rice, cover tightly, and simmer until lentils and rice are tender, about 1 hour. Up to 2 cups more water may be needed to cook the rice. Stir occasionally. Add more salt, if necessary.

Mjeddrah is traditionally eaten with a salad and the following dressing on top (like a tostada without the tortilla). Choose among lettuce, spinach, tomatoes, green onions, cucumber, radishes, bell pepper, and sprouts. For the dressing, combine 3 tablespoons olive oil, 2 tablespoons lemon juice, ½ teaspoon paprika, ¼ teaspoon dry mustard, 1 clove garlic, minced, ¼ teaspoon honey, and salt to taste, and toss with salad.

Complementary protein: lentils + rice

Greek-Style Skillet with Mint

3 to 4 servings

This combination of foods and seasonings is typically Greek or Turkish. For a very special dinner, serve with a Greek salad combining lettuce, tomatoes, Greek olives, anchovies, and feta cheese.

2 tablespoons olive oil
1 medium onion, chopped
1 clove garlic, minced
1 small or medium eggplant, peeled and diced (1-inch cubes)
¼ pound green beans or other green vegetable (optional — adds a beautiful touch)
½ to 1 teaspoon mint*

½ to 1 teaspoon dillweed*
1 tablespoon parsley
2 tablespoons lemon juice
1 cup canned tomatoes
One 8-ounce can tomato sauce
3 cups cooked brown rice and soy grits (1 cup uncooked rice and ¼ cup uncooked grits)
2 cups yogurt

Heat olive oil and sauté onion and garlic until onion is translucent. Add eggplant and green beans and sauté 5 minutes. Add herbs and sauté 1 minute. Add lemon juice, tomatoes, and tomato sauce, cover, and cook 15 minutes. Heat up rice and serve vegetables over it. Put a large dollop of yogurt on or beside each serving.

Complementary protein: rice + soy

---

*If fresh herbs, use larger amount. Adjust to taste.

Roman Rice and Beans

8 to 10 servings

This dish has been one of my family's favorites since the 1971 edition. With a green salad and Italian bread, it is a satisfying meal. (It's great for serving large gatherings, too.)

Olive or other oil for sautéing
2 cloves garlic, crushed
1 large onion, chopped
1 to 2 carrots, chopped
1 stalk celery or 1 green pepper chopped
2/3 cup chopped fresh parsley
2 to 3 teaspoons basil
2 teaspoon oregano

2 to 3 large tomatoes, coarsely chopped
Salt and pepper to taste
2 cups cooked pea or kidney beans (¾ cup uncooked)
5 cups cooked brown rice (cooked with 1 teaspoon salt)
½ cup or more grated Parmesan cheese

Heat oil and sauté garlic, onion, carrots, celery, parsley, and dried herbs until onion is translucent. Add tomatoes, salt and pepper, and beans. Combine rice and Parmesan cheese. Add bean mixture to rice mixture. Garnish with more fresh parsley and grated cheese.

Complementary protein: beans + rice

Potato Latkes

2 to 3 servings

Kids love potato pancakes. They make a quick supper when the cupboard seems bare.

1 large potato
½ onion
2 tablespoons whole wheat flour
2 tablespoons chopped fresh parsley

2 egg whites, beaten stiff
Salt and pepper to taste*
5 tablespoons instant dry milk
Oil for frying

*I find that by adding extra pepper I can reduce the salt a lot.

Grate potato and drain liquid, grate onion, and combine with flour, parsley, egg whites, salt and pepper, and milk.

Drop spoonfuls of batter into hot oil in a skillet, flatten with the back of a spoon, and brown well on both sides. Top with applesauce, or serve with a cottage cheese and tomato salad.

Variation: Make Potato Corn Cakes by adding 1 small can drained whole-kernel corn.

Complementary protein: potato + milk

Sweet and Sour Stuffed Cabbage

4 servings

The contrast of the green cabbage and red tomato sauce makes this dish quite beautiful. It is especially good topped with yogurt.

12 whole cabbage leaves
2 tablespoons oil
1 onion, chopped
½ cup pignolia nuts, chopped cashews, or toasted sunflower seeds
1 scant tablespoon caraway seeds

½ cup raisins
One 15-ounce can tomato sauce
1 tablespoon lemon juice
3 cups cooked brown rice and soy grits (1¼ cups uncooked rice and ⅛ cup uncooked grits, cooked together with ½ teaspoon salt)
1 cup yogurt

Steam cabbage leaves until limp and set aside. Heat oil and sauté onion until translucent. Add nuts, caraway seeds, and raisins and sauté 2 minutes. Combine tomato sauce and lemon juice. Combine rice with sautéed ingredients and add enough sauce to moisten.

Put about 3 tablespoons of filling on each leaf and roll up, securing with a toothpick if necessary. Put the rolls in a skillet and pour the remaining sauce over them. Cover and cook until cabbage is quite tender, about 15 minutes. Serve topped with yogurt.

Variation: To give this dish an unusual flavor, add ½ teaspoon cinnamon to the stuffing mixture.

Complementary protein: soy + rice + seeds + nuts + milk
product

Homemade Tofu Burgers

8 patties

A favorite dish of Bill and Akiko Shurtleff of the Soyfoods Center, Lafayette, California. They write: "You won't believe the delicious flavor of these easy-to-make cholesterol-free meatless entrees. A favorite in Japan for over 400 years. Watch out, McDonald's!" The "batter" can be kept in the refrigerator, so you can make fresh burgers as you want them. Great for breakfast, too.

30 ounces tofu
1/3 cup grated carrot
¼ cup minced leeks, scallions, or onions

2 tablespoons ground roasted sesame seeds, sunflower seeds, peanuts, or chopped nutmeats
Oil for frying

Cut tofu into thin slices and arrange between two layers of dishtowel. Let stand for 15 minutes, then put firm pieces in the middle of a dry dishtowel, gather the corners, twist to form a sack, and squeeze tofu firmly to drain off as much moisture as possible.

In a shallow bowl, combine tofu with carrot, leeks, and sesame seeds. Knead, as if kneading bread, for about 3 minutes. When dough is smooth and holds together well, moisten palms with oil and shape dough into patties, 3 to 3½ inches in diameter.

Pour oil into a wok (to a depth of 1½ inches) or skillet (to a depth of ¼ to ½ inch). Heat oil to 375°F. (If you don't have a thermometer, test the temperature with a ½-inch ball of the dough; it should fry, sizzling vigorously, to golden brown in about 1 minute. The oil should be fragrant but never smoking.) Fry burgers until crisp and nicely browned, about 4 minutes on one side, 3 minutes on the other. Drain and serve hot, with a sprinkling of soy sauce, on a bun with lettuce, tomato, ketchup, mustard, dill pickle slices, alfalfa sprouts, or other burger trimmings.

Complementary protein: soy (tofu) + seeds + wheat (bun)

Creamed Celery Saute

4 servings

This is such a simple idea, but so good. The cottage cheese and yogurt give a delicious sour cream flavor. Serve with sliced tomatoes and hearty rye bread.

Margarine for sautéing
4 stalks celery with leaves, chopped
1 to 2 tablespoons chopped fresh parsley
1 to 2 scallions, chopped

Salt and pepper to taste
1 teaspoon lemon juice
1½ cups combined cottage cheese and yogurt (or all cottage cheese), blended smooth
Garnish: chopped fresh parsley

Heat margarine and sauté celery, parsley, scallions, and salt and pepper until celery is tender. Stir in lemon juice. Remove from heat, and add cottage cheese–yogurt blend just before serving. Serve over halved baked potatoes or your favorite pasta. Garnish with parsley.

Complementary protein: milk product + potato or wheat

4.

Pie-in-the-Sky Suppers

"Pat-in" supper pie crusts
* * Sesame—Whole Wheat "Pat-In" Crust
   Parmesan Rice Crust
   Quick Cornmeal Crust
* * One-Egg Tofu Quiche
   Crusty Corn-Bean Pie
   Garden Vegetable Pie

---

*New recipe.

IF YOU ARE like me, you hesitate to make pies very often because of the ordeal of making and rolling a pie crust. Here are three ideas for supper pies that do not require rolling out a crust. (And they do not rely on the nutritionally meager store-bought crusts, either!) The trick is simply patting the dough ingredients right into the pie plate. It is so simple, in fact, that you will probably wonder why you didn't think of it before. So here are ideas for cheese, bean, and vegetable pies—each with infinite possibilities for delicious variation depending on what you have on hand and your own imagination.

Sesame—Whole Wheat "Pat-In" Pie Crust

1 pie crust

From Perri Sloane of Davis, California, who improved the original Easy Whole Wheat Crust in the 1975 edition.

1 cup whole wheat floor
¼ cup margarine, softened
¼ cup sesame seeds

1 tablespoon brown sugar
  (optional; for dessert pie)
2 tablespoons water

Mix together and pat into 9-inch pie plate. Bake in a preheated 350°F oven for 10 minutes before filling.

Complementary protein: wheat + sesame

Parmesan Rice Crust (and Pie)

1 pie crust

1 egg
2 tablespoons grated Parmesan
  cheese
Juice of ½ lemon
Pepper to taste

2½ cups cooked brown rice
  (1¼ cups uncooked)
¼ cup chopped fresh parsley
  (optional)
2 tablespoons ground toasted
  sesame seeds

Preheat oven to 350°F. Beat egg, mix with remaining ingredients, and pat into a 9-inch pie pan. Bake until it begins to get crusty, about 15 minutes.

Remove from oven, fill with your favorite sautéed vegetables, add a cream sauce if you wish, and sprinkle with more ground toasted sesame seeds. Return to the oven to heat through, another 10 to 15 minutes.

Complementary protein: rice + sesame seeds + milk
product

Quick Cornmeal Crust

1 pie crust

2 cups yellow cornmeal
½ teaspoon salt
2 tablespoons brewer's yeast

3 tablespoons oil
½ to ¾ cup hot Seasoned Stock
  (or enough to make a stiff
  batter)

Preheat oven to 350°F. Mix and pat into an oiled deep 9-inch pie pan or cake dish. Bake for 10 minutes before filling. A spicy bean filling complements the protein in the cornmeal.

One-Egg Tofu Quiche

6 hearty servings

If you love quiche but would like to avoid some of the cholesterol and dairy fat, try Perri Sloane's delicious alternative. Perri is from Davis, California, and is active in Food for All, a hunger action group.

Oil for sautéing
2 cloves garlic, minced
1 onion, chopped
5 to 6 mushrooms, sliced
½ cup zucchini, spinach, or other
  green vegetable, chopped
1 teaspoon herbs (basil, rosemary,
  thyme, etc.)

12 ounces tofu
4 ounces grated Muenster or other
  cheese
One 13-ounce can low-fat
  evaporated milk
1 egg, beaten
Sesame–Whole Wheat "Pat-In"
  Pie Crust (p. 273)

Preheat oven to 350°F. Heat oil and sauté vegetables and herbs until tender. Squeeze tofu with a dry towel to drain off excess moisture and cut in small chunks. Combine tofu, cheese, milk, and egg with sautéed vegetables and pour into pie crust. Bake until browned, about 45 minutes. Let cool slightly before serving.

Complementary protein: soy (tofu) + wheat + milk
product

Crusty Corn-Bean Pie

4 to 6 servings

Oil for sautéing
1 onion, chopped
1 carrot, chopped
3 stalks celery, chopped
3 cups cooked kidney beans (1 cup uncooked, or use one 20-ounce can)

Pinch cayenne pepper
1 teaspoon ground cumin
1 tablespoon soy sauce
Quick Cornmeal Crust (p. 274)
1/3 cup or more grated sharp cheese

Preheat oven to 350°F. Heat oil and briefly sauté onion, carrot, and celery. Combine with beans, cayenne pepper, cumin, and soy sauce. Adjust seasoning to taste and turn into pie crust. Bake about 25 minutes, remove from oven and sprinkle with cheese, and bake 5 minutes more.

Complementary protein: beans + corn + milk product

Garden Vegetable Pie

6 servings

This is a beautiful dish that can be different every time, depending on what vegetables you have on hand.

2 tablespoons margarine or oil
¼ pound mushrooms, sliced
3 tablespoons whole wheat flour
1 cup low-fat milk
¼ pound grated cheese (optional)
1 teaspoon dry mustard (optional)
Salt and pepper to taste

Parsley and other herbs (tarragon, thyme, rosemary, etc.) to taste
4 cups lightly steamed or sautéed (not mushy) vegetables—carrots, cauliflower, broccoli, etc.
Sesame—Whole Wheat "Pat-In" Crust or Parmesan Rice Crust (p. 273), baked for 10 minutes
Topping: 2 tablespoons ground toasted sesame seeds

Preheat oven to 350°F. Heat margarine or oil and sauté mushrooms. Add flour and sauté, stirring, until browned. Gradually add milk and cook until sauce thickens. Add cheese, mustard, salt and pepper, and herbs. Put cooked vegetables in the pie crust and pour sauce over them. Bake just until vegetables are heated through and sauce bubbles. Sprinkle on topping.

Complementary protein: wheat + milk

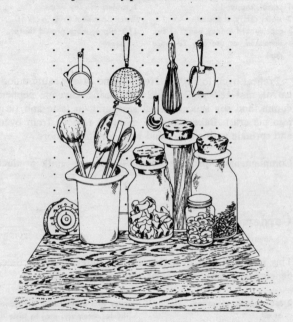

5.

The Universal Favorite: The Sandwich

---

*New recipe.

IT SEEMS THAT every culture faced with the question "What's for supper?" has come up with at least one similar answer: a round flatbread, be it corn or wheat, fried or baked, that can be filled in any number of delicious ways—or eaten plain as bread. In Mexico they call it the "tortilla," in India the "chapati," and in the Middle East the "pita." In my house it's known humbly as a filled sandwich. Since we are lucky enough to live in an area where we can get both tortillas and pita (even delicious whole wheat pita with sesame seeds!), we keep them on hand always for some of our favorite meals.

Here are filled sandwich recipes that are American takeoffs on traditional dishes. They make great buffet dinners because guests enjoy assembling their own.

In addition to sandwiches using tortillas or pita, I've included two other quick family favorites.

Tostadas

6 servings

This dinner makes a festive and delicious community meal.

Oil for frying
5 cups cooked or canned pinto beans (2 cups uncooked), cooked until quite soft
Salt to taste
1 dozen corn tortillas

Garnishes:
½ pound Monterey jack or cheddar cheese, grated
½ head lettuce, shredded
1 to 2 tomatoes, chopped
1 onion, finely chopped
1 can green chili sauce or taco sauce
1 cup yogurt (optional but good!)

In a deep, heavy skillet, heat enough oil to cover pan. Oil should be very hot but not smoking. Quickly add the beans, using a wooden spoon (some liquid is released this way). The oil should be hot enough to toast the beans. (*Refritos* means "well fried," not "refried.") Taste for salt.

Fry tortillas briefly in a little oil, or heat in the oven until crisp. To assemble, spread each tortilla with a sizable amount of beans, then add garnishes, sauce, and yogurt. Each person gets 2 tortillas.

Variation: For an authentic homemade sauce, peel and seed 4 ripe tomatoes and seed 6 green chili peppers. Chop the tomatoes, chilies, and 1 onion and mix well with 1 clove minced garlic, 1 teaspoon salt, ⅛ teaspoon black pepper, and 1 teaspoon vinegar.

Complementary protein: beans + corn + cheese

Middle Eastern Tacos

10 tacos

Wonderfully tasty and satisfying! Of all the recipes that appeared in the 1971 edition, this is the one my family has eaten most often. The bean-sesame mix makes a great cracker spread, too. With precooked beans, the whole thing can be put together in no time. Increase any of the spices to taste.

3 cups well-cooked garbanzo beans (1 cup uncooked)
½ cup ground toasted sesame seeds or ¼ cup sesame butter
2 cloves garlic
2 tablespoons lemon juice
¾ teaspoon ground coriander
Salt to taste
½ teaspoon ground cumin
¼ to ½ teaspoon cayenne pepper
10 pieces Middle Eastern flatbread (pita) or wheat tortillas
Garnishes:
   shredded lettuce
   chopped tomatoes
   chopped cucumber
   chopped onion
1½ cups yogurt or grated cheese

Purée together beans, sesame seeds, garlic, lemon juice, coriander, salt, cumin, and cayenne pepper, adding bean cooking liquid or water if necessary to make blending easy. Let stand at room temperature at least 30 minutes. Cut flatbread in half (to give 2 semicircles from each) and fill pockets with bean mixture. (If you like, heat filled pockets in oven before garnishing. If serving on wheat tortillas, fry until soft but not crisp.) Set out garnishes and let everyone assemble their own. Each portion should include yogurt or cheese topping to complete the protein complementarity.

Complementary protein: beans + sesame seeds + milk product + wheat

Tortillas Verdes

6 servings

A delicious light meal created by Bill and Akiko Shurtleff of the Soyfoods Center in Lafayette, California.

Up to 1 tablespoon margarine (optional)	2 tablespoons lemon juice
6 large (8-inch diameter) tortillas (preferably whole wheat)	¼ cup oil
	1 teaspoon dillseed
1 ripe avocado, peeled and seeded	½ teaspoon salt
	1 teaspoon soy sauce
8 ounces tofu	¼ cup water
	2 cups combined chopped lettuce, chopped tomatoes, sprouts

Heat margarine in a skillet and fry tortillas for 15 seconds on one side and 30 seconds on the other, or steam tortillas in a steamer. In a blender, purée the avocado, tofu, lemon juice, oil, dillseed, salt, soy sauce, and water. Put an equal amount of salad vegetables on each tortilla, top with purée, and serve immediately.

The purée can also be used as a dip, or add beans to make tostadas.

Protein complementarity: soy (tofu) + wheat or corn

Terry's Takeout Tofu

4 sandwiches

Writes Terry Gips of Princeton, New Jersey, about his recipe: "Fast food never had it so good. Look out, hamburger!"

1 tablespoon oil
1 to 2 medium onions, sliced into rings
1 cup sliced mushrooms (about 8 medium)
1 cup vegetables: sprouts, leafy greens, thinly sliced carrots, celery, shredded cabbage, etc.

1 tablespoon soy sauce
4 slices tofu, ½ inch thick and 4 inches long
¼ pound Swiss or Monterey jack cheese, cut into 4 slices
8 slices whole wheat bread or 4 pita breads

Heat oil in a large skillet and sauté onion rings for 2 minutes. Add mushrooms and vegetables and sauté briefly. Remove vegetables or push to one side and add soy sauce, tofu, and about 1 tablespoon water (to keep tofu from sticking). On each tofu slice put 1 slice of cheese. Turn heat down to low, cover skillet, and cook until cheese is melted, 3 to 5 minutes. Put tofu-cheese slices on bread or in pita and cover with vegetables. If you like, garnish with lettuce or additional sprouts.

Complementary protein: soy (tofu) +wheat

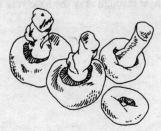

American Variations

For a meal that is simple and new each time, fill pitas or top wheat or corn tortillas with a variety of combinations, according to your taste. Here are some of the favorite filling ingredients at my house. Pick your favorites or try something new.

Bottom layer:
  Bolinas Soyburgers
  Homemade Tofu Burgers
  Broiled Falafel Patties
  Fried Spiced Tofu
  beans, especially pinto or
    garbanzo, whole or puréed
Top layer:
  chopped nuts
  chopped red onion
  sweet peas
  shredded lettuce or cabbage
  chopped spinach
  chopped cucumber
  sliced beets
  chopped apple

shredded cheese
toasted sunflower seeds
ground toasted sesame seeds
tomatoes
Seasonings:
  dill
  celery seed
  curry powder
  chili powder
  ground cumin
  ground coriander
Dressing:
  French dressing
  yogurt
  blue cheese dressing
  Vinaigrette Dressing

These sandwiches are good cold, so you can put all the ingredients on the table and let everyone make their own. They are equally good hot—make them up and put them in the oven to heat through. Try the following hot sandwich recipe.

Instant Pizza Miniatures

What might have been only a melted cheese sandwich becomes a quick supper when you just don't feel like cooking. Serve with a salad or soup.

English muffins or bread
Tomato paste
Mozzarella or other cheese, grated
Minced garlic (optional)

Garnishes (optional):
Parmesan cheese, grated
chopped scallions
chopped parsley
sliced green pepper
sliced mushrooms

Toast muffins, spread with tomato paste, and top with cheese and garlic. Toast under broiler until melted. Garnish and serve.

Complementary protein: milk product + wheat

6.

A Meal in a Soup Pot

---

* Golden Gate Minestrone
* Cream of Anything Soup
  Carrot and Onion Soup
* Tom's True Grits Chili
  Lentils, Monastery Style
  Hearty Tomato Soup
  Turkish Barley-Buttermilk Soup
* Millet-Cauliflower Soup
  Old-fashioned Potato Soup
* Mulligatawny
  Cold Zucchini and Buttermilk Soup
  Cold Curried Apple and Buttermilk Soup

---

*New recipe.

OUT OF THE world of delicious meatless soups, I have included those that I find myself making most often—because they are prepared with ingredients that I almost invariably have on hand: carrots, potatoes, canned tomatoes, and onions. You will see that I rely on low-fat milk, buttermilk, nonfat dry milk, and cheese to complement the grain or legume (bean, lentil) protein in most of these soups. Among your favorite soups are probably many from the legume family—black bean soup, navy bean soup, pea and carrot soup, for example. If you want to complement the protein when making these from your favorite recipes, just add a little milk protein in some form—a cheese sandwich served with the soup, or cheese stirred in or sprinkled on top.

If, while the soup is on the stove, you put some home-made muffins or bread in the oven, your **Meal in a Soup Pot** can become a genuine feast.

Golden Gate Minestrone

8 generous servings

A great soup to come home to after a long winter's day of birdwatching. Claire Greensfelder (see Betty the Peacenik Gingerbread) served 15 gallons of it to the Golden Gate Audubon Society Christmas Bird Counters! The flavor gets better and better with reheating.

1/3 cup olive oil
2 medium onions, chopped
½ green pepper, chopped
2 medium carrots, sliced in rounds
2 stalks celery, chopped
2 cloves garlic, minced
One 28-ounce can tomatoes
One 46-ounce can tomato juice
4 vegetable cubes (or 2 tablespoons vegetable seasoning)
1 bay leaf

1 teaspoon each rosemary and parsley
1½ cups cooked kidney beans (or one 15½-oz. can)
1½ cups cooked garbanzos (or one 15½-oz. can)
2 small zucchinis, sliced in rounds
2 small yellow squash, sliced in rounds
2 cups uncooked shells or other pasta
Garnish: Parmesan cheese or yogurt

Heat oil in a large pot and sauté onions, green pepper, carrots, celery, and garlic until onions are translucent. Add tomatoes, tomato juice, vegetable cubes, and herbs and cook over medium heat for 15 minutes. Add beans, zuc-chinis, squash, and pasta and cook over low heat for at least ½ hour. Taste for seasoning and add more herbs, if needed.

For a delicious spaghetti sauce, process in a blender 2 cups of leftover soup with 1 small can tomato paste, ⅛ to

¼ cup oil, and Italian herbs to taste. Toss in ½ cup cottage cheese, too, for exact smoothness and flavor. Ladle into bowls, garnish, and serve.

Complementary protein: beans + wheat

Cream of Anything Soup

6 servings

This recipe and the variation are favorites of Kevin Onderdonk of Woodcliff Lake, New Jersey, who wrote his own cookbook, *Spaceship Earth Cookery*, for the students in a nutrition course he taught.

4 cups of vegetables (your choice), chopped	1 teaspoon arrowroot powder (optional)
½ cup margarine	½ gallon low-fat milk
2 to 3 tablespoons whole wheat flour	2 to 3 tablespoons soy sauce
	1 teaspoon basil
	1 cup cooked rice (optional)

Steam vegetables in a steamer or simmer in a pot until tender. In a blender, purée a third to half the vegetables with the steaming water. Melt margarine in a large pot. Add flour and arrowroot (optional), stirring until flour begins to brown. Slowly add milk. Add both puréed vegetables and steamed vegetables, soy sauce, basil, and rice. Simmer for 20 minutes. Do not boil.

Variation: For Dairyless Cream of Anything Soup, soak 1 part cashews overnight in 4 parts water. Process for a few seconds in a blender. Now you have cashew milk to replace the low-fat milk.

Complementary protein: milk product + rice

Carrot and Onion Soup

4 servings

This soup is simple yet has a unique quality that makes it a favorite with my family and with guests. I like it especially because I almost always have the ingredients on hand. Any homemade bread would make this soup into a special supper. I cut the carrots and onions into big chunks and reduce them to tiny slivers in the blender.

3 tablespoons margarine	Pinch tarragon
4 to 5 medium carrots, grated	½ cup rice
1 medium onion, minced	4 cups Seasoned Stock
1 teaspoon salt	1 to 1¼ cups hot milk
	Croutons (optional)

Heat margarine in a heavy pot or pressure cooker and gently sauté carrots, onion, salt, and tarragon for about 5 minutes. Add rice and stir into mixture. Add stock and cook until rice is very well done, about 45 minutes (only 25 with a pressure cooker). You may want to sieve the soup or purée it in a blender; I purée only half, so that some chewiness is left. Return it to the pot and add milk to your preferred consistency; do not let it boil. Add a pat of margarine and serve with croutons.

Complementary protein: rice + milk

Tom's True Grits Chili

7 to 8 servings

A favorite of Tom Greensfelder of Chicago. Like his sister Claire (see Betty the Peacenik Gingerbread), Tom has a flair for cooking. Due to popular vegetarian demand, he changed his hamburger-based chili into what you see here. Meat eaters love it too.

1/3 cup vegetable oil
1 cup soy grits
1½ medium onions, coarsely chopped
3 cloves garlic, minced
Two 8-ounce cans tomato sauce
3 medium tomatoes, coarsely chopped

Two 15½-ounce cans kidney beans
3 canned green chilies
1 tablespoon each cumin and chili powder
Oregano to taste
1 cup grated cheddar cheese (optional)

Heat oil in a large skillet and sauté grits until golden. Add onions and garlic and sauté until onions are translucent. Stirring, add tomato sauce, tomatoes, beans, chilies, cumin and chili powder, and oregano. If not spicy enough, add more chili powder or cayenne pepper. If it's too thick, add water. Simmer for 5 to 10 minutes. Serve in bowls and pass the cheddar.

Complementary protein: beans + milk product

Lentils, Monastery Style

4 to 6 servings

This soup is especially delicious when served with corn muffins.

¼ cup olive oil
2 large onions, chopped
1 carrot, chopped
½ teaspoon each thyme and marjoram
3 cups Seasoned Stock

1 cup lentils, rinsed
Salt to taste
¼ cup chopped fresh parsley
One 1-pound can tomatoes
¼ cup dry sherry
2/3 cup grated Swiss cheese

Heat oil in a large pot and sauté onions and carrot for 3 to 5 minutes. Add herbs and sauté 1 minute. Add stock, lentils, salt, parsley, and tomatoes and cook, covered, until lentils are tender, about 45 minutes. Add sherry. To serve, put 2 tablespoons cheese in each bowl and fill with soup.

Complementary protein: lentils + milk product

Hearty Tomato Soup
(Like Campbell's Never Dreamed of)

6 servings

The great virtue of this recipe is that something very special is created from foods that you probably have on hand most of the time. Serve with oatmeal bread and enjoy the hurrahs. The variations are from Myra Levy and Charlie Varon of San Francisco.

2 tablespoons oil for sautéing
1 clove garlic, minced
1 onion, chopped
1 stalk celery, chopped (optional)
1 carrot, chopped
2 tablespoons whole wheat flour
1½ cups cooked rice (¾ cup uncooked)

One 28-ounce can tomatoes, chopped and mashed with a spoon
Salt to taste
4 white peppercorns or lots of freshly ground black pepper
1 teaspoon each oregano and basil
3 cups hot milk
1 tablespoon margarine

Heat oil in a heavy pot and sauté garlic, onion, celery, and carrot until onion is translucent. Add flour, stirring until toasty. If using uncooked rice, add it with the flour and sauté, stirring, until it's a little toasty. Add tomatoes, salt, pepper, herbs, and cooked rice (if you are using it) and cook at least 15 minutes (about 45 minutes with raw rice; cook until rice is done). Remove from heat. For an elegant soup, purée in the blender or put through a sieve. Add milk and margarine and more salt and pepper if needed. Heat through but do not let boil.

Variations: Substitute 1½ cups uncooked rice-soy shells or other noodles for flour and rice. Add 1 small eggplant, cut into ½-inch cubes.

Add chopped broccoli and zucchini.

Complementary protein: rice + milk

Turkish Barley-Buttermilk Soup

4 servings

Don't let the simplicity of this soup fool you. Once I made it for a demonstration of nonmeat cooking, and the moderator could not stop eating it for the entire program.

2 tablespoons oil for sautéing	5 cups Seasoned Stock
2 large onions, chopped	2 cups buttermilk or yogurt
1 cup barley	1 teaspoon dillweed
	1 pat or more margarine

Heat oil in a heavy pot and sauté onions until translucent. Add barley and sauté, stirring lightly, until translucent and slightly toasty-smelling. When onion is well browned, add stock and cook until barley is well done, 45 minutes to 1 hour (25 minutes in a pressure cooker). Remove from heat, let cool a bit, and slowly add buttermilk, and more stock to thin it if necessary. Sprinkle in dill and add margarine.

Complementary protein: barley + milk

Millet-Cauliflower Soup

2 quarts

Here's our variation of a favorite of Robin Bryce Lasobeck of Gainesville, Florida. She says everyone enjoys its homestyle flavor. She teaches a course called "Journey into Natural Foods."

2 tablespoons oil plus oil for
  sautéing
½ cup millet
1½ cups water
3 stalks celery, chopped
1 green pepper, chopped
1 small onion, chopped
2 cloves garlic, minced
1 large carrot, grated or chopped
6 cups water
1 medium head cauliflower, very
  coarsely chopped
1 bay leaf
2 tablespoons dry vegetable soup
  base
½ teaspoon each basil, mint,
  chervil, thyme, and ground
  celery seed
2 tablespoons white miso (dark
  miso will make the soup tan
  instead of creamy)
¾ cup raw cashews
1 cup water
½ cup nutritional yeast
Salt to taste

Heat 2 tablespoons oil in a soup pot and toast millet until golden brown and beginning to pop. Remove from heat, add 1½ cups water, bring to a boil, and simmer for 20 minutes. In a medium skillet, heat oil and sauté celery, green pepper, onion, garlic, and carrot until onion is translucent. To millet pot add 6 cups water (for thick soup), cauliflower, bay leaf, sautéed mixture, soup base, and herbs and celery seed, stirring occasionally so millet doesn't stick. Simmer for 20 minutes. In a blender, process miso, cashews, 1 cup water, and yeast. Add to soup and simmer 10 minutes. Taste for salt and adjust consistency with more water if you like.

Complementary protein: millet + cashews + cauliflower
+ miso + yeast

Old-fashioned Potato Soup

4 servings

Even when your cupboard is bare, you probably have on hand the ingredients for this soup. Serve with grilled-cheese sandwiches for a quick winter lunch.

2 tablespoons oil for sautéing
1 medium onion, chopped
3 stalks celery with leaves, chopped
3 medium or 2 large potatoes, peeled and diced
3 to 4 cups Seasoned Stock or water
Salt and pepper to taste
1 small bay leaf
1 cup instant dry low-fat milk
1 to 2 tablespoons margarine
Garnish: parsley, chives, green onion, or dill

Heat oil in a heavy pot and sauté onion and celery until onion is translucent. Add potatoes, stock, salt and pepper, and bay leaf and cook until potatoes are tender, about ½ hour. Let cool briefly. Stirring, slowly add milk and margarine. Taste for salt. Heat through but do not let boil. Garnish and serve.

Variations: Use leeks instead of onion. Add canned minced clams, diced carrots, canned asparagus, or cooked cauliflower.

Complementary protein: potato + milk

Mulligatawny

2 quarts

The San Francisco Ecology Center is famous for its great soups. Ed Lubin of the Center offers this one, which he says is "a favorite of our lunchtime patrons." It is delicious and easy to make. The longer it cooks, the better it tastes.

3 to 4 tablespoons margarine
2 onions, coarsely chopped
2 to 3 cloves garlic, minced
1 carrot, chopped
2 stalks celery, chopped
1 green pepper, chopped
1 small turnip or parsnip, grated
1 large or 2 small Pippin or other apples, cored and chopped
1 teaspoon curry powder
3 ounces tomato paste
2 tablespoons parsley
5 cups water
2 cups cooked garbanzos (2/3 cup uncooked) or one 1-pound can, undrained
Salt or vegetable seasoning powder to taste

Heat margarine in a large pot and sauté onions and garlic until onions are translucent. Add carrot, celery, green pepper, turnip, apple, curry powder, tomato paste, parsley, and water and cook for 30 minutes to 1 hour. Purée beans in a blender until smooth and add to soup pot, with more water if the soup is too thick. Taste for salt and spices. Heat through and serve or continue to simmer, the longer the better.

Cold Zucchini and Buttermilk Soup

4 servings

Buttermilk, so much cheaper than yogurt, can be the basis for many delightful and practically instant summer soups. Here are just two ideas; many other vegetables and fruits might be used.

Oil for sautéing
1 medium zucchini, coarsely chopped
1 medium onion, chopped
1 clove garlic, minced
3 cups buttermilk
Salt and pepper to taste
Garnish: fresh dillweed or parsley

Heat oil and sauté zucchini, onion, and garlic until soft but not mushy. Purée in a blender and add buttermilk and salt and pepper. Chill and garnish.

Cold Curried Apple and Buttermilk Soup

4 servings

You can vary this by substituting a seeded cucumber for the apple.

Oil for sautéing
1 medium onion, chopped
1 apple, cored and chopped
2 teaspoons curry powder
Pinch mustard seed (optional)
3 cups buttermilk
Garnish: fresh dillweed or parsley

Heat oil and sauté onion, apple, curry powder, and mustard seed until soft but not mushy. Let cool and add buttermilk. Chill and garnish.

7.

A Meal in a Salad Bowl

Exotic Rice Salad
Macaroni Salad Ricotta
Tabouli
Vegetable Salad Carousel
Tempeh and Bulgur Salad
Garbanzo and Cheese Salad
Lentil Salad
Fine Fruit Salad and Other Ideas
* Ultimate "Egg" Salad
Tempeh Mock Chicken Salad

---

*New recipe.

MY DAUGHTER CALLS me a "salad freak." Sometimes in the summertime salads are about the only food that seems appetizing to me. So I have had to learn ways to fill my protein need from the salads I love—and it is not difficult. The recipes here demonstrate some of the many, many possibilities.

TIPS FOR PROTEIN-ENRICHED SALADS

To lettuce salads add:
  Parmesan cheese
  cheese cubes
  ground toasted sesame seeds
  toasted sunflower seeds
  cooked beans
  leftover cooked beans and grains
  cooked broccoli, green peas, cauliflower
To fruit salads add:
  nuts
  ground toasted sesame seeds
  toasted sunflower seeds
  low-fat yogurt
  low-fat cottage cheese

Exotic Rice Salad

4 servings

On a summer's eve this tangy salad (served with sliced beets and cucumber in Vinaigrette Dressing) could be just the meal to refresh the palate.

1½ cups cold* cooked rice (¾ cup uncooked)
½ cup coarsely chopped celery
½ cup coarsely chopped peanuts
1½ cups yogurt

2 tablespoons chutney (or more to taste), or 2 tablespoons apricot preserves plus a dash of lemon juice and grated or powdered ginger to taste

Toss in a salad bowl.

Complementary protein: rice + milk product + peanuts

---

*Room temperature is best. If rice is too cold, it will be gritty.

Macaroni Salad Ricotta

4 servings

Serve on a bed of lettuce. Colorful, light, and satisfying.

½ pound whole wheat macaroni
1 cup ricotta cheese
2 teaspoons prepared mustard
Yogurt as needed
¼ cup sliced or chopped black olives
1 bell pepper, coarsely chopped

2 scallions with tops, chopped
1 tablespoon chopped fresh parsley
Red pimientos to taste
½ teaspoon each dillweed and basil
Salt and pepper to taste

Cook macaroni until tender, drain, and chill. Mix ricotta cheese and mustard and thin with yogurt to the consistency of mayonnaise. Combine macaroni and remaining ingredients and toss with dressing.

Variation: Substitute cottage cheese for part or all of the ricotta, buttermilk or milk for part or all of the yogurt.

Complementary protein: wheat + milk product

Tabouli
(Zesty Lebanese Salad)

6 servings

This recipe is adapted from a traditional Lebanese dish often served on festive occasions. If you want to be truly authentic, let your guests or family scoop it up with lettuce leaves instead of spoons. For a group, I've often served Tabouli with Middle Eastern Tacos—a great combination. The variation was suggested by Camille Gilbert of California.

4 cups boiling water
1¼ cups bulgur
¾ cup cooked white or garbanzo
    beans (¼ cup uncooked)
1½ cups minced fresh parsley*

¾ cup minced fresh mint leaves*
    or additional parsley
¾ cup chopped scallions
3 medium tomatoes, chopped
½ cup or more lemon juice
¼ cup olive oil
Salt and pepper to taste

Pour boiling water over bulgur, cover, and let stand until light and fluffy, about 2 hours. Shake in a strainer and squeeze out excess water. Combine it with remaining ingredients and chill for at least 1 hour. Serve on raw grape, lettuce, or cabbage leaves.

----

*Mince by hand or in a blender, using a wooden chopstick to scrape the herbs from the container sides into the blade action.

Variation: Use 1 cup bulgur and ½ cup soy grits.

Complementary protein: wheat + beans

Vegetable Salad Carousel

4 servings

These recipes are intended to stimulate your imagination to think of delicious ways to use leftover vegetables in salads. (My favorite combination is the cauliflower-lima.) The flavor is best when served at room temperature. Add your favorite herbs to the basic Vinaigrette Dressing.

Potato

6 medium potatoes, cooked, sliced,
    and cooled to room temperature
2 stalks celery, chopped
1 to 2 green onions, finely

chopped, and/ or ¼ cup
    chopped fresh parsley
¼ cup chopped sweet pickles
¼ to ½ pound Swiss cheese, cut
    in chunks

Complementary protein: potatoes + milk product

Lentil-Mushroom

3 cups cooked lentils (1 cup uncooked), cooked with 1 whole onion and 1 bay leaf until tender but not mushy; remove onion and bay leaf before using

2 stalks celery, chopped
1 to 2 green onions, finely chopped
¼ to ½ pound Muenster or other cheese, cut in chunks
¼ cup finely chopped fresh parsley
¼ pound raw mushrooms, sliced

Complementary protein: beans + milk product

Cauliflower-Lima

1 small head cauliflower, cooked until barely tender
2 to 3 cups cooked lima beans (1 cup uncooked)

1 red onion, thinly sliced
¼ to ½ pound Swiss cheese, cut in chunks

Complementary protein: beans + milk product

Vinaigrette Dressing

3 to 4 parts oil

1 part vinegar
Salt and pepper to taste

Mix well. Pour over vegetables, toss, and serve.

Tempeh and Bulgur Salad

Serves 3 to 4

When Bill and Akiko Shurtleff, authors of the *Book of Tempeh* (as well as the *Book of Tofu* and the *Book of Miso*), discovered that there were no tempeh recipes in the first draft of this edition, they were determined that I come to appreciate this traditional Indonesian food, tempting me with delicious recipes like this one. I'm convinced.

2 tablespoons oil
4 ounces tempeh, cut in ½-inch cubes
½ onion, chopped
½ cup bulgur
1 to 4 large mushrooms, chopped
1 cup water
1 tablespoon soy sauce
1 stalk celery, diced
½ large carrot, diced or grated

1 tomato, diced, or 10 cherry tomatoes, quartered
2 tablespoons minced fresh parsley
1 tablespoon vinegar
1 tablespoon lemon juice
1½ teaspoons honey
½ teaspoon dillweed
⅛ teaspoon oregano
Dash white pepper

Heat 1 tablespoon oil in a large skillet and sauté tempeh, onion, bulgur, and mushrooms for 3 to 4 minutes. Add water and soy sauce, bring to a boil, cover, reduce heat, and simmer for 15 minutes. Let cool to room temperature. Combine with remaining ingredients, mix well, and chill for at least 2 hours before serving.

Complementary protein: soy (tempeh) + wheat

Garbanzo and Cheese Salad

4 to 5 servings

Use any combination of fresh vegetables; just be sure to include the garbanzos and cheese.

1½ cups cooked garbanzo beans (½ cup uncooked), cooled to room temperature
2/3 cup grated Swiss or cheddar cheese
Red leaf lettuce, torn into pieces
Spinach, torn into pieces
½ cup sliced scallions

1 green pepper, chopped
½ cup raw shelled peas or defrosted frozen peas
½ cup diced or sliced yellow crookneck squash
½ cup chopped or sliced cucumber
1 cup mung bean or alfalfa sprouts

Toss with your favorite dressing.

Complementary protein: beans + cheese

Lentil Salad

4 servings

Good by itself for lunch or with soup for supper.

½ cup lentils	2 tablespoons mayonnaise
1 small onion, chopped	1 teaspoon garlic powder
4 cups Seasoned Stock	1 teaspoon Dijon or other
Oil for sautéing	prepared mustard
½ cup bulgur	2 teaspoons lemon juice (or more
¼ cup soy grits	to taste)
1 cup yogurt	6 cups chopped spinach, scallions,
	and red onions

Cook lentils and onion in 2 cups stock until tender but not mushy, about 25 minutes. Drain extra water. Heat oil in a heavy skillet over medium heat and sauté bulgur and soy grits for 5 to 10 minutes, to toast, stirring constantly. Heat remaining 2 cups stock, add to bulgur and grits, cover tightly, and cook over low heat until light and fluffy, about 10 minutes. Let cool. Mix yogurt, mayonnaise, garlic powder, mustard, and lemon juice. Combine grain with lentils and vegetables, and toss with dressing. Chill if desired.

Complementary protein: beans + wheat + milk product

Fine Fruit Salad and Other Ideas

8 servings

¾ cup roasted peanuts	1 cup sliced fresh peaches
1 cup raw or roasted sunflower	1 cup seedless grapes
seeds	½ cup raisins
1 cup sliced apples	½ cup shredded coconut
1 cup sliced bananas	2 to 4 tablespoons honey
½ cup tangerine or orange	Juice of ½ lemon
sections	½ cup white wine
	Garnish: 10 to 15 fresh mint leaves

In a large bowl, combine peanuts, seeds, fresh fruit, raisins, and coconut. Mix honey, lemon juice, and wine and toss with salad. Garnish.

Other delicious salads using peanuts and sunflower seeds:

Peanut, Sunflower, and Carrot Salad

Toss grated carrots, raisins, peanuts, sunflower seeds, and crushed pineapple (optional) with a dressing of 1 part peanut butter and 2 parts mayonnaise.

Peanut and Sunflower Waldorf Salad

Sprinkle lemon juice over diced apples (or pineapple chunks) and celery. Add chopped peanuts and sunflower seeds. Moisten with a dressing of mayonnaise and peanut butter.

Complementary protein: peanuts + sunflower seeds

Ultimate "Egg" Salad

4 to 6 sandwiches

Now you can have egg salad taste with no cholesterol. It was adapted from Robin Bryce Lasobeck's recipe by Myra Levy and Charlie Varon, who live on Army Street in San Francisco. They tested so many tofu salad recipes for this edition that they began calling themselves the Army Street Labs.

1 pound tofu (soft works best)
2 tablespoons oil for sautéing
1 clove garlic, minced
1 teaspoon dillweed
½ teaspoon each turmeric, celery seeds, and caraway seeds
2 tablespoons sesame seeds
2 tablespoons brewer's yeast
3 to 4 tablespoons eggless mayonnaise

1 to 2 tablespoons prepared mustard
½ small onion or 2 scallions, minced
1 stalk celery, chopped
½ green or red pepper, chopped
½ cup minced fresh parsley
Paprika, black pepper, and salt or tamari to taste

Drain excess water from tofu and crumble. Heat oil and sauté tofu briefly. Drain excess water, if necessary. Mix with remaining ingredients and serve on whole wheat bread or crackers with tomato slices and alfalfa sprouts.

Complementary protein: soy (tofu) + wheat (bread)

Tempeh Mock Chicken Salad

3 servings

This is another tempeh recipe from Akiko and Bill Shurtleff of the Soyfoods Center, Lafayette, California. Akiko and her friend Valerie Robinson of Soyfoods Unlimited brought samples to a lunch party at the Institute. None of us had ever tasted tempeh before. The praise stopped only for as long as it took us to eat it.

6 ounces tempeh
¼ cup mayonnaise (regular or eggless)
1 stalk celery, finely chopped

2 tablespoons each minced dill pickle, onion, and fresh parsley
1 teaspoon each prepared mustard and natural soy sauce
Dash garlic

Steam tempeh 20 minutes, let cool enough to handle, and cut into cubes slightly smaller than ½ inch. Combine with remaining ingredients and mix lightly. This makes a great sandwich filling or a beautiful salad, mounded on a bed of lettuce.

Complementary protein: soy (tempeh) + wheat (bread)

Part III

Meatless Menus for Special Occasions

1.

The Indian Feast (Version One)

Menu:

> *Fruit and Vegetable Cup*
>
> *Sweet and Pungent Vegetable Curry*
>
> *Sesame Dream Bars (p. 367)*

Fruit and Vegetable Cup

Pineapple chunks (preferably fresh)	Mandarin orange slices
	Diced carrot
Diced apple	Chopped celery

Dress with yogurt and honey, with a dash of grated orange rind.

Sweet and Pungent Vegetable Curry

6 servings

A delightful combination—perfect for the most festive occasion. It can be prepared well in advance.

2 cups cooked soybeans, kidney beans, or limas (or a mix of the three (2/3 cup uncooked); reserve 1 cup cooking liquid	1 tablespoon hot curry powder (or more to taste)
	¼ cup flour
2 or 3 tablespoons oil for sautéing	¾ cup raisins
4 carrots, sliced diagonally	¾ cup raw or roasted cashews
2 onions, thinly sliced	3 tablespoons mango chutney (or more to taste)
1 zucchini, sliced (optional)	3½ cups cooked brown rice and bulgur (1 cup uncooked rice and ¾ cup uncooked bulgur)

Heat oil and sauté carrots, onion, and zucchini until onions are translucent. Add curry powder and flour and sauté 1 minute. Add beans and reserved bean cooking liquid (or water) and simmer until carrots are tender but not soft. Add raisins, cashews, and chutney, and more liquid if necessary (sauce should be thick). Taste for seasoning and simmer until raisins are soft. Serve over the cooked grain.

Complementary protein: beans + wheat + rice

2.

The Indian Feast (Version Two)

Menu:

Honeyed Curry Platter

Spinach and mushroom salad

Cypress Point Carrot Cake (p. 370)

Honeyed Curry Platter

6 servings

The fruit makes this dish an incredible feast for the eyes and mouth.

2 tablespoons margarine
1 tablespoon arrowroot powder or 2½ tablespoons whole wheat flour
2 cups low-fat milk
¾ cup instant nonfat dry milk
1 tablespoon lemon juice
1 tablespoon honey
2 teaspoons curry powder
Salt to taste
Oil for sautéing

¼ cup ground sesame seeds
1 medium onion, diced
2 cloves garlic, minced
2 medium carrots, diced
2 small zucchini, diced
Other vegetables in season
4 cups cooked brown rice (2 cups uncooked)
Whole cooked shrimps (optional)
Garnishes (optional):
  sliced fresh nectarines
  fresh green grapes

Melt margarine in a saucepan. Add arrowroot powder and cook for a few minutes, stirring constantly. (If you are using flour, cook until it is slightly browned.) Add liquid and dry milk and cook, stirring, until thickened to sauce consistency. Add lemon juice, honey, curry powder, and salt.

Heat oil in a skillet and sauté the ground sesame, onion, garlic, carrots, zucchini, and other vegetables until tender. Put rice on a large platter and arrange vegetables and shrimp on top. Pour cream sauce over all and garnish.

Complementary protein: rice + milk + sesame + beans

3.

Middle Eastern Specialty

Menu:

Eggplant spread on crackers (well-cooked eggplant blended with sesame butter, garlic, lemon, and herbs of your choice)

Sweet and Sour Couscous for Arabian Nights

Tossed salad

Sesame Dream Bars (p. 368)

Sweet and Sour Couscous for Arabian Nights

Serves 6

Couscous is a light, partially refined wheat product that is a basic ingredient in many Middle Eastern dishes. It gives a very special quality to this recipe.

Oil for sautéing
1 large onion, chopped
3 stalks celery, chopped
½ pound fresh mushrooms, sliced
4 medium carrots, sliced
1 to 2 teaspoons dillweed
1 bay leaf
1 to 2 teaspoons parsley
1 to 2 teaspoons horseradish
Salt and pepper to taste
1 teaspoon dry mustard
1 clove garlic, mashed
2 cups Seasoned Stock

½ to 1 cup dry white wine
2 to 3 cups cooked garbanzos
    (¾ cup uncooked) or one
    20-ounce can
1 egg
1 cup milk
¼ cup instant dry milk
¼ cup brown sugar
One 8-ounce can tomato sauce
¼ cup vinegar
5 cups cooked couscous (2 cups
    uncooked, prepared according
    to directions on package) or
    bulgur or rice

Heat oil in a deep skillet or Dutch oven and sauté onion, celery, mushrooms, and carrots until onion is translucent. Add herbs, horseradish, salt and pepper, ½ teaspoon mustard, and garlic and cook for 10 minutes. Add stock and wine and cook, covered, for 10 minutes. Add garbanzos, taste for salt and pepper, and adjust seasoning. Consistency should be like that of a thick soup; if necessary, you can thicken with cornstarch.

Over simmering water in a double boiler, beat the egg and liquid milk together. Add dry milk, sugar, and tomato sauce, then vinegar and remaining ½ teaspoon mustard, stirring with a whisk all the while.

To serve, put a portion of couscous on each plate and top with the garbanzo-vegetable mix and then the sauce. This dish has a flavor unlike any other—definitely worth the trouble!

Complementary protein: beans + wheat + milk

4.

Brazilian Evening

Menu:

Feijoada (Tangy Black Beans)

Rice with Green Chili Sauce

Greens with Sesame Seed Topping and Orange Slices

Feijoada (Tangy Black Beans)

6 servings

This recipe was one of my favorites from the last edition. A Brazilian friend embellished it for this edition.

Oil for sautéing
1 large onion, chopped
2 cloves garlic, minced
2 green onions, chopped
1 green pepper, chopped
1 tomato, chopped
1 teaspoon cilantro (optional)
1 cup black beans
3 cups Seasoned Stock (or substitute wine for up to half the stock)
1 bay leaf
¼ teaspoon pepper
1 teaspoon vinegar (omit if using wine)
1 orange, washed but unpeeled, whole or halved
½ teaspoon salt
2 stalks celery, chopped
1 tomato, chopped
1 carrot, chopped (optional)
½ sweet potato, diced

Heat oil in a large heavy pot and sauté onion, garlic, green onions, green pepper, tomato, and cilantro until onion is translucent. Add beans, stock, bay leaf, pepper, and vinegar. Bring to a boil, reduce heat, and simmer for 2 minutes. Take off stove and let sit, covered, for 1 hour.

Add remaining ingredients and simmer, with lid ajar, for 2 to 3 hours more, until beans are tender. Remove a ladleful of beans, mash them, and return them to the pot to thicken the mixture.

I have done the whole thing in a pressure cooker, after first sautéing the onion and garlic. It is much quicker and still *very* good.

Rice with Green Chili Sauce

Rice

2 tablespoons olive oil
1 onion, chopped
3 cloves garlic, minced

2 tomatoes, peeled, seeded, and
coarsely chopped
About 4½ cups cooked brown rice
(2 cups uncooked)

Heat oil and sauté onion and garlic until onion is translucent. Add tomatoes and simmer a few minutes. Stir in the cooked rice and keep warm over low heat.

Sauce

1 tomato, peeled and seeded
California green chiles, seeded,
to taste (start with half a
2-ounce can)
1 teaspoon salt

2 cloves garlic
Juice of 1 lemon
1 onion, cut in chunks
Scallions and parsley to taste
¼ cup vinegar

In a blender, purée tomato, chilies, salt, and garlic until smooth. Add lemon juice, onion, scallions and parsley, and vinegar, and blend coarsely (do not purée).

Just before serving, stir in a little liquid from the Feijoada pot.

Greens with Sesame Seed Topping and Orange Slices

1½ pounds trimmed greens
(turnip or mustard greens,
collards, etc.)
Olive oil for sautéing

1 clove minced garlic
½ cup toasted sesame seed meal
Garnish: 1 orange, sliced

Steam greens until barely wilted. Heat oil and briefly sauté greens with garlic. Sprinkle 1 heaping tablespoon sesame seed meal on each serving and garnish with orange slices on top or around edges.

Serve the rice with sauce along with the beans and greens for a splendid three-course Brazilian dinner.

Complementary protein: beans + rice

5.

Greek Gala

Menu:

> *Greek salad (lettuce, black olives, tomatoes, cucumber, onions, feta cheese, lemon juice, oil, dillweed, pepper)*
>
> *Moussaka*
>
> *Easy Apple-Cheese Pie (p. 375)*

Moussaka

6 servings

The flavor of this dish improves overnight in the refrigerator; reheat before serving. Note: Eggplant can absorb an awful lot of oil if you're not careful. Use as little as possible—just enough to keep the eggplant from sticking as you stir—or brush eggplant slices with oil and bake at 350°F until quite soft.

Oil for sautéing
1 large eggplant, sliced ½ inch thick
6 tablespoons margarine
1 large onion, finely chopped
2 cloves garlic, minced
1½ cups cooked brown rice (½ cup uncooked)
1 cup cooked soybeans (1/3 cup uncooked), seasoned to taste with salt and puréed (or cook ¼ cup soy grits with the rice)
3 tablespoons tomato paste
½ cup red wine
¼ cup chopped fresh parsley

¼ teaspoon each basil and rosemary (optional)
⅛ teaspoon cinnamon
Salt and pepper to taste
½ cup bread crumbs
½ cup grated Parmesan cheese
3 tablespoons whole wheat flour
2 cups low-fat milk
2 eggs (omit 1 yolk if you want to reduce cholesterol)
1 cup part-skim-milk ricotta cheese or low-fat cottage cheese, blended smooth
⅛ teaspoon nutmeg (or more to taste)

Heat oil and sauté eggplant slices until softened but not mushy. Set aside. In a separate skillet heat 2 tablespoons margarine and sauté onion and garlic until onion is translucent. Add rice, beans, tomato paste, wine, herbs, cinnamon, and salt and pepper and stir to mix. Put eggplant slices in a casserole and top with bean-rice mixture. Sprinkle on bread crumbs and Parmesan cheese.

Preheat oven to 375°F. Melt remaining 4 tablespoons margarine in a saucepan and stir in the flour with a wire whisk. Gradually stir in the milk, and continue stirring over low heat until the mixture thickens and is smooth. Remove from heat, let cool slightly, and stir in the eggs, ricotta, and nutmeg.

Pour custard sauce over casserole layers and bake until top is golden and a knife comes out clean from the custard, about 45 minutes. Remove from oven and cool 20 to 30 minutes. Cut into squares and serve.

Complementary protein: soybeans + rice + milk

6.

Mexican Banquet (Version One)

Menu:

Vegetarian Enchiladas

Mexican fried rice (sauté precooked rice with onions, green pepper, garlic, etc.)

Fresh fruit salad (try a dressing of lime juice, yogurt, and honey)

Vegetarian Enchiladas

4 servings

Warning: The sauce for this is very hot. You may want to reduce the amount of hot sauce and chili powder.

Olive oil for sautéing
1½ cups chopped onions
2 cups canned tomatoes
One 8-ounce can tomato sauce
2 cloves garlic, minced
Pinch cayenne pepper
10 drops hot sauce
½ tablespoon plus 1 teaspoon chili powder
1 tablespoon honey
Salt to taste

¼ teaspoon ground cumin seed
¼ pound black olives, pitted and sliced (reserve some for garnish)
1½ cups cooked pinto beans (½ cup uncooked), mashed or ground
8 soft corn tortillas
¼ pound Monterey jack or other cheese, grated

Heat oil and sauté two-thirds of the onions until translucent. Add tomatoes, tomato sauce, half the garlic, the cayenne pepper, hot sauce, ½ tablespoon chili powder, honey, salt, and cumin seed and simmer, uncovered, for 30 minutes.

Heat olive oil and sauté remaining onions and garlic and black olives until onions are translucent. Add remaining 1 teaspoon chili powder, taste for salt, and add beans (and some sauce if mix seems too sticky). Stir well.

Preheat oven to 350°F. Fill each tortilla with 2 to 3 tablespoons filling and 1 tablespoon grated cheese. Roll up and put in a shallow baking pan. Cover with sauce, sprinkle with remaining cheese, and garnish with reserved olives. Bake until bubbling hot, about 30 minutes.

Complementary protein: beans + corn

7.

Mexican Banquet (Version Two)

Menu:

> Guacamole (avocado, garlic, lemon juice dip) with toasted tortillas
>
> Rice con Queso
>
> Lettuce and red cabbage salad
>
> Lemon sherbert with Tofu Apple Nut Loaf (p. 367)

Rice con Queso

6 servings

This is an ideal dish for a buffet dinner. My guests always ask for the recipe.

3 cups cooked brown rice (1½ cups uncooked), cooked with salt and pepper

1 1/3 cups cooked black beans or black-eyed peas, pinto beans, etc. (½ cup uncooked)

3 cloves garlic, minced

1 large onion, chopped

1 small can chiles, chopped

½ pound ricotta cheese, thinned with a little low-fat milk or yogurt until spreadable

¾ pound shredded Monterey jack cheese

½ cup shredded cheddar cheese

Garnishes (optional): chopped black olives, onions, fresh parsley

Preheat oven to 350°F. Mix together rice, beans, garlic, onion, and chilies. In a casserole, spread alternating layers of the rice-beans mixture, ricotta cheese, and jack cheese, ending with a layer of rice and beans. Bake for 30 minutes. During the last few minutes of baking, sprinkle cheddar cheese over the top. Garnish before serving.

Complementary protein: rice + beans + milk products

8.

Dinner in Italy

Menu:

Minestrone con Crema

Garlic bread

Tossed green salad with Caesar dressing

Poppy Seed Cake (p. 366)

Minestrone con Crema

6 to 8 servings

Seems like a lot of vegetables? Believe me, it works—this soup is truly delicious. A friend who swears he dislikes both greens and turnips ate it with gusto.

½ cup fresh basil, spinach, or parsley
1 clove garlic, minced
1 cup grated Parmesan cheese
Olive oil
1½ cups barely done cooked garbanzos (½ cup uncooked), undrained
5 kohlrabis or turnips, with leaves chopped and bulbs diced (about 2 cups)
1 head cabbage, fiinely chopped or grated
2 cups beet greens or spinach, without stems, chopped
¼ cup fresh parsley
Salt to taste
3 cups low-fat milk

In a mortar or blender, make pesto by mashing or blending basil, garlic, and Parmesan cheese with enough oil to make a smooth paste. In a large pot combine the beans, bean cooking liquid, kohlrabis, cabbage, beet greens, parsley, and salt with enough water to cover. Bring to a boil, reduce heat, and simmer 1 hour. Add milk and simmer 15 minutes more; do not let it boil. Stir in the pesto, heat 5 minutes, and serve at once.

Complementary protein: beans + milk

9.

Oriental Specialty

Menu:

Sweet and Sour Vegetables with Tempura

Fried rice with sesame (stir-fry precooked rice with ¼ cup ground toasted sesame seeds)

Sweet and Sour Vegetables with Tempura

6 servings

Stir-fry the vegetables while the tempura is frying. You can make the rice (about 5 to 6 cups cooked rice and soy grits; 2 cups uncooked rice and ¼ cup uncooked grits) ahead of time or at the last minute.

Tempura

Oil for frying
3 cups sliced raw vegetables
(carrots, broccoli, onion,
cauliflower, zucchini, etc.) and
tofu (optional)

1 batch Quick Mix pancake batter
(use 2 eggs; beat egg whites
until stiff and fold them into
batter just before frying
vegetables)
Shredded cabbage

Pour oil into a wok, deep skillet, or pot to a depth of 2 inches. Heat to very hot but not smoking. Using chopsticks, tongs, or your fingers, pick up a vegetable slice, dip it into the batter, and drop into hot oil. Cook, turning once or twice, until golden brown. Cook several slices at a time, but do not crowd. Remove from hot oil with another set of chopsticks, tongs, or a slotted spoon. Drain on shredded cabbage (beautiful for serving) or paper towel.

Stir-fried Vegetables

2 tablespoons peanut oil
3 cups sliced raw vegetables
(same as above) and tofu
(optional)

1 or 2 sliced onions
One 1-pound can pineapple
chunks, drained (reserve juice)

Heat oil in a large pan and sauté vegetables briefly. Add onion and pineapple chunks and sauté for 1 minute or so.

Sweet and Sour Sauce

2½ tablespoons cornstarch
Reserved pineapple juice
¼ cup brown sugar

¼ cup vinegar
1 tablespoon soy sauce

Make a smooth paste of the cornstarch and a few tablespoons pineapple juice and combine with remaining ingredients. Add to the stir-fried vegetables and cook, stirring, until the sauce thickens and is clear and glutinous.

To serve, spoon the cooked (and reheated, if necessary) rice onto a large platter (you may need two). Spread the tempura vegetables (on shredded cabbage, if you used it) around the edges and spoon the sauced stir-fried vegetables over rice. If you like, sprinkle some finely chopped scallions over all. A beautiful dinner.

Complementary protein: wheat + soy + rice

10.

Harvest Dinner

Menu:

Walnut-Cheddar Loaf

Steamed broccoli with lemon sauce

Fried sliced apples

Indian Pudding or Soybean Pie (p. 373, 376)

Walnut-Cheddar Loaf

5 to 6 servings

This is especially nice served with a cheese sauce, with whole walnuts sprinkled on top.

2 tablespoons oil for sautéing
2 cups chopped onions
1 cup coarsely ground black walnuts
1 cup grated cheddar cheese
2 tablespoons lemon juice

2 eggs, beaten
Salt to taste
2 tablespoons nutritional yeast
1 teaspoon caraway seeds
1¼ cups cooked brown rice (½ cup uncooked)

Preheat oven to 350°F. Heat oil and sauté onions until translucent. Mix with remaining ingredients and put in an oiled loaf pan. Bake for 30 minutes.

Complementary protein: rice + milk product

11.
Pizza Party

Menu:

Complementary Pizza

Caesar salad

Complementary Pizza

4 ten-inch pizzas

The pizza looks like work, but it makes a wonderful supper dish—high protein in amount *and* quality.

2 tablespoons dry baking yeast
1¼ cups warm water
3 teaspoons honey
¼ cup olive oil plus 3 tablespoons for sautéing
1 teaspoon salt (optional)
2½ cups whole wheat flour
½ cup soy flour
1 cup finely chopped onions
1 tablespoon minced garlic
4 cups canned tomatoes, chopped
1 small can tomato paste

1 tablespoon oregano
1 tablespoon fresh or 1 teaspoon dried basil
1 bay leaf
Salt and pepper to taste
Cornmeal for dusting
1 pound mozzarella cheese, grated
½ cup freshly grated Parmesan cheese
Garnishes (optional): sliced garlic, onion, mushrooms, green pepper

Dissolve yeast in water with 1 teaspoon honey. Mix with ¼ cup oil, salt, and flours in a large bowl. Turn out on a floured board and knead until smooth and elastic. Oil the bowl, return the dough to it, and set in a warm place for about 1½ hours, until dough doubles in volume. Punch down and knead again for a few minutes to make dough easy to handle.

Heat remaining 3 tablespoons oil in a large pot and sauté onions and garlic until soft. Add tomatoes, tomato paste, herbs, remaining 2 teaspoons honey, and salt and pepper and bring to a boil; lower heat and cook 1 hour, stirring occasionally. Remove bay leaf. If you want a smooth sauce, sieve or purée it.

Preheat oven to 500°F. Divide dough into quarters and stretch each into a 5-inch circle, then roll out to a circle 10 inches in diameter and about ⅛ inch thick. Dust baking pans with cornmeal, put pizzas on top, and pinch a small rim around the edge of each. For each pizza use ½ cup tomato sauce, ½ cup mozzarella cheese, and 2 tablespoons Parmesan cheese. Top with your choice of garnishes and bake 10 to 15 minutes.

Complementary protein: wheat + soy + milk products

Part IV

And
All
The
Extras

1.

Snacks, Appetizers, and Candies That Count

Snacks that count
    Instant Cottage Cheese Pudding
    Instant Buttermilk Pudding
    Peanut Butter Protein Sandwich
    Low-Calorie Cheese Spread

Appetizers that count
  * Cool Spinach Appetizer
    Cold Gallentine
    Sesame Crisp Crackers
    Bean Dip, Arab Style
    Bean Dip, Mexican Style
    Cottage Cheese and Seafood Dip
    Party Snacks
    (For other appetizer ideas, see the Menus in Part III.)

Candies that count
    Peanut Butter Log
    Sesame Seed Delight
    Tiger's Candy

---

*New recipe.

The recipes in this section prove that a snack or a sweet doesn't have to be considered just an energy food, a filler, or a mere self-indulgence. It can also contribute substantially to meeting your body's need for protein.

Snacks That Count

Instant Cottage Cheese Pudding

To cottage cheese add:
  chopped nuts
  applesauce

toasted sunflower seeds
dried fruit
dash cinnamon

Choose your favorite ingredients and mix together to your taste for a great snack.

Instant Buttermilk Pudding

This has a great sweet-sour taste that is addicting. If you think you don't like buttermilk, try it this way.

To leftover rice add:
  buttermilk
  brown sugar or honey

nuts or seeds
raisins
½ teaspoon cinnamon

Peanut Butter Protein Sandwich

Remember that when you eat peanut butter by itself your body can use only about 40 percent of the protein in it. The rest is wasted because the amino acids are unbalanced. This is why commercials that promote peanut butter as a good source of protein are misleading *unless* you know how to combine it with other protein sources to create an amino acid balance that the body can use more fully.

So, go get your jar of peanut butter. If it is partly eaten, there'll be room to add some nonfat dry milk powder. The exact proportion is 2 parts peanut butter to slightly less than 1 part milk powder (or slightly less than ½ cup milk powder for every cup of peanut butter). However, this much powder will make the peanut butter too stiff, so either add less powder (any at all is helpful, protein-wise) or add honey to soften it up. Or, if the peanut butter-milk mix is stiff, I like to add a quarter of a mashed banana when I am making a sandwich for my little girl. She loves it that way.

Make your peanut protein count.

Complementary protein: peanut + milk

Low-Calorie Cheese Spread

Ricotta cheese or low-fat cottage cheese

Optional:
chopped dried fruit
chopped nuts

Try either cheese on toast, English muffins, or a bagel. Add just a touch of marmalade. Delicious!

If you want more protein and fewer calories, ricotta is a great substitute for cream cheese. It has one-third the calories and 75 percent more protein.

Appetizers That Count

Cool Spinach Appetizer

2 cups

Claire Greensfelder (see Betty the Peacenik Gingerbread) developed this recipe in an effort to re-create the great taste she had in an Afghanistan restaurant. I don't know whether she succeeded, but my kids love it, even though spinach is not their favorite vegetable.

1 pound spinach
1 cup plain yogurt

1 tablespoon tahini (sesame
  butter) or more to taste
Juice of 1 lemon
1 clove garlic, minced

Cook spinach, drain, and let cool. Mix thoroughly with remaining ingredients. Great on pita bread, crackers, or pumpernickel.

Complementary protein: milk product + wheat (bread)

Cold Gallentine

6 servings

Makes a fine hors d'oeuvre or lunchtime dish.

2 tablespoons margarine
1 medium onion, chopped
¼ pound mushrooms, coarsely
  chopped
2 eggs, beaten
Salt and pepper to taste
Pinch nutmeg
1¼ cups cooked brown rice (½
  cup uncooked)

2 tablespoons brewer's yeast
¾ cup bread crumbs
¼ cup nuts or ground toasted
  seeds
Spread (optional):
  2 tablespoons ricotta cheese
  2 tablespoons yogurt
  2 tablespoons mayonnaise

Preheat oven to 375°F. Heat margarine and sauté onion and mushrooms until onion is translucent. Mix eggs with salt and pepper and nutmeg and add rice, yeast, bread crumbs, and nuts; then mix in sautéed vegetables. Put in an oiled casserole and bake for 30 minutes. Let cool. Cut in 2-inch squares. Combine spread ingredients and serve on or with cold gallentine.

Complementary protein: rice + yeast + wheat + seeds
                         + milk products

Sesame Crisp Crackers

3 to 4 dozen crackers

These crackers go well with soups as well as sweets. Serve them with your favorite dips, spreads, and cheeses.

1½ cups whole wheat flour
¼ cup soy flour
¼ cup ground sesame seeds

Salt to taste
1/3 cup oil
About ½ cup water

Preheat oven to 350°F. Stir together whole wheat and soy flour, sesame seeds, and salt. Add oil and blend in well, then add enough water to make the dough soft enough to roll out very easily into a thin sheet. Gather the dough into a ball, then roll out to ⅛ inch thick. Cut in cracker shapes or sticks and put on an unoiled baking sheet. Bake until crackers are crisp and golden.

Complementary protein: rice + sesame seeds + wheat + soy

Bean Dip, Arab Style

See filling for Middle Eastern Tacos. It combines garbanzo beans (chickpeas) and sesame butter with an incredible assortment of spices. Serve on wheat crackers.

Complementary protein: beans + sesame

Bean Dip, Mexican Style

Cook pinto beans until very soft. Purée, adding a little oil to improve the texture if you wish. For extra flavor, add chili powder, garlic, and cumin to taste. Fry as in the recipe for Tostadas. Stir in lots of grated cheddar or jack cheese. Use as a dip with corn chips or quartered and toasted tortillas.

Complementary protein: beans + milk product

Cottage Cheese and Seafood Dip

Blend cottage cheese with chopped onion and drained canned minced clams. Add herbs if you like. Great as a light dip with fresh vegetables.

Party Snacks

18 servings (4½ cups)

¾ cup roasted peanuts
1 cup roasted sunflower seeds
1 cup roasted cashews

1 cup raisins
1 cup toasted shredded coconut
Salt (optional)

Combine and serve as a party snack. This also makes a simple dessert after a big meal. You can vary the recipe by leaving all of the ingredients raw. Try subsituting sliced dates for the raisins and walnuts for the cashews; this makes a richer snack.

Complementary protein: peanuts + sunflower seeds

Candies That Count

Peanut Butter Log

10-inch log

Many mothers have told me that when their children ask for sweets, they give them a piece of this log—with a clear conscience. I know of a nursery school that let the children make their own, and the kids loved it.

½ cup peanut butter
2 tablespoons honey
2½ tablespoons nonfat dry milk
  (3½ tablespoons instant) or
  more as needed

½ cup raisins
Shredded coconut (optional)

Blend peanut butter and honey, then work in as much powdered milk as you need to make the mixture easy to handle and fairly stiff. Pick up the mixture and knead in the raisins, distributing them evenly. Roll into a 1x10-inch log. Then roll in coconut for eye appeal. Chill, and slice or pull apart.

This mixture can be molded into balls or any shape, and even pressed into cookie molds to make an exciting snack for small children (and big ones, too).

Complementary protein: peanuts + milk

Sesame Seed Delight

18 pieces

You can vary this by adding ¾ teaspoon mace, cinnamon, or cardamom.

¼ cup margarine	½ cup grated coconut (optional)
¼ cup sesame butter	¼ cup ground nuts (optional)
1 cup ground sesame seeds	¼ cup honey
1/3 cup instant dry milk	¼ cup raisins
½ cup wheat germ	2 teaspoons vanilla or almond extract

Cream together margarine and sesame butter. Blend with remaining ingredients and form into 1-inch balls. Chill several hours.

Complementary protein: sesame seeds + milk + wheat

Tiger's Candy

2 dozen balls

½ cup peanut butter
2/3 cup ground sunflower seeds
1 tablespoon brewer's yeast
   (optional)
¼ cup instant dry milk
1 to 2 tablespoons honey

¼ cup finely chopped raisins
¼ cup finely chopped dates or
   other dried fruit (or more
   raisins)
Shredded coconut or carob
   powder

Blend together peanut butter and ground sunflower seeds, then stir in yeast, milk, honey, raisins, and dates and mix well (probably the easiest way is with your hands). If the mixture is too dry to hold together, add liquid milk; if too wet, add more powdered milk. Form into balls and roll in coconut.

Complementary protein: peanuts + sunflower seeds + milk

2.

Start-Right Breakfasts

Quick Mix
(Complementary protein mix for pancakes, waffles, biscuits, muffins,
coffeecake, etc.)

Pancakes
Oatmeal-Buttermilk Pancakes
Johnnycakes
Fruit Pancakes

Waffles
Wheat-Soy Waffles
Cornmeal-Soy Waffles

Cereal
Easy Crunchy Granola
Chunky Granola
Rice Cream and Sesame Cereal
* Nut French Toast
* California Scrambled Tofu

*New recipe.

Most breakfast foods lend themselves easily to spiking with protein.

1. To make instant protein-rich cold breakfast cereal, add to leftover grain (rice, bulgur) your choice of:

Toasted sunflower seeds	Milk
Ground toasted sesame seeds	Cottage cheese
Wheat germ	Ricotta cheese
Peanuts	Honey
Yogurt	Dried fruit
Buttermilk	Fresh fruit

2. To make your hot cereal into a protein-rich breakfast *while cooking* add your choice of:

Soy grits (1 tablespoon per serving—they cook in just a few minutes)	Extra nonfat dry milk powder (1 tablespoon per serving)
Wheat germ (to taste)	Ground toasted sesame seeds (to taste)

3. If you like just toast in the morning, you can still have a healthy breakfast.

Make your own bread and include extra nonfat dry milk, wheat germ, soy flour or grits, ground sesame or sunflower seeds. The Whole Wheat Quick Bread is a terrific breakfast bread.

Spread your toast with low-fat cottage cheese. One of my favorites is a toasted pumpernickel bagel with a thick coat of cottage cheese and a little orange marmalade.

4. For waffles or pancakes that give you protein as well as energy, add:

Soy flour (¼ cup soy flour to 1 cup whole wheat flour)	3 tablespoons nonfat dry milk to 1 cup whole wheat flour)
Extra nonfat dry milk (at least	Wheat germ

or top your pancakes with ricotta cheese or low-fat cottage cheese and fruit.

Quick Mix

This complementary protein mix is all-purpose—great for making pancakes, waffles, biscuits, muffins, coffeecake, or tempura.

6½ cups whole wheat regular or pastry flour	1 tablespoon salt (or to taste)
1½ cups soy flour	1 cup instant dry milk
	1/3 cup baking powder
	2½ cups wheat germ

Mix thoroughly and store in a tightly covered jar in the refrigerator.

Complementary protein: wheat + soy + milk product

Pancakes

About 8 pancakes

1 egg	3 tablespoons oil
1 cup low-fat milk, buttermilk, or yogurt	1½ cups Quick Mix

Beat egg and combine with milk and oil. Stir in mix and fry on a griddle.

Waffles

About 6 waffles

2 eggs	3 tablespoons melted margarine or oil
1½ cups low-fat milk	2 tablespoons honey
	1¼ cups Quick Mix

Beat eggs and combine with milk, margarine, and honey. Stir in mix. Bake in a preheated waffle iron. To make lighter waffles, separate the eggs and beat whites until stiff; fold into batter just before baking.

Biscuits

About 16 biscuits

1/3 cup oil or melted margarine

2/3 cup low-fat milk, buttermilk, or low-fat yogurt
2¼ cups Quick Mix

Preheat oven to 450°F. Combine oil and milk and stir in mix. Turn out on floured board and knead lightly. Pat or roll out 1 inch thick, cut with a biscuit cutter, and put on a greased baking sheet. Bake for 12 to 15 minutes.

Variation: Cut dough in triangles, fill with brown sugar and cinnamon, and roll up.

Muffins

2 eggs
1 cup low-fat milk, buttermilk, or low-fat yogurt
2 tablespoons oil
2 tablespoons honey or molasses
2½ cups Quick Mix

Optional:
   chopped dried fruit (dates, apricots, raisins, etc.)
   chopped nuts
   fresh berries
   canned fruit, drained and chopped

Preheat oven to 400°F. Beat eggs and combine with milk, oil, and honey. Stir in mix and dried fruit or other addition. Pour into muffin pans or cups and bake for 15 minutes. For lighter muffins, separate the eggs and beat the whites until stiff. (Fold into batter just before baking.)

Coffeecake

1 egg
¼ cup oil plus 1 tablespoon
¾ cup low-fat milk, buttermilk, or low-fat yogurt
¾ cup tightly packed brown sugar

1½ cups Quick Mix
Dried fruit (as above) (optional)
1½ teaspoons cinnamon
½ cup nuts
½ cup shredded coconut

Preheat oven to 375°F. Beat egg and combine with ¼ cup oil, milk, and ½ cup sugar. Stir in mix and dried fruit. Combine cinnamon, remaining ¼ cup sugar and 1 tablespoon oil, nuts, and coconut. Sprinkle crumbly mixture over batter and bake for 30 minutes.

Oatmeal-Buttermilk Pancakes

6 servings (18 to 24 four-inch pancakes)

These pancakes are moist and deliciously chewy.

½ cup water
½ cup instant dry powdered milk
1 tablespoon honey
2 cups buttermilk or milk with
  1 tablespoon vinegar

1½ cups rolled oats
1 cup whole wheat flour
1 teaspoon baking soda
Salt (optional)
1 to 2 eggs, beaten

Mix water, milk, and honey and stir in buttermilk and oats. If using unrefined rolled oats, refrigerate overnight so the oats can soften. Beat in remaining ingredients and fry on a hot griddle. For even better results, let stand for 1 to 24 hours. If batter becomes too thick, add more milk or water.

Complementary protein: wheat + milk + oats

Johnnycakes

6 servings (about 24 four-inch cakes)

These cakes have a different flavor and texture from pancakes; a welcome change.

1 cup water
½ cup instant dry milk powder
1 egg
1 tablespoon honey

2 tablespoons oil
1 cup freshly ground cornmeal
1/3 cup soy flour
¼ cup whole wheat flour (or more as needed)

Mix water and dry milk. Beat egg and add to milk, along with honey and oil. Combine cornmeal, soy flour, and whole wheat flour and add to liquid ingredients. Add more whole wheat flour to the consistency you prefer. Pour like pancakes onto a hot oiled griddle or skillet. Serve with honey and margarine or other favorite topping.

Complementary protein: corn + soy + milk + wheat

Fruit Pancakes

6 servings

You can omit 1 egg yolk if you want to reduce cholesterol.

1 cup whole wheat flour	1½ cups low-fat milk (or more for a thin batter)
1/3 cup sesame seed meal	¼ cup oil
1 tablespoon baking powder	2 cups cooked brown rice (¾ cup uncooked)
1 tablespoon brown sugar	
½ teaspoon salt	1 cup fruit chunks (apples, pears, peaches, bananas, berries, etc.)
3 eggs, separated	

Mix together flour, sesame seed meal, baking powder, sugar, and salt. Mix egg yolks, milk, oil, and cooked rice and stir into dry ingredients, using the fewest strokes possible—just enough to wet the dry ingredients. Beat egg whites until stiff and gently fold into batter along with fruit. Bake on a hot oiled griddle.

Complementary protein: rice + sesame seed + milk

Wheat-Soy Waffles

About 5 waffles

These are delicious, light waffles. They are especially good with the addition of about ½ cup chopped nuts. Make a lot and keep leftovers for toasting.

1 cup whole wheat flour	2 eggs
¼ cup soy flour	1½ cups milk
1 teaspoon salt	3 tablespoons melted margarine
2 teaspoons baking powder	or oil
	2 tablespoons honey

Combine flours, salt, and baking powder. Combine eggs, milk, margarine, and honey and beat well. Stir into dry ingredients. (Lumps are okay.) Bake on a hot oiled waffle iron. For an even lighter waffle, separate the eggs, beat the whites until stiff, and fold them in as the last step. To reduce cholesterol, omit 1 egg yolk.

Top leftover toasted waffles with creamed tuna, sliced tomato and melted cheese, or whipped cottage cheese with fruit topping.

Complementary protein: wheat + soy + milk

Cornmeal-Soy Waffles

6 waffles

These are surprisingly delicious waffles, golden and crunchy, easy to make. Make lots and freeze leftovers. They are just as good popping out of a toaster. I love them with cottage cheese and honey on top.

2 eggs	3 tablespoons molasses
1 cup milk plus 1 tablespoon	1 cup cornmeal
nonfat dry milk	1/3 cup soy flour
3 tablespoons oil	Salt (optional)
	2 teaspoons baking powder

Beat eggs and add milk, oil, and molasses. Blend well. Stir together cornmeal, flour, salt, and baking powder and add to liquid ingredients. Bake in a hot oiled waffle iron, using about ½ cup batter per waffle.

Complementary protein: corn + soy + milk

Easy Crunchy Granola

About 12 cups

7 cups rolled oats
1 cup rolled wheat (or more oats)
1 cup wheat germ
1¼ cups ground sesame seeds
1/3 cup instant dry milk or ¼ cup noninstant dry milk

2 tablespoons brewer's yeast
½ to 2 cups shredded coconut
½ cup vegetable oil
½ to 1 cup honey
1 tablespoon vanilla

Preheat oven to 400°F. Put oats and wheat in a large baking pan (or Dutch oven) and toast in the oven until nicely browned, shaking every few minutes. When they are done, add wheat germ, sesame seeds, milk, brewer's yeast, and coconut. Toast for about 5 minutes. Stir in oil, honey, and vanilla and toast for 5 more minutes. Store in a loosely covered jar.

Variation: Along with the sesame seeds add 1 cup each or combined whole or ground peanuts, walnuts, sunflower seeds.

Complementary protein: sesame seeds + milk + wheat

Chunky Granola
(With No Oil Added)

Susan Weber of Willits, California, volunteered several weeks' work at the Institute. She brought with her this recipe, which appeals to me because it doesn't call for added oil, unlike most granola recipes. Susan's family calls it "Cookie Crunch Granola," but she thought that sounded too much like General Foods' creation.

8 cups rolled oats
1 to 2 cups nuts
½ cup sunflower seeds
½ cup sesame seeds
½ cup whole millet or buckwheat
  groats

3 cups or more whole wheat flour
  (or part cornmeal, rice flour,
  or other whole-grain flour)
1 to 2 teaspoons salt (optional)
½ to 1 cup honey
1 to 2 cups hot water (more water
  makes it chunkier, less makes it
  crumbly)
1 teaspoon vanilla

Preheat oven to 350°F. In a large bowl or pot, combine oats, nuts, seeds, millet, flour, and salt. Mix together honey, water, and vanilla, and stir into dry ingredients. Spread on a lightly oiled baking sheet and squeeze mixture together to form small chunks, but don't crowd; the chunks need to bake clear through. Roast until golden brown, about 10 to 20 minutes. (With the larger amount of water, reduce heat and bake longer.) As it bakes the granola may need stirring to brown evenly. Cool thoroughly before storing.

Variations: Replace part of the water with the freshly squeezed juice of 2 oranges (and add the grated rinds if the oranges were not sprayed with pesticides), or use 2 teaspoons orange oil.

For "gingerbread" granola, use half molasses (for half the honey) and add 2 teaspoons cinnamon, 1 teaspoon ginger, and ¼ teaspoon ground cloves.

For a nice change, substitute maple syrup for honey.

Complementary protein: sesame seeds + wheat + oats + nuts + sunflower seeds

Rice Cream and Sesame Cereal

4 servings

If you like cream of wheat or cream of rice cereal and would like the same good taste with the food value of whole grains, try this simple recipe. Roasting the rice is optional but gives it a slightly nuttier taste.

Rice Cream Powder

¾ cup brown rice, washed

Roast in a dry skillet over medium heat, stirring until browned. Grind in a blender or food processor until fine. Roast again in dry skillet. Store cooled powder in a tightly covered container.

Cereal

4 cups low-fat milk
1 teaspoon salt
1 cup rice cream powder

1 tablespoon brewer's yeast
2 tablespoons ground raw or toasted sesame seeds

Bring milk and salt to a boil and stir in rice cream powder. Lower heat and simmer, covered, until thick, about 10 minutes. Stir in brewer's yeast and sesame seeds. Serve with more ground toasted sesame seeds, milk, margarine, honey, or molasses.

Variation: Instead of rice cream try wheat, rye, or corn.

Complementary protein: rice + milk

Nut French Toast

6 to 8 slices

A favorite of Irma Timmons of Shawano, Wisconsin, and a great way to enjoy French toast with no cholesterol. For a more traditional texture, blend in an egg white or two.

1 cup water	½ teaspoon tamari sauce
1 cup raw cashews	1 tablespoon honey
	2 tablespoons whole wheat flour

Purée in a blender. Dip whole wheat bread slices into the batter (keep stirring the batter—the nuts tend to settle to the bottom) and brown well on both sides on a griddle or in a skillet brushed with safflower oil. Serve with applesauce or your favorite fruit topping. I like it with low-fat cottage cheese on the side.

Complementary protein: cashews + wheat

California Scrambled Tofu

2 servings

A favorite of Karla Peterson of Pt. Richmond, California. She writes, "We've enjoyed experimenting with tofu. The scrambled tofu recipe is our favorite. What a delight to find an alternative to eggs for breakfast!"

2 teaspoons margarine or oil
1 large green onion, sliced
1 cup sliced mushrooms (4 to 5 medium)

11 ounces tofu, drained (squeeze in dry towel) and crumbled
¼ teaspoon ground turmeric
Dash white pepper
¾ cup grated cheddar cheese

Heat margarine and lightly sauté green onion and mushrooms. Add tofu, turmeric, pepper, and cheese and cook over low heat until tofu is thoroughly heated, 5 to 10 minutes. Drain off excess water. Serve with toasted whole-grain bread or English muffins.

Variations: Add ½ diced bell pepper and 1 small diced tomato.
Add 1 to 2 teaspoons chili salsa.
Serve topped with avocado slices.

Complementary protein: cheese + soy (tofu)—both highly usable

3.

Baked-In Protein

---

*New recipe.

Bread and other baked items can be a good source of protein with only minor (and taste-improving) changes in the way they are usually made. Only two slices of most of the breads in this section will provide at least one-fifth of your daily protein allowance—about twice what you would get from the best commercial bread. And that is before you put anything on it! Making the protein in baked goods count will become second nature once you become acquainted with the simple ways any recipe can be adapted. (Also see Quick Mix for biscuits, muffins, and coffeecake.)

1. When one of your favorite recipes calls for flour, for every cup add ¼ cup soy flour or powder or ⅛ cup soy grits (adds a nice crunchy texture), or delete some and substitute your choice of:

Wheat germ
Wheat bran
Brewer's yeast

Ground sesame or sunflower seeds
Instant nonfat dry milk

2. When the recipe calls for cornmeal, for every cup add ⅓ cup soy flour (or ¼ cup soy grits) plus ⅓ cup instant nonfat dry milk or ¾ cup cooked beans (ever try beans in cornbread?).

3. When the recipe calls for nuts, for every ½ cup substitute ¼ cup sunflower seeds.

4. When the recipe calls for milk, add extra nonfat dry milk (or throw it in even if recipe doesn't call for milk!), or substitute cottage cheese (more protein).

Whole Wheat Quick Bread

1 loaf

A lovely bread, especially for breakfast.

2 cups whole wheat flour
½ cup soy flour
½ teaspoon baking soda
1½ teaspoons baking powder
½ teaspoon salt (optional)

¼ cup wheat germ
¼ cup instant dry milk
6 tablespoons corn oil
1½ cups sour milk (or 1½ cups milk plus 2 teaspoons vinegar)
½ cup molasses

Sift together flours, baking soda, baking powder, and salt. Stir in wheat germ and dry milk. Combine oil, milk, and molasses and add to dry ingredients, stirring just enough to moisten thoroughly. Pour into an oiled 9x5-inch loaf pan and let stand for 20 minutes. Preheat oven to 350°F and bake until bread is nicely browned and a toothpick comes out clean, about 35 minutes.

Complementary protein: wheat + soy

Jenny's Tofu Corn Bread

1 medium loaf

A favorite of Jennifer Raymond of Littleriver, California, from *The Best of Jenny's Kitchen*. This corn bread is a bit moister, and probably chewier, than what you're used to. It is packed with protein, as the tofu is complementary with the cornmeal and the whole wheat flour. You can omit 1 egg yolk to reduce the cholesterol; add a little extra milk to compensate.

1½ cups cornmeal	½ pound tofu
¼ cup whole wheat flour	2 eggs
1 teaspoon salt (optional)	3 tablespoons oil
1½ teaspoons baking powder	¼ cup honey
½ teaspoon baking soda	1 cup low-fat milk

Preheat oven to 425°F. Stir together cornmeal, flour, salt, baking powder, and baking soda. In a blender, process tofu, eggs, oil, honey, and milk until smooth. Add to dry ingredients and stir until just blended. Pour into a greased and floured 9x9-inch baking dish and bake for 25 to 30 minutes.

Complementary protein: soy (tofu) + wheat + corn + milk

No-Wait Wheat-Oat Bread

2 large loaves

This earthy, substantial bread is fantastic with soup. It can be made in an hour and needs no rising. It is best warmed fully.

1½ cups oatmeal	1 teaspoon salt (optional)
2 to 3 packages yeast	¼ cup oil
4 cups warm water	¼ cup wheat germ
2 tablespoons honey, plus ¼ cup honey or part molasses	1 cup soy grits
	10 cups whole wheat flour

Warm oatmeal in a low oven. In a large bowl, dissolve yeast in warm water and 2 tablespoons honey. Let stand in a warm place until foamy, about 10 minutes. Add remaining ¼ cup honey, salt, and oil and stir in warm oatmeal. Let stand a few minutes. Preheat oven to 275°F.

Add wheat germ, grits, and 9 cups flour and knead well, using remaining flour as needed, until elastic. Divide dough between 2 large loaf pans or 3 small ones. Bake for 15 minutes, then increase oven temperature to 350°F and bake for 45 minutes to 1 hour more.

Complementary protein: wheat + soy

Quick and Easy Pumpernickel

1 large loaf

A delightful pumpernickel—rich, smooth taste and good cutting quality.

1 cake, package, or tablespoon yeast	1/3 cup powdered milk
¼ cup warm water	2 eggs
1½ cups warm Seasoned Stock	2 tablespoons caraway seeds
¼ cup molasses	1/3 cup soy grits
2 tablespoons oil	2 tablespoons brewer's yeast (optional)
1 teaspoon salt (optional)	2½ cups whole wheat flour (plus extra for kneading)
2½ cups rye flour	

Combine yeast, warm water, warm stock, molasses, oil, salt, and rye flour and beat about 3 minutes, preferably with an electric beater. One at a time, beating after each addition, add the powdered milk, eggs, seeds, soy grits, and brewer's yeast. Add the wheat flour a little at a time, mixing it in with your hands. Let stand 10 minutes.

Knead the dough about 5 minutes. You will need to use extra flour during kneading, as the dough is very sticky. Shape into 1 long or 2 small loaves and brush with oil. Put loaf pan in a large pot or roaster and pour about 1 inch of boiling water into the pot. Cover tightly and set on top of a radiator, in the sun, or in any warm place. Let rise 30 minutes, or a little longer if you think it has some more rising to do. Remove pan from water and bake in a 200°F oven for 10 minutes, then for 30 minutes in a 350°F oven.

Complementary protein: rye + milk + wheat + soy

Wheat-Soy-Sesame Bread

2 loaves

This bread is excellent. Many people have told me it is their favorite yeast bread.

2 packages or 3 tablespoons dry baking yeast	1 teaspoon salt (optional)
	¾ cup ground sesame seeds
2 cups warm Seasoned Stock or water	½ cup soy flour
	2 tablespoons soy grits
¼ cup oil	4 to 5 cups whole wheat flour
¼ cup honey	(enough to make a stiff dough)

In a large bowl, dissolve yeast in warm stock and add remaining ingredients. Turn out on a floured board and knead until smooth and elastic. Put dough in a large oiled bowl and set in a warm place to rise until doubled in volume, about 1½ hours. Punch down and knead a few minutes, adding flour as needed. Shape into 2 loaves and put in oiled pans. Let rise again until nearly doubled, about 1 hour, and bake in a preheated 350°F oven for about 30 minutes.

Complementary protein: wheat + soy + sesame

Triti-Casserole Bread

1 loaf of 12 wedges

Triticale flour (tritiflour) is from a hybrid plant, a cross
of rye and wheat. It has more protein than the best wheat
and is reported to have a better amino acid balance, too.
This recipe, adapted slightly, comes from the Triticale
Foods Corporation, Suite 101 Park Place, Lubbock, Texas
79408. The loaf is low but rich and goes beautifully with
any spread.

1 package dry yeast	1 teaspoon salt (optional)
2 tablespoons sugar	¼ teaspoon baking soda
¼ cup lukewarm water	1 egg
1 tablespoon margarine	1½ cups tritiflour (or use wheat or
1 tablespoon minced onion	rye)
1 cup cottage cheese	½ to 1 cup whole wheat flour
2 tablespoons dillseed or caraway	(enough to make a stiff dough)
seeds, or 1 tablespoon dillweed	Softened margarine

In a large bowl, dissolve the yeast and sugar in water
and let sit until foamy. Heat margarine in a small saucepan
and gently cook the onion, cottage cheese, and seeds until
the onion softens, then add to yeast. Add salt, soda, egg,
tritiflour, and whole wheat flour. Mix well, cover, and let
rise until doubled. Stir down and put in a greased 8x1½-
inch casserole dish. Let rise. Preheat oven to 350°F and
bake until bread is browned and sounds hollow when
tapped, about 45 minutes. Remove from oven and brush
with margarine.

Complementary protein: grain + milk product

Boston Brown Bread

1 large loaf

Try this bread with ricotta cheese mixed with chopped dates and nuts. It is dark and rich but not at all heavy.

1¾ cups whole wheat flour	1 teaspoon baking powder
1 cup finely ground yellow cornmeal	1 teaspoon salt (optional)
1/3 cup soy flour	¾ cup molasses
1 teaspoon baking soda	2 cups low-fat milk
	1 cup raisins

Preheat oven to 350°F. Stir together dry ingredients. Combine molasses and milk and stir in dry ingredients and raisins. Pour into a well-oiled loaf tin and bake for 50 to 60 minutes.

Traditionally, this bread is steamed in cans. To do this, grease the insides and lids of molds or cans with tightly fitting lids (one 2-quart mold or two smaller ones; tin foil can be used instead of lids). Fill three-fourths full, cover, and put on a trivet in a heavy kettle over 1 inch of boiling water. Cover the kettle tightly and turn heat high until steam begins to escape; then lower heat for rest of cooking. Steam 3 hours, replenishing boiling water as needed.

Complementary protein: cornmeal + soy + milk

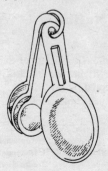

Perri's Best Bran Muffins

About 20 muffins

As a cook in a whole-foods restaurant in Davis, California, Perri Sloane tested many of the recipes in this book. This is one of her all-time favorites. It dates from when she worked at the Greenery Restaurant in Fullerton, California.

2 cups buttermilk
1 egg
2 tablespoons oil
½ cup honey

2 cups whole wheat flour
1½ cups wheat bran
1 cup chopped nuts
1 teaspoon baking soda
1 teaspoon baking powder

Preheat oven to 350°F. Combine buttermilk, egg, oil, and honey. Stir together flour, bran, nuts, baking soda, and baking powder and add liquid ingredients. Pour into oiled muffin tins and bake 15 to 17 minutes.

Variation: Instead of nuts, use 1 cup raisins, 1 mashed banana, ½ cup peanut butter, or ½ cup dates.

Complementary protein: wheat + milk

Orange Bran Muffins

About 15 muffins

This is a favorite of Elsie Nasatir of Santa Barbara, California. She writes: "It has neither salt nor sugar and has been very well accepted by my friends." You can omit 1 of the egg yolks to reduce cholesterol.

1 small can frozen orange-juice
    concentrate
1 large banana, thinly sliced
¼ cup oil

2 eggs, separated
½ cup whole wheat flour
1 teaspoon baking soda
2 cups raw bran
½ cup raisins or sunflower seeds

Preheat oven to 375°F. With an electric mixer, mix juice, banana, oil, and egg yolks until smooth. Add flour and baking soda, then bran and raisins. Beat egg whites until stiff and fold in. Spoon into greased muffin tins and bake about 20 minutes.

Variations: Substitute 1 heaping tablespoon peanut butter for the raisins, or simply add peanut butter to the other ingredients.

Complementary protein: wheat + sunflower seeds

Orange Sesame Muffins

About 12 muffins

This fairly sweet muffin goes well with a light meal. You can omit 1 egg yolk to reduce cholesterol.

1½ cups whole wheat flour	2 eggs
½ cup soy flour	½ cup yogurt or buttermilk
1 teaspoon salt (optional)	¼ cup oil
¼ cup ground sesame seeds	½ cup honey
2 teaspoons baking powder	1 tablespoon grated orange peel
	Juice of 2 oranges

Preheat oven to 375°F. Mix together the flours, salt, seeds, and baking powder. With an electric mixer, beat together eggs, yogurt, oil, honey, orange peel, and juice and pour into the dry ingredients. Stir just enough to moisten them and fill oiled muffin tins two-thirds full. Bake until muffins are golden, about 20 minutes.

Complementary protein: wheat + soy + sesame seeds

Peanut Butter Corn Sticks

12 sticks

These corn sticks are not too sweet. They accompany vegetable soups or stews very nicely.

1 cup whole wheat flour
1 tablespoon baking powder
½ teaspoon salt (optional)
½ cup yellow cornmeal

¼ cup peanut butter
2 tablespoons honey
1 egg, beaten
2/3 cup low-fat milk

Preheat oven to 425°F. Combine flour, baking powder, salt, and cornmeal. In another bowl, blend peanut butter, honey, egg, and milk; stir into dry ingredients. Fill oiled corn stick, gem, or shallow muffin pans two-thirds full. Bake for 12 to 15 minutes.

Complementary protein: peanuts + milk + wheat

4.

Protein for Dessert

Cookies
   Chock-Full Chocolate Chip Cookies
   Peanut Butter Cookies with a Difference

Cakes
   Chameleon Spice Cake (Apple, Banana, or Carob)
  * The Thinking Person's Cheesecake
   Poppy Seed Cake
  * Tofu-Apple-Nut Loaf
   Sesame Dream Bars
   Applesauce-Ginger Squares (or Banana Bread)
   Cypress Point Carrot Cake
  * Betty the Peacenik Gingerbread

Puddings
   Sweet Rice Delight
   Tangy Rice-Sesame Pudding
   Indian Pudding

Pies
   Easy "Pat-In" Dessert Pie Crust
  * Winter Fruit Pie
   Easy Apple-Cheese Pie
   Soybean Pie
  * Frozen Peach Treat

---

*New recipe.

These cookies, cakes, puddings, and pies hopefully will give you some sense of the range of possibilities for making complementary protein desserts. Make up your own with favorite recipes by simply following these rules of thumb.

1. For baking, see "Tips for Baked-In Protein," page 366.

2. For dessert fillings, when a recipe calls for sour cream or cream cheese, substitute any combination of cottage cheese, yogurt, ricotta, or buttermilk. (Sometimes it is better to mix ingredients gently with a fork. A blender can make them thinner than you would want for some recipes.)

3. In addition to the recipes that follow, here are common but often neglected desserts that are *not* empty calories:

Egg custard
Bread pudding
Rice pudding

Fruit cup with toasted nuts or
  seeds
Pumpkin pie

Chock-Full Chocolate Chip Cookies

About 45 cookies

I include this recipe to show that I am definitely not a purist. Actually, this is one of my favorite recipes in the book.

½ cup soft margarine
¾ cup lightly packed brown sugar
2 to 3 egg whites, beaten stiff
1 teaspoon vanilla
1/3 cup instant dry milk (¼ cup
  noninstant)

½ cup water
2 cups whole wheat flour
1 teaspoon baking soda
1 cup chocolate chips
¾ cup chopped peanuts
1 cup sunflower seeds

Preheat oven to 375°F. In a large bowl, cream together margarine and sugar. Add egg whites, vanilla, milk, and water and beat until fluffy. Stir together flour and baking soda and add to wet ingredients. Stir in chocolate chips, peanuts, and seeds. Drop by teaspoonfuls onto a greased baking sheet and bake until browned, 10 to 15 minutes.

Remember, you can add complementary protein ingredients to any cake or cookie recipe that calls for nuts. Just add peanuts and sunflower seeds in place of the nuts or seeds called for in the recipe.

Complementary protein: peanuts + sunflower seeds

Peanut Butter Cookies with a Difference

About 30 cookies

You can omit 1 egg yolk to reduce cholesterol—just add 2 tablespoons water to compensate.

½ cup oil	½ teaspoon salt (optional)
1 cup honey	1 teaspoon cinnamon
¾ cup peanut butter	½ teaspoon mace
2 eggs, beaten	¼ teaspoon cloves
½ cup instant dry milk (1/3 cup noninstant)	½ cup rolled oats or Granola
	½ cup raisins
2 tablespoons baking powder	1½ cups whole wheat flour

Preheat oven to 325°F. In a large bowl, beat oil and honey with an electric mixer until creamy and light. Beat in peanut butter, then eggs, milk, baking powder, salt, and spices. By hand stir in oats, raisins, and flour. Mix well and drop by teaspoonfuls on an unoiled baking sheet. Bake 10 to 12 minutes.

Complementary protein: peanuts + milk + wheat

Chameleon Spice Cake (Apple, Banana, or Carob)

12 servings

This is so yummy, your child may not be able to resist sneaking a fingerful of frosting off the cake. You can omit 1 or 2 egg yolks to reduce cholesterol, replacing each with 1 tablespoon milk.

½ cup honey
½ cup oil
3 eggs
2 teaspoons vanilla
½ cup low-fat milk or buttermilk
2 cups whole wheat pastry flour
½ cup soy flour
½ cup instant dry milk powder
½ cup wheat germ
2 teaspoons baking powder
Spices (for apple or banana cake only):
　1 teaspoon cinnamon
　½ teaspoon nutmeg
　½ teaspoon allspice

Flavoring:
　apple cake: 2 to 3 cups finely chopped cored but unpeeled apples
　banana cake: 1½ cups mashed bananas (about 3 medium)
　carob cake: ½ cup carob powder plus 1 teaspoon instant coffee, mixed with 1/3 cup water
2/3 cup ground sunflower seeds or chopped nuts

Preheat oven to 350°F. In a large bowl cream together honey and oil. Add the eggs one at a time, beating well after each addition, and then the vanilla and liquid milk. In another bowl stir together flours, dry milk, wheat germ, baking powder, and, for apple or banana cake, spices. Add to liquid ingredients and beat well. The mixture should be like normal cake batter; if too dry, add some more milk. Stir in flavoring and beat well again. Fold in sunflower seeds and pour into an oiled 9x13-inch pan. Bake until a toothpick comes out clean, about 45 minutes.

Variation: For banana or carob cake, add ½ cup shredded coconut along with flour.

Frosting

2 tablespoons softened margarine
¼ cup honey
1 teaspoon vanilla
2 to 3 tablespoons low-fat milk
   or buttermilk

1 cup instant powdered milk (for
   spice frosting) or 2/3 cup
   instant powdered milk plus ¼
   cup carob powder (for carob
   frosting)
Dash each cinnamon, nutmeg, and
   allspice (or more to taste)

Cream together margarine, honey, and vanilla. Beat in liquid and dry milk and spices. Beat until smooth, adding more liquid or dry milk for desired consistency.

Variation: For a fruit frosting, substitute fruit juice for milk and grated orange rind for spices.

Complementary protein: wheat + soy + milk + seeds

The Thinking Person's Cheesecake

8 servings

Why eat a cheesecake full of fat, cholesterol, and sugar when you can make this cake—just as delicious—with little fat or cholesterol?

1 pound cottage cheese or part-
   skim-milk ricotta
1 cup plain yogurt
3 egg whites

1¼ teaspoons vanilla (or more to
   taste)
1/3 cup honey
Easy "Pat-In" Dessert Pie Crust

Preheat oven to 350°F. Blend cottage cheese, yogurt, egg whites, vanilla, and honey until smooth and pour into crust. Bake until the center is firm, about 35 minutes.

Serve with fresh berries. If you have no berries, combine ¾ cup yogurt with a few tablespoons honey (to taste) and spread over the cake after it has cooled.

Complementary protein: milk product + wheat

Poppy Seed Cake

10 servings

This cake can be whipped together in 10 minutes. It originated with a very close friend, who always delights her guests (especially me) and her children when she makes it.

One 2½-ounce box poppy seeds
1 cup low-fat milk
2 eggs
¾ cup oil
¾ cup honey

½ teaspoon vanilla or almond
  extract
2 cups whole wheat flour
¼ cup instant milk powder
Dash cinnamon and/or nutmeg
2½ teaspoons baking powder

Soak poppy seeds in milk for 1 hour. Preheat oven to 350°F. Add eggs, oil, honey, and vanilla to seeds and beat together. In another bowl mix flour, dry milk, cinnamon, and baking powder. Add dry ingredients to wet and mix. Bake in a greased and floured cake pan for 45 minutes.

This cake is delicious plain but can be made more special by adding a lemon frosting. Use the frosting recipe for Chameleon Spice Cake, omitting the spices, substituting 2 to 3 tablespoons lemon juice for the milk, and adding the grated peel of 1 lemon. If you frost the cake while it is hot, the frosting will drip down the sides.

Complementary protein: wheat + milk

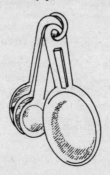

Tofu-Apple-Nut Loaf

1 loaf or 12 squares

This recipe is a favorite of Bill and Akiko Shurtleff of the Soyfoods Center in Lafayette, California. They write, "This delectable, slightly sweet whole wheat bread . . . has a light, well-risen texture but requires the use of no eggs, milk, or other dairy products. The secret lies in the use of tofu."

1 cup tofu	1 tablespoon lemon juice
2 cups applesauce (if using unsweetened applesauce, increase honey to ½ cup)	½ teaspoon cinnamon
	¼ teaspoon salt (optional)
	2 cups whole wheat flour
½ cup oil	1½ teaspoons baking soda
¼ cup honey	½ to ¾ cup chopped walnuts
Grated rind of 1 lemon	1 cup raisins

Preheat oven to 350°F. In a blender, combine tofu, applesauce, oil, honey, lemon rind, lemon juice, cinnamon, and salt and purée until smooth. Sift together flour and baking soda and combine with puréed ingredients in a large bowl. Stir in walnuts and raisins. Pour into a well-greased 9-inch ring mold or large loaf pan and bake until a toothpick comes out clean, about 50 minutes. Cool for 5 minutes in the mold or pan, then remove. Serve hot or cold.

Variation: For banana bread, substitute 2 to 3 mashed bananas for the applesauce.

Complementary protein: soy (tofu) + wheat

Sesame Dream Bars

2 dozen

A heavenly taste combination.

Cookie Base

½ cup margarine, softened
½ cup honey

1¼ cups whole wheat flour
¼ cup soy flour

Preheat oven to 350°F. Cream together margarine and honey until light and fluffy. Add flours and blend well. Spread in an oiled 13x9x2-inch pan (a smaller pan will give you a cakey bar) and bake about 20 minutes until firm and just beginning to brown. Cool 5 minutes before adding top layer.

Top Layer

2 eggs
¾ cup honey or brown sugar
1 teaspoon vanilla
¼ cup whole wheat flour

½ teaspoon baking powder
½ cup unsweetened shredded
   coconut
¼ to ½ cup ground sesame seeds

Beat eggs until light. Beat honey and vanilla; add flour and baking powder. Stir in coconut and sesame seeds. Spread in an even layer over cookie base. Return to oven and bake 20 minutes. Let cool for about ½ hour before cutting into squares.

Complementary protein: wheat + soy + sesame seeds

Applesauce-Ginger Squares
(or Banana Bread)

16 two-inch squares

The banana and peanut variation is especially good-tasting. Victoria Phare of Ferndale, California, suggests adding ½ cup yogurt with the bananas.

1 cup applesauce
½ cup honey
1/3 cup oil or melted margarine
1¼ cups whole wheat flour
1/3 cup soy flour
1 teaspoon baking soda

½ teaspoon each salt, cinnamon, ginger, and cloves
1/3 to 2/3 cup ground or chopped roasted peanuts
½ to 1 cup ground or whole sunflower seeds

Preheat oven to 350°F. Mix together applesauce, honey, and oil. Combine dry ingredients and mix into wet ingredients. Stir in peanuts and seeds. Bake in an 8-inch-square pan for 30 minutes.

Variation: Substitute 2 mashed ripe bananas, 1 teaspoon vanilla, and 1 egg for the applesauce. Reduce honey to taste. Bake in a small oiled bread pan at 350°F for about 1 hour.

Complementary protein: peanuts + sunflower seeds

Cypress Point Carrot Cake

12 servings

Cypress Point refers to my former home in Pt. Richmond, California, a lovely community nestled right on San Francisco Bay. It was there that I wrote the first edition of *Diet for a Small Planet*.

The sauce is optional, and you can reduce cholesterol by omitting 1 egg yolk from the cake. Still, this is an incredibly rich treat, suitable for New Year's Eve and other celebrations.

1½ cups whole wheat flour
½ cup soy flour
2 teaspoons cinnamon
2 teaspoons baking soda
2 cups grated carrots
1 cup crushed pineapple, drained
½ cup chopped nuts

½ cup ground sesame seeds
3½ ounces shredded coconut
3 eggs
¾ cup oil
¾ cup buttermilk
½ cup honey or 1 cup brown sugar

Sauce

½ cup buttermilk
¼ cup honey or ½ cup brown sugar

½ teaspoon baking soda
½ to 1 stick margarine

Preheat oven to 350°F. Combine flours, cinnamon, and baking soda. In another bowl, mix carrots, pineapple, nuts, sesame seeds, and coconut. In a large bowl, beat together eggs, oil, buttermilk, and honey. Add carrot mixture to egg mixture, then add flour. Bake in an angel food cake or fluted-edge pan for 1 hour.

Combine sauce ingredients and simmer for 5 minutes. Take the cake out of pan, punch tiny holes in the top, and pour the sauce over it.

Complementary protein: wheat + soy + sesame seeds + milk

Betty the Peacenik Gingerbread

9 to 12 servings

A favorite of Claire Greensfelder, San Francisco. She earned the name "Betty the Peacenik" in 1970, when simultaneously she was the Betty Crocker Homemaker of Tomorrow and a leader of Students for Political Action in her high school in Oakland.

½ cup margarine, cut up	¼ cup soy flour
½ cup brown sugar	½ teaspoon each baking powder
½ cup molasses	and baking soda
½ cup boiling water	½ teaspoon salt (optional)
1 egg	1 teaspoon each ginger and
1¼ cups whole wheat flour	cinnamon

Preheat oven to 350°F. Put margarine, sugar, and molasses in a large bowl and add boiling water, stirring until well mixed. Add the egg and stir again. In a separate bowl, mix flours, baking powder and soda, salt, and spices. Pour dry ingredients into wet and beat until smooth. Pour into a 9-inch square or round pan and bake for 35 minutes. Serve with applesauce or yogurt.

Complementary protein: wheat + soy

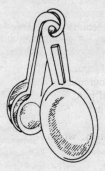

Sweet Rice Delight

4 servings

This is a good way to use up leftover brown rice and makes a nice change from rice pudding. It is best made several hours ahead of time and refrigerated to let the flavors blend.

1½ cups cooked brown rice (½ cup uncooked)
½ cup toasted sesame seed meal
¼ cup honey
½ cup coconut

1 cup canned pineapple chunks, drained
1 banana, sliced
½ to 1 cup other fruit, fresh or canned and drained
1 cup low-fat yogurt
Chopped nuts (optional)

Gently mix together everything but the nuts. Just before serving, stir again and sprinkle nuts on top, or stir them in if you like.

Complementary protein: rice + sesame seeds + milk product

Tangy Rice-Sesame Pudding

6 servings

Especially good served warm. Arrange fresh orange slices on each dessert bowl for an elegant ending to a meal. You can omit 1 egg yolk to reduce cholesterol (add another egg white).

1¾ cups cooked brown rice (¾ cup uncooked)
2 cups orange juice
3 tablespoons ground sesame seeds
½ cup well-packed brown sugar
Grated rind of 1 orange

2 eggs, well beaten
½ teaspoon each cinnamon and ginger
¼ teaspoon nutmeg
1 teaspoon vanilla extract
½ cup raisins (optional)
Garnish: 2 oranges, peeled and sectioned

Preheat oven to 350°F. Combine all ingredients except oranges and mix well. Put in an oiled baking dish and bake until firm, about 1 hour. Spoon into bowls and garnish.

Complementary protein: rice + sesame seeds

Indian Pudding

4 to 6 servings

This pudding is delicious both hot and cold, especially with yogurt, sour cream, or ice cream. To reduce cholesterol, omit 1 egg yolk.

4 cups low-fat milk
1 cup yellow cornmeal
¼ cup soy grits soaked in ½ cup water
1/3 cup margarine*
2/3 cup light molasses

½ teaspoon ground cinnamon
¼ teaspoon each ground cloves and ginger
⅛ teaspoon each ground allspice and nutmeg
2 eggs, beaten

Preheat oven to 325°F. Bring milk to a boil and gradually add cornmeal and grits. Lower heat and beat with a whisk until it begins to thicken. Remove from heat and add margarine, molasses, and spices. Let cool slightly and add eggs. Pour into a greased baking dish and bake until firm, about 45 to 60 minutes.

Variation: Add ½ cup dried fruit.

Complementary protein: corn + soy + milk

---

* An unmessy way to measure margarine: fill a cup two-thirds full of water, then add margarine until cup is brimming. Drain off water.

Easy "Pat-In" Dessert Pie Crust

1 pie crust

Great for any cheesecake or dessert pie. It's easier and healthier than using graham crackers.

2 cups Granola ¼ cup orange or other fruit juice

In a blender, process Granola to a coarse powder. Transfer to a bowl and add juice. Mix thoroughly and pack into a 9-inch pie dish. I usually brown the crust in a 350°F oven for 10 minutes before filling it.

A delicious dessert pie crust can also be made simply by adding a couple of tablespoon brown sugar to the Sesame–Whole Wheat "Pat-In" Crust.

Complementary protein: wheat + nuts

Winter Fruit Pie

One 9-inch pie

On a lecture trip to St. Louis' Webster College, I was treated to dinner in a delightful whole-foods restaurant, the Sunshine Inn. The hit of the evening was this unusual pie. No one, including me, guessed that the topping was made of tofu. Nor did I guess that a pie so elegant could be so simple to make. Thank you, Martha McBroom.

Juice of ½ lemon
2 2/3 cups cored and sliced
  baking apples (peeled if
  sprayed)
1 1/3 cups cranberries, washed
1/3 cup honey plus 1/3 to ½ cup
  honey (to taste)

1 teaspoon cinnamon
2 2/3 tablespoons tapioca
1 pound tofu
½ teaspoon sea salt
1 tablespoon vanilla
Easy "Pat-In" Dessert Pie Crust

Squeeze lemon juice over apples, just enough to coat them, and combine apples, cranberries, ⅓ cup honey, cinnamon, and tapioca. Let sit for at least 15 minutes.

Preheat oven to 425°F. In a blender or food processor, process tofu, remaining honey, salt, and vanilla until smooth. (Or mix tofu with a fork or electric mixer until fairly smooth, then blend in remaining ingredients.) Fill pie crust with fruit mixture and then spread with topping. Bake for 15 minutes, then reduce oven temperature to 350°F and bake until golden, about 25 minutes more.

Complementary protein: soy (tofu) + wheat

Easy Apple-Cheese Pie

6 servings

This simple-to-make pie is very special. It goes well with many different types of dinners—from the traditional to the exotic.

3 to 4 tart green eating apples	Up to ½ cup brown sugar (to
Juice of ½ lemon	taste)
Easy "Pat-In" Dessert Pie Crust	1 egg
8 ounces ricotta cheese	½ cup low-fat yogurt
	1 teaspoon vanilla

Preheat oven to 350°F. Peel, core, and slice the apples and sprinkle with lemon juice. Arrange slices on pie crust in circles, overlapping slightly. In a bowl, beat with a fork (*not* an electric mixer) the ricotta cheese, sugar, egg, yogurt, and vanilla. Pour over the apples and bake until pie is lightly browned and a knife comes out clean, about 30 minutes. Cool and chill in refrigerator for at least 1 hour.

Complementary protein: wheat + milk product

Soybean Pie

6 servings

This tastes incredibly like pumpkin pie.

1½ cups very well-cooked
  soybeans (½ cup uncooked)
¾ cup honey
Salt to taste
1 teaspoon cinnamon

½ teaspoon ginger
¾ teaspoon nutmeg
2 eggs, slightly beaten
¾ cup low-fat milk
4 tablespoons instant dry milk
Easy "Pat-In" Dessert Pie Crust

Preheat oven to 450°F. Purée soybeans in a blender or with the fine blade of a food grinder. Combine with remaining ingredients except pie crust and pour into crust. Bake for 15 minutes, then reduce oven temperature to 350°F and bake until a knife comes out clean, about 30 minutes more.

Complementary protein: wheat + soy + milk

Frozen Peach Treat

8 to 10 servings

My children did a blind taste test of four versions of this recipe. They loved them all, but this one was the winner. It's from Claire Greensfelder (see Betty the Peacenik Gingerbread), who once wrote a food column for the *East Bay Voice*.

6 ripe peaches, peeled and
  chopped
1 quart plain yogurt

Juice of ½ lemon
Honey to taste

In a large bowl, mash peaches with a potato masher or pastry cutter. (If you use a blender, more of the water will be drawn from the fruit and you will have more crunchy water crystals.) Add yogurt, lemon juice, and honey and stir. Ladle into serving bowls or paper cups. Set in the freezer for at least 2½ hours. An incredibly refreshing treat.

Appendixes

Appendix A. Education for Action: Recommended Books and Periodicals

It is hard to sustain hope and energy for change when we are bombarded each day by the media. War, crime, AIDS, poverty, environment. . . . We easily feel overwhelmed. To develop an understanding of how one's own efforts can make a difference, to learn about work for positive change, we need to expand the news and analysis coming into our lives. We can select analyses as well as news about citizen initiatives that would rarely appear in the daily paper or on the evening news.

Here are some reading suggestions you might consider from the two organizations I have helped to found:

From the Institute for the Arts of Democracy, 36 Eucalyptus Lane, Suite 100, San Rafael, California 94901:

Building Citizen Democracy: Concepts and Citizen Arts for Renewing Public Life. A lively booklet presenting the philosophy behind citizen democracy and its practical implications for renewing public life. Includes questions for group discussion. Frances Moore Lappé $4.00

Rediscovering America's Values. Written as a lively dialogue about freedom, democracy, and fairness, this book is sparking discussion about the values that shape our society. Frances Moore Lappé   Paperback, $12.95

Please write for a complete list of publications and membership information.

From the Institute for Food and Development Policy (Food First), 145 Ninth Street, San Francisco, CA 94103.

World Hunger: Twelve Myths, 208 pages with photographs. A good next-step for understanding world hunger after reading *Diet for a Small Planet*. It also includes a resource guide. Frances Moore Lappé and Joseph Collins, 1986.   Paperback, $9.95

Alternatives to the Peace Corps: A Directory of Third World and U.S. Volunteer Opportunities. Brings together resources and information that will help the prospective volunteer find an appropriate placement abroad. 1991 Edition. $6.95

Don't be Afraid Gringo: A Honduran Woman Speaks from the Heart. A gripping narrative that tells about courage and hope in face of injustice and violence, it captures powerful lessons about the causes of third world poverty and the role of U.S. foreign policy. Elvia Alvarado. Translated and edited by Medea Benjamin, with photographs by Susan Meiselas. 1987. $7.95

Taking Population Seriously. Explores the critical lessons to be learned from third world societies most successful in bringing down birth rates. Frances Moore Lappé and Rachel Schurman. 1990. $7.95

Please write for a complete list of publications and membership information.

My recommended alternatives to mass-media news includes:

Broad coverage:

Weeklies:

The Nation, Box 1953, Marion, OH 43306. Hard-hitting analysis. Short pieces.

In These Times, 1300 W. Belmont, Chicago, IL 60657. News providing critical perspective.

Monthlies/bi-monthlies/quarterlies:

The American Prospect, quarterly, P.O. Box 7645, Princeton, NJ 08543-7645. New journal from the country's most creative liberals; insightful, in-depth pieces.

Mother Jones, monthly, 1663 Mission St., San Francisco, CA 94103. Social, cultural, political analysis.

New Options Newsletter, monthly, 2005 Massachusetts Avenue, Washington, DC 20036. Analysis of trends, books, organizations, and ideas leading to a sustainable society.

Organize Training Center Clipping Service, quarterly, Organize Training Center, 1095 Market, #419, San Francisco, CA 94103. You get a well-organized compilation of newspaper and magazine articles from around the country—all about citizens making change. It's a terrific service for busy people.

The Progressive, monthly, 409 E. Main St., Madison, WI 53703. Provides valuable in-depth critical coverage of current events and social issues.

Sojourners, monthly, 1321 Otis NE, Washington, DC 20017. Progressive analysis of social issues grounded in a commitment to living religious values.

Tikkun, 5100 Leona St., Oakland, CA 94619, bi-monthly. More than progressive and Jewish—particularly thoughtful essays on a broad range of critical social issues.

Utne Reader, bi-monthly, Box 1974, Marion, OH 43305. Reprints the best articles from a wide cross-section of the alternative press and features guides to other alternative periodicals.

Specific concerns:

Monthlies/Quarterlies:

Building Economic Alternatives, quarterly, c/o Coop America, 2100 M. St. NW, Suite 403, Washington, DC 20063. Focuses on how to spend, save, invest, boycott, and change our habits to contribute to a healthier world.

Democracy in Education, quarterly, The Institute for Democracy and Education, 119 McCracken Hall, Ohio University, Athens, OH 45701-2979. Inspiring articles about teaching for active citizenship, for teachers and non-teachers alike. A great antidote to despair about public schools.

Dollars and Sense, 38 Union Square, Room 14, Somerville, MA 02143. Easy-to-understand, short pieces demystifying economics.

The Ecologist, Whitehay, Withiel Bodmin, Cornwall UK. The best single source of in-depth, critical looks at environmental problems and activism.

Multinational Monitor, P.O. Box 19405, Washington, DC, 20036. Gripping exposés of multi-national corporations' role here and abroad.

Nutrition Action, Center for Science in the Public Interest, 1875 Connecticut Ave. NW, Washington, DC 20009. Highly usable, cutting-edge info on healthy, ecological eating. Zesty writing. Fun to read.

Vegetarian Times P.O. Box 570, Oak Park, IL 60303. A broader focus than you might think from the title. Makes non-meat eating an adventure into a variety of social arenas.

Focusing on hunger, poverty and international development:

New Internationalist, 113 Atlantic Avenue, Brooklyn, NY 11201. Published in England. Popularly accessible, moving writing.

Seeds, 222 East Lake Drive, Decatur, GA 30030. Approaches development from a Christian values base.

WHY, Challenging Hunger and Poverty, 261 West 35th Street, #1403, New York, NY 10001-1906. Excellent source about hunger here and abroad. The voice of World Hunger Year, co-founded by Harry Chapin, who you'll read about in Part IV, Chapter 1.

Appendix B. Basic Cooking Instructions for Beans, Grains, Nuts, and Seeds

Definitions

Soy grits (or soy granules) = partially cooked cracked soybeans.

Soy powder = soybean flour.

Bulgur wheat = partially cooked (parboiled) wheat, usually cracked.

Ground sesame seed = sesame meal. (Can be easily made at home; see cooking instructions below.)

Seasoned stock = any leftover liquid from cooking beans, vegetables, etc., or water with a small amount of powdered or cubed vegetable seasoning. (Available without additives in health food stores; can be substituted for stock in any recipe.)

Here are instructions for preparing the basic ingredients often called for.

Cooking Beans

1. Regular cooking: wash beans in cold water, and soak overnight in three times the volume of water; *or* bring the beans and water to a boil, cover tightly, and let sit for 2 hours. Simmer the beans, partially covered, adding water if necessary, for about 2 hours, depending on the type of bean and the consistency you want. If you want to mash or purée the beans, you will want to cook them until they are quite soft.

2. *Pressure cooking:* a pressure cooker is a real advantage in cooking beans as well as grains. Since the foods cook so much more quickly, a meal doesn't require as much forethought. Pressure cooking also gives you a more tender bean. Soaking or precooking saves a little time, but with pressure cooking it really is not necessary. Bring the washed beans, and three to four times their volume in water, to a boil in the cooker. Cover and bring to 15 pounds pressure. Cook beans for 25 to 45 minutes. Cool immediately. Don't attempt to cook split peas, or any bean that tends to foam, in a pressure cooker or you may find yourself with a clogged cooker and a big mess.

3. *Roasting:* cook beans by one of the above methods for a firm bean. Spread the beans on a lightly oiled baking sheet. Sprinkle with salt, if desired, and bake at 200°F for about 1 hour, until they are well browned. When they are hot, they will be crunchy outside and tender inside. When they are cool, they will be hard and crunchy throughout. You can also roast the beans in a lightly oiled frypan over medium heat on top of the stove. Stir constantly. Soybeans, when roasted, or when chopped or ground in a blender, can be eaten alone. They make a garnish to be sprinkled on a variety of dishes; or use them when nuts or nutmeal are called for.

4. *Making tofu (soybean curd):* tofu is now widely available throughout the United States at most natural food stores and at many supermarkets. Tofu has the best flavor and is least expensive when made at home. For an easy to follow recipe that gives consistently good results see *The Book of Tofu* (Ballantine paperback, $2.95), which also contains over 250 recipes for using the eight basic types of tofu, plus detailed nutritional information and a list of U.S. tofu shops.

Cooking Grains

1. Regular cooking: wash the grains in cold water. Bring stock or water, equal to twice the volume of the grains, to a boil (for millet or buckwheat, use three times the volume). Put in the grains, bring to a boil again, lower heat, and simmer (covered) for 30 to 45 minutes, until all of the liquid is absorbed.

2. Pressure cooking: in the pressure cooker follow the same method, but instead of simmering the grain bring to 15 pounds pressure and cook for about 20 minutes. Cool under cold water when cooking time is up. You may wish to vary the amount of water in order to create the texture of grain you prefer. If you have trouble with sticking, here's the trick I use: put about 1 inch of water in the bottom of the pressure cooker. Put the grain into a stainless-steel bowl that will fit easily into the pressure cooker (with plenty of room between the top of the bowl and the lid of the pressure cooker). Add water to the level of about ¾ inch above the level of the grain. Put the bowl inside the pressure cooker, cover, and begin cooking. This method is also handy when I need to cook both grains and beans at the same time, but separately. I merely put the small stainless-steel bowl inside the pressure cooker. I then put the beans with adequate water around the outside of the bowl, and the grains inside the bowl.

3. Sautéing: this method is most frequently used in cooking bulgur wheat and buckwheat groats, but can be used with any grain to achieve a "nuttier" flavor. Wash the grains and put in a dry saucepan or pressure cooker over low heat. Stir until dry. Add just enough oil to coat each kernel. Sauté the grains, stirring constantly, until all of the grains are golden. Stir in boiling water or stock (amounts as for regular cooking, above) and bring the mixture to a boil. Cover and simmer 30 to 45 minutes; or, if using a pressure cooker, bring to 15 pounds pressure and cook 20 minutes. Cool cooker immediately.

Cooking Nuts and Seeds

1. To roast whole seeds or nuts: place in a dry pan and roast over medium flame until they have desired brownness; or spread them on a baking sheet and toast them in a 200°F oven. Use the seeds whole, or grind them in a blender, a few at a time, or with a mortar and pestle. Add salt if desired.

2. To roast or toast ground seeds or nuts: buy the meal or, to make it yourself, grind the seeds or nuts in a blender. Then roast the meal in a dry pan, stirring constantly, adding salt if desired. Or spread the meal on a baking sheet and bake at 200°F, stirring often. (You can also grind small quantities of whole grains in your blender.)

3. Nut and seed butters: it is easy to make your own fresh nut and seed butters if you have a blender. From whole roasted or raw seeds or nuts: grind as for meal, adding a little oil to "start" the butter; continue adding as many nuts or seeds as your blender can handle. From roasted or raw ground nuts or seeds: stir a little oil, and honey if desired, into the meal, and you will have creamy nut or seed butter.

Appendix C. Protein-Calorie Guidelines for Evaluating Foods

One way to demonstrate that most plant foods are good protein sources is to ask: do most plant foods provide adequate protein without exceeding calorie needs? By this test, most plant foods not only qualify as good protein sources, they excel.

First, from a day's diet, let's subtract those foods that provide *no* protein—oil, butter, sugar, honey, alcohol, and most fruits (fruits provide so little as to be almost insignificant). In a diet of people conscious of the need for moderation in fat and sugar, these foods provide roughly 25 percent of the calories. (In the day's menu in Figure 10, such foods provide about 25 percent of the calories.)

So this means that the remaining 75 percent of one's calories—or 2,025 calories for an "average" American male of 154 pounds—comes from foods containing some protein. The average American male, according to the National Academy of Sciences, needs 56 grams of protein a day. This allowance assumes a diet with considerable animal protein. In a diet with much less animal and more plant protein than the typical American diet, that allowance would rise to 65 grams. And since each gram of protein has 4 calories, this average male needs a total of 260 calories from protein out of a total of 2,025 calories from foods with protein, or 13 percent. Now we have a basis for judging what protein foods will meet the average person's needs on a plant food diet.

Using this guideline, if a food has 13 percent or more of its calories from protein, it qualifies as a protein source that can fill our protein needs without going over our calorie limit. All this means is that if you got all of your protein from this one food, your protein allowance would be covered. This is hypothetical, of course. Few people try to exist on one food

Just because a food—such as rice or carrots, for example—does not qualify on this list does not mean that it is not a good food and should not be eaten. Many are nutritious and should be eaten with food containing a higher percentage of protein-calories.

The following list demonstrates that almost all plant foods qualify as good protein sources, and many are exceptionally strong:

Percent of Calories from Protein

VEGETABLES			
The following qualify:		Lima beans	27%
Spinach	49%	Pintos	26%
Watercress	46%	Peas	26%
Kale	45%	Chickpeas	23%
Broccoli	45%	Peanuts	18%
Collards	43%		
Cauliflower	40%	*The following do not:*	
Mushroom	39%	None	
Lettuce (iceberg)	28%		
Okra	27%	GRAINS	
Radish	24%	*The following qualify:*	
Cucumber	24%	Wheat (hard spring)	17%
Squash	23%	Oatmeal	15%
Cabbage	22%	Rye	14%
Celery	21%		
Eggplant	19%	*The following do not:*	
Onion (green)	17%	Millet	12%*
Corn	15%	Barley (light)	11%*
Beets	15%	Bulgur	10%
Pumpkin	15%	Rice	8%
Turnips	13%		
		NUTS AND SEEDS	
The following do not:		*The following qualify:*	
Potato	11%	Sunflower seeds	17%
Carrot	10%	Sesame seeds	13%
Sweet Potato	6%	Black walnuts	13%
LEGUMES		*The following do not:*	
The following qualify:		Almonds	12%*
Soybeans	33%	Cashews	12%*
Lentils	29%	Pecans	5%

---

* Please note that if a person is eating considerably less than 25 percent of their calories in nonprotein foods such as butter, oil, honey, sugar, alcohol, or fruits, then these foods would definitely be adequate to meet protein needs.

Appendix D. Protein Tables and Tips for Complementing Proteins

The tables in this appendix supply the raw material for your more complete understanding of the whys and hows of combining proteins in order to increase their usability.

The first two columns in the protein tables tell you what percent of your daily protein need is met by an average serving of a given food. The items are ranked in *decreasing* order according to the percent of their contribution to your daily protein requirement, both within each food category and by food category.* *To fulfill your protein allowance, these percentages must add up to 100 each day.*

The last three columns of the tables show you the basis on which I arrived at these percentages: the *total* grams of protein have been reduced by the NPU score of the food in order to arrive at the grams of protein *your body can use.* This amount of usable protein I then divided by the daily protein allowance to get the percent of the daily protein allowance that an average serving fills. Simple enough.

To remind you of the importance of adjusting for protein usability, let me give you a graphic example. If, for instance, we considered that eating ½ ounce of egg protein was the same as eating ½ ounce of peanut protein, we

---

* Except for meat and poultry, placed last, because they are included primarily for the sake of comparison with nonmeat protein sources.

would be greatly mistaken. The amino acid pattern of the egg protein (NPU of 94) is one that the body can use almost completely; but the body can only use half of the peanut protein (NPU of 43), because its amino acids deviate considerably from the body's one utilizable pattern. So if you eat ½ ounce each of egg and peanut protein, you get twice as much protein from the egg as from the peanut. The percentages shown in the charts have been calculated to correct for these differences in the availability of protein to your body.

The only difficulty in adjusting for differences in protein usability is that research to determine the NPU scores of food proteins is still rudimentary. Many plant foods have not been tested, and the NPU scores that we do "know" are often based on a limited number of experiments. We can hope that this research will progress. In the meantime, even with rough estimates of protein quality, we are on better ground than if our calculations were based on *total* protein, knowing full well that 5 to 70 percent of this total is not usable by the body.

The percentages in the first two columns apply to the average American adult—a 154-pound male and a 128-pound female. If you are not quite so average, use the following guideline for determining the appropriate protein intake for your body weight.

For ages 15 to 18, add 10 to the percentage total given for your weight in Table I.

For children (either sex), use the second column on each protein table that follows. If a child, aged 1–3, with an approximate weight of 28 pounds, is getting enough protein, the percentages should add up to 50 percent for the day. For ages 4–6, weight approximately 44 pounds, percentages should add up to 65 percent. And for ages 7–10, weight approximately 66 pounds, percentages should add up to 78 percent.

Add up your protein intake for a few days to see whether or not you are meeting your protein allowance. If you're not, use the tables to figure out ways to increase your intake and let it become a habit!

TABLE I.
ARE YOU GETTING THE RIGHT AMOUNT OF
PROTEIN FOR YOUR BODY?

In the following
Protein Tables . . .

Male Adult		Female Adult		
if you weigh:	the %'s should add up to:	the %'s should add up to:	Total %'s if pregnant:	Total %'s if nursing mother:
108		85	143	123
118	75	90	151	131
128	85	100	168	145
138	90	110	185	160
148	95	115	193	167
154	100	120	202	174
164	105	130	218	187
174	115	135	227	196
184	120	145	244	210
194	125	155	260	225

Mixing Your Own Proteins

Next to the percentages in the tables are letter ratings that allow you to make up your own complementary protein combinations. The letter ratings indicate how well each type of food supplies you with a key amino acid. (Of the eight essential amino acids, only the four likely to be deficient in a diet of nonmeat protein are shown here.) Since egg protein is considered to be the most nearly perfect protein, the ratings are based on how closely the particular amino acid content of a food matches the amount of that amino acid found in egg protein.* Thus:

---

* The amino acid content of egg protein used by scientists as the model is that established by the U.N. Expert Group, reported in *Protein Requirements* (WHO, FAO), 1965.

Letter Ratings: Percent of Egg Amino Acid Content

A + ≥ 100	C = 40–60
A = 80–100	D = 20–40
B = 60–80	E = 1–20

Using the protein tables, you can match the deficiencies in some foods (C and D ratings) with adequacies (A and B ratings) in other foods in order to achieve higher biological values than those of the same foods eaten separately. Discovering the patterns of amino acid strengths and weaknesses in the different food groups will enable you to do your own "protein matching." To help you I provide two guides:

1. For foods having no serious amino acid deficiencies, such as seafood (Protein Table I), dairy products (Protein Table II), and meat and poultry (Protein Table IX), I have emphasized their particular strengths by putting their A + ratings in boldface. These foods need no supplementation from other foods but make excellent supplements themselves.

2. All the other protein tables have foods with serious amino acid deficiencies. The one or two most important weaknesses of each food are indicated by boxed letters. Compensation for these deficiencies can come either from the foods in category 1 above or from other foods having an *opposite* pattern of amino acid deficiency. Rather than concentrating on the names of amino acids, it might be easier simply to note the columns in which weaknesses tend to occur.

Please refer back to page 179 for a chart summarizing the complementary protein combinations. The following protein tables will give you a fuller understanding of the amino acid patterns in foods that make these combinations "work." Following each of the nine protein tables, I also include tips for complementing that particular food's protein.

Protein Table I. SEAFOOD

Average Serving of Seafood, 3½ oz. (100 g), in Decreasing Order of Usable Protein	Percent of Daily Protein Allowance in an Average Serving		Ratings of Amino Acid Content as Compared to Egg Protein				Total Grams of Protein	NPU	Grams of Protein Your Body Can Use[2]
	M	F	Tryp.	Iso.	Lys.	SC.[1]			
					STRENGTH →				
1. Tuna,* canned in oil, drained, ⅔ cup	45%	58%	B	B	A+	B	24	(80)	19
2. Mackerel, Pacific	43	55	B	B	A+	B	21	(80)	18
3. Halibut	40	52	B	B	A+	C	22	(80)	17
4. Humpback salmon	38	48	B	B	A+	B[8]	20	(80)	16
5. Swordfish[3]	36	45	B	B	A+	B	19	(80)	15
6. Striped bass	36	45	B	B	A+	B[8]	19	(80)	15
7. Rockfish	36	45	B	A	A+	B	19	(80)	15
8. Shad	36	45	B	B	A+	B	19	(80)	15
9. Shrimp	36	45	B	B	A+	B[4]	19	(~80)[5]	15
10. Sardines, Atlantic, 8 med., canned in oil	33	42	B	A	A+	B	21	(69)	14
11. Carp	33	42	B	B	A+	A[8]	18	(80)	14
12. Catfish	33	42	B	B	A+	A	18	(80)	14

*Warning: large oceangoing fish like blue-fin tuna and swordfish, which are at the end of long food chains, have shown to be heavily contaminated with mercury.

Seafood Continued

Average Serving of Seafood, 3½ oz (100 g), in Decreasing Order of Usable Protein	Percent of Daily Protein Allowance in an Average Serving		Ratings of Amino Acid Content as Compared to Egg Protein				Total Grams of Protein	NPU	Grams of Protein Your Body Can Use[2]
	M	F	Tryp.	Iso.	Lys.	SC.[1]			
					STRENGTH →				
13. Cod	33%	42	B	B	A+	A	18	(80)	14
14. Pacific herring	33	42	B	A	A+	B	18	(80)	14
15. Haddock	33	42	B	B	A+	A	18	(80)	14
16. Crab	33	42	B	B	A+	B[4]	17	(~80)	14
17. Northern lobster	33	42	B	B	A+	B[4]	17	(~80)	14
18. Squid	31	39	A	B	A+	B	16	(~80)	13
19. Scallops, 2 or 3	29	36	A	B	A+	B	15	(~80)	12
20. Flounder or sole	29	36	B	B	A+	C	15	(80)	12
21. Clams, 4 large, 8 small	26	33	A	B	A+	B	14	(~80)	11
22. Oysters, 2 to 4	21	27	A	B	A+	B	11	(~80)	9

[1] Amino acids: Tryp. = Tryptophan. Iso. = Isoleucine; Lys. = Lysine; SC. = Sulphur-containing amino acids.
These are the four essential amino acids likely to be deficient in plant protein.

[2] Loss calculated from the Net Protein Utilization score (NPU). See page 68 for an explanation of NPU.

[3] Also slightly deficient in the aromatic amino acids, phenylalanine, and tyrosine.

[4] Also slightly deficient in valine.

[5] ~ = estimated.

Protein Table II. DAIRY PRODUCTS

Average Serving of Dairy Products	Percent of Daily Protein Allowance in an Average Serving		Ratings of Amino Acid Content as Compared to Egg Protein				Total Grams of Protein	NPU	Grams of Protein Your Body Can Use
	M	F	Tryp.	Iso.	Lys.	SC.[1]			
					STRENGTH				
1. Cottage cheese, 6 tbsp, 3½ oz (100 g)									
Uncreamed	31	39	B	A	A+	B	17	(~75)	13
Creamed	26	33	B	A	A+	B	14	(~75)	11
2. Egg white, dried, powdered, ½ oz (14 g)	21	27	A+	B	A+	A+	11	(83)	9
3. Milk, non-fat dry solids, 4 tbsp, 1 oz (5½ tbsp inst.)	19	24	A	B	A+	B	10	(82)	8
4. Parmesan cheese, 1 inch sq, 1 oz (28 g)	17	21	B	A	A+	B	10	(~70)	7
5. Milk, skim, whole or buttermilk, 1 c (244 g)	17	21	A	A	A+	B	9	(82)	7
6. Yogurt from skim milk, 1 c (244 g)	17	21	A	A	A+	B	8	(82)	7
7. Swiss cheese, 1 inch sq, 1 oz (28 g)	14	18	B	A	A+	B	8	(~70)	6

Dairy Products Continued

Average Serving of Dairy Products	Percent of Daily Protein Allowance in an Average Serving		Ratings of Amino Acid Content as Compared to Egg Protein				Total Grams of Protein	NPU	Grams of Protein Your Body Can Use
	M	F	Tryp.	Iso.	Lys.	SC.[1]			
					STRENGTH →				
8. Edam cheese, 1 inch sq, 1 oz (28 g)	14	18	B	A	A+	B	8	(~70)	6
9. Egg, 1 medium (48 g)	14	18	A	A	A+	A	6	(94)	6
10. Ricotta cheese, ¼ c (60 g)	12	15	B	A	A+	B	7	(~75)	5
11. Cheddar cheese, 1 inch sq, 1 oz (28 g)	12	15	B	A	A+	B	7	(70)	5
12. Roquefort cheese or Blue mold, 1 inch sq, 1 oz (28 g)	10	12	B	A	A+	B	6	(~70)	4
13. Camembert cheese, 1 inch sq, 1 oz (28 g)	10	12	B	A	A+	B	5	(~70)	4
14. Ice cream, about 1/5 pint (100 g)	10	12	A	A	A+	B	5	(~82)	4

The following dairy products are not good protein sources because they contain too many calories for the amount of protein you get:[1] cream, sour cream, cream cheese, butter (no protein).

[1]See page 130 for an explanation of the selection of good protein sources based on their calorie-to-protein ratio.

Tips for complementing other foods with seafood

The lysine strength (A+) of seafood means that it can complement well the protein of foods low in lysine, such as grains and certain nuts and seeds.

Tips for using dairy products to complement the protein in other foods

1. **Amino Acid Makeup:** dairy products have excellent amino acid ratings, as you would suppose from their high NPU scores. Thus they make good supplements to any food. But dairy products have notable amino acid strengths in isoleucine, and especially in lysine. These strengths can be used to advantage in combination with cereal grains (Protein Table V), which are low in both of these same amino acids. And it doesn't take much! Only 2 tablespoons of nonfat dried milk added to 1 cup of wheat or rye flour increases the protein quality about 45 percent. Thus, bread with cheese, cheese-rice casseroles, and cereal with milk are all good protein mixes. These same amino acid strengths allow dairy products to complement the protein of nuts and seeds (Protein Table IV): sesame, peanuts, black walnuts, etc.

2. Experimentally determined complementary protein mixes include milk products:

plus Grains, for example:

Milk + Rice
Milk + Wheat
Milk + Corn + Soy
Milk + Wheat + Peanuts

plus Nuts and seeds, for example:

Milk + Peanuts
Milk + Sesame

plus Legumes, for example:

Milk + Beans

plus Potatoes:

Milk + Potatoes

Protein Table III. LEGUMES: Dried Beans, Peas, and Lentils

Average Serving of Legumes, ¼-½ c dry[1] (Approx. 50 g)	Percent of Daily Protein Allowance in an Average Serving		Ratings of Amino Acid Content as Compared to Egg Protein				Total Grams of Protein	NPU	Grams of Protein Your Body Can Use
	M	F	Tryp.	Iso.	Lys.	SC.[1]			
	If complemented, add 5%		DEFICIENCY →		DEFICIENCY	→			
1. Soybeans or soy grits	24	30	A	B	A	C[3]	17	(61)	10
2. Mung beans	17	21	C	C	A+	D	12	(57)	7
3. Broad beans	14	18	C	B	A	D	13	(48)	6
4. Peas	14	18	C	B	A+	D	12	(47)	6
5. Black beans	12	15	B	A+	A	C	12	(42)	5
6. Cowpeas (black-eyed)	12	15	B	C	A+	D	12	(45)	5
7. Kidney beans	12	15	C	B	A+	D	12	(38)	5
8. Chick-peas (garbanzos)	12	15	C	B	A+	C	11	(43)	5
9. Lima beans	12	15	C	B	A+	C	10	(52)	5
10. Tofu (soybean curd), wet weight, 3½ oz, 2"x2"x2½"	12	15	A	B	A	C	8	(65)	5
11. Lentils	10	12	C	B	A+	D	13	(30)	4
12. Other common beans, navy, pea bean, white	10	12	C	B	A+	D[2]	11	(38)	4

[1] Makes ¾-1 c when cooked.

[2] Also deficient in valine. See page 413 for an explanation of C and D ratings.

Protein Table IV. NUTS AND SEEDS

Average Serving of Nuts and Seeds, Approx. 1 oz (28 g)	Percent of Daily Protein Allowance in an Average Serving		Ratings of Amino Acid Content as Compared to Egg Protein				Total Grams of Protein	NPU	Grams of Protein Your Body Can Use
	M	F	Tryp.	Iso.	Lys.	SC.[1]			
1. Pignolia nuts, 2½ tbsp	If complemented, add 3–4%		—[1]	—	—	—	9	(~50)	5
	12	15		DEFICIENCY →	→				
2. Pumpkin and squash seeds, 2 tbsp	If complemented, add 2–3%		A	B	B	—	8	(~60)	5
	12	15							
3. Sunflower seeds, 3 tbsp, or sunflower meal, 4 tbsp	10	12	A	B	C	B	7	(58)	4
4. Peanuts, 2 tbsp	7	9	B	C	C	C[2]	8	(43)	3
5. Peanut butter, 2 tbsp	7	9	A+	C	C	C[2]	8	(43)	3
6. Cashews, 12–16 nuts	7	9	A+	B	B	B	5	(58)	3
7. Sesame seeds, 3 tbsp, or sesame meal, 4 tbsp	7	9	A	C	C	A	5	(53)	3
8. Pistachio nuts, 3 tbsp	7	9	B	C	B	B[2]	5	(~50)	3
9. Black walnuts,[3] 4 tbsp, 16–20 halves	7	9	B	C	D	B	6	(~50)	3
10. Brazil nuts, 8 medium	5	6	A+	C	C	A+	4	(50)	2

The following nuts are not good protein sources because they contain too many calories for the amount of protein you get: pecans, chestnuts, coconuts, filberts, hazelnuts, macadamia nuts, almonds, pine nuts, English walnuts.

[1]Amino acid content unknown.

[2]Also deficient in threonine.

[3]Black walnuts have about 40 percent more protein than English walnuts.

Tips for complementing the protein in legumes

1. **Amino Acid Makeup:** notice in Protein Table III that the major amino acid deficiencies of legumes appear in the two **outside** columns: tryptophan and the sulfur-containing amino acids. But among the nuts and seeds in Protein Table IV and among grains in Protein Table V, deficiencies appear most frequently in the two **inside** columns: isoleucine and lysine. It is now clear why legume protein, on the one hand, and the protein in grains and certain nuts and seeds, on the other hand, complement each other. Having exactly the opposite strengths and weaknesses, in combination they become more complete proteins.

2. Experimentally determined complementary protein mixes include legumes:

plus Grains, for example:

> Legumes + Rice
> Soybeans + Rice + Wheat
> Beans + Wheat
> Soybeans + Corn + Milk
> Beans + Corn
> Soybeans + Wheat + Sesame

plus Dairy products, for example:

> Beans + Milk

plus Nuts and seeds, for example:

> Soybeans + Peanuts* + Sesame
> Soybeans + Peanuts* + Wheat + Rice
> Soybeans + Sesame + Wheat

---

* Peanuts are botanically classified as legumes.

Tips for complementing the protein in nuts and seeds

1. **Amino Acid Makeup:** the amino acid pattern that emerges among the nuts and seeds is one of deficiency in the two **inside** columns, isoleucine and lysine, and strength in the two **outside** columns, tryptophan and the sulfur-containing amino acids. Sesame seed strikingly exemplifies this contrast. Seeds and many nuts, therefore, make good complements of legumes, which have just the opposite pattern—as you recall from Protein Table III.

Remember also the potential of dairy products to fill the amino acid "gaps" of nuts and seeds. The strength of dairy products in the two **inside** columns, isoleucine and lysine, means they have exactly what is needed by the nuts and seeds. It is not at all surprising, then, that experimentation has resulted in the complementary combinations below.

2. Experimentally determined complementary protein mixes include nuts and seeds:

plus Legumes, for example:

> Peanuts* + Sesame + Soybeans
> Sesame + Beans
> Sesame + Soybeans + Wheat

plus Dairy products, for example:

> Peanuts + Milk

plus Other nuts or seeds, for example:

> Peanuts + Sunflower seeds

plus Grains (because grains and nuts and seeds are low in the same amino acids, their complementarity seems to depend usually on the presence of legumes or dairy products), for example:

> Peanuts + Wheat + Milk
> Sesame + Wheat + Soybeans
> Exception: Sesame + Rice

---

* Peanuts are botanically classified as legumes.

Protein Table V. GRAINS, CEREALS, AND THEIR PRODUCTS

Average Serving of Grains, Cereals, and Their Products[1]	Percent of Daily Protein Allowance in an Average Serving		Ratings of Amino Acid Content as Compared to Egg Protein				Total Grams of Protein	NPU	Grams of Protein Your Body Can Use
	M	F	Tryp.	Iso.	Lys.	SC.[1]			
	If complemented, add 2–3%			DEFICIENCY					
1. Triticale	14	18	—[2]	—	—	—	10	(~60)[3]	6
2. Wheat, whole grain hard red spring, 1/3 c (55–60 g)	12	15	B	C	C	B	8	(60)	5
3. Rye, whole grain, 1/3 c (55–60 g)	10	12	C	C	C	B	7	(58)	4
4. Egg noodles, cooked tender, 1 c (160 g)	10	12	B	B	C	C	7	(~60)	4
5. Bulgur (parboiled wheat), 1/3 c (50–55 g), or Cracked wheat cereal, 1/3 c (35–40 g)	10	12	B	C	C	B	6	(~60)	4
6. Barley, pot or Scotch, 1/3 c (60–65 g)	10	12	A	C	C	B	6	(60)	4
7. Millet, 1/3 c (55–60 g)	7	9	A+	B	C	A	6	(~55)	3

Grains Continued

Average Serving of Grains, Cereals, and Their Products	Percent of Daily Protein Allowance in an Average Serving		Ratings of Amino Acid Content as Compared to Egg Protein				Total Grams of Protein	NPU	Grams of Protein Your Body Can Use
	M	F	Tryp.	Iso.	Lys.	SC.[1]			
				DEFICIENCY →	→				
8. Spaghetti or Macaroni cooked tender, 1 c (140–150 g)	7	9	B	B	C	C	5	(~50)	3
9. Oatmeal, 1/3 c (30–35 g)	7	9	B	C	C	B	4	(66)	3
10. Rice, 1/3 c (60–65 g)									
a. Brown	7	9	B	C	C	B	5	(70)	3
b. Parboiled (converted)	7	9	B	B	C	A	5	(~70)	3
c. Milled, polished	5	6	A	B	C	B	4	(57)	2
11. Wheat germ, commercial, 2 level tbsp (11–12 g)	5	6	C	B	A+	B	3	(67)	2
12. Bread, commercial, 1 slice, whole wheat or rye	3	4	—	—	—	—	2.4	(~45)	1.2
13. Wheat bran, crude, 2 round tbsp (10 g)	2	3	A	C	B	A	1.6	(55)	0.9

[1]Raw unless otherwise stated.
[2]Amino acid pattern unknown.
[3]At least one triticale producer claimed a usability score (PER) comparable to soybeans.

Protein Table VI. FLOUR

For ease in calculating the amount of protein in the bread you make, protein values for flours are given here per cup rather than per average serving.

One Cup of Flour	Ratings of Amino Acid Content as Compared to Egg Protein				Total Grams of Protein	Grams of Protein Your Body Can Use		If complemented, add usable grams[1]
	Tryp.	Iso.	Lys.	SC.		NPU		
		DEFICIENCY						
		→	→					
1. Soybean flour, defatted (138 g)	A	B	A	C[2]	65	(61)	40	5
2. Gluten flour (140 g)	B	B	D	B[3]	85	(39)	23	?
3. Peanut flour, defatted (100 g)	B	C	C	C	48	(43)	21	9
4. Soybean flour, full fat (72 g)	A	B	A	C	26	(61)	16	3
5. Whole wheat flour, or Cracked wheat cereal (120 g) (see Appendix F for comparison with white flour)	B	C	D	B	16	(60)	10	2

Flour Continued

One Cup of Flour	Ratings of Amino Acid Content as Compared to Egg Protein				Total Grams of Protein	Grams of Protein Your Body Can Use NPU	If complemented, add usable grams[1]
	Tryp.	Iso.	Lys.	SC.			
		DEFICIENCY →	→				
6. Rye flour, dark[4] (119 g)	C	C	C	B	16	(58) 9	2
7. Buckwheat flour, dark[4] (100 g)	B	C	C	B	12	(65) 8	2
8. Oatmeal (80 g)	B	C	C	B	11	(66) 7	1
9. Barley flour (112 g)	B	C	C	B	11	(60) 7	2
10. Cornmeal, whole ground (118 g)	C	C	C	B	10	(51) 5	2
11. Wheat bran, crude (55 g)	A	C	B	A	9	(55) 5	1

[1] Approximate amount of protein saved by complementing the protein in the flour. Refer to the beginning of Table V for tips on complementing grain protein.

[2] Also slightly deficient in valine.

[3] Also deficient in threonine.

[4] Both dark rye and dark buckwheat flours have almost twice as much protein as the light varieties.

Tips for complementing the protein in grains, cereals, and
their products

1. **Amino Acid Makeup:** Like many nuts and seeds on
the previous protein table, the amino acid deficiencies of
grains, cereals, and their products, including flour (Protein Table VI), generally appear in the two inside columns,
isoleucine and lysine. (This pattern is broken primarily by
processed cereal products and by legume flours that I have
included here only for convenience.) As we have already
noted, legumes are the obvious match for grains because
they have the reverse pattern of deficiencies. Except for
black-eyed peas and mung beans, legumes are moderately
strong in the second column, isoleucine; and without exception legumes are very strong in the third column, lysine.
Perhaps the simplest way to regularly use legumes to complement grains is merely to add about 2 tablespoons of soy
grits (partially cooked, cracked soybeans) to every cup of
grain—in any dish from your morning oatmeal to your
supper casserole. The dish will taste better, too. Certain
commercial cereals such as "Protein Plus" have already
added soy grits for you. So be sure to check the labels of
commercially made cereals for a fortuitous complementary
protein combination!

For the same reasons—strengths in both center columns,
isoleucine and lysine—milk products make good complements to grains. But there's a "natural" complement that
you might not notice. Yeast, on Protein Table VIII, is also
well endowed with these two amino acids in which grains
are deficient. Nutritional, or brewer's, yeast, as it is called,
can be mixed into breads and pancakes or sprinkled on
breakfast cereals.

2. Experimentally determined complementary protein mixes include grains:

plus Legumes, for example:
> Rice + Legumes
> Corn + Legumes
> Wheat + Legumes

plus Dairy products, for example:
> Rice + Milk
> Wheat + Cheese
> Wheat + Milk

plus Nuts and seeds (because grains and nuts and seeds are low in the same amino acids, their complementarity seems to depend usually on the presence of legumes or dairy products), for example:
> Wheat + Peanuts* + Milk
> Wheat + Sesame + Soybean
> Exception: Rice + Sesame

plus Yeast, for example:
> Rice + Brewer's yeast

---

* Peanuts are botanically classified as legumes.

Protein Table VII. VEGETABLES

Average Serving of Vegetables Based on a Fresh, Uncooked Weight of 3½ oz (100 g)[1]	Percent of Daily Protein Allowance in an Average Serving		Ratings of Amino Acid Content as Compared to Egg Protein				Total Grams of Protein	NPU	Grams of Protein Your Body Can Use
	M	F	Tryp.	Iso.	Lys.	SC.			
			DEFICIENCY		DEFICIENCY				
	If complemented, add 2–5%		→	→					
1. Lima beans, green, 4 rounded tbsp, about ½ c when cooked	10	12	A	A	A	D	8	(~52)	4
2. Soybean sprouts, 1 c	7	9	—	C	C	F	6	(56)	3
3. Peas, green, ¾ c, shelled	7	9	B	B	A+	D	6	(53)	3
4. Brussels sprouts, 9 med.	7	9	B	B	A	D	5	(<60)[2]	3
5. Corn, one medium ear	7	9	D	C	C	B	4	(72)	3
6. Broccoli, 1 stalk, 5½ inches	If complemented, add 1–2% 6	8	B	B	B	C	4	(<60)	2–3
7. Kale, w/ stems, ¾ c when cooked	5	6	B	C	C	D	4	(54)	2
8. Collards, ½ c when cooked	5	6	A	C	A	C	4	(~45)	2
9. Mushrooms, 10 small, 4 large	5	6	B	D	B	A[3]	3	(72)	2
10. Asparagus, 5–6 spears	4	5	B	D	B	D	3	(<60)	1.8
11. Artichoke, ½ large bud	4	5	—	—	—	—	3	(<60)	1.8

Vegetables Continued

Average Serving of Vegetables Based on a Fresh, Uncooked Weight of 3½ oz (100 g)[1]	Percent of Daily Protein Allowance in an Average Serving		Ratings of Amino Acid Content as Compared to Egg Protein				Total Grams of Protein	NPU	Grams of Protein Your Body Can Use
	M	F	Tryp.	Iso.	Lys.	SC.			
	If complemented, add 1–2%			DEFICIENCY		DEFICIENCY			
12. Cauliflower, 1 c flower pieces	4	5	A	B	A	D	3	(<60)	1.8
13. Spinach, ½ c when cooked	4	5	A	B	A+	B	3	(~50)	1.5
14. Turnip greens, ½ c when cooked	3	4	A	C	B	D	3	(45)	1.4
15. Mung bean sprouts, 1 c (100 g)	3	4	—	—	—	—	4	(36)	1.4
16. Mustard greens, ½ c when cooked	3	4	A+	C	B	C	3	(~45)	1.4
17. Potato, white, ½ med. baking potato	3	4	A	C	B	D	2	(60)	1.2
18. Okra, 8–9 pods, 3 inch long	2	4	B	B	B	C	2	(<60)	1.2
19. Chard, 3/5 c when cooked	2	3	B	B	B	—	2	(~50)	1

[1] Shopping hint: 100 g (or 3½ oz) is equivalent to slightly less than ¼ lb on the grocery scale.

[2] Where the NPU of a vegetable is unknown, I have judged it to be less than 60 (<60), based on typical NPU scores of other vegetables.

[3] The SC content of mushrooms is disputed in my sources. I chose the high (A) level because it is in line with the unusually high NPU (72) of mushrooms.

Tips for complementing the protein in fresh vegetables

Since the most striking feature of fresh vegetables is their very low ratings in the last amino acid column, sulfur-containing amino acids, you would first want to look for foods with a high rating in that column. In Protein Table IV we find **sesame seeds** and **Brazil nuts**—both unusually strong (A and A+ rating) in the last column. Sesame and Brazils would probably serve best as complements to those fresh vegetables such as lima beans, green peas, Brussels sprouts, and cauliflower, which are very deficient in the last column while strong (A or B rating) in the second column, isoleucine. This is true because sesame and Brazils are themselves somewhat weak (C rating) in the second column.

In Protein Table V, among the grains, we can also find some possible complements to these fresh vegetables. **Millet** and **parboiled rice** (converted) stand out as exceptions among the grains; they are both very strong (A rating) in the last column, sulfur-containing, and moderately strong (B rating) in the second column, isoleucine. They, therefore, might well complement the protein in many fresh vegetables, especially the greens, which have just the opposite pattern.

Some vegetables might complement the protein in other vegetables. **Mushrooms,** high (A rating) in the last column, sulfur-containing, could be combined with lima beans, green peas, Brussels sprouts, broccoli, or cauliflower—all lacking in this amino acid.

Protein Table VIII. NUTRITIONAL ADDITIVES

Average Serving of Nutritional Additive	Percent of Daily Protein Allowance in an Average Serving		Ratings of Amino Acid Content as Compared to Egg Protein				Total Grams of Protein	NPU	Grams of Protein Your Body Can Use
	M	F	Tryp.	Iso.	Lys.	SC.			
					STRENGTH →				
1. Egg white, dried, powdered, ½ oz (14 g)	21	27	A+	B	A+	A+	11	(83)	9
2. "Tiger's Milk," ¼ c, 1 oz (28 g)	14	18	–	–	–	–	8	(~75)	6
3. Brewer's yeast, powder, 1 level tbsp (9–10 g)	5	6	B	A	A+	C	4	(50)	2
4. Wheat germ, commercial, 2 level tbsp (11–12 g)	5	6	C	B	A+	B	3	(67)	2

Tips for complementing other foods with the protein in nutritional additives

Amino acid strength in the two center columns (isoleucine and, especially, lysine) make nutritional additives likely complements for foods having the opposite amino acid pattern. Likely complementary protein combinations include nutritional additives:

	See Table:
plus Certain nuts and seeds, for example: sesame seed, black walnuts	IV
plus Many grains, for example: wheat, barley, oatmeal, rice	V

An experimentally determined complementary protein combination is nutritional yeast:

plus Rice

Protein Table IX. MEAT AND POULTRY

Average Serving of Meat and Poultry, Cooked, 3½ oz (100 g)	Percent of Daily Protein Allowance in an Average Serving		Ratings of Amino Acid Content as Compared to Egg Protein				Total Grams of Protein	NPU	Grams of Protein Your Body Can Use
	M	F	Tryp.	Iso.	Lys.	SC.[1]			
					STRENGTH →				
1. Turkey, roasted, 3 slices, 3"x2½"x¼"	52	67	—	B	A+	B	31	(~70)	22
2. Pork, loin chop, lean and fat	45	58	A	A	A+	B[1]	29	(~67)	19
3. Porterhouse steak, lean and marbled only (½ lb raw)	40	52	B	B	A+	B[1]	25	(67)	17
4. Hamburger, medium (¼ lb raw)	40	52	B	B	A+	B[1]	26	(67)	17
5. Chicken, fryer, breast	36	45	B	A	A+	B	23	(~65)	15
6. Lamb, rib chop, lean and fat	31	39	B	B	A+	B[1]	20	(~65)	13

[1]Also slightly deficient in valine.

Tips for using meat and poultry to complement the protein in plant food

High amino acid ratings (especially lysine) give even small portions of meat and poultry the ability to complement plant foods, particularly those, such as grains, which are low in lysine.

Turkey apparently surpasses all other meat and poultry in its ability to complement plant protein. Experiments show that if you add only one-fifth as much turkey to a meal of wheat, peanuts, or black-eyed peas, the protein quality of the combination will be the same as if the entire meal had been beef!

How the Food Groups Rate— Protein-Wise

SEAFOOD

Seafood rates first place as a source of protein. Fish is near meat in protein content and superior to meat in protein usability (NPU), except for shark and skate. Some fish, like cod and haddock (#13 and #15 on Protein Table I), are practically *pure* protein; that is, they contain *no* carbohydrates and only about .1 percent fat. Though the average protein portion I have given is small (less than ¼ pound), even at this level some fish can fill 40–50 percent of your daily allowance. It doesn't take much: even small chunks of fish in soups and lightly cooked vegetable mixes can give the dish a taste and protein boost.

The next-to-the-last column of the table tells you about the protein usability of seafood: the high NPU of most fish, 80, reflects excellent amino acid ratings. Notice particularly the high lysine content (A+ rating) of seafood. It is now easy to explain why fish and rice are sucessfully eaten as a staple by so many people. Rice, as you will see, is deficient in lysine and isoleucine—defects that seafood can effectively remedy.

I have given the values for raw as opposed to cooked seafood only because the best data available to me was in this form. No significant amount of protein is lost in cooking seafood.

DAIRY PRODUCTS

You may have been surprised to discover that dairy products appear low on the quantity scale of the "Food Protein Continuum." It is true that their percent protein on a weight basis is low. However, the fact that milk (#5 in Protein Table II) is only 4 percent protein and eggs (#9) are only 13 percent protein should not mislead you. Remember that the quality of these products is higher than any other food. On the right side of Table II, you can read their NPU scores—the measures of protein usability. The NPU of milk is over 80 and that of egg is 94 as compared to beef, for example, with an NPU of 67.

An example will remind you of the importance of NPU. Although eggs *appear* to have much *less* protein than beans (that is, eggs are only 13 percent protein, while beans are 21 percent protein), as far as your body is concerned their protein content is nearly equal. Why? Because the high NPU of eggs means that its protein is almost fully used by the body while the low NPU of beans makes its protein only partly available.

Also, the relatively low protein content of some dairy products is made up for by the fact that they are in forms that we normally eat in large quantities. For example, two cups of milk (#5 on Table II) supplies more than one-third of your daily protein allowance. Let's compare this with another food, noodles (#4 on Protein Table V), whose protein content is *three times* that of milk. To get the same proportions of your daily protein allowance from noodles as from 2 cups of milk, you would have to eat *4* cups of cooked noodles. The point is that whereas you might easily drink 2 cups of milk a day, you are not likely to eat 4 cups of noodles!

The protein cost and calorie comparisons (Appendixes F and D) show that dairy products fare quite well on these counts also. And dairy products have another virtue to recommend them: they are our major source of calcium. This nutritional strength takes on special importance in light of the fact that the majority of American women consume considerably less than the recommended allowance of calcium. But some people hesitate to increase their intake of dairy products because of their fat content. This shouldn't be a stumbling block—not when there are so many delicious ways to enjoy *low-fat* dairy products.

Legumes: Dried Beans, Peas, and Lentils

Legumes are one of the earliest crops cultivated by man. Even in biblical times their nutritional value was known. When Daniel and other favored children of Israel were offered the meat usually reserved only for the King of Babylon, Daniel refused. He asked only for pulses (legumes) and water. After ten days, the Bible passage relates, the faces of the children "appeared fairer and fatter than all the children that ate of the king's meat." This is not too surprising, because the protein content of some legumes is actually equal to, or greater than, that of meat! But maybe you are registering surprise that anyone would *choose* legumes. It is true that dried beans and peas can be the dullest food in the world, but they can also be the basis of the most savory dishes in your menu. Lentils, peas, black beans, and soybeans make delicious and satisfying soups. Kidney beans and garbanzos (chickpeas) make a great cold salad, or they can top off a fresh green salad. Pea beans with maple syrup is the old favorite: Boston baked beans.

Since legumes are all at least 20 percent protein, why don't they contribute even more to meeting our daily protein allowance than the typical 10–20 percent indicated on the table? The answer is twofold: first, their NPU scores are on the average lower than any other food group recommended as a protein source. Lentils (#11 in Protein Table III) have the lowest NPU score, 30, of any food included in these tables. But legumes also include some of the highest-quality plant protein. Soybeans and mung beans (#1 and #2) have NPU scores of 61 and 57 respectively—reflecting protein usability approaching that of meat. Note that tofu (soybean curd) has an even higher NPU, 65, than the untreated soybean. Second, we tend to eat legumes in small quantities. A serving of ¾ cup of legumes actually weighs only 50 grams before cooking. We usually eat other high-protein food, like meat, in quantities at least twice this amount. But remember that the percentages I have given you here are for legumes eaten *without* the benefit of supplementation with other protein sources. Eating legumes with cereals can make the protein *in both* more valuable to you, increasing the availability of their combined protein content as much as 40 percent.

Perhaps no two people have done more to bring the Eastern art of cooking with legumes to the West than William and Akiko Shurtleff. Authors of *The Book of Tofu, The Book of Miso* (Ballantine Books, New York) and *The Book of Tempeh* (Harper/Colophon Books, New York), they offer hundreds of mouth-watering recipes. For more information on soyfoods cookery (and these books), write directly to Bill and Akiko at the Soyfoods Center, Box 234, Lafayette, CA 94549. (Send long, self-addressed envelope.)

NUTS AND SEEDS

Nuts and seeds follow legumes in their ability to meet your daily protein need. They rank behind legumes only because we tend to eat them in much smaller quantities and they therefore contribute less to our dietary needs. Actually, they are as rich in protein as the legumes, and they often have higher NPU values.

First let's compare the two seeds, sesame and sunflower. Sunflower seed is definitely richer in protein than is sesame—24 percent as compared to 19 percent. The usability of sunflower protein is also better than sesame protein; this is probably the result of the lower lysine and isoleucine content of sesame seed. Experimentally, sunflower seeds show even greater ability to promote growth than meat. Both types of seed have higher NPU scores than most legumes.

You might also wish to note that sesame seeds lose most of their calcium, iron, thiamine, and all of their sodium, potassium, and Vitamin A when they are decorticated. To avoid this loss you can purchase the "unhulled" variety. However, some studies have shown that in order for the body to digest the sesame seed it must be ground. This can be done in any good blender or with a mortar and pestle.

Now look at the nuts. The quantity and usability of their protein is generally lower than the seed meals. A surprise is cashew nuts, whose NPU matches sunflower seeds (and nearly equals soybeans). If you find that your favorite nuts (such as pecans or English walnuts) are not listed here, it's because they are too calorific! To illustrate: if you (a woman) wanted to get your daily protein allowance solely from pecans (hypothetical, of course), you would have to consume almost 1½ pounds of pecans, which contain over 4,000 calories—or about twice what you should consume. This illustrates the rationale I have used for including only those items that can provide protein without exceeding caloric needs. The one exception here is Brazil nuts, which have been included because of their unusual strength in the sulfur-containing amino acids (rare in plant protein). For a complete analysis of the calorie "cost" of the foods given here, see Figure 17.

Finally, notice that the portions given here are quite conservative. A 1-ounce serving of peanuts provides 7 to 8 percent of your daily protein needs. But if you ate a small package of peanuts (1½ ounces), you would actually be fulfilling 10 to 12 percent of your daily allowance.

GRAINS, CEREALS, AND THEIR PRODUCTS

Cereals provide almost half the protein in the world's diet. This might surprise you, since the percent of protein in cereals is not high. Someone must be eating a lot of grain. Not us, of course, but other people in the world.

Let's take a look at grains from several points of view.

First, as to the *quantity* of protein they contain. Among the various grains we find wide differences. In first place is triticale, a newly developed cross between rye and wheat which is reported to have 16–17 percent protein. Wheat, rye, and oats have from 30 to 35 percent *more* protein by weight than rice, corn, barley, and millet. The protein content of one type of grain can also vary significantly: wheat, for example, ranges between 9 and 14 percent protein. The values you find for wheat in Protein Tables V and VI are based on the highest-protein wheat: hard red spring wheat. You may wish to check the labeling on wheat products to see what type of wheat is used. Durum wheat, often used in pasta, has the second-highest protein content, 13 percent.

These differences may suggest to you that if rice is a staple in your diet, you may wish to increase the protein content by adding some whole wheat, rye, or oats. Did you know that you can cook whole-grain wheat, oats, and rye in the same way that you do rice? The mix has a nutty, rich flavor, which you may prefer to rice alone.

Oatmeal is low (#9) on Table V only because we usually eat it in a rolled form that is much lighter than the whole grains. (Less weight: therefore, less protein.)

But what about the usability of cereal protein? Their NPU values generally range from the low 50s to the low 60s, but there are some important exceptions. The NPU of whole rice, 70, is probably the highest of any of the whole grains and equal to the NPU of beef! Wheat germ and rice germ (not listed) come next, with NPUs of 67. Oatmeal and buckwheat follow, with NPUs of 66 and 65 respectively. These values are higher than most vegetable protein and are comparable to the quality of beef. On the other hand, the lowest NPU of cereal products is that of wheat gluten (#2 under "Flour," Protein Table VI). Although gluten flour is 41 percent protein, its NPU of 39 means that only about *one-third* of its protein is available to the body. A deficiency of lysine (D rating) appears to be the culprit. These differences in usability and quantity among the grains mean that the price you pay and the calories you have to eat to get a given amount of protein also vary significantly. You may wish to take careful note of these differences in Figures 17 and 18.

Cereal products such as bulgur (#5 on Table V) may stump you if you've only read traditional cookbooks. Bulgur is partially cooked, usually cracked wheat. Its processing is both an asset and a liability. Thus, while the lysine in bulgur is more available than that in whole wheat, from 2 to 28 percent of its B vitamins are destroyed.

VEGETABLES

A glance at Protein Table VII will show you that vegetables, in general, will not be large contributors to your daily protein intake. On a moisture-free basis, some green vegetables have a protein content equivalent to nuts, seeds, and beans. But their water content gives them bulk that limits their usefulness in our diets—as protein suppliers, that is. However, don't forget their valuable role in providing essential vitamins and minerals. So if you enjoy these vegetables, eat lots of them. Whereas I have given ½ cup of cooked greens as an average serving, you may enjoy twice this amount. With the exception of potato, all these vegetables are low in calories; so there is no need to limit your intake on this account.

The NPU scores of these vegetables provide some interesting surprises. Among the legumes in Table III, we saw that mung beans had an NPU of 57. But here, as mung bean sprouts, their NPU is only 36. Soybean sprouts also take a slight dip in NPU, with 56 as compared to 61 for the dried bean.

To increase the protein content and taste interest of vegetable dishes, experiment with milk- and cheese-based sauces. I have discovered that buttermilk makes an excellent sauce base. Since it is already somewhat thick, one needn't add as much flour. In addition, its tartness highlights many green vegetables.

Also, sliced or crumbled hard-boiled egg is very tasty on green vegetables such as spinach or asparagus. Adding nuts is another way to increase the protein value of vegetable dishes. Your favorite vegetable dishes in Chinese restaurants probably include walnuts or cashews. Why not do the same? Broccoli, peas, and cauliflower are especially good with nuts.

NUTRITIONAL ADDITIVES

If you have doubts about the adequacy of your protein intake, even a small amount of the first two items in the nutritional additives protein table (VIII) can give you a real protein boost. Only one tablespoon of dried egg white or one-fourth cup of "Tiger's Milk" mixed into your favorite drink can fill 14 to 17 percent of your daily protein need.

The other two nutritional additives (#3 and #4 in the table) are used by most people because of their high vitamin and mineral content. (Yeast is from two to ten times richer than wheat germ in these nutrients.) I have included them because a very small amount (1 or 2 tablespoons) can meet 5 percent of your protein allowance and, second, because of their amino acid strengths.

FOR COMPARISON: MEAT AND POULTRY

Notice, on Protein Table IX, that only 3½ ounces of meat contribute from 30 to 61 percent of your daily protein allowance. These figures make very clear that the enormous quantities of meat we now consume are hardly needed! In Eastern cuisine, small amounts of meat supplement staple vegetable dishes. This dietary tradition, although perhaps determined by the limited availability of meat, more correctly reflects the body's actual needs.

Gelatin, an animal protein, is often recommended as a protein supplement. Actually, it should be your last choice. Several important amino acids are virtually lacking in gelatin. It has an NPU of 2! Moreover, gelatin can *reduce* the usability of the protein in food eaten with it.

Appendix E. Cost of One Day's Protein Allowance

1. *Dairy products*

Dried nonfat milk solids (@ $2.25 / lb.)	$0.58
Whole egg (AA large @ $1.93 / doz.)	1.02
Cottage cheese from skim milk @ $1.19/lb.)	.73
Whole milk, nonfat milk (@ 65¢ / qt.)	1.10
Buttermilk @ 81¢ / qt.)	1.23
Swiss cheese (@ $2.99/lb.)	1.50
Cheddar cheese (@ $2.49/lb.)	1.42
Parmesan cheese (@ $6.39/lb.)	2.46
Ricotta cheese (@ $1.70/lb.)	1.99
Blue mold cheese (@ $5.72/lb.)	3.65
Yogurt from non-fat milk (@ 47¢/pt.)	2.43
Camembert cheese (@ $6.50/lb.)	5.11

2. *Legumes (dry seed)*

Soybeans, soy grits, and flour (@ 59¢/lb.)	$0.28
Split peas (@ $1.05/lb.)	.73
Cowpeas (black-eyed peas) (@ $1.09/lb.)	1.09
Lima beans (@ $1.25/lb.)	1.11
Black beans (@ $1.39/lb.)	1.27
Kidney beans (@ $1.35/lb.)	1.50
Common white beans (@ $1.15/lb.)	1.31
Chick peas (garbanzos) (@ $1.35/lb.)	1.46
Lentils (@ $1.35/lb.)	1.89
Mung beans (@ $1.49/lb.)	1.07

3. *Grains, cereals, and their products*

Whole-grain wheat, "wheatberries" red spring (@ 28¢/lb.)	$0.28
Wheat bran (@ 39¢/lb.)	.43
Oatmeal in bulk (@ 59¢/lb.)	.59
Rye flour, dark (@ 49¢/lb.)	.49
Whole wheat flour (@ 39¢/lb.)	.44
Millet (@ 65¢/lb.)	1.11
Cornmeal (@ 37¢/lb.)	.73

Brown rice (@ 45¢/lb.)	.81
"Roman Meal" (@ 73¢/lb.)	.78
Gluten flour (@ $3.44/lb.)	2.09
Barley, pot or Scotch, and flour (@ 69¢/lb.)	1.16
Spaghetti, macaroni (@ 84¢/lb.)	1.24
Egg noodles (@ $1.45/lb.)	1.84
Buckwheat flour (@ $1.23/lb.)	1.53
Bulgur, red (@ $1.09/lb.)	1.41
Whole wheat bread (@ 95¢/lb.)	1.64
Rye bread (@ 93¢/lb.)	1.61

4. Seafood

Squid (@ 99¢/lb.)	$0.51
Cod (@ $3.99/lb.)	1.75
Turbot (@ $2.25/lb.)	1.06
Tuna, canned in oil (@ $2.16/lb.)	1.08
Perch (@ $3.59/lb.)	2.26
Sardines, Atlantic, canned in oil (@ $3.20/lb.)	2.08
Catfish (@ $5.29/lb.)	3.62
Crab in shell (@ $3.99/lb.)	5.68
Oysters (@ $3.80/lb.)	4.18
Salmon (@ $7.99/lb.)	5.54
Shrimp meat (@ $5.99/lb.)	4.79

5. Nutritional additives

Wheat germ (@ 64¢/lb.)	$0.37

"Tiger's Milk" (@ $8.98/lb.)	3.85
Brewer's yeast (nutritional yeast) (@ $3.65/lb.)	1.65

6/ Nuts and seeds

Sunflower seed kernels or meal (@ 99¢/lb.)	$0.83
Raw peanuts (@ $2.15/lb.)	1.87
Peanuts (@ $1.65/lb.)	1.36
Pumpkin and squash kernels (@ $2.65/lb.)	1.57
Brazil nuts (@ $2.95/lb.)	3.92
Peanut butter (@ $2.29/lb.)	2.04
Raw cashews (@ $3.70/lb.)	3.36
Sesame seeds or meal (@ $3.39/lb.)	3.92
Cashews (@ $3.09/lb.)	2.81
Pistachio nuts in shell (@ $3.89/lb.)	7.75

7. Meats and poultry

Hamburger, regular grade (@ $1.78/lb.)	$1.44
Chicken breast with bone (@ $2.28/lb.)	2.05
Pork loin chop medium fat with bone (@ $2.58/lb.)	2.71
Porterhouse steak, choice grade, with bone (@ $5.08/lb.)	5.37
Lamb shoulder chop, choice grade, with bone (@ $3.99/lb.)	4.85

Appendix F. Whole Wheat Flour Compared to White Flour

	Composition of Whole Wheat Flour (per 100 g, or 3½ oz)		Composition of All-Purpose White Flour Compared to Whole Wheat Flour		
			White Flour		Enriched White Flour
1. Protein	13.3	g	10.5 g	79%	10.5 g	79%
2. Minerals						
Calcium	41	mg	16 mg	39%	16 mg	39%
Phosphorous	372	gm	87 mg	23%	87 mg	23%
Iron	3.3	mg	0.8 mg	24%	2.9 mg	88%
Potassium	370	mg	95 mg	26%	95 mg	26%
Sodium	3	mg	2 mg	67%	2 mg	67%
3. Vitamins						
Thiamin	0.55	mg	0.06 mg	11%	0.44 mg	80%
Riboflavin	0.12	mg	0.05 mg	42%	0.26 mg	216%
Niacin	4.3	mg	0.9 mg	21%	3.5 mg	81%

Appendix G. Brown Rice Compared to Other Types of Rice

	Composition of Brown Rice (per 100 g, or 3½ oz)	Composition of Other Types of Rice					
		White Rice		Enriched White Rice		Converted Rice (Enriched)	
1. Protein	7.5 g	6.7 g	90%	6.7 g	90%	7.4 g	99%
2. Minerals							
Calcium	32 mg	24 mg	75%	24 mg	75%	60 mg	190%
Phosphorous	221 mg	94 mg	43%	94 mg	43%	200 mg	90%
Iron	1.6 mg	0.8 mg	50%	2.9 mg	180%	2.9 mg	180%
Potassium	214 mg	92 mg	43%	92 mg	43%	150 mg	70%
Sodium	9 mg	5 mg	56%	5 mg	56%	9 mg	100%
3. Vitamins							
Thiamin	0.34 mg	0.07 mg	21%	0.44 mg	130%	0.44 mg	130%
Riboflavin	0.05 mg	0.03 mg	60%	0.03 mg	60%	0.03 mg	60%
Niacin	4.7 mg	1.6 mg	34%	3.5 mg	74%	3.5 mg	74%

Appendix H. Sugars, Honey, and Molasses Compared

Composition (per 100 g, or 3½ oz)

	White Sugar (Granulated)	Brown Sugar (Best or Cane)	Molasses (Third Extraction or Blackstrap)	Honey (Strained or Extracted)	Maple Sugar
1. Minerals	mg	mg	mg	mg	mg
Calcium	0	85	684	5	143
Phosphorus	0	19	84	6	11
Iron	0.1	3.4	16.1	0.5	1.4
Potassium	3.0	344	2927	51	242
Sodium	1.0	30	96	5	14
2. Vitamins					
Thiamin	0	0.01	0.11	trace	—
Riboflavin	0	0.03	0.19	0.04	—
Niacin	0	0.2	2.0	0.3	—

Source: "Composition of Foods," Agriculture Handbook, No. 8, USDA. Values given vary in other sources.

Appendix I. Food Additives: What's Safe? What to Avoid?

Safe

These additives appear to be safe.

ALGINATE, PROPYLENE GLYCOL ALGINATE Thickening agents; foam stabilizer. *Ice cream, cheese, candy, yogurt*

ALPHA TOCOPHEROL (Vitamin E) Antioxidant, nutrient. *Vegetable oil*

ASCORBIC ACID (Vitamin C), **ERYTHORBIC ACID** Antioxidant, nutrient, color stabilizer. *Oily foods, cereals, soft drinks, cured meats*

BETA CAROTENE Coloring; nutrient. *Margarine, shortening, non-dairy whiteners, butter*

CALCIUM (or **SODIUM**) **PROPIONATE** Preservative. *Bread, rolls, pies, cakes*

CALCIUM (or **SODIUM**) **STEAROYL LACTYLATE** Dough conditioner, whipping agent. *Bread dough, cake fillings, artificial whipped cream, processed egg whites*

CARRAGEENAN Thickening and stabilizing agent. *Ice cream, jelly, chocolate milk, infant formula*

CASEIN, SODIUM CASEINATE Thickening and whitening agent. *Ice cream, ice milk, sherbet, coffee creamers*

CITRIC ACID, SODIUM CITRATE Acid, flavoring, chelating agent. *Ice cream, sherbet, fruit drink, candy, carbonated beverages, instant potatoes*

EDTA Chelating agent. *Salad dressing, margarine, sandwich spreads, mayonnaise, processed fruits and vegetables, canned shellfish, soft drinks*

FERROUS GLUCONATE Coloring, nutrient. *Black olives*

FUMARIC ACID Tartness agent. *Powdered drinks, pudding, pie fillings, gelatin desserts*

GELATIN Thickening and gelling agent. *Powdered dessert mix, yogurt, ice cream, cheese spreads, beverages*

GLYCERIN (GLYCEROL) Maintains water content. *Marshmallow, candy, fudge, baked goods*

HYDROLYZED VEGETABLE PROTEIN (HVP) Flavor enhancer. *Instant soups, frankfurters, sauce mixes, beef stew*

LACTIC ACID Acidity regulator. *Spanish olives, cheese, frozen desserts, carbonated beverages*

LACTOSE Sweetener. *Whipped topping mix, breakfast pastry*

LECITHIN Emulsifier, antioxidant. *Baked goods, margarine, chocolate, ice cream*

MANNITOL Sweetener, other uses. *Chewing gum, low-calorie foods*

MONO- and DIGLYCERIDES Emulsifier. *Baked goods, margarine, candy, peanut butter*

POLYSORBATE 60 Emulsifier. *Baked goods, frozen desserts, imitation dairy products*

SODIUM BENZOATE *Fruit juice, carbonated drinks, pickles, preserves*

SODIUM CARBOXYMETHYLCELLULOSE (CMC) Thickening and stabilizing agent; prevents sugar from crystallizing. *Ice cream, beer, pie fillings, icings, diet foods, candy*

SORBIC ACID, POTASSIUM SORBATE Prevents growth of mold and bacteria. *Cheese, syrup, jelly, cake, wine, dry fruits*

SORBITAN MONOSTEARATE Emulsifier. *Cakes, candy, frozen pudding, icing*

SORBITOL Sweetener, thickening agent, maintains moisture. *Dietetic drinks and foods; candy, shredded coconut, chewing gum*

STARCH, MODIFIED STARCH Thickening agent. *Soup, gravy, baby foods*

VANILLIN, ETHYL VANILLIN Substitute for vanilla. *Ice cream, baked goods, beverages, chocolate, candy, gelatin desserts*

Caution

These additives may be unsafe, are poorly tested, or are used in foods we eat too much of.

ARTIFICIAL COLORING—YELLOW NO. 6 Artificial coloring. *Beverages, sausage, baked goods, candy, gelatin*

ARTIFICIAL FLAVORING Flavoring. *Soda pop, candy, breakfast cereals, gelatin desserts; many others*

BUTYLATED HYDROXYANISOLE (BHA) Antioxidant. *Cereals, chewing gum, potato chips, vegetable oil*

CORN SYRUP Sweetener, thickener. *Candy, toppings, syrups, snack foods, imitation dairy foods*

DEXTROSE (GLUCOSE, CORN SUGAR) Sweetener, coloring agent. *Bread, caramel, soda pop, cookies, many other foods*

GUMS: Guar, Locust Bean, Arabic, Furcelleran, Ghatti, Karaya, Tragacanth. Thickening agents, stabilizers. *Beverages, ice cream, frozen pudding, salad dressing, dough, cottage cheese, candy, drink mixes*

HEPTYL PARABEN Preservative. *Beer*

HYDROGENATED VEGETABLE OIL Source of oil or fat. *Margarine, many processed foods*

INVERT SUGAR Sweetener. *Candy, soft drinks, many other foods*

MONOSODIUM GLUTAMATE (MSG) Flavor enhancer. *Soup, seafood, poultry, cheese, sauces, stews; many others*

PHOSPHORIC ACID; PHOSPHATES Acidulant, chelating agent, buffer, emulsifier, nutrient, discoloration in-

hibitor. *Baked goods, cheese, powdered foods, cured meat, soda pop, breakfast cereals, dehydrated potatoes*
PROPYL GALLATE Antioxidant. *Vegetable oil, meat products, potato sticks, chicken soup base, chewing gum*
SULFUR DIOXIDE, SODIUM BISULFITE Preservative, bleach. *Sliced fruit, wine, grape juice, dehydrated potatoes*

Avoid

These additives are unsafe in the amounts consumed or are very poorly tested.

ARTIFICIAL COLORINGS
    BLUE No. 1 *Beverages, candy, baked goods*
    BLUE No. 2 *Pet food, beverages, candy*
    CITRUS RED No. 2 *Skin of some Florida oranges only*
    GREEN No. 3 *Candy, beverages*
    ORANGE B *Hot dogs*
    RED No. 3 *Cherries in fruit cocktail, candy, baked goods*
    RED No. 40 *Soda pop, candy, gelatin desserts, pastry, pet food, sausage*
    YELLOW No. 5 *Gelatin dessert, candy, pet food, baked goods*
BROMINATED VEGETABLE OIL (BVO) Emulsifier, clouding agent. *Soft drinks*
BUTYLATED HYDROXYTOLUENE (BHT) Antioxidant. *Cereals, chewing gum, potato chips, oils, etc.*
CAFFEINE Stimulant. *Coffee, tea, cocoa (natural); soft drinks (additive)*
QUININE Flavoring. *Tonic water, quinine water, bitter lemon*
SACCHARIN Synthetic sweetener. *"Diet" products*
SALT (SODIUM CHLORIDE) Flavoring. *Most processed foods, soup, potato chips, crackers*
SODIUM NITRITE, SODIUM NITRATE Preservative, coloring, flavoring. *Bacon, ham, frankfurters, luncheon meats, smoked fish, corned beef*

SUGAR (SUCROSE) Sweetener. *Table sugar, sweetened foods*

Glossary

ANTIOXIDANTS retard the oxidation of unsaturated fats and oils, colorings and flavorings. Oxidation leads to rancidity, flavor changes, and loss of color. Most of these effects are caused by reaction of oxygen in the air with fats.

CHELATING AGENTS trap trace amounts of metal atoms that would otherwise cause food to discolor or go rancid.

EMULSIFIERS keep oil and water mixed together.

FLAVOR ENHANCERS have little or no flavor of their own, but accentuate the natural flavor of foods. They are usually used when very little of a natural ingredient is present.

THICKENING AGENTS are natural or chemically modified carbohydrates that absorb some of the water that is present in food, thereby making the food thicker. Thickening agents "stabilize" factory-made foods by keeping the complex mixtures of oils, water, acids, and solids well mixed.

Copyright by Center for Science in the Public Interest 1978. Posters with this information available from CSPI, 1755 S Street N.W., Washington, D.C. 20009.

Appendix J. Recommended Paperback Cookbooks

1. Ewald, Ellen, *Recipes for a Small Planet*. Ballantine, 1973. A wealth of creative complementary protein recipes.
2. Hewitt, Jean, *The New York Times Natural Foods Cookbook*. Avon, 1972. Highly recommended by friends.
3. Hunter, Beatrice Trum, *The Natural Foods Cookbook*. Pyramid, 1961. My early bible. Just reading through all the incredible ideas is mind-expanding!
4. Katzen, Mollie, *Moosewood Cookbook*. Ten Speed Press, P.O. Box 7123, Berkeley, Calif. 94707. Simple and elegant dishes.
5. Robertson, Laurel, Carol Flinders, and Bronwen Godfrey, *Laurel's Kitchen. A Handbook for Vegetarian Cookery and Nutrition*. Bantam Books, 1976. A classic.
6. Thomas, Anna, *The Vegetarian Epicure*. Vintage, 1972. Elegant dishes.
7. Schandler, Michael and Nina, *The Complete Guide and Cookbook for Raising Your Child as a Vegetarian*. Schocken Books, 1981. Also includes advice for pregnant and breast-feeding women.
8. Shurtleff, William, and Akiko Aoyagi, *The Book of Tofu* (1979) and *The Book of Miso* (1981), Ballantine Books, and the *Book of Tempeh*, Harper & Row. Much

more than excellent cookbooks, these provide fascinating information about the cultures that developed these versatile foods. For more information about soyfoods and a catalogue of publications, send a long, self-addressed stamped envelope to The Soyfoods Center, P.O. Box 234, Lafayette, CA 94549.

Notes

Diet for a Small Planet Twenty Years Later—An Extraordinary Time to Be Alive

1. National Academy of Sciences, "Alternative Agriculture," Washington DC, September 1989.
2. Marty Strange, *Family Farming: A New Economic Vision* (Lincoln and San Francisco: University of Nebraska Press and the Institute for Food and Development Policy, 1988).
3. Helvetius, *de l'esprit*, Paris, 1758, cited in Jane Mansbridge, *Beyond Self-Interest* (Chicago: University of Chicago Press, 1990), 6.
4. John Adams, quoted by Clinton Rossiter, *Conservatism in America*, 2d ed., rev. (New York: Vintage, 1962), 111.
5. See, for example, Frances Moore Lappé, *Rediscovering America's Values* (New York: Ballantine Books, 1989), Part II, "What's Fair?" and Kevin Phillips, *The Politics of Rich and Poor* (New York: Random House, 1990).
6. Adam Smith, *The Theory of Moral Sentiments*, ed. D. D. Raphael and A. L. Macfie (Indianapolis: Liberty Classics, 1982), pt. 1, sec. 1, ch. 5, 25.
7. Charles R. Darwin, *The Descent of Man and Selection in Relation to Sex.* (New York: D. Appleton, 1909), pt. 1, 121.
8. Martin L. Hoffman, "The Development of Empathy," in J. Philippe Rushton and Richard M. Sorrentino, eds., *Altruism and Helping Behavior* (Hillsdale, NJ: Lawrence Erlbaum Associates, 1981).
9. Alfie Kohn, *The Brighter Side of Human Nature* (New York: Basic Books, 1990).

10. See, for example: *In Defense of the Land Ethic: Essays in Environmental Philosophy* (Albany: State University of New York Press, 1989), and *Companion to A Sand County Almanac: Interpretive and Critical Essays* (Madison: University of Wisconsin Press, 1987).

11. "Marx Meets Muir, Toward a Synthesis of the Progressive Political and Ecological Visions," *Tikkun*, vol. 2, no. 4, Sept./Oct. 1987.

12. Jim Mason and Peter Singer, *Animal Factories* (New York: Crown, 1980).

13. John Robbins, *Diet for a New America* (Walpole, NH: Stillpoint Publishing).

14. Wes Jackson, "Making Sustainable Agriculture Work," *The Journal of Gastronomy*, vol. 5, no. 2, Summer/Autumn 1989, 133.

15. "Democracy's Next Generation," People for the American Way, Washington, DC, 1989.

16. Harry C. Boyte, *CommonWealth: A Return to Citizen Politics* (New York: Free Press, 1989).

17. Harry C. Boyte, *Community Is Possible: Repairing America's Roots* (New York: Harper and Row, 1984).

18. Bernard Crick, *In Defence of Politics* (Baltimore: Penguin, 1964), 25.

19. Kentuckians for the Commonwealth, P.O. Box 864, Prestonburg, KY 41653.

20. Bill Elasky, "Becoming" in *Democracy & Education*, 1990 Conference Issue (Athens, OH: Institute for Democracy in Education, 1990).

21. Financial Democracy Campaign, 329 Rensselaer St., Charlotte, NC 28203.

22. Barry Commoner, *Making Peace with the Planet* (New York: Pantheon, 1990).

23. Frances Moore Lappé and Family, *What To Do After You Turn Off the TV* (New York: Ballantine Books, 1985).

24. Listening Project, Rural Southern Voice for Peace, 1898 Hannah Ranch Road, Burnsville, NC 28714.

Book One: Diet for a Small Planet

PART I.
RECIPE FOR A PERSONAL REVOLUTION

Chapter 2. My Journey

1. *Impact of Market Concentration on Rising Food Prices,* Hearing Before the Subcommittee on Antitrust, Monopoly and Business Rights of the Committee on the Judiciary, United States Senate, 96th Congress, 1st Session on Rising Food Prices in the United States, April 6, 1979, U.S. Government Printing Office, 1979. Testimonies of Drs. Russell Parker, John Conner, and Willard Mueller. (Based on their testimony of $10 to $15 billion in 1975, I estimate monopoly overcharges to have reached close to $20 billion by 1981.)
2. U.S. Agency for International Development, Congressional Presentation, Fiscal Year 1982, main volume, p. 239.
3. Ibid. p. 250.
4. William Lin, George Coffman, and J. B. Penn, *U.S. Farm Numbers, Size and Related Structural Dimensions: Projections to the Year 2000,* Technical Bulletin No. 1625, Economics and Statistics Service, U.S. Department of Agriculture, 1980, p. iii.
5. U.S. Department of Agriculture, *Landownership in the United States,* 1978, p. 1.
6. Donald Paarlberg, *Farm and Food Policy: Issues of the 1980s,* University of Nebraska Press, 1980, p. 68.
7. *Impact of Market Concentration,* op. cit.
8. Industry profits from *Handbook of Agriculture Charts,* 1980, U.S. Department of Agriculture, p. 39. Overcharges estimate from *Impact of Market Concentra-*

tion, op. cit., adjusted upward to account for increased profits and inflation since 1975.

9. *Washington Resource Report,* Environmental Policy Center, Washington, D.C., July 1981.

10. "The Pesticide Industry: What Price Concentration?" *Farmline,* U.S. Department of Agriculture, March 1981, p. 10.

11. Council on Wage and Price Stability, Executive Office of the President, *Report on Prices for Agricultural Machinery and Equipment,* Washington, D.C., 1976.

12. U.S. Department of Agriculture, *Status of the Family Farm,* Second Annual Report to Congress, Economics and Statistics Service, Agricultural Economic Report No. 441, 1979, p. 40.

13. James Rowen, "Oxy Takes a Very Big Bite," *The Nation,* October 31, 1981, p. 435.

14. V. James Rhodes, "The Red Meat Food Chain: Horizontal Size and Vertical Linkages," presented at Midwestern Conference on Food, Agriculture and Public Policy, S. Sioux City, Nebraska, November 18, 1980.

15. *Western Livestock Journal,* August 1979.

16. *An Analysis of the Futures Trading Activity in Live and Feeder Cattle Contracts of Large (Reporting) Traders on the Chicago Mercantile Exchange,* staff report to the Small Business Committee of the House of Representatives, September 1980, pp. 13, 21, 23.

17. Our estimate comes from the following sources: profits in the late 1960s averaged $14 million/yr. according to *Feedstuffs,* January 11, 1969. Profits for 1979 estimated at $150 million by *Business Week,* April 16, 1979. In constant 1967 dollars this is a 441 percent increase; in current dollars, over 1,000 percent increase.

18. "Cargill: Preparing for the Next Boom in Worldwide Grain Trading," *Business Week,* April 16, 1979, pp. 3 ff.

19. *Multinational Corporations and United States Foreign Policy,* Hearing Before the Subcommittee on Multinational Corporations, Senate Foreign Relations Committee, June 18, 23, 24, 1976, Part II, p. 241.

20. *Wall Street Journal,* March 6, 1979.

21. Dan Morgan, *Merchants of Grain* (Viking, 1979), pp. 234–235.
22. *Feedstuffs,* November 1, 1979, p. 1.
23. Ibid.
24. *Small Business Problems in the Marketing of Meat and Other Commodities* (Part 3—Beef in America: An Industry in Crisis), by the staff of the Committee on Small Business, House of Representatives, 96th Congress, 2nd Session, October 1980, U.S. Government Printing Office, 1980, pp. 28–29.
25. *Relationship Between Structure and Performance in the Steer and Heifer Slaughtering Industry,* Committee on Small Business, House of Representatives, 96th Congress, 2nd Session, September 1980, U.S. Government Printing Office, 1980, p. 44. (This study indicates that 30 percent of the rise in beef prices in recent years can be attributed to concentration in the industry. But the study is widely disputed.)
26. *Impact of Market Concentration on Rising Food Prices,* op. cit.

PART II.
DIET FOR A SMALL PLANET

Chapter 1. One Less Hamburger?

1. *Food and Agriculture Organization, Production Yearbook,* Rome, 1979.
2. *World Hunger, Health, and Refugee Problems, Summary of a Special Study Mission to Asia and the Middle East* (Washington, D.C.: U.S. Government Printing Office, 1976), p. 99.
3. Letter from Dr. Marcel Ganzin, Director, Food Policy and Nutrition Division, FAO, Rome, April 1976.
4. Calculations based on Food and Agriculture Organization, *Yearbook of International Trade Statistics,* 1974; *Production Yearbook,* 1974 and 1975; and *Trade Yearbook,* 1975. For a complete discussion see

Chapter 11, *Food First: Beyond the Myth of Scarcity* (Ballantine Books, 1979).

5. Food and Agriculture Organization, *Report on the 1960 World Census of Agriculture,* Rome, 1971. (And since then, landholdings in most countries have become even more concentrated.)

6. Food and Agriculture Organization, *State of Food and Agriculture,* 1978, Rome, pp. 66–71.

7. Ho Kwon Ping, "Profit and Poverty in the Plantations," *Far Eastern Economic Review,* July 11, 1980, pp. 53 ff.

8. James Parsons, "Forest to Pasture: Development or Destruction?" *Revista de Biologia Tropical,* vol. 24, Supplement 1, 1976, p. 124.

9. The first part of *Food First: Beyond the Myth of Scarcity* by Frances Moore Lappé and Joseph Collins (Ballantine, 1979), discusses the reasons behind the high birthrates in the third world and includes references to many excellent sources.

10. U.S. Agency for International Development, *Congressional Presentation,* Fiscal Year 1980, p. 128.

Chapter 2. Like Driving a Cadillac

1. *Raw Materials in the United States Economy 1900–1977;* Technical Paper 47, prepared under contract by Vivian Eberle Spencer, U.S. Department of Commerce, U.S. Department of Interior Bureau of Mines, p. 3.

2. Ibid. Table 2, p. 86.

3. U.S. Department of Agriculture, *Livestock Production Units, 1910–1961,* Statistical Bulletin No. 325, p. 18, and *Agricultural Statistics, 1980,* p. 56. Current world imports from *FAO At Work,* newsletter of the liaison office for North America of the Food and Agriculture Organization of the United Nations, May 1981.

4. David Pimentel et al., "The Potential for Grass-Fed Livestock: Resource Constraints," *Science,* February 22, 1980, volume 207, pp. 843 ff.

5. David Pimentel, "Energy and Land Constraints in

Food Protein Production," *Science,* November 21, 1975, pp. 754 ff.

6. Robert R. Oltjen, "Tomorrow's Diets for Beef Cattle," *The Science Teacher,* vol. 38, no. 3, March 1970.

7. The amount varies depending on the price of grain, but 2,200 to 2,500 pounds is typical. See note 13 for more detailed explanation of grain feeding.

8. U.S. Department of Agriculture, Economic Research Service, *Cattle Feeding in the United States,* Agricultural Economics, Report No. 186, 1970, p. 5.

9. Ibid. p. iv.

10. U.S. Department of Agriculture, *Agricultural Statistics, 1979 and 1980,* Tables 76 & 77.

11. Norman Borlaug in conversation with Frances Moore Lappé, April 1974.

12. U.S. Department of Agriculture, *Agricultural Statistics, 1980,* Table 76.

13. How many pounds of grain and soy are consumed by the American steer to get 1 pound of edible meat?

    (a) The total forage (hay, silage, grass) consumed: 12,000 pounds (10,000 pre-feedlot and 2,000 in feedlot). The total grain- and soy-type concentrate consumed: about 2,850 pounds (300 pounds grain and 50 pounds soy before feedlot, plus 2,200 pounds grain and 300 pounds soy in feedlot). Therefore, the actual percent of total feed units from grain and soy is about 25 percent.

    (b) But experts estimate that the grain and soy contribute more to weight gain (and, therefore, to ultimate meat produced) than their actual proportion in the diet. They estimate that grain and soy contribute (instead of 25 percent) about 40 percent of weight put on over the life of the steer.

    (c) To estimate what percent of edible meat is due to the grain and soy consumed, multiply that 40 percent (weight gain due to grain and soy) times the edible meat produced at slaughter, or 432 pounds: $.4 \times 432 = 172.8$ pounds of edible portion contributed by grain and soy. (Those who state a 7:1 ratio use the entire 432 pounds edible meat in their computation.)

(d) To determine how many pounds of grain and soy it took to get this 172.8 pounds of edible meat, divide total grain and soy consumed, 2850 pounds, by 172.8 pounds of edible meat: 2850 ÷ 172.8 = 16–17 pounds. (I have taken the lower figure, since the amount of grain being fed may be going down a small amount.) These estimates are based on several consultations with the USDA Economic Research Service and the USDA Agricultural Research Service, Northeastern Division, plus current newspaper reports of actual grain and soy currently being fed.

14. U.S. Department of Agriculture, Economic Research Service and Agricultural Research Service, Northeastern Division, consultations with staff economists.

15. In 1975 I calculated this average ratio and the return to us in meat from *Livestock-Feed Relationships*, National and State Statistical Bulletin #530, June 1974, pp. 175–77. In 1980 I approached it differently and came out with the same answer. I took the total grain and soy fed to livestock (excluding dairy) from *Agricultural Statistics, 1980*. The total was about 145 million tons in 1979. I then took the meat and poultry and eggs consumed that year from *Food Consumption, Prices, and Expenditures*, USDA-ESS, Statistical Bulletin 656. (I included only the portion of total beef consumed that was put on by grain feeding, about 40 percent, and reduced the total poultry consumed to its edible portion, i.e., minus bones.) The total consumption was about 183.5 pounds per person, or 20 million tons for the whole country. I then divided the 145 million tons of grain and soy fed by the 20 million tons of meat, poultry, and eggs produced by this feeding and came up with the ratio of 7 to 1. (Imports of meat are not large enough to affect this calculation appreciably.)

16. Calculated as follows: 124 million tons of grain "lost" annually in the United States × 2,000 pounds of grain in a ton = 248 billion pounds "lost" divided by 4.4 billion people = 56 pounds per capita divided by 365 days equals .153 pound per capita per day × 16

ounces in a pound — 2.5 ounces per capita per day— 1/3 cup of dry grain, or 1 cup cooked volume.

17. R. F. Brokken, James K. Whittaker, and Ludwig M. Eisgruber, "Past, Present and Future Resource Allocation to Livestock Production," in *Animals, Feed, Food and People, An Analysis of the Role of Animals in Food Production,* R. L. Baldwin, ed., An American Association for the Advancement of Science Selected Symposium (Boulder, CO: Westview Press, 1980), pp. 99–100.

18. J. Rod Martin, "Beef," in *Another Revolution in U.S. Farming,* by Lyle Schertz and others, U.S. Department of Agriculture, Washington, D.C., 1979, p. 93.

19. D. E. Brady, "Consumer Preference," *Journal of Animal Science,* vol. 16, p. 233, cited in H. A. Turner and R. J. Raleigh, "Production of Slaughter Steers from Forages in the Arid West," *Journal of Animal Science,* vol. 44, no. 5, 1977, pp. 901 ff.

20. *Des Moines Register,* December 8, 1974.

21. *Cattle Feeding in the United States,* op. cit., pp. 78–79.

22. "Past, Present and Future Resource Allocation to Livestock Production," op. cit., p. 97.

23. Ibid. p. 91.

24. U.S. Department of Agriculture, Economics and Statistics Service, *Status of the Family Farm,* Second Annual Report to the Congress, Agricultural Economic Report No. 434, p. 48.

25. Quantities of each fuel used from *Energy and U.S. Agriculture: 1974 and 1978,* U.S. Department of Agriculture, Economic and Statistics Service, April 1980. Conversions to BTUs used Cervinka, "Fuel and Energy Efficiency," in David Pimentel, ed., *Handbook of Energy Utilization in Agriculture* (Boca Raton, Fla.: CRC Press, 1980). Fossil fuel imports from *Monthly Energy Review,* March 1981, U.S. Department of Energy, Energy Information Administration, p. 8.

26. Georg Borgstrom, Michigan State University, presentation to the Annual Meeting of the American Association for the Advancement of Science (AAAS), 1981.

27. Ibid.

28. "The Browning of America," *Newsweek*, February 22, 1981, pp. 26 ff.

29. To arrive at an estimate of 50 percent, I used *Soil Degradation: Effects on Agricultural Productivity*, Interim Report Number Four of the National Agricultural Lands Study, 1980, which estimates that 81 percent of all water consumed in the United States is for irrigation. And I used the *Fact Book of U.S. Agriculture*, U.S. Department of Agriculture, Misc. Publication No. 1065, November 1979, Table 3, which shows that about 64 percent of irrigated land is used for feed crops, hay, and pasture. Sixty-four percent of 81 percent is 52 percent.

30. Philip M. Raup, "Competition for Land and the Future of American Agriculture," in *The Future of American Agriculture as a Strategic Resource*, edited by Sandra S. Batie and Robert G. Healy, A Conservation Foundation Conference, July 14, 1980, Washington, D.C. , pp. 36–43. Also see William Franklin Lagrone, "The Great Plains," in *Another Revolution in U.S. Farming?*, Lyle Schertz and others, U.S. Department of Agriculture, ESCS, Agricultural Economic Report No. 441, December 1979, pp. 335–61. The estimate of grain-fed beef's dependence on the Ogallala is from a telephone interview with resource economist Joe Harris of the consulting firm Camp, Dresser, McKee (Austin, Texas), part of four-year government-sponsored study: "The Six State High Plains Ogallala Aquifer Agricultural Regional Resource Study," May 1980.

31. William Franklin Lagrone, "The Great Plains," op. cit., pp. 356 ff.

32. "Report: Nebraska's Water Wealth is Deceptive," *Omaha World-Herald*, May 28, 1981.

33. Giannini Foundation of Agricultural Economics, *Trends in California Livestock and Poultry Production, Consumption, and Feed Use: 1961–1978*, Information Series 80-5, Division of Agricultural Sciences, University of California Bulletin 1899, November 1980, pp. 30–33.

34. General Accounting Office, *Groundwater Overdraft-*

ing Must Be Controlled, Report to the Congress of the United States by the Comptroller General, CED 80–96, September 12, 1980, p.3.

35. Donald Worster, *Dust Bowl: The Southern Plains in, the 1930's* (New York: Oxford University Press, 1979), p. 236.

36. William Brune, State Conservationist, Soil Conservation Service, Des Moines, Iowa, testimony before Senate Committee on Agriculture and Forestry, July 6, 1976. See also Seth King, "Iowa Rain and Wind Deplete Farmlands," *New York Times,* December 5, 1976, p. 61.

37. "In Plymouth County, Iowa, the Rich Topsoil's Going Fast. Alas," Curtis Harnack, *New York Times,* July 11, 1980.

38. Pimentel et al., "Land Degradation: Effects on Food and Energy Resources," in *Science,* vol. 194, October 1976, p. 150.

39. National Association of Conservation Districts, Washington, D.C., *Soil Degradation: Effects on Agricultural Productivity,* Interim Report Number Four, National Agricultural Lands Study, 1980, p. 20, citing the 1977 National Resources Inventory.

40. Calculated from estimates by Medard Gabel for the Cornucopia Project, c/o Rodale Press, Inc., Emmaus, Pa. 18049. See the description of this project among the organizations in Part IV.

41. Seth King, "Farms Go Down the River," *New York Times,* December 10, 1978, citing the Soil Conservation Service.

42. Ned D. Bayley, Acting Assistant Secretary for Natural Resources and Environment, "Soil and Water Resource Conservation Outlook for the 1980's," 1981 Agricultural Outlook Conference, Washington, D.C.

43. *Soil Degradation: Effects on Agricultural Productivity,* op. cit., p. 21.

44. W. E. Larson, "Protecting the Soil Resource Base," *Journal of Soil and Water Conservation,* vol. 36, number 1, January-February 1981, pp. 13 ff.

45. Soil and Water Resources Conservation Act—Summary of Appraisal, USDA Review Draft, 1980, p. 18.

46. David Pimentel, "Land Degradation: Effects on Food and Energy Resources," op. cit., p. 150, estimates $500 million costs of sediment damage. Philip Le Veen, in "Some Considerations for Soil Conservation Policy," unpublished manuscript, Public Interest Economics, 1981, p. 29, estimates $1 billion.

47. Soil Degradation: Effects on Agricultural Productivity, op. cit., p. 28.

48. U.S. Department of Agriculture, Economics and Statistics Service, Natural Resource Capital in U.S. Agriculture: Irrigation, Drainage and Conservation Investments Since 1900, ESCS Staff Paper, March 1979.

49. Ag World, April 1978, citing work of Clifton Halsey, University of Minnesota conservationist.

50. U.S. Department of Agriculture, Handbook of Agricultural Charts, 1979, p. 19.

51. U.S. Department of Agriculture, Fertilizer Situation, 1980, p. 14.

52. Medard Gabel, Cornucopia Project, Preliminary Report, Rodale, Inc., Emmaus, Pa. 18049, p. 33.

53. C. A. Wolfbauer, "Mineral Resources for Agricultural Use," in Agriculture and Energy, William Lockeretz, ed. (New York: Academic Press, 1977), pp. 301–14. See also Facts and Problems, U.S. Bureau of Mines, 1975, pp. 758–868.

54. General Accounting Office, Phosphates: A Case Study of A Valuable Depleting Mineral in America, Report to the Congress by the Comptroller General of the United States, EMD-80-21, November 30, 1979, p. 1.

55. Environmental Science and Technology, vol. 4, no. 12, 1970, p. 1098.

56. Barry Commoner, The Closing Circle (Knopf, 1971), p. 148.

57. Georg Borgstrom, The Food and People Dilemma (Duxbury Press, 1973), p. 103.

58. U.S. Department of Agriculture, Economics and Statistics Service, Natural Resource Capital in U.S. Agriculture: Irrigation, Drainage and Conservation Investments Since 1900, ESCS Staff Paper, March 1979.

59. General Accounting Office, Federal Charges for Irrigation Projects Reviewed Do Not Cover Costs, Report

to the Congress of the United States from the Comptroller General, PAD-81-07, March 3, 1981, p. 43.

60. Ibid. p. 26.
61. Julia Vitullo-Martin, "Ending the Southwest's Water Binge," *Fortune*, February 23, 1981, pp. 93 ff.
62. Ibid.
63. *Federal Charges*, op. cit., pp. 3–4.
64. "Ending the Southwest's Water Binge," op. cit.
65. U.S. Department of Agriculture, *Farmline*, September 1980.
66. Milton Moskowitz, Michael Katz, and Robert Levering, eds., *Everybody's Business: An Almanac* (Harper and Row, 1980), p. 643.
67. U.S. Department of Agriculture, Economics and Statistics Service, *Status of the Family-Farm*, Second Annual Report to the Congress, Agricultural Economic Report No. 434, p. 47.
68. Ibid. p. 45.
69. Joseph C. Meisner and V. James Rhodes, *The Changing Structure of U.S. Cattle Feeding*, Special Report 167, Agricultural Economics, University of Missouri-Columbia, November 1974, p. 13.
70. "Past, Present and Future Resource Allocation to Livestock Production," in *Animals, Feed, Food and People, An Analysis of the Role of Animals in Food Production*, op. cit.
71. U.S. Department of Agriculture, *Agricultural Statistics, 1979*, pp. 435–38.

Chapter 3. The Meat Mystique

1. Winrock International Livestock Research and Training Center, *The World Livestock Product, Feedstuff, and Food Grain System: An Analysis and Evaluation of System Interactions Throughout the World*, with Projections to 1985, Winrock, Arkansas, 1981.
2. U.S. Department of Agriculture, *Utilization of Grain for Livestock Feed*, Washington, D.C., May 1, 1980, pp. 4–6.
3. Kenneth Bachman and Leonardo Paulino, *Rapid*

Growth in Food Production in Selected Countries: A Comparative Analysis of Underlying Trends, 1961–76, Research Report 11, International Food Policy Research Institute, October 1979, p. 29.

4. "Replacing Energy as the Inflation Villain: Agriculture," Business Week, June 1, 1981, p. 71.

5. Maurice Brannan, "Trade Patterns," Feedstuffs, September 1, 1980.

6. Interview with J. Dawson Ahalt, Chairman, World Food and Agricultural Outlook and Situation Board, U.S. Department of Agriculture, July, 1980.

7. For a complete discussion of promotion of agricultural exports by the U.S. government, see Food First: Beyond the Myth of Scarcity, by Frances Moore Lappé and Joseph Collins with Cary Fowler (Ballantine Books, 1979), Parts VII and IX.

8. C. W. McMillan, "Meat Export Federation to Be Newest Cooperator," Foreign Agriculture 13 (May 26, 1975), p. 14.

9. Ibid.

10. U.S. Department of Agriculture, Handbook of Agricultural Charts 1980, pp. 63, 69.

Chapter 4. Democracy at Stake

1. General Accounting Office, Report by the Comptroller General of the United States, An Assessment of Parity as A Tool for Formulating and Evaluating Agricultural Policy, CED 81-11, October 10, 1980, p. 18.

2. U.S. Department of Agriculture, Status of the Family Farm, Second Annual Report to Congress, 1979, p. 3.

3. Marvin Duncan, "Farm Real Estate: Who Buys and How," Monthly Review of the Federal Reserve Bank of Kansas City (June 1977), p. 5.

4. William Lin, George Coffman, and J. B. Penn, U.S. Farm Numbers, Size and Related Structural Dimensions: Projections to the Year 2000, Technical Bulletin No. 1625, Economics and Statistics Service, U.S. Department of Agriculture, 1980, p. iii.

5. Lyle Schertz and others, Another Revolution in U.S.

Farming?, Agricultural Economic Report No. 441, Economics and Statistics Service, U.S. Department of Agriculture, 1979, pp. 300 ff.

6. Diocesan Coalition to Preserve Family Farms, *Fourteen-County Land Ownership Study 1980*, Diocese of Sioux City, Iowa, 1980.

7. U.S. Department of Agriculture, *A Time to Choose: Summary Report on the Structure of Agriculture*, Washington, D.C., January 1981. Table 24, p. 58, indicates that 100 percent of the economies of scale are, on average, reached when sales average $133,000. From Table 5, p. 43, one can calculate that roughly 50 percent of sales are from farms above this size.

8. Leo V. Mayer, *Farm Income and Farm Structure in the United States*, Congressional Research Service, Library of Congress, Report No. 79-188 S, September 1979, Table 11, p. 31. The lowest per unit costs of production—expenses per dollar of gross farm income—are found on farms with gross sales between $20,000 and $99,999 a year; the highest on farms with sales over $200,000.

9. *A Time to Choose*, op. cit., p. 56.

10. *Another Revolution in U.S. Farming?*, op. cit., p. 31.

11. *A Time to Choose*, op. cit., pp. 46–47, 144–45.

12. Ibid.

13. E. Phillip LeVeen, "Towards a New Food Policy: A Dissenting Perspective," *Public Interest Economics-West*, April 1981, Berkeley, California, Table 1.

14. Alfred J. Kahn and Sheila B. Kamerman, "Cross-National Studies of Social Service Systems and Family Policy," Columbia University, School of Social Work, 622 W. 113th St., New York, N.Y. 10025.

15. Warren Weaver, "House Unit Finds Aged Getting Poorer," *New York Times*, May 2, 1981.

16. National Advisory Council on Economic Opportunity, *Critical Choices for the 1980s*, 12th Report, August 1980, p. 15.

17. Ibid. pp. 16–17.

18. Census Bureau figures, as quoted in the *San Francisco Chronicle* of August 21, 1981.

19. Mike Feinsilber, Philadelphia *Enquirer*, December 24,

1980, quoted by Loretta Schwartz-Nobel, *Starving in the Shadow of Plenty* (G. P. Putnam's Sons, 1981).

20. Tom Joe, Cheryl Rogers, and Rick Weissbourd, *The Poor: Profiles of Families in Poverty*, Center for the Study of Welfare Policy, The University of Chicago, Washington office, March 20, 1981, p. iii.

21. Ibid.

22. Robert Greenstein, Director on Food Assistance and Poverty (former administrator of the Food and Nutrition Service, U.S. Department of Agriculture), statement before the Senate Committee on Agriculture, Nutrition and Forestry, April 2, 1981.

23. Interview with Robert Greenstein, May 30, 1981.

24. Nick Kotz, *Hunger in America: The Federal Response*, The Field Foundation, 100 East 85th Street, New York, N.Y. 10028, p. 13.

25. Interview with Dr. Livingston by research assistant Sandy Fritz, May 1981.

26. President's Commission for a National Agenda for the Eighties, *Government and the Advancement of Social Justice, Health, Welfare, Education and Civil Rights in the Eighties*, Washington, D.C., 1980, p. 33.

27. M. E. Wegman, *Pediatrics*, December 1980, p. 832.

28. Ibid.

29. *Statistical Abstract*, 1978.

30. "Infant Mortality Highest in U.S. Capital," *New York Times*, December 13, 1981.

31. *Starving in the Shadow of Plenty*, op. cit.

32. *Hunger in America*, op. cit.

33. Robert Greenstein, testimony (see note 22).

34. *Access to Food: A Special Problem for Low-Income Americans*, Community Nutrition Institute, Washington, D.C., April 1, 1979, p. 17.

35. Interview with Nancy Amidei of the Food Research and Action Center, December 1981.

36. Greenstein, testimony, and Gar Alperovits and Feff Faux, "Controls and the Basic Necessities," *Challenge*, May–June 1980.

37. "Poverty Rate on Rise Even Before Recession," *The New York Times*, February 20, 1982.

38. *Dietary Goals for the United States*, Second Edition,

prepared by the staff of the Select Committee on Nutrition and Human Needs, U.S. Senate, December 1977, reproduced by the Library of Congress, Congressional Research Service, March 31, 1978, p. xxxi.

Chapter 5. Asking the Right Questions

1. U.S. Department of Agriculture, *Food Consumption, Prices and Expenditures*, Economics and Statistics Service, Statistical Bulletin No. 656, February 1981, pp. 4–5.

2. *Wall Street Journal*, May 8, 1981.

PART III.
DIET FOR A SMALL PLANET REVISITED

Chapter 1. America's Experimental Diet

1. Patricia Hausman, *Jack Sprat's Legacy: The Science and Politics of Fat and Cholesterol*, Center for Science in the Public Interest (Richard Marek Publishers, 1981), p. 97.
2. *Dietary Goals for the United States*, Second Edition, prepared by the staff of the Select Committee on Nutrition and Human Needs, United States Senate, December 1977, reproduced by the Library of Congress, Congressional Research Service, March 31, 1978, p. xxviii. See also W. Haenszel and M. Kurihara, "Studies of Japanese Immigrants," *Journal of the National Cancer Institute*, vol. 40, 1968, p. 43.
3. M. Hindhede, "The Effect of Food Restriction During War on Mortality in Copenhagen," *Journal of the American Medical Association*, vol. 74, no. 6 (February 7, 1920), p. 381, cited by Keith Akers, *Vegetarianism* (forthcoming). See also H. D. McGill, Jr., "Appraisal of Dietary Fat as a Causative Factor in

Atherogenesis," *American Journal of Clinical Nutrition,* vol. 32, 1979, pp. 2637–43.

4. Erik Eckholm and Frank Record, "The Affluent Diet: A Worldwide Health Hazard," in *Sourcebook on Food and Nutrition,* First Edition, Dr. Loannis S. Scarpa and Dr. Helen Chilton Kiefer, editors, Marguis Academic Media, 100 East Ohio St., Chicago, Ill. 60611, p. 20.

5. *Journal of the American Dietetic Association,* vol. 77, July 1980, p. 66.

6. Letitia Brewster and Michael Jacobson, *The Changing American Diet,* Center for Science in the Public Interest, 1744 S St. NW, Washington, D.C. 20009, pp. 64–65.

7. Ibid. pp. 35, 43.

8. *Dietary Goals,* op. cit., p. xl.

9. Lindsay H. Allen et al., "Protein-induced Hypercalciuria: a Longer Term Study," *The American Journal of Clinical Nutrition,* vol. 32, April 1979, pp. 741–49; and *Journal of Dental Research,* vol. 60, 1971, p. 485.

10. *Jack Sprat's Legacy,* op. cit., pp. 58–59.

11. *Dietary Goals,* op. cit., p. xxx.

12. *Jack Sprat's Legacy,* op. cit., pp. 105–106.

13. Ibid. p. 59, and *Clinical and Developmental Hypertension,* vol. 3, no. 1, 1981, pp. 27–28.

14. *The Changing American Diet,* op. cit., p. 22.

15. Charles Frederick Church and Helen Nichols Church, *Food Values of Portions Commonly Used,* Tenth Edition, J. B. Lippincott Co., 1975.

16. *Dietary Goals,* op. cit., p. 46.

17. Jane Brody, *Jane Brody's Nutrition Book* (W. W. Norton, 1981), p. 397.

18. *Dietary Goals,* op. cit., p. 46.

19. *The Changing American Diet,* op. cit., p. 46, and U.S. Department of Agriculture, Economics and Statistics Service, *Food Consumption, Prices and Expenditures,* Statistical Bulletin No. 656, February 1981, p. 2.

20. *Dietary Goals,* op. cit., p. 32.

21. *The Changing American Diet,* op. cit., p. 17.

22. *Dietary Goals,* op. cit., p. 31.

23. Ibid. p. 31.

24. Milton Moskowitz, Michael Katz, and Robert Levering, *Everybody's Business: An Almanac* (Harper and Row, 1980), p. 66.
25. *The Changing American Diet*, op. cit., 44–45.
26. *Everybody's Business*, op. cit., p. 34.
27. *Dietary Goals*, op. cit., pp. 40–49.
28. Ibid. p. 49.
29. *Jane Brody's Nutrition Book*, op. cit., p. 397.
30. U.S. Department of Agriculture, *The Sodium Content of Your Food*, Home and Garden Bulletin No. 233, pp. 11–12.
31. Ibid. pp. 17, 19.
32. Ibid. p. 28.
33. Gene A. Spiller with Ronald J. Amen, *Topics in Dietary Fiber Research* (Plenum Press, 1978), p. 78.
34. U.S. Department of Agriculture, *Handbook of Agricultural Charts, 1978*, p. 56.
35. Dr. Sharon Fleming, personal correspondence, February 26, 1981.
36. M. G. Hardinge, A. C. Chambers, H. Crooks, and F. J. Stare, "Nutritional Studies of Vegetarians III. Dietary Levels of Fiber," *American Journal of Clinical Nutrition*, 1958, 6:523.
37. *The Changing American Diet*, op. cit., p. 25.
38. Ibid. p. 30.
39. Ibid. p. 13.
40. *Everybody's Business*, op. cit., p. 785.
41. Wayne Anderson, "More Meat—or less—on the Dinner Table," *Feedstuffs*, May 12, 1975, p. 116.
42. *The Changing American Diet*, op. cit., p. 58.
43. *Everybody's Business*, op. cit., p. 784.
44. *The Changing American Diet*, op. cit., pp. 27–28.
45. "Antibiotic Feed Additives: The Prospect of Doing Without," *Farmline*, U.S. Department of Agriculture, December 1980.
46. U.S. Department of Health, Education and Welfare, Public Health Service, Food and Drug Administration, Bureau of Foods, *Compliance Program Report of Findings*, FY77 Total Diet Studies—Adult (7320.73), pp. 8, 9.
47. Talbot Page, Joel Babien, and Stephanie Harris, "The

Effect of Diet on Organochlorine Concentration in Breast Milk," unpublished study. Contact through the Environmental Defense Fund, Washington, D.C. For report of women eating no animal food, see Jeffrey Hergenrather, Gary Hlady, Barbara Wallace, and Eldon Savage, Ethos Research Group, letter to the *New England Journal of Medicine*, March 26, 1981, p. 792. See also *Birthright Denied: The Risks and Benefits of Breast-Feeding,* by Stephanie G. Harris and Joseph H. Highland, Second Edition, revised, The Environmental Defense Fund, Washington, D.C., 1977.

48. *Compliance Program Report,* op. cit., p. 10.
49. Randall Ment, "Pestiscam," *Greenpeace Examiner,* Spring 1981, p. 25.
50. *The Changing American Diet,* op. cit., p. 50.
51. Graham T. Molitor, "The Food System in the 1980s," *Journal of Nutrition Education,* volume 12, no. 2 Supplement, 1980, pp. 103 ff.
52. *The Changing American Diet,* op. cit., p. 58.
53. *New England Journal of Medicine,* vol. 304, no. 16 (April 6, 1981), pp. 930–33.
54. *Journal of the American Dietetic Association,* vol. 77, July 1980, p. 67.

Chapter 2. Who Asked for Fruit Loops?

1. Daniel Zwerdling, "The Food Monsters: How They Gobble Up Each Other—and Us," *The Progressive,* March 16, 1980, p. 20.
2. "Judge Admonishes ITT Bakery Division on Price Tactics," *San Francisco Chronicle,* May 13, 1981.
3. Frances Moore Lappé and Joseph Collins with Cary Fowler, *Food First: Beyond the Myth of Scarcity* (Ballantine, 1979), p. 324 ff. discusses agri-business expansion abroad.
4. Milton Moskowitz, Michael Katz, and Robert Levering, *Everybody's Business: An Almanac* (Harper and Row, 1980), p. 1.
5. *Impact of Market Concentration on Rising Food Prices,* Hearing Before the Subcommittee on Antitrust,

Monopoly and Business Rights of the Committee on the Judiciary, United States Senate, 96th Congress, 1st Session on Rising Food Prices in the United States, April 6, 1979. U.S. Government Printing Office, 1979, Testimonies of Drs. Russell Parker, John Connor, and Willard Mueller, p. 46.

6. Ibid. (These authorities estimated consumer overcharges to be as much as $15 billion a year by 1975. From this, I estimate them to have reached about $20 billion a year by 1982.)

7. "FTC Asserts Big 3 Cereal Makers Reap Over $1 Billion," *Wall Street Journal,* October 2, 1980.

8. Frederick F. Clairmonte, "U.S. Food Complexes and Multinational Corporations, Reflections on Economic Predation," *Economic and Political Weekly,* vol. XV, nos. 41, 42, 43, special no. 1980, p. 1815.

9. *Everybody's Business,* op. cit., p. 29.

10. "FTC Asserts" (see note 7).

11. *Impact of Market Concentration,* op. cit., p. 13.

12. Ibid. p. 47.

13. "The Food Monsters," op. cit., p. 22.

14. *Impact of Market Concentration,* op. cit., p. 47.

15. "The Food Monsters," op. cit., p. 22.

16. A. Kent MacDougall, "Market-Shelf Proliferation—Public Pays," *Los Angeles Times,* May 27, 1979, pp. 1 ff.

17. Anthony E. Gallo and John M. Connor, "Packaging in Food Marketing," *National Food Review,* U.S. Department of Agriculture, Spring 1981.

18. "Market-Shelf Proliferation—Public Pays," op. cit.

19. Ibid.

20. *Everybody's Business,* op. cit., p. 45.

21. U.S. Department of Agriculture, *Handbook of Agricultural Charts,* 1978, p. 31.

22. David Pimentel, "Land Degradation: Effects on Food and Energy Resources," *Science,* vol. 194, October 8, 1976, pp. 151–55.

23. Georg Borgstrom, *The Food and People Dilemma* (Duxbury Press, 1973), pp. 102–103.

24. *San Francisco Examiner,* May 3, 1981.

25. Graham T. Molitor, "The Food System in the 1980s,"

Journal of Nutrition Education, vol. 12, no. 2, Supplement, 1980, p. 109.

26. Judith J. Wurtman, "The American Eater: Some Nutritional Problems and Some Solutions," *Vital Issues,* Center for Information on America, vol. XXIX, no. 2, Washington, Conn. 06793.

27. *Everybody's Business,* op. cit., p. 19.

28. "Market-Shelf Proliferation—Public Pays," op. cit.

29. *Everybody's Business,* op. cit., p. 66.

30. Ibid. p. 127.

31. Ibid. p. 64.

32. "Branded Foods," *Forbes,* January 5, 1981.

33. *Everybody's Business,* op. cit., p. 49.

34. Ibid. pp. 28–29.

35. Robert Choate, Chairman, Council on Children, Media and Merchandising, in *Edible TV: Your Child and Food Commercials,* prepared by the Council on Children, Media and Merchandising for the Select Committee on Nutrition and Human Needs, United States Senate, September 1977, U.S. Government Printing Office, p. 9.

36. Ibid. p. 21.

37. Ibid. p. 63.

38. Ibid. p. 66.

39. Ibid. p. 69.

40. "Branded Foods," *Forbes,* January 5, 1981.

41. Kathryn E. Walker, "Homemaking Still Takes Time," *Journal of Home Economics,* vol. 61, no. 8, October 1969, pp. 621 ff.

42. Michelle Marder Kamhi, "Making Diets Healthy at P.S. 166," *Nutrition Action,* January 1980.

Chapter 3. Protein Myths: A New Look

1. R. J. Williams, "We Abnormal Normals," *Nutrition Today,* 1967, 2:19–28.

2. Dr. Donald R. Davis, Clayton Foundation Biochemical Institute, University of Texas, Austin, Texas 78712, personal correspondence, May 5, 1981.

3. Jessica Wade et al., "Evidence for a Physiological Regu-

lation of Food Selection and Nutrient Intake in Twins," *The American Journal of Clinical Nutrition,* vol. 34, February 1981, pp. 143–47.

4. *Energy and Protein Requirements,* report of Joint FAO/WHO Ad Hoc Expert Committee, WHO Technical Report Series No. 522, Rome, 1973, pp. 66–69.

Chapter 4. Protein Complementarity: The Debate

1. "Nutritional Evaluation of Protein Foods," Peter L. Pellett and Vernon R. Young, eds., The United Nations University World Hunger Programme, Food and Nutrition Bulletin, Supplement 4, pp. 59–60.

2. A. E. Harper, "Basic Concepts," in *Improvement of Protein Nutriture,* National Academy of Sciences, 1974.

3. H. T. Ostrowski, "Nutritional Improvement of Food and Feed Proteins," in *Advances in Experimental Medicine and Biology,* Melvin Freedman, ed., vol. 105 (Plenum Press, 1978).

4. Nevin Scrimshaw, personal correspondence, April 23, 1981.

Index

ABOUT THE AUTHOR

Frances Moore Lappé is the author of many books. She and Joseph Collins co-founded the San Francisco-based Institute for Food and Development Policy (also known as Food First), a not-for-profit public education and documentation center. An authority on world hunger, Ms. Lappé is best known for *Diet for a Small Planet*, which has sold almost three million copies since it was first published in 1971. In 1990 she co-founded with Paul Martin DuBois the Institute for the Arts of Democracy.